Window and Mirror

RTÉ television: 1961–2011

JOHN BOWMAN

The Collins Press

FIRST PUBLISHED IN 2011 BY
The Collins Press
West Link Park
Doughcloyne
Wilton
Cork

The following photographs are from sources other than RTÉ Stills Library. They are listed by page number.
Where more than one photograph appears on a page, a key word is added to the page number.

pp.5, 200, 236, Irish Times; p.15, Scandinavian Radio; p.21, Guardian News & Media Ltd.; p.22, Mary Evans Picture Library; p.24
(Macmillan), p. 49, Getty Images; p.29 (Edwards), North Western University; p.34, Kennelly Archive; p.36, Failte Ireland; pp.42 and
134, BBC Pictures; p.48, Flann O'Brien drawing, courtesy of Michael Ó Nualláin; pp.56 and 204 (Child), Time Magazine; p.58
[Edwards and Richards], courtesy of Michael Johnston; p.59, Cork GAA; p.67 (Dunn), Radharc Archive; pp.85, 94 and 100, courtesy
of Declan McCourt; p.88 (Andrews), An Post; p.180, courtesy, Charlie Bird; p.207, Sportsfile; P.208 (O'Gara), courtesy of Six Nations
Rugby; p.235 (Obama), Press Association; Frontispiece: Patrick Collins drawing of proposed Television Building, courtesy of Ronnie
Tallon, Scott Tallon Walker. p.246, Cathal O'Neill's water colour of RTÉ Administration Building, courtesy Cathal O'Neill.

British Library Cataloguing in Publication data

Bowman, John, 1942-
  Window and mirror : RTE television – 1961-2011.
  1. Radio Telefís Éireann–History. 2. Television
broadcasting–Social aspects–Ireland. 3. Television and
politics–Ireland. 4. Television broadcasting–Religious
aspects–Catholic Church.
  I. Title
384.5'54065'417-dc22

ISBN: 978-18488-9135-7

Design and typesetting by Susan Waine
Typeset in 11pt on 12.5pt Scala
Printed in Italy by L.E.G.O. S.p.A.

Contents

BBCWA:	BBC Written Archives
DDA:	Dublin Diocesan Archives
FCO:	Foreign and Commonwealth Office
GAA Archives:	Gaelic Athletic Association Archives
NAI:	National Archives of Ireland
NAUK:	National Archives of the United Kingdom
NIO:	Northern Ireland Office
NLI Ms. Dept:	National Library of Ireland Manuscripts Department
PRONI:	Public Records Office of Northern Ireland
RTÉWA:	Radio Telefís Éireann Written Archives
TCD Ms. Dept:	Trinity College Dublin Manuscripts Department
UCDAD:	University College Dublin Archives Department

'Sure, what is it only a glorified mirror?'

THE HISTORIAN OF AMERICAN TV, Erik Barnouw, complained that the medium of television 'never sat still for its portrait' but remained in a state of constant flux,[1] a point that resonated with this author as he attempted a historical portrait of RTÉ television over its first half-century. Conscious that this could not be a comprehensive institutional history, I have during its writing often thought of it as a portrait composed of various brushstrokes representing a number of themes exploratory of the story of RTÉ television – its provenance; how the politicians underestimated the professionalism and the 'can-do' approach of the first generation of broadcasters; and the story over its first half-century.

Emphasis is placed here on the achievements of the 1960s and 1970s, the pioneering years when the template of public service broadcasting was established. At the end of the 1970s, one of the pioneers, Jack White, recalled the challenge of almost twenty years before when the staff had had minimal training and less experience. In other countries a newly launched television service was expected to offer a two- or three-hour schedule each night. But the Irish case was different: much of the country was in the multi-channel area with competition from arguably the best television anywhere. White believed that any contentment by Telefís Éireann with just providing 'short rations' – what he termed 'a thin smear of home production' – would have rendered the new station uncompetitive. From the beginning, White concluded, the television service was committed to working 'beyond its resources'. He believed that broadcasting tended to defeat analysis. Broadcasters themselves took 'refuge in mystique about communication'; management analysts were defeated by an industry in which both input and output were 'largely intangible'.[2] And it is this

Jack White was among the pioneers of Telefís Éireann. He believed that from the beginning the station was working 'beyond its resources'. As he assumed ever more senior responsibilities, Jack White remained an occasional reporter. He is shown here outside Buckingham Palace, London for the programme 'No Country for Old Men', broadcast on 16 April 1980 as part of the *Insight* documentary series. The broadcast was introduced by Michael Garvey as an obituary tribute to Jack White, who had died suddenly some days before.

1 Erik Barnouw, *Tube of Plenty: The Evolution of American Television* (Oxford, 1990), p.v.
2 Jack White, Director of Broadcasting Resources, to RTÉ Authority, 6 September 1979. From 'a digest, prepared at the request of the Chairman, of my remarks at the meeting of the RTÉ Authority on 9 July 1979.'

very intangibility that renders difficult the shaping of a history.

Programmes are porous, as are departments: turf wars are endemic so television's story can never be told very tidily. Religious programming differs from relations between the hierarchy and the station. The hierarchy was as likely – perhaps more likely – to comment on *The Late Late Show* as on a religious programme. Likewise, politicians also paid particular attention to the *Late Late*, quickly sensing a rival forum to their own. Yet any chapter dealing chronologically with that programme would introduce a number of policy issues that could apply equally to other programmes. The solution I have adopted brings me back to the concept of a portrait: what I have included are discrete accounts of episodes, challenges, themes; memorable programmes and some not remembered because they were censored or cancelled; major national debates about the second television channel; the *Sit Down and Be Counted* controversy; coverage of the North; Irish language policy; issues of bias; the liberal agenda; how drama, sport, agriculture, food, politics and much else might be covered on television; why the RTÉ Authority came to be sacked; the pay of top presenters; Eurovision; the visits of President Kennedy and Pope John Paul II; the 1916 Golden Jubilee; how investigative programmes triggered tribunals – in the 1960s into *the making of the programme*, more recently into the clerical sexual abuse exposed. It is hoped that by writing about such a variety of aspects of the station's history the sum will be greater than the parts and the reader will gain an insight into the manner in which RTÉ responded to the challenge initially offered to the station by the Lemass government in 1961.

The book does not follow particularly conventional rules. There is some emphasis on the wonder of television as a medium when it was first introduced: this may recapture some of that feeling of awe experienced by older readers; but, more importantly, oblige younger readers to imagine what Irish society was like before the television age. In choosing these themes, the book takes into account, to some extent, the earlier work of individual scholars such as Savage,[3] Horgan[4] and others and – while not ignoring some of the issues covered by them – does not attempt to duplicate their work. The book brings the story up to 'late last night' as it were, although, to allow for the difficulties of making historical judgments of events that are very close, and with the thirty year-rule keeping many archives covering the most recent period closed, I have used a device late in the book to compare the 1960s to the most recent decade. In doing that I have taken a wide range of examples. Older readers who remember being viewers in both the first and fifth decades of RTÉ's history may need this reminder to notice the scale of the changes – since change, when incremental, can remain largely

---

3   Robert J.Savage, *Irish Television: The Political and Social Origins* (Cork, 1996), and *A Loss of Innocence? Television and Irish Society: 1960-1972* (Manchester, 2010).
4   John Horgan, *Broadcasting and Public Life* (Dublin, 2004).

unnoticed. But younger viewers who take today's choice of channels for granted will benefit from this reminder of how little it took to excite their parents' and grandparents'. It is worth recalling that in autumn 1961 crowds gathered around the windows of television dealers in Dublin trying to catch a glimpse of the test card from the Kippure transmitter. One of them even told Norris Davidson for a radio documentary that the test card was not as good as the BBC's. With the new television service, the complaints department opened early: even before the station itself.

This book has been a most complex challenge: there were limitations on scale, sources and, above all, the time in which to research and write it. It should not – and indeed, given the timeframe, could not – be compared to the history of British broadcasting such as that completed by Asa Briggs. That ran to five volumes, included radio, employed a team of researchers, had total access to a fully accessioned BBC Written Archives and took some decades to complete. Such a history of RTÉ remains to be written and it is hoped this book will not be without some insights to whomever eventually takes on that challenge.

In the course of its writing I have many times become aware and concerned at what is absent; about how arbitrary some of the judgement calls had to be. When a book is the most comprehensive attempt yet at capturing the story of RTÉ television in its first half century – and for all its failings and limitations, this book is, I suppose, that – one is all the more aware of what is not between its covers. I have tried to cast my net wide. That is a duty, of course. But, inevitably, one is drawn to write on what one knows most about. And the focus of the research has always been on the impact that RTÉ television has made on Irish society over the past half-century.

A note on the book's title: *Window and Mirror*. It suggests that the television service was both a window on Ireland and the world; but also a mirror reflecting Irish society to itself, warts and all. The title was prompted by a story recounted in the *RTV Guide* by Ciaran MacMathuna, 'A flying visit to meet and film the people of Ireland'. MacMathuna accompanied the first three continuity announcers, Kathleen Watkins, Nuala Donnelly and Marie O'Sullivan to meet the people and make a programme for the opening night.

RTV Guide, 15 December 1961, featuring Nuala Donnelly, Kathleen Watkins and Marie O'Sullivan, who accompanied Ciaran MacMathuna on a tour around Ireland introducing the announcers to the public before the station opened.

> Of course, we met the inevitable faintly cynical Irishman (more humorous than malicious) who refuses to be impressed or even if he is, won't show it. We met him in a town in Munster standing in front of a closed circuit television unit that accompanied us. He was seeing his own face on the screen for the first time. After looking at himself for a little while he turned and walked away. His words came back in a loud whisper: 'Sure, what is it only a glorified mirror?'[5]

---

5   Ciaran MacMathuna, 'A flying visit to meet and film the people of Ireland', *RTV Guide*, 15 December 1961.

Incidentally, having settled on the title, the author, some six months later, came across this exchange in an early interview with the incoming director-general, George Waters, in the *RTÉ Guide* in 1978.

> Q. Do you see television primarily as a mirror of Irish society or as a window on the world?
> A. Both. It must reflect Irish society as we see it now. It must also bring to viewers a picture of what's happening throughout the world.[6]

Finally, a declaration of interest. That such a book should be written and that I should write it was suggested by a publisher, by RTÉ and it was also an idea which I had entertained myself. It must be a complicating factor that I am both an insider as a broadcaster and am attempting to play the role of an independent historian of an institution for which I have some regard and for which I have worked all my adult life. Manifestly there are advantages and disadvantages in such an arrangement. I will leave it to the reader to judge how that dilemma has been coped with. This book has entailed me writing about contemporaries, colleagues and, sometimes, friends. There could even be some points of controversy which some of them would rather I had not included. In all such cases I applied one rule: if I were not a colleague, what would my judgement have been? Was the evidence important to an understanding of that dimension of RTÉ's history under consideration? Through this method, any dilemmas were resolved for the author; whether others are content with the results is for them to decide. In no case was any of the content approved by any individual, still less by RTÉ. In only one instance did I seek permission from an individual to include some material. The photograph on page 146 was not normally available from the RTÉ Library without consultation with its main subject, Madelyn Erskine, who is posing for a nude scene in the life class in *The Spike*. When I telephoned her to seek her permission, I thought I recognised some hesitation. But I later discovered that this was solely because I was inattentive to the fact that I was phoning on April the First and she was wary lest that date was the explanation for my request. When I explained that the scene had been an integral part of the controversy and was central to the text, she quickly assented.

Finally the work is entirely the responsibility of the author: in this case he alone will be in charge of the complaints department.

---

6   John Walsh, interview with George Waters, *RTÉ Guide*, 14 April 1978.

1

one carping voice was heard declaring it to be a 'far too ambitious project'

I N THE OPENING BROADCAST on Telefís Éireann on New Year's Eve 1961, President Eamon de Valera admitted that sometimes when he considered television and its 'immense power', he felt 'somewhat afraid'. Never before in history was there 'an instrument so powerful to influence the thoughts and actions of the multitude'. It had the potential to 'build up the character of the whole people, inducing a sturdiness and vigour and confidence'. But, on the other hand, it could 'lead through demoralisation to decadence and disillusion'.[1]

Such foreboding was probably shared by some of the other

---

1. RTÉ archives, 31 December 1961.

One of the attractions of the opening night schedule was a Telefís Éireann film made of the state visit to Ireland some months before of Princess Grace of Monaco. Her appeal was enhanced by her Irish roots and her earlier fame as a Hollywood star, Grace Kelly.

Edward J. Roth, director-general, President Eamon de Valera and chairman, Eamonn Andrews, at the Telefís Éireann studios on the opening night of the new television service, New Year's Eve 1961.

A toast to the new station at the opening night party at Dublin's Gresham Hotel. (Left to right) E.J.Roth, Roibeard Ó Faracháin, Milo O'Shea [partly obscured], Michael Barry, Denis O'Dea, Joe Linnane, Ria Mooney, Eamonn Andrews. Back to camera: Jimmy O'Dea with his wife, Ursula Doyle.

Some trouble-shooting behind the scenes on opening night. So much could go wrong. Would Murphy's Law apply?

establishment figures present at the opening night ceremonies. But for most viewers the arrival of an Irish television service was a matter of pride and excitement. For some, it was their first sighting of a live television broadcast, and for many it was certainly their first experience of reliable television reception. Those who had for years enjoyed fringe reception from British stations could now expect a signal from Telefís Éireann that was free from interference. That first night much of the country was watching, some communally.

In the months preceding the launch, television had gripped the country's imagination. Crowds had swarmed around the shop windows of television dealers looking in awe at the new station's test card. The American director-general, Edward J. Roth, had admitted to nervousness 'a couple of weeks' before the opening. By his reckoning the station had reached an 80 per cent efficiency rating but had then stayed becalmed for 'an alarmingly long time' until a breakthrough came.[2] The station's management could scarcely have been faulted had they sought some postponement of the station's opening. Controller of programmes, Michael Barry was adamant: 'Postponements can grow like mushrooms.'[3]

For those who had purchased a television receiver, there was the liability that neighbours without one might invite themselves to join

2 *RTV Guide*, 8 December 1961.
3 *ibid.*, 1 December 1961.

January 1st, 1962.

Very well done and thank you for the hard and long weeks of work that went to start us off so well last night. Now we have much to do, and without pause, but everybody acquitted themselves splendidly and some were heroes last night. It is not possible to say this without embracing all of Engineering Division. Robert Fraser of ITA whispered to me at 11:30 "100 marks" and this goes for everyone connected in any way with the programmes, the preparation, transmission or the plans for people or material that went into them.

On 1 January Michael Barry sent a memo to all staff involved in the production. He told them that Sir Robert Fraser, director-general of the Independent Television Authority, had come from London for the opening night and had whispered to him as the transmission was nearing completion: '100 marks'. Barry thanks all staff involved in the production and shares the compliment.

in a communal viewing of the station's launch. Nor did Telefís Éireann lack ambition in the scale of programmes it hoped to provide – and in a very short time frame. Industry professionals were impressed. It was known that first nights were fraught with danger. Risks had to be taken with new systems, many of them ad hoc improvisations. And those operating them had minimal training and scarcely any experience. So much could go wrong. Would Murphy's Law apply? It had in Australia. On ABC's opening night the Bach gavotte was seen but not heard and when the first newsreel film broke down, the presenter was caught on camera with a drink in one hand and a cigarette in the other.[4]

Gabriel Fallon, as a lifelong man of the theatre, knew all about the adrenalin of opening nights and had the imagination to appreciate how much more complex this one was. He felt an especial sympathy for Roth, given the Irish talent for begrudgery. Fallon reckoned that Roth must have been 'aghast at the spate of prenatal criticism'; but, in the event, where the cynic 'anticipated chaos ... everything moved at an orderly speed'. Fallon added that 'at least one carping voice was heard declaring it to be a far too ambitious project.'[5]

First edition of the *RTV Guide*, 8 December 1961.
A promise had been made to be on the air before the end of 1961. The television licence would be introduced on 1 January 1962 and it was considered politic that the licence payers – especially those in the multi-channel area – would have an Irish station among their choices

---

4 K.S.Inglis, *This is the ABC: The Australian Broadcasting Commission: 1932-1983* (Melbourne, 1983), p.198; hereafter, Inglis, *ABC*.
5 Gabriel Fallon, 'A critic's view of our start', *RTV Guide*, 5 January 1962.

The 'Out of Our Census' cover, *Dublin Opinion*, July 1956. A national census had been carried out some weeks previously. One topical controversy was that emigration figures were so high that the future of the country was threatened. This Charles E.Kelly cartoon prompted T.K.Whitaker to initiate what became the seminal policy document of recovery, *Economic Planning*.

Author interview, T.K.Whitaker, 2003.

A television cameraman balances on scaffolding outside the Gresham Hotel, Dublin on opening night to capture the scenes in O'Connell Street.

IRELAND HAD AN AGEING POPULATION in the 1950s, blighted by what Garvin has called 'the growth of something that looked like gerontocracy', with the exclusion from power of younger people.[6] There were complaints of a 'great inertia' oppressing the country, resulting from thirty years when the economy had been 'economically rudderless – or perhaps, steered in the wrong direction'.[7] On the fortieth anniversary of the Easter Rising in 1956 an *Irish Times* editorial pointing to high figures for both unemployment and emigration argued that if current trends were to continue, Ireland would die 'not in the remote unpredictable future, but quite soon'. This theme had been the subject of a controversial book, *The Vanishing Irish*, published by Fr John O'Brien published by University of Notre Dame in 1954.[8] Bryan MacMahon – among the book's contributors – privately reported that 'the whole countryside' was 'crawling with ancient spinsters and bachelors'. Marriage and birth rates for the previous quarter indicated 'a further decline'. When MacMahon and other contributors to the book came under attack from someone whom he regarded as 'spouting off fantastic nonsense', MacMahon drafted a riposte in his *Irish Press* column. When the editor declined to publish it, MacMahon resigned. 'It's very depressing when one is denied the right of utterance', he confided to a friend; 'silence and atrophy spell death'.[9]

Throughout the 1950s Irish governments looked 'unstable, weaker and more unsure of their own longevity' than they had been in the 1930s and 1940s.[10] Seán Lemass, when asked whether he regretted not having inherited the Fianna Fáil leadership in 1948, replied that the party was unsure about the extent to which its appeal derived from Eamon de Valera's legendary reputation and his charisma as a 1916 leader. Certainly the 1950s was an uncertain period for the party. Bew suggests that the 1957 election was 'perhaps Fianna Fáil's last chance, but it was a chance that was taken.'[11] Soon de Valera was prevailed upon to retire from the leadership and to seek the Presidency. Without a contest, Lemass succeeded to the party leadership and to the office of

6 Tom Garvin, *News from a New Republic: Ireland in the 1950s* (Dublin, 2010); hereafter, Garvin, *New Republic*.
7 'Point counterpoint', *Irish Times*, 14 December 1956.
8 John A. O'Brien, *The Vanishing Irish: The Enigma of the Modern World* (Notre Dame, 1954).
9 Diarmaid Ferriter, *Occasions of Sin: Sex and Society in Modern Ireland* (London, 2009), pp. 216-17; hereafter, Ferriter, *Occasions of Sin*.
10 Garvin, *New Republic*, 37.
11 Paul Bew, *Ireland: The Politics of Enmity, 1789-2006* (Oxford, 2007), p.477.

Taoiseach. Garvin reckoned him 'a tired workaholic, an ageing man in a hurry, fighting the onset of ill-health and a fading of energies.'[12]

Lemass was impatient to bring about fundamental economic reform: he thought of the new television service – in so far as he thought about it at all – as an enabler of the urgent changes he would presently seek to accelerate. To him a television service was akin to a public utility. Scarce wavelengths were allocated to governments by international agreement, just as landing rights at foreign airports were negotiated on an intergovernmental basis. Lemass had specific expectations from the new service and he prepared a script for his Minister for Posts and Telegraphs, Michael Hilliard, to be addressed to the inaugural meeting of the television Authority. He forwarded it to the minister asking that any proposed changes – he would have had department secretary, Leon Ó Broin in mind as the likely culprit – should be referred back to him for approval. Lemass was especially conscious of the national image. He was somewhat wary of the medium of television, following what he thought was a deeply unsatisfactory experience with an American CBS documentary team.[13]

Lemass argued that because the image of themselves reflected in a national television service could 'influence the people of any nation to aspire to a better life, the pretext of objectivity should not be allowed to excuse the undue representation of our faults.' What the new

Tom Garvin suggested that Ireland was blighted by something 'that looked like gerontocracy.' Eamon de Valera's Council of State meeting in June 1966. Front row (left to right): Andrias Ó Caoimh, S.C. Attorney General; Seán MacEntee, Tánaiste and minister for Health; Seán Lemass, Taoiseach; President de Valera; Martin O'Flaherty, Secretary to the President; Conor A. Maguire, Chief Justice; Cahir Davitt, President of the High Court; James Dillon, TD, leader of Fine Gael. Standing (left to right) General Richard Mulcahy, TD; Senator Liam Ó Buachalla, Cathaoirleach of the Senate; Patrick Hogan, TD, Ceann Comhairle; Seán T. O'Kelly; Senator Robert P. Farnan; Maurice Dockrell, TD, Lord Mayor of Dublin; Domnhall Ó Buachalla; John A. Costello, TD; William Norton, TD; Patrick J. Little. Notice the number of women. When President Kennedy landed at Dublin airport in 1963, there was only one woman in the fifty-strong reception party – his sister, Jean Kennedy Smith. Members of the Council of State had all been invited to the special lunch in Dublin on New Year's Eve 1961 to mark the launch of the new television service.

---

12 Garvin, *New Republic*, 60.
13 Robert J. Savage, 'Introducing Television in the Age of Seán Lemass', in Brian Girvan and Gary Murphy (eds), *The Lemass Era, Politics and Society in the Ireland of Seán Lemass* (Dublin, 2005), pp. 191-214.

It snowed in Dublin on the opening night but a good-humoured crowd saw in the New Year, outside the Gresham Hotel in Dublin, where they welcomed the new television station and were entertained by the Army No. 1 Band.

Taoiseach Seán Lemass on a monitor for guests at the opening night ceremony at the Gresham Hotel. He was, by now, 'a tired workaholic, an ageing man in a hurry, fighting the onset of ill-health and a fading of energies.'

broadcasting Authority 'should aim to present is a picture of Ireland and the Irish as we would like to have it, although our hopes and aims may well be helped by the objective presentation of facts in association with constructive comment.'[14] Hilliard, in his address to the first meeting of the new Authority, suggested that no service would be acceptable if it did not 'maintain worthy standards from the moral point of view'. But his government colleague, Erskine Childers, who had taken a close interest in television, argued that it was generally accepted by experts that television as a medium invariably put the government and the whole of the Establishment of the day 'inevitably on the defensive'.[15]

Would this prove to be the fate of the establishment now gathered in the Gresham Hotel to introduce this new upstart? Even that night there were some indications of how the old deferential order was endangered. Earlier that evening the archbishop's driver Robert was startled as they arrived together at the still unfinished television studios for the live Benediction service which formed part of the opening night's schedule. Drama producer Chloe Gibson – casually dressed in jeans – had been assigned to direct the broadcast. When McQuaid presented himself, accompanied by Robert, now carrying his lordship's vestments, she greeted Robert with the words: 'Sweetheart, you can leave the gear down here.'[16]

14 Lemass to Moynihan, 4 May 1960, NAI DT S14996.
15 Seanad Debates, vol. 66, col. 368, 15 January 1969.
16 John Cooney, *John Charles McQuaid: Ruler of Catholic Ireland* (Dublin, 1999), pp. 346-47; hereafter, Cooney, *McQuaid*.

This photograph was almost certainly taken during the live Benediction ceremony celebrated on opening night by Dr John Charles McQuaid. On the left of picture is his religious adviser, Canon Cathal McCarthy, presumably there to advise the director, Chloe Gibson [right] on any liturgical questions. In the centre is vision mixer, Max Mulvihill. Note the number of onlookers. Michael Barry would soon be comparing the control room to an Eastern bazaar. He complained that 'up to four separate conversations' could be taking place in different parts of the presentation gallery, 'where operators should be learning to concentrate'. It was imperative that 'an atmosphere that allows concentration must be established', with ideally 'lowered voices and perhaps, with advantage, shaded background lighting.'

Michael Barry to all members of Programme Division, 'Television Control Gallery Discipline', [n.d. but 1962], Radio Telefís Éireann Written Archives; hereafter, RTÉWA.

'snoring gently behind the Green Curtain'

AS THE NEW TELEVISION SERVICE was being launched the Roman Catholic church was arguably at the peak of its influence and power in Irish society. One in eight boys among Leaving Certificate students for the previous four years was studying for the priesthood. Explaining this phenomenal figure, Maynooth sociologist and future Bishop of Limerick, Jeremiah Newman, drew attention to the increasing number of priests needed 'for the regular hearing of nuns' confessions'.[17] The society which was about to be exposed to television had been a historically sheltered one. It had further reinforced its isolation by enacting some of the most draconian censorship laws governing print and film in the English-speaking world: the Church was an enthusiastic cheer-leader, approving this cultural and intellectual isolation of the country. This had been further reinforced by the south's neutrality during World War II. O'Faoláin believed that Ireland had been 'snoring gently behind the Green curtain' that she had been 'rigging up' for the previous thirty years – 'Thought-proof, World-proof, Life-proof.'[18]

And this was essentially the Ireland bequeathed to Lemass

One of two articles in the *RTV Guide* of 12 April 1963, on a documentary, *Men for the Harvest*, about Maynooth, the 'largest English-speaking seminary in the world'. The article noted that the producer, Chloe Gibson, with her production assistant Patricia Hughes, 'were the first women to be allowed enter several parts of the college which was founded in 1795.'

17 Jeremiah Newman, 'The Priests of Ireland: A Socio-Religious Survey', *Irish Ecclesiastical Record*, Vol. XCVIII, July 1962, 1-27, August 1962, 65-91. Newman reports on 3,180 vocations from 24,339 school-leavers: i.e. 12.5 per cent.
18 *The Bell*, March 1951, 18.

In the summer of 1961 auditions were held to assess the talent of those many aspiring performers who had written to the new station to be considered. On 25 August, the theatre director Jim Fitzgerald – who was one of the first producer-director recruits – wrote this assessment of one singer.

Auditions at Marian College, Dublin: Arthur Murphy, singer. 'An interesting entertainer. Confident, professional. Light, pleasant tenor.' Murphy's singing of *The Rose of Tralee* 'somewhat inadequate since it calls "voice" – as such – into question. Patter following the number was amusing and showed that he was aware of his comparative vocal inadequacy.' Murphy also sang *Cockles and Mussels* which Fitzgerald reckoned 'bouncy, bright, witty and musically pointed'. He reckoned that Murphy had 'no television technique as yet but would learn fast. Personality "grates" a little due to slight brashness. Yes but will probably lose him to record companies. Generally by Frankie Vaughan out of Anthony Newley, own style still undeveloped.'

Arthur Murphy became a regular broadcaster with RTÉ and in the first month of the new television service he presented an interview programme *Visitors' Book*. In introducing him to its readers, the *RTV Guide* noted his reputation as a pop singer, his 'jazzed-up rendering' of *Cockles and Mussels* having become a best-seller.

It was still customary in 1961 to genuflect and kiss the ring of a Roman Catholic bishop. McQuaid after the Benediction ceremony in Telefís Éireann, 31 December 2011. On the right is Eamonn Andrews. He was wary of McQuaid's interest in the new station.

by his predecessor de Valera, himself a deeply conservative figure. Historians, writers and other observers all noted the significant role of the Roman Catholic Church in mid-twentieth-century Ireland – the country that was about to be exposed to television. Having studied Irish society as it was in the late 1950s, Garvin concluded that 'it appeared superficially that the Catholic Church was more powerful than it had been, arrogating to itself even more of what elsewhere might have been regarded as part of the civic and secular order.'[19] Joseph Lee suggests that since the mid-nineteenth century, the church had attracted 'some of the finer performer talent in the country' whose administrative and managerial abilities had found expression in religion, education, health and welfare.[20] Mercier characterised Ireland as 'priest-ridden, puritanical, philistine, hypocritical, snobbish, money-grubbing, provincial...'.[21] The anti-clerical polemicist Blanshard had in the mid-1950s characterised Irish Catholicism as a 'super-zealous and distinctive form of the original faith, more pugnacious, more self-centred, and more dogmatic than the spirit of Rome itself.'[22]

Although change was imminent, this was not yet appreciated by most church leaders. The most significant of them by far was the Archbishop of Dublin, John Charles McQuaid. He was astute enough

---

19 Garvin, *New Republic*, 37.
20 Joseph Lee, *Ireland, 1912-1985, Politics and Society* (Cambridge, 1989), pp.395-96; hereafter, Lee, *Ireland*.
21 Vivian Mercier, 'Literature in English: 1921-84', in J.R.Hill (ed), *A New History of Ireland: vii; Ireland, 1921-84* (Oxford, 2003), p.509; hereafter, Mercier, 'Literature in English'.
22 Paul Blanshard, *The Irish and Catholic Power* (London, 1954), p.28.

to anticipate the importance of television, and his ambition was nothing less than to determine that any discussion of catholic viewpoints would conform to his orthodox and conservative opinions. He sent two young and highly talented priests abroad for television training. This has been described by a generally unimpressed – and unsympathetic – biographer as 'arguably, the most far-sighted and progressive decision' of McQuaid's career.[23]

At their last meeting before the new service opened, the catholic hierarchy had expressed wariness. Television, while having great potential for good, could also do considerable harm, not merely 'in the diffusion of the erroneous ideas of those who are lacking in deep or accurate knowledge of religious truth, but also in the broadcasting of programmes which offend all reasonable standards of morals and decency.'[24] Cardinal D'Alton in his televised broadcast on opening night, hoped that television would not present viewers 'with a caricature of Irish life, such as we have had from our writers in recent years'.[25] He himself enthusiastically approved of the 'isolation of former days', and disapproved of the media's importation of 'views wholly at variance with Catholic teaching'.[26] Some measure of the paranoia of the hierarchy about new media can be gleaned from the correspondence of Bishop Browne of Galway with his friend and fellow-conservative McQuaid. Browne had complained that *The Furrow* – itself a serious monthly religious journal – 'was doing harm' and even described it as 'an escape route for heretics'. The metaphor was geographical: bishops – and most emphatically McQuaid – had a keen sense of their diocesan territory and it was *The Furrow*'s editorial base, located outside both their dioceses, which left them so powerless to influence the journal's content.

In fact, *The Furrow* provides one of the most interesting sources for commentary on the new television medium in Ireland during the 1950s. Along with Desmond Forristal's discriminating and liberal commentary and criticism, it chronicled just how eclectic was the speculation about the new medium. It published an optimistic prediction of how an Irish television service could influence the millions in Britain who were 'seeking in darkness and ignorance for the light of truth.' Eithne Conway had watched with some dismay how BBC programmes had covered homosexuality, prostitution and artificial insemination. While critical of these programmes coming from Britain, she was also certain that if Ireland had a television service

Kathleen Watkins introduces the opening night's viewing on Telefís Éireann, New Year's Eve, 1961. Cameraman is Chris Darby, floor manager is Tom McDermott. Watkins was asked to keep her harp in the studio in the station's early months. This enabled her to offer an improvised recital in the event of some breakdown.

---

23 Cooney, *McQuaid,* 347.
24 Hierarchy statement, Maynooth, 10 October 1961, *The Furrow*, 12/11, November 1961, 695-97.
25 *Irish Times*, 1 January 1962.
26 *Irish Independent*, 5 March 1962.

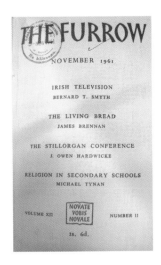

The Furrow took television seriously throughout the 1950s. Desmond Forrestal published regularly on the new medium; he would later be part of the *Radharc* team of priests making television documentaries. But Bishop Michael Browne of Galway thought *The Furrow* 'an escape route for heretics'.

capable of reaching the British public, 'the amount of good' that could be done would prove 'incalculable'. And she concluded that Irish television might yet prove 'the most powerful influence in a new age of missionary endeavour.'[27] Meanwhile, a leading British writer on television, Fr Agnellus Andrew, identified a potential opportunity to influence behaviour within Ireland; he suggested that in 'a Catholic country a daily televised family Rosary might, indeed, make of the entire nation a family at prayer.'[28]

Gaelic, specially coated and dressed for easy consumption

ANOTHER PART OF the traditional Irish establishment, the Gaelic world, also believed it needed to harness the new medium to its own purposes. As was repetitively emphasised at its Annual Congress, the GAA expected the new television service to aim at being Gaelic, national, cultural, educational and entertaining. The GAA presumed that those in charge would prove 'sound in their Gaelic and National outlook'.[29] There must be 'no truck nor truce with Irish servility...'. They considered the radio service already suspect for its 'high rate of Imperial preference' for foreign games such as soccer and rugby.[30] Historically the Gaelic Athletic Association had seen itself as more than the custodians of Gaelic football and hurling: the Irish language, dancing and music were also to be protected and encouraged. Delegates were informed that Irish dancing had received 'a very good reception' when televised in the North; another delegate encouraged support on the grounds that the difference between Irish and other dancing was that between 'civilization and licence'.[31]

From its agenda at the turn of the century, the Irish-Ireland movement had recorded two successes: Gaelic sport and traditional music. Radio had played a vital part in both. Why should not television be to the advantage of the language? That it would prove 'a great boost and fillip' was predicted, with every home a classroom, and 'Gaelic specially coated and dressed for easy consumption.' Television might yet prove to be the 'greatest medium' for the restoration of the Irish language.[32]

Others also expressed optimism – and duty. In the minister's

---

27 Eithne Conway, 'Ireland and television', *The Furrow*, 9/1, January 1958, 33-38.
28 Agnellus Andrew, 'Television and religion', *The Irish Ecclesiastical Record*, 83 (1955), 12-26; hereafter, Andrew, 'Television and religion'.
29 GAA archives, CC/1/19, 1956 volume; Seamus MacFerran was president.
30 Micheal Ó Donnchadha, presidential address, Annual Congress 1955, GAA archives, CC/1/18, 1955 volume.
31 GAA archives CC/1/25, 1962 volume.
32 GAA archives CC/1/21, 1958 volume.

"Bhí fear ann fadó agus fadó a bhí – will ye listen to me?"

The critic Vivian Mercier concluded that because of radio and television, 'the custom of oral story-telling in both Irish and English became almost extinct; even the Irish habit of leisurely, anecdotal conversation was on the wane.' This cartoon in *Dublin Opinion* as the new station went on the air catches this point.

Mercier, 'Literature in English', 516.

Cartoon by James O'Donovan, *Dublin Opinion*, March 1960.

address to the first meeting of the RE Authority, members were told that restoring Irish was 'not a mere pious aspiration but a vital national task', and the new television station would be expected 'to play its full part in ensuring that this aim will be achieved'.[33] Some sceptics believed that television policy would test the state's sincerity. It would be a touchstone 'of governmental honesty and initiative with regard to the language' and also had the potential to become among 'the most formidable opponents of the revival'.[34]

It was appreciated on all sides that television would not be neutral in its impact on the Irish language. Many saw it as a possible tipping point: accepting that television would become hugely popular, they believed it had the potential to save the language or to accelerate its decline. The Commission on the Restoration of the Language had submitted an interim report in March 1959 arguing that television 'should be effectively used to assist the language revival'. It called for an assurance that what it termed 'a satisfactory percentage of the television programmes would be in Irish and that that percentage would be increased gradually. The majority of children's programmes should be in Irish and a proportion of Irish should be used naturally and spontaneously in the other programmes.' It would be more important that Irish 'should be heard occasionally in the news bulletins, sports and entertainment programmes, etc., than that full programmes in Irish should be broadcast now and again.'

In 1962 Irish writers had mixed views about television. Seán O'Casey thought that, 'by and large, the programmes are frightful exhibitions, and I very seldom look at the damned thing.'[1] Patrick Kavanagh had 'some belief' in Telefís Éireann. He thought it was not as committed to 'the weary commercialised convention of entertainment as the Yankee and British outfits.'[2] But on the station's opening night, Austin Clarke – who was at the launch party – offered what Gabriel Fallon thought 'the most amusing response' when interviewed. He told the nation 'in anything but Yeatsian tones' that he 'liked nothing' about television.[3]

1 O'Casey to Lorraine Beaver, 5 December 1962, Krause, *O'Casey Letters*, 340-41.
2 *Hibernia*, December 1962.
3 *RTV Guide*, 5 January 1962.

33 BBCWA EI/2092/2.
34 Eoin McKiernan, *The Will of a Nation: Ireland's Crisis* (St. Paul, Minnesota, 1964), p.10.

The Commission also recommended that Irish should be the administrative language of the new television service from the beginning and if technicians or specialists who were not Irish speakers had to be appointed because of the unavailability of qualified Irish speakers, such appointments should be temporary. 'Appointments could be made permanent when they had acquired a satisfactory knowledge of Irish or when qualified Irish speakers would be available.'[35]

The three key leaders of the new television service by opening night appreciated that the Irish language issue was going to prove even more controversial than might have been expected: each addressed the issue in interviews in the *RTV Guide* during December. Michael Barry said that anyone with a knowledge of another language used it colloquially, 'sometimes seeking the most expressive words from different languages to colour his speech. Something of this can spread right across nearly all programmes and be developed.'[36] Eamonn Andrews allowed himself the complaint that the language groups differed in what they wanted from the new service, leaving it in a no-win situation, but he insisted that the station knew its 'duties to the language, to the people who will pay to watch our service, and to the advertisers who will pay to use it. It is a realistic attitude, and that does not mean that it is just a commercial attitude.'[37]

Edward Roth, when asked about the place of Irish in the new service, would not have given great reassurance to the Gaelgeoirs with his reply: 'I shall work towards giving the Irish people the kind of service they want. And we shall abide by our statutory obligation to the language.' Nor would they have been reassured by one of his asides: 'One of the results of audience research might be that the ratings of programmes in Irish might seriously injure the progress of the Irish revival movement.' On minorities – he was probably thinking of the language lobby – Roth said that minorities would be catered for 'in a minor way. But minorities here seem to be able to look after themselves. They are more vigorous and articulate here than in any other country.'[38]

The problem was that the government had given the new station contradictory instructions which would be quickly appreciated by any television scheduler anywhere: to be popular enough to ensure that the station not become a burden on the exchequer; but also to be pro-active in its support of the Irish language. Thus did the government move the station into the line of fire of those critics who wanted it to save the Irish language with an incremental policy of ratcheting up the proportion of programmes which would use Irish.

'Television production was a rough-hewn affair from the first; before the great vulgarities of later decades set in. There was a freebootery about the licence given to the first producers. A parallel has been made with the licence given to the privateers of an earlier period to go and chart routes where none existed. Someone, after all, had to find the way – and fast. During the course of an impatient century, the cinema film, sound broadcasting, and then television broadcasting passed through progressively accelerating periods of adolescence. It is arguable that, by giving the television programme-makers their heads, the best advantage was taken of the brief anonymity before authoritativeness and then commercial and public interest began to exert their separate pressures. The sense of freedom and the relative anonymity lead to a heady exhilaration.'

Michael Barry, *From the Palace to the Grove* (London, 1992), Royal Television Society, p. 134.

---

35 John Horgan, *Seán Lemass, The Enigmatic Patriot* (Dublin, 1997), pp.309-10; hereafter, Horgan, *Lemass*.
36 *RTV Guide*, 1 December 1961.
37 *ibid.*, 29 December 1961.
38 *ibid.*, 8 December 1961.

2

television 'would be robbed of many of its terrors' if P and T ruled itself out of ever running a TV station – Department of Finance

I T COULD NOT BE CLAIMED that there was any coherent state policy on television in the 1950s. Most politicians were not especially interested. The debate happened behind closed doors, with the all-powerful Department of Finance keeping a very persistent Ó Broin at bay: Finance's attitude moved from one of ignorance, through suspicion, disdain and dithering, to a reluctant acquiescence that the Irish public, like others in the modern world, would want to watch television, and better that they have an Irish channel among their choices than none.

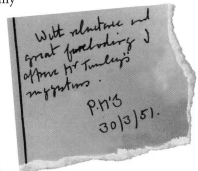

Insofar as there was a policy, Ó Broin embodied it. He was a tireless advocate of public service television. Assiduously, relentlessly, he scourged Finance, requesting support in anticipation of television's arrival. His copious memoranda on the subject were invariably based on the assumption that television was inevitable. His initial foray as early as 1950 was modest enough. He sought permission to buy a television set for the department. The nay-sayers in Finance – who were not being asked for fresh money but rather that Ó Broin could spend from his existing budget – wrote of him in a disdainful manner. A verdict on one of his memoranda elicited the comment that it was difficult 'to take it seriously' or, indeed, 'to have any patience' with him. The public had expressed 'no interest' in television and would probably be reluctant to spend large sums 'on such a luxury'.[1]

Patrick McGilligan, TD, Minister for Finance 1948-51, reluctantly approved the purchase of a television set by the Department of Posts and Telegraphs.

One of the earliest pessimists on this front was Patrick McGilligan, a politician who had established his formidable reputation as a far-sighted, imaginative enabler when he had championed the state investment in the Shannon Scheme in the 1920s. In 1951, as Finance minister, he was reluctantly persuaded by his department to acquiesce in one of Ó Broin's modest proposals to invest in television research. McGilligan minuted that it was with 'reluctance and great foreboding' that he approved such expenditure and it could be agreed only on the understanding that any such service 'must pay its way'. And he added

---

1   Memo to McHenry, 23 February 1950, NAI Fin S104/1/50.

If there was a policy on television, it was the disparate contributions of Leon Ó Broin. His memoir, *Just Like Yesterday*, gives his account.

a query of his own to the permission: 'How many people will be able and prepared to buy TV sets and pay the personal charges?'[2] Reluctance and foreboding would be a fair description of Finance's attitude to Ó Broin for the rest of the decade.

But he was not deterred. As he liked to say himself, he was 'a Finance man'; he had served his apprenticeship in the department and he knew its mind. This might explain an early heresy from him when he was accused of breaking the rules by sending a memorandum directly to cabinet without first giving Finance an opportunity to comment. To Finance this gave his initiative 'an ugly look'. The civil servants in Finance did not profess to know why this had happened but could not believe it was 'a mere accident'. From their reading of earlier proposals from Ó Broin, it was 'abundantly clear' to them that a state-operated TV service 'in some shape or other was in mind'. Despite some tacking and weaving by him, they still believed that his long-term strategy was to ratchet government policy towards a BBC-style model of public service television.

Moreover, Finance's experience of kites from Posts and Telegraphs was not 'too happy' and they would not place 'too much reliance' on Ó Broin's 'change of front'. But they conceded that television 'would be robbed of many of its terrors as far as we are concerned' if Posts and Telegraphs was indeed ruling itself out of ever running a TV service. The advice was proffered that Ó Broin's disclaimer should now be taken at face value and negotiations on research spending reopened on the basis that Finance's attitude had been 'altered by the disclaimer'. They hoped that this would 'not provoke another display of petulance, but one never knows!'[3]

Finance remained determined to exclude any possibility that the state would be encumbered with the responsibility of running a television service. The department believed it to be a luxury service and capable of distorting the balance of payments, given that the station and transmission network – to say nothing of television receivers – would all be imported. But inexorably, as Ó Broin had always predicted, television widened its popular appeal across the developed world. His goal – and his achievement – was to accelerate policy decisions about television by forcing the pace and making it happen while he could still influence the legislative framework within which a television service would be delivered. He effectively retained custodianship of television policy such as it was throughout the 1950s. And he was met with a stonewalling performance from successive finance ministers, no matter which government was in power.

2 McGilligan, note, 30 March 1951, NAI Fin S104/1/50.
3 Finance minute, 10 May 1951, *ibid*.

and what if a schedule was 'unbalanced, trivial and unpalatable'?

BY THE SUMMER OF 1957 as many as fifteen proposals had been received from the private sector interested in winning a licence to provide an Irish television service. Two individuals in particular sought and won special attention: Charles Michelson, a Romanian based in Paris, and Gordon McLendon of the McLendon Investment Corporation from Texas. Both promised to provide a television service at *no* cost to the state in return for permission to establish a commercial radio station in Ireland which would illegally beam commercial programmes into Britain. Commercial television had recently been established in Britain but radio remained a public service monopoly run by the BBC.

McLendon believed it would impress the television commission if he gave his testimony to them in a ten-gallon hat and cowboy boots. Michelson combined a strong anti-communist spin with recommendations from senior Vatican figures. He had spent weeks lobbying politicians and state-sponsored bodies and had made surprising progress. He had even brought Monsignor Georges Roche from Rome to argue that with such a powerful radio station Ireland could play a critical role in the struggle against communism, irreligion and materialism. This latter agenda was emphasised especially to impress McQuaid. In this it failed. McQuaid noted in the margin of the Michelson document that the proposal was 'truly not proved'; moreover its realisation 'would seem to involve this country in a scheme of piracy'. And there was no evidence that Michelson would 'not sell this station, as he did his other stations – and to whom?'[4]

In a logical, well-expressed advocacy of the public service model, Ó Broin argued that there was a 'particular objection' to a private monopoly in a medium such as television. What he termed 'negative external supervision' would scarcely be enough to curb a concessionaire who had introduced a schedule which was 'unbalanced, trivial and unpalatable to intelligent Irish viewers.' But he was especially scathing about the funding proposals from McLendon and Michelson whereby the price of their providing a free television service would be government support for a commercial radio station beamed at the British market on the model of Radio Luxembourg. This, wrote Ó Broin, would mean the 'abandonment' of the international rule of law which

Gordon McLendon, one of two foreigners who offered a free television service – but at a price which Ó Broin, at least, thought much too high.

Charles Michelson also proposed a free television service. He came with letters of introduction from the Vatican to seek McQuaid's support. McQuaid – unlike so many others – was not impressed. It would amount to 'a scheme of piracy.'

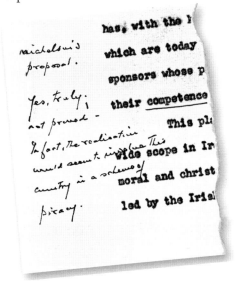

---

4 McQuaid's marginal note on statement of Monsignor Georges Roche, 18 July 1958.

regulated the broadcast spectrum by allocating agreed wavelengths and transmitter power to each state.

Ó Broin was manifestly shocked to find that this proposal was being given serious consideration. He did not shirk from introducing his blunderbuss: Ireland would be the first of 25 countries to break the law and this without having expressed any dissatisfaction with it. Moreover, there was 'no guarantee whatever' that such renunciation of the international agreement would enable a reasonably interference-free wavelength to be obtained. On the contrary, 'defensive action by the countries affected would probably render Ireland's step ineffective and leave our ultimate position worse', since the country would – after such transgressions – be in no position to complain if others encroached on dedicated Irish wavelengths. But having excoriated the notion of the radio proposal, he undermined it further by asking why – even if it were to be proceeded with – the government should not remain the arbiters of who should use such profits to fund a television service. The commercial radio groups concerned were 'hardly the kind of people who should be given specially favourable consideration for the grant of an internal television monopoly.'[5]

IRISH TELEVISION

PROPOSALS FOR A FULL TELEVISION SERVICE REACHING EVERY PART OF THE ISLAND WITH PROGRAMMES OF HIGH STANDARD, PLANNED AND EXECUTED IN IRELAND TO MEET IRISH NEEDS, UNDER THE CONTROL AND WITH THE PARTICIPATION OF A STATE AUTHORITY, BUT WITHOUT CHARGE TO THE EXCHEQUER; LINKED WITH SOME PROPOSALS REGARDING SOUND BROADCASTING.

The Michelson proposal. Note that it promised a television service 'reaching every part of the island'

5   [Ó Broin], memorandum for the government, 'Post Office observations; section on public control and private monopoly', 10 January 1958, RTÉWA: RE 105/58-1.

In December 1952 Erskine Childers, then Minister for Posts and Telegraphs, expressed an interest in television, as is attested in the archives of the British Embassy in Dublin. Childers confided to Ross Williamson, the press attaché, that he was 'madly enthusiastic' to see a sponsored television service in the Republic. But when he was introduced to British advertising executives at a British Embassy dinner, they showed little interest. Childers stated preference was that the capital cost would be borne by a commercial investor and that the government would rent transmission time with an option to buy the station after twenty years. Childers, it should be emphasised, was notoriously prone to flying kites – and this was probably a solo effort. What was elicited from this initiative was that the British did covet the engineering contract for any putative television service and were not unaware of other dimensions. Williamson wrote to the Commonwealth Relations Office that it would be very much to their advantage 'to have the new service controlled financially and influenced culturally' by British business interests. 'It could so easily happen that other influences – not friendly or potentially not friendly – took over this important new instrument of propaganda. But let us hope that won't happen.'

Williamson to A.H.Joyce, 16 February 1953, NAUK, DO 35/9567/58/9/1.

Radio Éireann would remain 'the shabbiest of Cinderellas while our new ugly sisters ... show off their "finery".'

THAT SUCH PROPOSALS were being seriously entertained by some ministers caused Radio Éireann's director Maurice Gorham alarm. He spoke to Ó Broin and – probably prompted by him – expressed his reservations in writing, with the intention that his letter be shown to Lemass. Gorham warned that the government might yet find itself supporting 'a rip-roaring commercial television system' which would primarily be selling foreign goods and 'a rip-roaring commercial international broadcasting system' which would infringe international agreements, and all being done 'in the belief that television is a good thing so long as it is free, and that any international infringements in sound broadcasting can be justified by the possibility of promoting exports, tourism, and the sale of sweep tickets.' Both the radio station and the 'free' television service would, in Gorham's opinion, be beyond government control. Meanwhile Radio Éireann would be starved and controlled; 'its content limited to whatever was held not to conflict with Government policy in every sphere – but with hardly anybody listening to it.'

Gorham allowed that what he had outlined 'may be merely a nightmare', but when he considered how badly treated Radio Éireann had been with all expenditure 'resisted on grounds of economy', while 'strong backing' was being given to these other schemes, it was easy to imagine how Radio Éireann 'would become something rather like a folk museum, standing back from the busy street, which is a source of pride to its founders, although nobody ever goes in.'[6] Ó Broin duly passed what he described as this 'absolutely on the mark' analysis to Maurice Moynihan, secretary in the Taoiseach's office, inviting him to show Gorham's letter to Lemass. Ó Broin could not resist the opportunity to pour further scorn on the 'free' proposals. He objected to all the attention being focused on television, to the neglect of radio; if this trend were to continue, Radio Éireann would remain 'the shabbiest of Cinderellas while our new ugly sisters (and how ugly they may be) show off their "finery".'[7]

Ó Broin argued that he would prefer Ireland to have no television service 'if the alternative was to allow private commercial interests to take over'. The labyrinthine process by which the Lemass government eventually reached its final decision on how an Irish television service would be established and financed has already been told.[8] The saga

---

6 Gorham to Ó Broin, 10 February 1958, NAI, DT S 14996B.
7 Ó Broin to Moynihan, 11 February 1958, *ibid.*
8 See Robert J.Savage, *Irish Television: The Political and Social Origins* (Cork, 1996); hereafter, Savage, *Irish Television*.

The Department of External Affairs were told that the Michelson proposal had Vatican approval 'at the very highest level', presumably Pope Pius XII himself.

'Irish television: proposals for a full television service reaching every part of the island.' What came to be known as the Michelson proposal came with Vatican approval. Monsignor Georges Roche, speaking in strict confidence to Leo McCauley, Irish ambassador to the Vatican, wanted the Murnaghan commission to treat the proposal as 'an ordinary commercial application'. He requested the strictest secrecy lest it fell to be handled in the Department of External Affairs 'by someone whose prejudices would cause him to look with suspicion on an activity backed by the Church and so create difficulties not justified by the intrinsic nature of the scheme.' Roche had told McCauley that the Church was 'deeply and actively interested in this scheme as an anti-communist weapon'. If adopted, Ireland would become a centre 'from which would radiate [radio] programmes conforming to the ideals of Christendom and western civilization and competing with Communist propaganda'. McCauley reported that Roche had left him 'in no doubt' that an interest was being taken in the scheme 'at the very highest level'.

McCauley to secretary DEA, 11 September 1958, NAI DT S 14996B. Emphasis probably added within the Department of External Affairs.

included another commission – set up by Finance minister, Seán MacEntee in February 1958 – whose majority findings favouring a commercially run service were rejected precipitately and, to everyone's surprise, by Lemass. Ó Broin described this in his autobiography as 'an extraordinary *volte-face*', ascribing it to pragmatism. It was not at all surprising to him that such a practical politician would come to this conclusion. But he may have understated his own influence: Lemass had called him in for a briefing and had contented himself with listening to the Ó Broin line.[9]

Meanwhile, another body, 'The Commission for the Restoration of the Irish Language', brought out a special interim report solely devoted to television's role in the language revival. The Commission was not without ambition. It suggested that Irish rather than English should be used in the day-to-day running of the station; that all staff should be fluent in Irish; and that the schedule include strict quotas of Irish language content. Such a policy was needed 'in order that the television public, including viewers, advertisers, administrators, artists, technicians... may realise that the Irish language is to be accorded its due status as the national language.'

This report was sent to de Valera, by then in his final months as Taoiseach and he forwarded it to the Michael Hilliard Minister for Posts and Telegraphs for any observations. Ó Broin's reply was masterly. He again called for public service custodianship: if all or most of the putative television service was 'to be operated by a commercial group, Irish or foreign, with financial profits as its primary objective, the revival movement might be regarded as dead.' But he combined this attitude with a rebuttal of what he deemed the unrealistic proposals from the language commission.[10] He did allow that Irish language programmes would have a limited place in the sort of service he had in mind: it would 'probably be necessary as a token of the government's sincere desire to advance Irish that some programmes in Irish be broadcast even in the knowledge that their public will be extremely small. Gestures of this sort, though necessary, do little to advance the cause of Irish and it will probably be necessary to restrict them within reasonable limits.'[11]

9 Leon Ó Broin, *Just Like Yesterday* (Dublin, n.d. [1982]), pp.210-11; hereafter, Ó Broin, *Yesterday*.
10 Robert J. Savage, *A Loss of Innocence? Television and Irish Society, 1960-72* (Manchester, 2010), p. 196; hereafter, Savage *Loss*.
11 Savage, *Irish Television*, 196-97.

Although couched as a response to the interim report of the language commission, this was Ó Broin regaining the initiative for the host department in what he saw as the wholly unsatisfactory manner in which other more senior departments had been unsupportive, irresponsible and dilatory in their handling of television policy. If television was to be used positively for national objectives, it was Posts and Telegraph's conviction that the television Authority 'should itself operate the programmes – that is, *all* the programmes'.[12]

If there was a policy on television, it was composed of the disparate contributions of Ó Broin: his haggling challenges to Finance on the need to have a policy; his authorship of departmental responses to key documents; his evidence to the commission; his semi-official private correspondence with BBC leaders; his face-to-face meeting with Lemass; and his excoriating rebuttal of the arguments of those who offered a 'free' television service in return for permission to beam pirate commercial radio to Britain. Ó Broin had had a life-long interest in broadcasting. As a young man he had rigged up his own reception aerial to listen in to the new radio station 2RN on its opening night in 1926. Thirty-five years later he would be again at home as the new television service was launched in Dublin's Gresham Hotel. He was not among those invited to the station's launch.

Throughout the 1950s Leon Ó Broin took the keenest interest in the new medium of television and believed an Irish service was inevitable. That it should be based on a public service model was his primary objective and he assiduously worked to that end. He was not among the guests at the opening night party at the Gresham Hotel. He could still remember the snub many years later: 'The world and his wife were there. I wasn't. I wasn't invited.'

Author interview with Ó Broin, 1976.

12 Horgan, *Lemass*, 312.

In August 1959, Sir Robert Fraser, director-general of the Independent Television Authority, alerted the regulatory authorities in Britain that he had had a letter from his chairman, Sir Ivone Kirkpatrick, informing him that Erskine Childers had invited him to join the forthcoming Irish Television Board (the Radio Éireann Authority). Kirkpatrick knew he must decline, but wondered how he could do so as tactfully and diplomatically as possible. He asked whether or not legally he could be on two boards, one for Ulster (the ITA's remit covered UTV) and one for the Republic, adding that any such individual 'would probably be shot by both sides simultaneously'.

The incoming permanent secretary of the Commonwealth Relations Office, Sir Alexander Clutterbuck – lately ambassador in Dublin – was consulted and agreed that any such appointment would be 'highly undesirable'. The file notes that Childers was being 'very persistent' about the matter and he was not even the minister in the Irish government with responsibility for broadcasting. It is possible that this was another 'solo run' by Childers; but it is also possible that he was acting with the approval of his colleagues or even at the prompting of Eamon de Valera, who had met Kirkpatrick – and discussed television with him – the previous October. Nothing came of the initiative but, whereas the British establishment was against any such involvement, they also appreciated that there was no need for ITV 'to stand at arm's length from the new Board. On the contrary, we would hope that, in the interests of Anglo-Irish relations, they would be ready to guide the fledgling's first uncertain flights – but from the shadow of the woods, not *in coram populo*.'

Sir Robert Fraser [ITA] to W.A. Wolverson [GPO HQ, London], 17 August 1959; J. Chadwick to P. Bridges, 26 August 1959, NAUK, HO 256/467; Ivone Kirkpatrick to Eamon de Valera, 8 October 1958, NAI DT S14996A.

'television: the very word is half-Latin and half-Greek. No good can come of it.'

THROUGHOUT THE 1950S a debate continued about the impact which this new phenomenon of television would have on society. Readers of *The Irish Ecclesiastical Record* were advised to give 'long and careful preparation before you admit the monster to your homes.'[13] Orson Welles had warned that if the home were 'to become a non-stop movie house, God help the home.'[14] The Pope agreed with Welles. His concern was the deplorable cinema atmosphere of 'materialism, fatuity and hedonism' which would, through television, 'penetrate within the very walls of the home'.[15]

Such warnings about the new medium could be read in the Irish religious press. Readers of *The Irish Monthly* were informed as early as 1950 that television had 'swept the United States like a prairie fire.' The social historian of the future would 'mark television as *the* greatest influence on American civilization since the internal combustion engine.'[16] That children, especially, needed protection from television was widely argued. Readers of *The Irish Ecclesiastical Record* were reminded of the 'obvious obligation of supervision, on civic and religious authorities and on parents': selective viewing was all important. 'The practice of sitting hour after hour and letting the television programme drip over you is less than human.'[17] Another writer asked if television might not 'create and confirm the habit of merely *looking* at life instead of studying and reflecting upon it?' Would a diet of 'spoon-fed instruction and entertainment' not result in 'the desire for ever-new and easier assimilation?'[18] A priest contributed an article to *The Furrow*, 'The teaching sister and the modern girl', suggesting how nuns could impart to their pupils 'a facility for moderate use and prudent selection' of their future television viewing.[19]

Throughout the developed world the new medium was under scrutiny. The Church of England's submission to the Pilkington Committee on the future of British broadcasting struck a note of alarm. It condemned some television programmes as 'vicious' on the grounds that they contained 'brutality, sexual incitement, or the condoning of moral depravity'.[20] An Irish submission to Pilkington

'Action-adventure' was the euphemism used by American television executives as they fought a ratings war based on thrillers and crime series which included ever-increasing violence. During 1960-61 ABC Television used this advertisement to emphasise their leadership over Network Y [CBS] and Network Z [NBC].

Broadcasting, 9 September 1960.

13 Andrew, 'Television and religion', 25.
14 Asa Briggs, *The BBC: the First Fifty Years* (Oxford, 1985), pp.243-44.
15 Andrew, 'Television and religion', 23.
16 Patrick Purcell 'TV or not TV?' *Irish Monthly*, vol. lxxviii, December 1950, 576.
17 Andrew, 'Television and religion', 24.
18 S.St. Clair Morrison, 'The writer and TV', *The Irish Monthly*, May 1954, vol.lxxxii, 182-84.
19 Edward Murphy, 'The teaching sister and the modern girl', *The Furrow*, 9/9, September 1958, 563
20 The speaker was Dr F.A.Cockin, recently retired bishop of Bristol. Church of England, oral evidence to Pilkington Committee, 'Responsibility of Broadcasters: effect of television', NAUK HO 244/261.

anticipated the influence of television serials, so-called, 'soaps'. The submission noted the special importance of 'the set values and attitudes of hero figures.' They were not stating that

> every play or dramatic programme should have a 'moral'; we are emphasizing that every such programme *has* a moral and that the main impact of television on values and attitudes derives from such programmes, especially those in serial form and that such programmes should be so designed as not to debase standards.[21]

In America where many of these programmes originated, it was becoming apparent that those winning the ratings wars were the series that were most violent. The historian of American television, Erik Barnouw, noted that the networks in their orders to the Hollywood studios demanded more action. 'They never – or seldom – said "violence," but that is what they got'.[22]

As the television service was awaited in Ireland, there was a fair amount of scepticism about whether the net effect of television would benefit society or otherwise. And this debate was worldwide. Intellectuals were especially suspicious. Had not the celebrated editor of the *Manchester Guardian*, C.P.Scott, warned the world about television: the very word was 'half-Latin and half-Greek. No good can come of it.' [23]

C.P.Scott, editor of the *Manchester Guardian*. 'Television: no good can come of it.'

---

21 'Social Study Conference (Ireland)' file, Pilkington Committee papers, NAUK, HO 244/764. The authors were Michael O'Flanagan, Ena Meehan and Brian McGuigan.
22 Erik Barnouw, *Tube of Plenty: The Evolution of American Television* (Oxford, 1990, second revised edition), p.263; hereafter, Barnouw, *Tube of Plenty*.
23 Asa Briggs, *The History of Broadcasting in the United Kingdom: Sound and Vision: iv, 1945-55* (Oxford, 1995) p.1; hereafter, Briggs, *Sound and Vision*.

The possible impact of television on radio listening was widely debated as the new medium became more popular. In 1951 – when television was still in its infancy – the *Irish Times* commented on television enthusiasts who were asserting 'that the new medium must inevitably replace the old', and that radio would 'shortly be as dead as the dodo'. Their argument was that radio, because it had been the only source of home entertainment, had 'undertaken a vast amount of work' unsuited to the medium. Television, on the other hand, possessed 'all the powers of radio, film and theatre combined, together with advantages enjoyed by none of these.' This left radio 'akin to that of a one-legged dancer', who had done 'very well in view of his natural limitations', but who now must retire, since 'an accomplished two-legged rival' had arrived. The newspaper's radio critic, however, was not so pessimistic. He thought it 'most unlikely' that radio would meet the fate of the silent movies. Rather, it would continue to provide 'a pleasant accompaniment to the rattle of the housewife's dust-pan and pot-lids.'

G.H. 'Television threat to radio's future', *Irish Times*, 11 May 1951.

'this thing', 'the peepshow', 'a torture-chamber'

HISTORICALLY IRISH BROADCASTING had not suffered from party pressures: this, for the simple reason that it was insulated entirely from politics. But on their rare incursions into the broadcasting arena in the early days, the instinct of the politicians had been 'to steer clear, as far as possible, of politics and religion.'[24] When a suggestion was made during the 1932 general election that some 'short speeches or statements' by the political parties might be broadcast, it withered through lack of support. The civil service advice was that it would be best to avoid 'the abuse which might ensue if unrestricted political broadcasts were permitted.'[25] Finance minister Ernest Blythe – who would be a member of the first television Authority thirty years later – did not need any such discouragement. His own policy was expressed in his decision on the file: 'I am against political broadcasting.'[26] Fianna Fáil, soon to be in power for a sixteen-year period, proved equally conservative, accepting the advice to eschew election debates on radio because they were 'obviously full of dangers in an inflammatory atmosphere such as ours'.[27]

Nor was this caution coming merely from the politicians and civil servants. The broadcasters, too, lacked adventure, as was attested by

24 J.J.Walsh to P.S.O'Hegarty, 21 May 1926, Posts and Telegraphs file, RTÉWA.
25 O'Hegarty, 4 February 1932, *ibid*.
26 Blythe, memo, 5 February 1932, *ibid*.
27 O'Hegarty to Traynor, 10 April 1937, RTÉWA.

Not what it seems; not Ireland's earliest television broadcast. Cumann na nGaedheal leader W.T.Cosgrave uses 'a talking film' – shortly after the 'talkies' were invented – as a means of widening his party's appeal to voters in the 1932 election. The *Illustrated London News* reported that the innovation had made a favourable impression, with sound reproduction being excellent.

the first chairman of the new television authority, Eamonn Andrews. Drawing on his own early experience as a broadcaster in Dublin, he had found that 'the greatest care' was taken to avoid topics 'that were at all likely to evoke even a whiff of party controversy and, if possible, any controversy at all.' Radio Éireann, he believed, was 'one of the worst but best-meaning radio services in the world'.[28] Indeed radio waited until television had carved out a new frontier for current affairs before being emboldened to take its own early steps. So reticent and tardy had Radio Éireann been – prior to television's arrival – that, insofar as current affairs was concerned, this could justly be described as the golden age of *silent* radio.

The introduction of an Irish television service presented an entirely new challenge to politicians. In other democracies throughout the 1950s it was recognised that television was changing the very nature and style of political communication: it was no longer a matter of words alone. According to one of the world pioneers in current affairs television, Grace Wyndham Goldie, it consisted

> not only of what a speaker said but what he conveyed by his manner and bearing; by the turn of his head; by the lines on his face; by the way in which he used his hands; by the gestures and mannerisms which were part of him. Seen on television political leaders became at once more human and more vulnerable.

It all came down to the viewer's 'personal assessment of the calibre and trustworthiness' of the politician on the screen.[29] Irish politicians were becoming aware of these arguments. They were hearing that television had the reputation of being both powerful and fickle.

They were not alone in their wariness: the Australian prime minister, Robert Menzies, had expressed the hope that television – what he termed 'this thing' – might be delayed until he had completed his political career. In Britain, Winston Churchill had termed the new medium 'the peepshow', limiting the public to only one peep in his own case, on his eightieth birthday.[30] And Harold Macmillan had warned that any successful political television programme seemed 'to be more and more a cross between a music-hall turn and a scene in a torture-chamber.'[31] Macmillan was fond of

One Finnish woman in the 1960s recalled, for an oral history project, her indebtedness to television in its early years: 'nothing could beat the feeling of freedom' when her husband shared the housework and Finnish television's broadcasting hours were extended to midnight. 'A granny living downstairs had done some baking. We had a bun circle, because I couldn't bake. We went to the sauna and ate Janssonin kiusaus [casserole of potatoes and anchovies] or cabbage pie and then went to watch the TV. That's what I call happiness. We would have gone on watching TV until the morning.'

Jukka Kortti and Tuuli Anna Mahonen, 'Reminiscing Television: Media ethnography, oral history and Finnish third generation media history', in *European Journal of Communication*, vol.24, 2009, 64-65.

---

28 *Irish Times*, 1 November 1967.
29 Grace Wyndham Goldie, *Facing the Nation: Ttelevision and Politics: 1936-76* (London, 1977), p.188.
30 Inglis, *ABC*, 193.
31 Harold Macmillan's speech to the parliamentary press gallery, 14 March 1962; Antony Jay (ed), *The Oxford Dictionary of Political Quotations* (Oxford, 1996), p.245. I am grateful to my late son Jonathan Philbin Bowman for drawing this reference to my attention.

Harold Macmillan compared a television studio to 'a torture-chamber', complaining of the camera's 'hot probing eye'.

More than fickle, television could prove decisive, most tellingly in its impact on the 1960 U.S. presidential election. In the first ever televised debates between the candidates, Richard Nixon looked uncomfortable and ill-prepared in the reaction cut-away shots as John F.Kennedy emphasised his points. And Nixon suffered from 'five o'clock shadow': he had not been advised to shave just before the broadcast. Most tellingly, opinion polls showed that television viewers believed Kennedy had come out best in the exchanges; radio listeners believed Nixon had. Kennedy's verdict on television's impact: 'We wouldn't have had a prayer without that gadget.'

this metaphor, emphasising it again in an early party political broadcast which he opened by introducing viewers to the torture instruments: 'the camera's hot probing eye' and these other 'monstrous machines', all of which he had been advised to ignore and imagine that the viewers were 'sitting here in the room with me.'[32] More than fickle, television could in certain settings prove decisive, notably in the impact which the televised debates had had on the Kennedy-Nixon presidential election in the United States in 1960.

As we have already seen, Irish politicians had historically been wary of broadcasting. When they declined to participate in live political debates during the 1948 election, it was suggested that they feared the medium of radio because 'without sincerity at the mike there will be no truth trickling through the receiver set'. Radio was 'the domestic lie-detector, and, as such, may well be passed up by the politicians in favour of the open-air forum.'[33] A decade later Hilton Edwards had another open-air forum in mind when he thought of the new medium of television. He believed that it had 'taken the place of the Roman Circus. In the old days when you made a political *faux pas* and you wanted to divert the public, you got a few Christians and you chucked them to a few mangy lions. Now you just chuck them to the television reporters. In other words, it's essentially a sadistic form of entertainment.' Having made this point, he added – perhaps fortunately since he was a senior executive in the new service – television could also be 'much more than that'.[34]

32 Opening to Conservative Party political broadcast, 24 January 1962, 'Call for "A little extra effort"', *The Times*, 25 January 1962.
33 O.G.D[owling], 'Air Space for politicians?', *Evening Herald*, 15 January 1948.
34 Hilton Edwards, 'RTÉ: Drama on Television' [interview by Cyril Farrell], *Aquarius*, 1973, pp.104-09; hereafter, Edwards, *Aquarius*.

3

'a catholic of Irish ancestry ... a go-getter ... and no strings attached'

THE GREATEST CHALLENGE to the first Radio Éireann Authority was to seek an experienced chief executive for the new television service. At least one Irish candidate was available. In late 1959 Maurice Gorham, director of Radio Éireann since 1953, terminated his contract, which was not due to expire until June 1961. This was in the context of an imminent vacancy for the new post of director-general of the combined radio and television service, 'to leave both the Minister and himself free in the matter when the time comes'.[1] Gorham's broadcasting career had been spent at the BBC at the most senior levels in radio and television and he was author of *Television: Medium of the Future*, published as early as 1949. Where other intellectuals were filled with foreboding, Gorham believed that television – while it would draw audiences from the cinema and radio – would not deplete the numbers who attended theatres, concert halls, art galleries, libraries and sports terraces; 'at least the man who has television will have more to come home to, and will know far more about what he might go to when he does choose to go out.'[2]

He was considered for the position of director-general and certainly had a champion in a key administrative position, his friend Leon Ó Broin. Some years earlier Ó Broin had characterised Gorham as indispensable to the country because of his wisdom on decisions concerning the putative television service: 'we would be seriously handicapped if we had to try to deal with the subject in his absence'.[3] But the Authority, to the disappointment of Ó Broin, preferred 'an unknown and relatively inexperienced American'.[4] Ó Broin reports Gorham as being 'none too happy', when he read of the persons 'likely to be given charge of television'.[5]

Ó Broin criticised the members of the first Radio Éireann Authority for not appreciating Maurice Gorham [below], the former director of Radio Éireann: otherwise they would have appointed this 'most cultivated Irishman who had unequalled experience of all forms of broadcasting to be their director-general instead of an unknown and relatively inexperienced American'.

Ó Broin, *Yesterday*, 211.

1 Memo, 25 August 1959, NAI, DT S16726.
2 Maurice Gorham, *Television: Medium of the Future* (London, 1949), p.140.
3 Ó Broin to Moynihan, memo, 25 November 1957, NAI, DT S3532D.
4 Ó Broin, *Yesterday*, 211.
5 *ibid.*, 182.

The successful candidate was a Bostonian of Irish-American parentage, Edward J.Roth. In his letter of application, Roth played the Irish card. Along with his impressive career details, he added a covering letter which he suggested 'might be of some interest to you'. In it emphasised his Irish roots. For the greater part of his life he had lived in an Irish-American home and community in Boston. His grandparents – and those of his wife – had all been born in Ireland. Indeed Roth supposed that 'there must have been times' in his younger years when he believed himself 'in Ireland...rather than Boston', so great was the Irish influence in his home. He believed that spending his first twenty-seven years in Boston had given him 'a considerable depth of insight to the Irish people, their likes and dislikes, their history and their culture...through my personal family inheritance, my experience and my independent study.'[6]

The Roth appointment file also suggests that Roth believed he ought to emphasise his catholicity in applying for this important public post in Ireland. This is reflected in the referees he nominated and in their concentration on this dimension. At least three of those supporting him mentioned his good Catholic home life and another wrote that he had 'that indefinable quality of being a moral and thinking Christian'.[7] Such an emphasis on the religious beliefs of a key employee was not exceptional in that era: the Board of Governors of the BBC sought a reassurance from Hugh Carleton Greene that he had no intention of converting to Roman Catholicism before appointing him director-general.

'I'm leaving so that my children can return and get jobs in Irish Television, that's why I'm leaving.'
– *Dublin Opinion*, October 1961

Eamonn Andrews, who took seriously his duties as chairman of the first Authority, was Roth's champion. Himself a television professional and aware of the challenges facing the first director-general, Andrews reckoned Roth the 'outstanding applicant'[8] with ability 'of a high degree'. He was especially impressed with Roth's experience as a manager of start-up stations in other countries. Andrews informed the Authority that, aside from Roth's impressive job interview, he had spent ten hours with him on Roth's visits to Dublin and could strongly recommend him. His weaknesses were

---

6   Covering letter, Roth to Irvine, 9 July 1960, along with formal application, Roth appointment file, RTÉWA.
7   Robert F.Stolfi [CBS television] to Irvine, 30 August 1960, *ibid.*
8   Note as to applications for DG post and opinion of Broadcasting Authority on E.J.Roth, 22 August 1960. RE Authority papers. There is an early list of applicants, not including Roth – possibly a 'long list' of those to be considered – in Blythe's papers. Of the 47 listed, only seven were Irish, UCDAD, P24/957.

'his lack of first-hand knowledge of Ireland and perhaps certain gaps in his intellectual make-up.' But balanced against this were 'such factors as his proven ability to adapt himself to other countries, his academic qualifications, his catholicity, and his Irish ancestry.' Andrews was impressed by Roth's negotiations 'on delicate subjects' with the Catholic hierarchy when at the University of Notre Dame 'and by his unprompted statement that he personally favoured a revival of the Irish language'. Above all, Andrews admired Roth's admission that he needed 'to take counsel initially in matters of policy affecting the day to day running of Irish television.' Such advice would be forthcoming.

Andrews believed that Roth's appointment would be popular if RE/TE 'presented him as he is – a catholic of Irish ancestry, a young man, a married family man, a go-getter with international experience and no strings attached.' For Andrews, Roth was the man 'to get the station on the air in the most economic and sensible way'.[9] At least one Authority member may have lacked such outright enthusiasm. Andrews had originally reported that the Trinity historian T.W. Moody 'had expressed agreement' with the decision to appoint Roth; but in the minutes those three words are scored through and replaced by 'would not disagree' with the decision.[10]

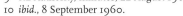

9 RE Authority, minutes, 22 August 1960.
10 ibid., 8 September 1960.

'There'll be no programmes with scenes of violence – does that eliminate the GAA ...?'

Nick's cartoon in the *Irish Times*, 17 November 1960, following the Andrews, Roth press conference.

The *Irish Times* lead story on 17 November 1960, introducing Edward Roth as the television service's first director-general. Roth had been appointed the previous week when the Radio Éireann Authority enjoined him to deliver a service that would have a 'distinctly Irish quality', reflecting traditional values and which would recognise its 'responsibilities as a public service concerned with cultural interests'. But it also emphasised the necessity to deliver 'a very high popular entertainment content' in order to build significant audiences. This dilemma of not becoming a burden on the tax-payers while also being a public service broadcaster with numerous cultural duties, remained a central dilemma for the new station throughout its existence. Roth got a favourable press after Andrews introduced him to the media. But the *Sunday Independent* thought him overpaid and unsuited to the task because of his lack of knowledge of contemporary Ireland.

Sunday Independent, 20 November 1960.

'Hilton Edwards boasted in a humorous self-deprecating way that he knew "nothing about television". In spite of his avowed ignorance, or more likely to prove that he really was not so ignorant at all, he wrote and spoke a great deal of eloquent nonsense, spiced with a few acute observations, when called upon to do so in the months leading up to the first transmissions.'

Fitz-Simon, *The Boys*, 242.

THE PIONEERING SPIRIT of the embryonic television service, combined with its naivete about the scale of the challenges ahead, could be illustrated from the records of many departments. Drama provides a telling example. It was at Eamonn Andrews's suggestion that Roth attempted to recruit Hilton Edwards as head of drama, arguably the most gifted theatre director then working in Ireland. Edwards was an Englishman who had lived in the country for decades and possessed 'a no-nonsense perception of Irish institutions, the Irish people, and of course the Irish theatre'.[11] He recalled that he had been approached by Roth on the strength of having done some work for Granada television.[12]

Roth 'over a series of lunches propounded the idea of making drama one of the staples of programming'. Edwards, initially shy of working for such a large organisation, found his reservations 'slowly evaporating'. Roth did not lack ambition. He suggested that the station should transmit 'one locally produced hour-long and one half-hour play a week, at least during the winter months, and perhaps a drama serial as well.' Edwards 'grew more enthusiastic', talked of a large staff and promised a policy document which Roth could bring to the Authority. Christopher Fitz-Simon – who, as well as being Edwards's biographer, had himself been a pioneer producer-director in the drama department – comments: 'There seems to have been little discussion on the matter of budget, and none on the availability of studio space.'

Denis Johnston offered congratulations to Edwards on his new appointment and further congratulations to RTÉ for selecting him. 'It is one of the really bright spots in what otherwise looks like a grim situation, and I was more than delighted to hear it. I hope that you will not let any Trolls[13] drive you potty...'.[14] Brian O'Nolan also expressed his pleasure – and surprise – to Edwards 'because heretofore, when a highly technical post with a decent salary had to be filled, some dreadful gobshite whose uncle is an FF T.D. disengaged himself from one of the peaks in Kerry, applied for the job, and was immediately appointed.' He saw Edwards's appointment as 'a very good sign', since nobody in Ireland had 'greater qualification and experience, not only of producing but of acting itself'.[15]

---

11 Christopher Fitz-Simon, *The Boys: A biography of Micheal MacLiammoir and Hilton Edwards* (Dublin, 2002), p.239; hereafter, Fitz-Simon, *The Boys*.
12 Edwards, *Aquarius*, 104.
13 Like much slang, 'trolls' has changed its meaning over time: as used here, manifestly an American term for those who tend to gratuitously exasperate or annoy others.
14 Johnston to Edwards, 27 June 1961, Edwards papers, RTÉWA.
15 O'Nolan to Edwards, 2 July 1961, *ibid*.

Edwards needed a production assistant who was 'familiar with the twisty paths through the cultural thickets of Dublin.' Sheila Carden, who worked closely with Edwards in his period as head of drama, believed that Roth had given him *carte blanche* on entertainment allowances and on expenditure on his office; it all 'contrasted markedly with the parsimony' which she observed in other departments. He invited the distinguished actor Donald Wolfit to come from London 'to discuss a programme idea and arranged for him and his wife to stay at the Russell Hotel, then the most expensive in the city; when the bill reached Accounts there was loud tut-tutting, though not yet loud enough to set off the alarm-bells.'

Fitz-Simon, *The Boys*, 243.

This referred to Edward's theatre experience: O'Nolan seemed unaware that television drama might call for specialist qualifications and experience which Edwards singularly lacked. But Edwards at least was aware of his limitations and to O'Nolan – who had included some film sequences in a proposed script – he wrote that 'although filming is not out of the question, there is naturally such a thing as pure TV technique as distinct from film. This I am learning and I am instructed as much as possible to see that productions are in this TV technique rather than in that of film.'[16] Edwards combined a note of diffident curiosity about the new medium with a constant emphasis on his lack of confidence concerning his competence.

In the summer of 1961 Edwards initiated a trawl for television scripts. He wrote to many established Irish writers inviting submissions. Assiduous, courteous and encouraging, he emphasised how experimental their approach could be. He explained to Austin Clarke that plays which had been written originally for the stage 'would have to be mechanically moulded or broken-down into visual television form', although this did not mean 'distortion of the script, only the breaking-down of the action in such a way as to give a more varied ocular interest'. He admitted to Clarke that he was 'only feeling' his way 'in this technique which is, after all, pretty new to all of us...'.[17] In format he encouraged Brian O'Nolan to be experimental, 'provided it can be got over through the TV medium'. In his case it need not necessarily be a comedy, although such a script would be very welcome, since there was 'not much good

The poet Austin Clarke on the opening night had told Michael O'Hehir – and the nation – that he liked nothing about television. But he was persuaded to make this documentary about himself. The producer, was Adrian Cronin [dark glasses] and the cameraman [lower right] was Godfrey Graham. Joe Kennealy is in the centre.

16 Edwards to O'Nolan, 4 July 1961, *ibid*.
17 Edwards to Clarke, 8 August 1961, Austin Clarke papers, NLI, Ms. 38,669/1.

Denis Johnston, in studio during the recording of RTÉ television's *Yeats Story* in 1964. Some footage survives; see *W. B. Yeats recalled* on RTÉ's MediaWeb.

Denis Johnston was rare among Irish writers in being interested in the theory of writing for television drama. As early as 1948 he had told the *Washington Post* that if television was approached 'from the movie point-of-view you get a bad imitation of the movies.... You can't compete with the movies in their own field but you can do things they can't do.'" Johnston had been a pioneering television director in the BBC in the late 1930s. Edwards now wooed him. In June 1961 – six months before the new station opened – Edwards wrote to Johnston that being himself 'a copycat and not an originator', he had not gone beyond an idea, prompted by seeing a BBC series on Churchill's war memoirs.

He suggested some significant Irish historical figures who might make a series: 'shall we say Erskine Childers (Papa of *The Riddle* of course, not Junior of the Ministry) would not be unsuitable, I am sure you can think of more interesting people. The obvious name that springs to mind is Roger C[asement], but I presume that this would not be acceptable for the moment unless the attitude were a purely defensive one.' Johnston replied promptly, agreeing that, given the prevailing climate, Casement was 'impossible, except on the mealy-mouthed Roger McHugh* basis that only makes him laughable.' As for Childers, his main claim was 'as a professional settlement-destroyer', but he had 'a son in a position to object to everything short of a halo'. Johnston reckoned Pearse to have had 'public adventures limited only to one week', the rest being 'mostly speeches in graveyards'. He believed that a good subject 'for romantic treatment' was Collins. 'The obvious objection is that the present Government killed him. But this is not an aspect of the story that need be laboured, and if consciences are still so bad on the subject that Ireland's best soldier cannot yet be honoured, then things are really in a bad way.' He invited Edwards to consider it 'and discuss it as a suggestion.... There are so many adventures that could be serialised about Collins that need not be fabricated, as they would with almost anybody else.'

Bernard Adams, *Denis Johnston: A Life* (Dublin, 2002), p.298; Edwards to Johnston, 23 June and Johnston's reply, 27 June 1961, Edwards papers, RTÉWA.

* Roger McHugh, UCD academic and indefatigable champion of Casement's memory.

comedy being submitted.'[18] He also was at pains throughout this trawl for scripts to reassure these writers concerning remuneration: fees would 'compare very favourably' and would 'not be unacceptable'.[19] Denis Johnston was informed that while a rate of payment had yet to be struck and would hardly be 'on as lavish a scale as in England', Edwards reckoned it would 'be by no means unprofitable, particularly for anything coming from you. You are about the only Irish person I know who can write in the TV idiom. We are all having to learn it over here.'[20]

Johnston, for his part, was critical of what he characterised as American television's 'mad effort to imitate movies by fussy cutting and impossible montage tricks.'[21] This criticism was expressed in a letter in 1950 to his former fellow pioneer in BBC television drama, Michael Barry, himself a renowned practitioner in the infant art-form of putting drama on television. Barry believed that by 1950 in television drama, for better or worse, 'the guide-lines and methods of a complicated studio practice had already been laid down'. Right or wrong, 'they were the work-tools in the hands of the inventors – and a surprising number survived the test of the years.'[22]

Edwards's department had set itself initial goals which were to prove well beyond its capacity in the early months and yet where other new stations would have considered it impossible to even attempt drama, to the RTÉ pioneers it would have been unthinkable not to presume that they could emulate radio's achievement of large audiences for a weekly play. Playwrights too might expect work. The *RTV Guide* asked a cross-section of them what their expectations were of the new medium. David Hayes, Gerard Healy and John McCann reckoned that it would prove an encouragement, as did Brendan Behan, who added tellingly that the television schedule would need to fill a great deal of time and that once authors saw their play on television, they would be 'anxious to get going on another one as quickly as possible'. Behan believed that television would 'help many new playwrights to discover themselves'. Whereas John B. Keane feared that budding playwrights might 'become slaves of its technique' and reckoned that established writers for the stage would 'rebel against the impositions and restraints' of the medium – which he saw as few characters with short speeches.

Maura Laverty believed the arrival of television would not affect the writing of plays 'in the slightest', but allowed that it might prove

Brendan Behan believed television would encourage younger playwrights and anticipated how 'hungry' the schedules would be for new material; but he was too busy appearing on television to write for it. He was especially in demand in stations which thought an interview with a guest who was drunk was good for ratings. Controversy surrounds the circumstances in which two eminent broadcasters, Edward R. Murrow and Malcolm Muggeridge, proceeded with interviews with a heavily intoxicated Behan, the latter broadcast live on BBC's flagship *Panorama* programme on 18 June 1956. Historian of the BBC, Asa Briggs, wrote that Behan had been 'incoherent' with Muggeridge and 'ineffective' with Murrow, *Small World*, 8 November 1959. This screen grab from an RTÉ interview with Behan very shortly before he died is marked 'unclear if ever broadcast'.

Asa Briggs, *The History of Broadcasting in the United Kingdom: Competition: v, 1955-1974* (Oxford, 1995), p.175.

18 Edwards to O'Nolan, 30 June 1961, Edwards papers, RTÉWA.
19 Respectively to Maura Laverty, 16 June, Brian O'Nolan, 30 June 1961, *ibid*.
20 Edwards to Johnston, 23 June 1961, *ibid*.
21 Johnston to Barry, c. summer 1950, in Michael Barry, *From the Palace to the Grove* (London, 1992), pp.138-39.
22 Barry, *From the Palace to the Grove*, 133.

RTV Guide, 26 January 1962 published a survey of Irish playwrights offering their opinions on the new medium.

an encouragement and even result in what she called some 'real play*wrighting*'! Donagh MacDonagh's estimate was that it was impossible to anticipate television's impact –'Nobody knows' – while Austin Clarke foresaw a challenge awaiting the producers who would have to find a method which would give 'due value to the language of the play'. He may also have been prescient, predicting the importance of the soap opera when talking of 'a completely new field of drama of a popular kind'. John O'Donovan believed that television would have no effect on the art of the playwright and suggested that those who claimed otherwise were 'phonies and fakers'. In his opinion the television play presented no new challenges in dramatic technique: as with theatre and cinema, it needed 'arresting dialogue, observant characterisation and interesting situations', and any amount of 'lighting effects, camera gimmickry and hopping from one lens to another' would not turn a bad play into a good one.[23]

The arrival of television did provide employment and audiences for writers but also for others working in theatre. Fitz-Simon reports that Edwards's artistic circle 'was agog with excitement' over the prospect of him as head of drama at the new station: it 'quickly became plain to the theatre fraternity that a thoroughly Gate-orientated unit was being built up – but, had he been asked, Edwards would have declared with perfect justification that these were the best people available.'[24] Notoriously overcrowded, underfinanced and insecure, the theatrical profession in general – and not just actors – saw the coming of television as a potential source of more secure employment, and not just in the drama department. Were their skills not as relevant as those possessed by all the others aspiring to work for the new service? Workers in the theatre had one further advantage: in the main they were not abandoning secure pensionable jobs. Many now gravitated towards television.

within a week O'Hehir was sent terms 'which I could not refuse and I did not'

THE ENTIRE ECONOMY OF SPORT – whether played by amateurs or professionals – would be churned by the impact of television. Many governing bodies were wary. To refuse access might only result in rival codes filling the voracious television schedules. Were television to be embraced, would the broadcasters not want to concentrate on the most popular fixtures? And would the popularity of a particular sport on television necessarily be good for the grass-roots? One

23 *RTV Guide*, 26 January 1962.
24 Fitz-Simon, *The Boys*, 241.

matter was certain: the new medium could not be ignored. The international experience suggested that television policy was manifestly a strategic issue of importance to all governing bodies. Some few believed television inimical to their interests and wanted to ignore it. But soon enough it was recognised that live sport was destined to become a staple of television schedules and that no particular sport could afford to be absent from the small screen. The challenge for governing bodies was to develop a policy that would so ration television access that the

'Consider yourself suspended from the G.A.A., Doyle. Do you hear?'

wider interests of the sport in question were not damaged. Ideally they might be enhanced. It was quickly appreciated that the inevitable improvements in technology – the prospect of colour being the most obvious – would further add to the appeal of sports, and not only to its existing fan base but to new followers who might even confine their engagement to televised viewing.

In Ireland, as many as three codes of football were popular, as was another field game, hurling, which with Gaelic Football had flourished throughout the twentieth century at a time when many other countries were embracing the international codes – almost all of them first codified in Britain. The GAA's achievement in establishing Irish traditional games in the face of this tide of standardisation was remarkable – and owed not a little to their strict and effective use of the boycott of what they termed foreign games. These were soccer, rugby, cricket and hockey which the GAA claimed had been introduced into Ireland by the British army. Repeatedly they had requested Radio Éireann to provide a stand-alone programme devoted to the discussion of Gaelic games, not wishing these to be contaminated by being even discussed on the same sports programme as the 'foreign games' for which they reserved this special antipathy. The GAA could also claim to be the largest amateur sporting organisation in the world. Furthermore, they saw themselves as more than a sporting organisation but as a broad cultural movement to defend not just Gaelic games but also Irish music, dancing and the Irish language.

None of these tensions would make the challenges facing the sports department in the new television service any less demanding. The first head of sport, Michael O'Hehir, reassured the GAA that the new television service could be trusted. The GAA reciprocated, its general secretary reassuring Congress that O'Hehir was

This *Dublin Opinion* cartoon in March 1961 shows two GAA vigilantes whose task it had been for decades to spy on GAA members and recommend suspension for those found playing or even being a spectator at foreign games such as rugby. Here a GAA member watching rugby on television is spotted by two vigilantes, who promptly suspend him. I should add that in research for this book I found no trace of whether or not GAA members were expected to extend their boycott to watching foreign games on television.

Radio Éireann had played a major role in popularising Gaelic games. Communal listening was widespread in the 1930s before radio ownership was commonplacecommonplace as can be seen in this photograph by Christy O'Riordan. Neighbours are gathered at 19 O'Neill Street, Clonmel to listen to the commentary on the All-Ireland hurling final between Kilkenny and Limerick, 3 September 1933.

This is the first telecast of an All-Ireland Football final, 23 September 1962 in which Kerry defeated Roscommon 1-12 to 1-6. Communal viewing was commonplace, and for the same reason as communal listening had been in the early days of radio: not everybody owned a receiver. And this is well before the era of large-screen, high-definition reception. The small receiver is clearly being watched by a capacity crowd of Kerry supporters. Small children were allowed up front but were clearly expected not to block the view of those behind.

Already head of sport on radio, Philip Greene also expected to take on the responsibility for the new television service. He was surprised when it was announced that O'Hehir would be head of sport.

'100 per cent with us'.[25] Barry reckoned that O'Hehir was 'completely on top of his job', ensuring good relations with sporting bodies, and especially with the GAA, 'our "King-pin" in this respect'.

Barry added a somewhat less enthusiastic verdict on Philip Greene, deputy head of sport. Barry wrote that Greene placed 'a higher value' upon his services than did Barry, who admitted reliance on O'Hehir's advice on the matter. Greene was 'able enough, but limited' and 'inclined to minor resentment'.[26] Greene's resentment was more than minor. As head of sport on Radio Éireann, he had expected to inherit the leadership of an expanded department encompassing television and would not have been surprised had he been simply invited to take on the extra responsibility. Not all heads of department had been recruited through interview but Greene was obliged to go before an interview board – which included O'Hehir and Andrews – and presumed his appointment to be a formality. Then to everyone's surprise the announcement was made that O'Hehir would be head of department. Some presumed that the GAA had made representations. But they would scarcely have been necessary. Greene's broadcasting career was centred on soccer. It

25 GAA Archives, CC/1/26, 1963 volume.
26 Michael Barry, memorandum probably for the director-general or the RTÉ Authority, on the performance of department heads at the conclusion of the first year's television broadcasting, n.d. but probably January 1963. Barry papers, RTÉWA.

would certainly have been anticipated that the GAA's strong preference would be for 'one of their own' and that was how they – correctly – described O'Hehir. The new television service would well recognise that relations with the GAA and access to their games would be facilitated by having O'Hehir as head of department. He was credited with 'building Croke Park' through the popularity of his radio commentaries. And in his memoirs he tells how Andrews prompted him to make himself available; then within a week O'Hehir was sent 'terms which I could not refuse and I did not.'[27]

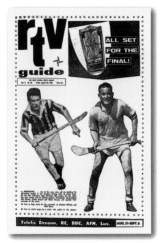

27 Michael O'Hehir, *My Life and Times* (Dublin 1996), pp.85-86.

Micheal O'Hehir, iconic radio broadcaster; his enthusiastic commentaries were world famous; but were they suited to television?

Michael O'Hehir was the first head of sport on Telefís Éireann. He was a legendary figure in GAA circles. His reputation had been earned on radio where his infectious enthusiasm and shrill distinctive voice often made matches more exciting to the listeners than they were to the spectators at the ground. Indeed O'Hehir explicitly admitted – and claimed it as an achievement – that he saw his role as delivering drama and excitement to the listeners whatever the quality of the match. Such an approach could scarcely work on television where viewers could judge the match for themselves and where, anyway, very different commentary skills were called for. Indeed, throughout the broadcasting world many professionals believed that it was an error to expect an established radio commentator to necessarily transfer successfully to television. But O'Hehir did not adapt his style for television commentary. Instead, throughout the 1960s he chose to use his radio commentary simultaneously on the television broadcast. Not only was his commentary style unsuited to television: as a radio style it concentrated on a word-picture rather than analysis. This, combined with a reluctance to be critical of the GAA, made for a one-dimensional performance. That as head of sport he insisted on broadcasting the *same commentary* on both radio and television compounded his limitations. What television needed was a minimalist style where the commentator's contribution was confined to adding interpretation and analysis to what the viewer could already see.

censorship snapped beneath the weight of films impervious to the censor's scissors

Cinema attendance in Ireland was exceptionally high in the 1950s. And the cinema owners lobbied against a television service because of the risk to employment in cinemas.

THE IMPACT of television on the cinema industry in Ireland proved to be 'almost fatal'.[28] It was the anticipation of just such an outcome which prompted Irish cinema and theatre owners to lobby the government in 1958 against the introduction of a television service, suggesting that the number of jobs at risk gave 'grave reason to doubt the economic advisability of the project.'[29] But the new medium would not only affect those showing feature films: those producing them were also fearful, including the powerful Hollywood studios. In 1954 Warner Brothers frowned even on the appearance of a television receiver in any of their films. The futility of such a policy was soon apparent and within a year Warner had signed a specialist contract to make telefilms for the ABC network. As a sop to the cinema industry, they included as part of an hour-long package a ten-minute feature on their next major movie. It was presumed that this would ease the anger of the cinema owners over Warner's 'dealing with the enemy'.[30]

But presently there was to be further dealing with the same enemy as the entire shape of the entertainment industry was reconfigured by the growing popularity of television. The major studios had another resource coveted by the new upstart: their back catalogues. In 1955, RKO, the only big Hollywood studio not by then producing films for television, sold the TV rights of its back catalogue of 740 feature films for $25 million. This created a domino effect and, in quick succession, Warner, Twentieth Century Fox, Paramount, Columbia and Universal had all sold their libraries of old films to television. These had all been made before 1948 and were owned outright by the studios, requiring no residual payments to those involved in the original productions.

The distributors who took this gamble found that it paid off 'with astonishing speed' because U.S. television stations 'reduced staffs, closed expensive studios, and took up round-the-clock film projection, alternating with occasional sports events'. Some indication of how fickle the station executives were – and how indifferent they could be to the content and range of their schedules – can be gleaned from the seismic shift in the output of WOR-TV NYK which in 1954 broadcast live drama every night and which within two years had

---

28 Rex Cathcart with Michael Muldoon, 'The mass media in twentieth-century Ireland' in J.R.Hill (ed.), *A New History of Ireland: vii; Ireland, 1921-84* (Oxford, 2003), p.695; hereafter, Cathcart, 'Mass Media'.

29 The Theatre and Cinema Association (Ireland), submission on television, 20 January 1958, NAI, Fin S104/1/50.

30 Barnouw, *Tube of Plenty*, 193.

WINDOW AND MIRROR

none at all, replaced by old movies which formed 88 per cent of the schedule.[31] This was the surest indication of how free enterprise television – without some mandatory public service commitments – could be driven by what some in the industry called 'the eyeball count'. The equations were simple: stations wanted profits; advertisers could be charged proportionate to audience size; the commercials mattered more than the programmes.

This upheaval in the American industry did have an effect on Telefís Éireann. Those who had bought the rights to the backlists from the Hollywood studios considered fees from smaller markets abroad as a bonus. They had already earned a return on their investment. When Telefís Éireann was launched, the Irish rights to these back catalogue films could be bought for little enough. And whereas American westerns and crime series were the butt of much of the criticism of the early Telefís Éireann, the programmes themselves were popular as audience ratings attest. As the station opened, executives defended their schedules: 'the widest and best selection of filmed programmes with which any television station has opened' was Barry's claim.[32] After his first year as controller, he gave much of the credit to Bill Harpur, describing him as 'a sensitive man of judgment and taste' who had been 'too little involved in the original contracting of the large overseas importations of film' – probably a tilt at Roth's purchasing expedition to London. Barry reckoned that 'excellent results' had obtained when,

Feature in *RTV Guide* of the western *Have Gun Will Travel*. Roth described the series as 'incomparably the finest thing of its kind that can be had.' It was then one of the most popular westerns on US television. Barry also defended the schedule: 'the widest and best selection of filmed programmes with which any television station has opened.'

Interviews, *RTV Guide*, December 1961.

Paladin (Richard Boone) arrives in time to save lovely Diana Coulter (Patricia Medina) from becoming the unwilling bride of a Texas cattle baron, in "Return of the Lady," to-night's *Have Gun, Will Travel* adventure on Telefís Éireann at 8.30.

But Boone really can shoot

IF viewers believed all they saw in westerns they'd be convinced that Hollywood is almost entirely populated ...

fired by the gunfighters of the old West. "The Colt, as knows," says ...

31 *ibid.*, 197-98.
32 Michael Barry, interview, *RTV Guide*, 1 December 1961.

Michael Barry praised Bill Harpur (right) whose 'meticulous viewing' of the prodigious amount of film to be pre-screened before transmission had resulted in 'no major trouble' in Telefís Éireann's first year. This was manifestly a reference to avoiding trouble with the self-appointed censors. But since the Hollywood back-catalogue had all been made under a prudish code – operating at least a decade before Irish television viewers saw the films – it would have been a very sheltered viewer who would have found them suggestive or indecent.

Barry, memo, n.d. but probably January 1963, Barry papers, RTÉWA.

eventually, he could empower Harpur 'in seeking out foreign film and in using his judgment.' He had a 'pliant and artistic temperament' and had worked 'unremittingly' when involved in influencing the programme schedule.[33] This was an era when strict film censorship laws were still on the Irish statute book and it would have been normal for the Dáil to have extended these to television. But to quickly establish the television service, the issue was postponed. It was to be the subject of separate legislation later but this was eventually superseded by wholesale reforms of all censorship provision – itself arguably accelerated by the modernising influence of television. Fanning suggests that the '*cordon sanitaire* of censorship snapped beneath the weight of films impervious to the censor's scissors'.[34]

33 Barry memo, n.d. but probably January 1963, Barry papers, RTÉWA.
34 Ronan Fanning, *Independent Ireland* (Dublin, 1983), p.200; hereafter, Fanning, *Independent Ireland*.

'Not always liked, but his manner does not always invite tolerability.' This was Michael Barry's verdict on Alpho O'Reilly, the television service's first Head of Design. He described him as an artist with 'a high reputation' but also 'a prickly personality'. He was sometimes to be 'found at the centre of small storm vortices'. Barry also wrote that O'Reilly was 'always amenable to reason, extremely hard-working and a thorough organizer within his sphere.'

Barry memo, n.d. but probably January 1963, Barry papers, RTÉWA.

4

The early newsroom: 'we were all scribes'

WHEN THE TELEVISION SERVICE was inaugurated, it inherited the old Radio Éireann newsroom, which now had the provision of a television news service added to its duties. The newsroom at the time believed it had least to learn about television. They tended to think of television news as a radio bulletin read to a camera with occasional pictures. And since almost all newsroom staff had come from the provincial press, they already thought of the radio bulletin as print news, read aloud to a microphone. It might also be stated that this was not wholly a disadvantage since in many embryonic TV news services film footage was determining news content irrespective of its significance. Barnouw found many early news bulletins in US stations to be distorted, being composed of 'newsfilm items threaded by an anchorman'. Except for 'catastrophes of some duration', the material filmed was invariably of predictable events, usually staged in anticipation of the news editor's interest. This reliance on the camera 'as arbiter of news value' had drastically curtailed content since beauty pageants now won airtime over expert analysis, 'a staple of radio news in its finest days'.[1]

Perhaps to avoid such distortion, the first Australian news service was compelled by the Commissioners of the ABC to maintain radio standards and not to be 'influenced by the availability of illustrations'. Despite protests from the broadcasters, the Commissioners initially limited film footage to a strict two minutes per bulletin, a ruling the news producers reckoned 'ridiculous'.[2] Something similar was happening at the BBC where the very reputation of its radio news inhibited how it approached the quite discrete challenge of news on television. Unlike its pioneering and

Charles Mitchel, RTÉ's first newsreader when the station opened and highly popular chief newsreader until his retirement in 1984. He had been a Gate Theatre actor before his recruitment as newsreader.

1   Barnouw, *Tube of Plenty*, 168-70.
2   Inglis, *ABC*, 211-12.

Early recruits as newsreaders, Andy O'Mahony (top) and Terry Wogan.

inventive approach to TV current affairs, the BBC's early record in news presentation was woeful. Its news bulletin was essentially a recorded radio bulletin with a clock filling the TV screen. The director-general of the time thought this was innovation enough. Meanwhile a separate department was responsible for a popular but inadequate *Newsreel* programme. It was then decided to merge the two programmes; but *News and Newsreel* proved to be an unsatisfactory compromise. It was as late as 29 March 1953 before the first live television news bulletin was broadcast by BBC Television. Some even suggested that the BBC's early efforts at television news must have sent its ITN rivals – who would soon set the pace in what television news could and should be – straight to the cellars to bring up a bottle of champagne.[3] Even as they developed a more coherent policy the BBC allowed its radio tradition to determine a crucial choice: broadcasters, often from an acting background, and not journalists would read the television news.

From the outset, the new Irish television service adopted this model, which had an inhibiting effect on the development of the news service. The emerging American model – and the ITN approach which would presently force the pace in Britain – was to recruit news-readers who were described as anchors, who themselves helped to write the bulletin and were thereby all the better placed to interview experts, newsmakers and their station's specialist correspondents as part of the news broadcast. It took RTÉ television news a full decade to appreciate this mistake. An internal report on the newsroom by Mike Burns and Eddie Liston argued that the station's news from its inception had been too formal. They believed the newsreader to be an 'antiquated invention' to disguise the medium's own failure to give visual treatment to all stories. 'The newsreader tended to be God and

3   Briggs, *Sound and Vision*, 538-43.

Barnouw describes television news in the United States in 1953 as 'an unpromising phenomenon', its 'main showpiece' being the fifteen-minute bulletin on NBC known as the 'Camel News Caravan'. In deference to its sponsor, this bulletin 'had a few special distortions', Camel stipulating that only cigarettes – never cigars – be shown in any news footage, with Churchill as the sole exception. They also insisted that all shots which included a 'No smoking' sign be excised: worse, these understandings were considered to be 'minor aspects of good manners rather than of news corruption'.

Barnouw, *Tube of Plenty*, 170.

created a barrier between viewers and the news. The Reithian concept of an impartial newsreader was false and no longer acceptable.' And since newsreaders were intelligent, it was unfair to employ them 'solely as parrots'; rather, they should have journalistic training, should be involved in writing the news and should do interviews like ITN presenters.

The Burns-Liston report was highly critical. Somebody somewhere must have decided that since the newsroom had proved so slow to accept criticism from outside, they might listen to the verdicts of some of their own. Burns and Liston did not pull their punches: foreign news was covered 'in a slap-dash, meaningless way'. The provinces were largely ignored. There was 'a lack of discipline, rehearsal and pride'; also a lack of analysis or of any element of news creation in the bulletins. As for newsroom reporters, they 'dressed badly, wore shaggy jackets, kept their hands in their pockets, and had poor diction.'[4]

Mike Burns, an insider and critic of the early Newsroom where there was a lack of awareness of television's potential; there were too many on the staff whose initial training was in provincial journalism. Burns would often explain: 'we were all scribes'.

---

4   Mike Burns, Eddie Liston, 'RTÉ News: 30 minute [television] bulletin, feasibility study, Ts. May 1971, RTÉWA.

As Telefís Éireann was established, one of the most important departments was agricultural programmes. Under the leadership of Paddy Jennings its role was predominantly educational, part of the drive to modernise Irish farming. The initial Radio Éireann Authority formed an agricultural sub-committee which, at its first meeting, agreed that Roth would approach the government for a preliminary grant of £20,000 to make 'educational and informational' programmes. Once broadcast, these films would be made available to the department for seminars around the country. If the government consented to the grant, it would be made clear that they would have 'no control whatsoever' on how the money might be spent. It was also agreed that no programmes should 'attempt to establish agricultural policy' and that 'all discussion programmes must provide for an opposing point of view'. Within two months, the department was informing the controller, Michael Barry, that the Minister, as 'a positive contribution', was willing to permit one of the department's leading educational communicators, Patrick Keenan, to be seconded to the station 'if you think well of the idea'. Keenan was recommended as being very knowledgeable on the advisory services and the rural community; it was envisaged that he could find the 'raw material' and otherwise assist the television producers. Barry accepted the offer, hoping that the initiative would prove of 'the greatest possible help', in coming closer 'to the agricultural side of things in our work on Telefís Éireann'.

Paddy Jennings interviewing farmer, *On the Land*, 1967.

Report of first meeting of agricultural sub-committee, RE Authority, 8 December 1961; Michael Barry [Department of Agriculture] to Michael Barry [TE], 9 February, and reply, 15 February 1962, RTÉWA.

somebody introduced... bubonic plague [into England...]
'Somebody is minded now to introduce sponsored broadcasting...'

Lord Reith, first director-general of the BBC: likened commercial television to the bubonic plague.

LORD REITH, the BBC's first director-general – and widely regarded as the architect of public service broadcasting – did not hide his loathing when the legislation to introduce commercial television to Britain was being enacted. He told the House of Lords: 'Somebody introduced dog racing into England ... and somebody introduced smallpox, bubonic plague and the Black Death. Somebody is minded now to introduce sponsored broadcasting into this country.'[5] Reith was not alone in the antipathy he reserved for the advertising break in the early years of television. The historian of the ABC in Australia asserted that the absence of commercials on that channel came 'to be widely perceived as an essential part of the national broadcaster's character, even a condition of its purity.'[6]

The GAA seemed to share this Reithian attitude, if one is to judge from the meticulous protocol which they insisted RTÉ follow in its first outside broadcast of Gaelic games on St Patrick's Day 1962. The programme controller, Michael Barry, after detailed negotiations, reported that the GAA was 'particularly anxious that advertisements should not directly impinge or interrupt' the broadcast from Croke Park but would be satisfied if the commercials were 'properly "buffered"'. Advertisements would be tolerable only if they were included in the introductory programme or the studio-based post-match analysis. The key requirement was that there was to be no advertising between the start of the game and the final whistle – including half-time – and Barry had to specifically promise that under no circumstances would RTÉ 'return directly from advertisements to Croke Park'.[7]

In negotiating Telefís Éireann's first broadcast from Croke Park, the GAA in 1962 seemed to take a Reithian attitude to television commercials: no contamination.

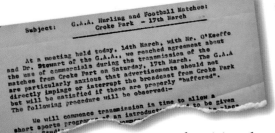

In this initial period there was much evidence of a general disdain for advertising's impact on the enjoyment of television: one Abbey playwright, Frank Carney, expressed no interest in the television adaptation of any of his plays were they to be interrupted by commercials. 'It offends natural Irish taste and I know it makes me feel like throwing my television set into the lily pond in the garden.'[8] Even John Irvine, a key architect of the new service, complained about the intrusion of advertising 'because of the way it generally shouts at one'.[9] But

5   Inglis, *ABC*, 441.
6   House of Lords Debates, vol.176, col.1297, 22 May 1952.
7   Michael Barry memo to Michael O'Hehir and others, 14 March 1962, RTÉWA.
8   *RTV Guide*, 26 January 1962.
9   Irvine to Séamus Ó Braonáin, 26 January 1965, Irvine papers, RTÉWA.

Niall Sheridan, Monica Sheridan and Michael Barry at the inaugural Jacobs Television Awards dinner, December 1962. There can be little doubt that among the topics they discussed was Edward Roth's insistence on boycotting the event because he believed it improper for him 'to intimately participate' in what was 'basically an undertaking to sell biscuits'. This attitude clearly surprised his colleagues since there had been a widespread welcome by broadcasters for Jacobs initiative in sponsoring these awards. But Roth's attitude remained aloof: he told the Radio Éireann Authority on 22 November 1962 that he had asked Sheridan to inform Gordon Lambert of Jacobs of his refusal to attend. Roth did acquiesce in Sheridan's attendance as a compromise and, as is clear from this photograph, Michael Barry joined him. Barry further distanced himself from Roth's line when he informed him on 26 November of his grave concern at the director-general's claim that he had already agreed with the Authority that the television service 'should not identify itself with any commercial undertaking in the community'.

The awards were to run for 31 years until 1993. Winners were decided by a jury of the television critics of the national newspapers. Radio awards were added from 1969. They were usually presented by a senior government minister, often the Taoiseach, as on this inaugural occasion. Incidentally, Monica Sheridan was to win one for her cookery programme the following year.

Sources: Barry papers, RTÉWA; Radio Éireann Authority papers, November 1962.

advertising remained essential to funding the new service.

When the broadcasting legislation was being drafted, Leon Ó Broin had privately solicited any advice which his friends among senior administrators in the BBC might offer. Among their 'major considerations' – which proved prescient in the context of Ray Burke's capping policy thirty years later – was a fear of the government retaining any 'detailed control' over the amount of advertising which would be permitted, since this could well prove an 'endless source of argument'.[10]

That television's advent would increase consumer spending was presumed. This indeed had been one of the Department of Finance's arguments in the 1950s when resisting television. The then level of advertising expenditure was considered 'very low', compared to Britain, and some experts predicted that there were 'frozen pools of purchasing power' which television could 'set flowing in a very special way'.[11] This line of argument was consistent with the thinking of the highly influential economist J.K.Galbraith, who had written persuasively that television was proving to be positive for modern economies. He scorned those 'solemn social scientists' who sneered at what they termed 'rhymed and singing commercials' promising 'highly improbable

---

10 Hugh Carleton Greene to Leon Ó Broin, 5 October 1959, informing him that he had 'not hesitated to write plainly' in reporting the BBC director-general Sir Ian Jacob's opinions. BBC Written Archives, 'Ireland: Radio Éireann', EI/2092/2.
11 C.P.Kelleher, 'The benefits of television advertising', *RTV Guide*, 29 December 1961.

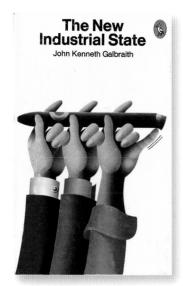

The New Industrial State

John Kenneth Galbraith

J.K.Galbraith, arguably the most influential economist of his day, insisted that economists who dismissed television commercials were merely protecting their reputations for 'Calvinist austerity'.

enjoyments'. Such criticism was 'a great mistake', for Galbraith reckoned that the contemporary industrial system was 'profoundly dependent on commercial television and could not exist in its present form without it'. Economists who dismissed commercial television as 'a wicked waste', were merely protecting their reputations for 'Calvinist austerity'. They were not 'adding to their reputation for relevance'.[12]

Meanwhile in the Irish case, historian Joseph Lee reckoned that the coming of television had encouraged begrudgery, making it 'more conspicuous, if not more intense'. One slogan from a motor car advertisement, 'If you've got it, flaunt it', captured in Lee's opinion 'the general ethos' of both advertising and programmes – 'especially American ones'. Television, he believed, 'encouraged an inflation of aspirations, and of exhibitionism, in an economy which, though growing unprecedentedly rapidly by its own standards, was still relatively poor by the standards of the societies whose values the advertisers transmitted.'[13] And it may be added that if housewives were especially targeted by the advertisers to join in the consumer boom, they were also the net beneficiaries, because a greater proportion of disposable family income was being spent at their discretion. Although much television advertising was criticised, RTÉ had introduced its own strict, prim, somewhat politically correct, code. Indeed, some industry sources hoped that Irish television would 'in avoiding more garish manifestations, set new standards of good taste'.[14]

With television, competition for advertising revenue in Irish media 'became acute' and the impact on Irish newspapers was estimated as being 'considerable'.[15] Niall Sheridan, who had responsibility for advertising on television, believed that this explained what he thought was some gratuitous hostility towards the new station by the Irish Press group; they were being 'more aggressive' than other newspapers, with 'a tendency to concoct news stories from hints, leaks and gossip, rather than to take a positive editorial line'. Sheridan believed that 'all this sniping' amounted to 'a definite policy of denigration of the television service'. In particular, he found that the paper's regular column by the former *Irish Times* editor, Alec Newman, to be 'so much out of character of what we know him in the past, as to suggest that his card was being marked.'[16]

12 John Kenneth Galbraith, *The New Industrial State* (London, 1967), p.213.
13 Lee, *Ireland*, 647.
14 C.P.Kelleher, 'The benefits of television advertising', *RTV Guide*, 29 December 1961.
15 Cathcart, 'Mass Media', 695.
16 Sheridan memo to director-general, 9 April 1963, RTÉWA.

'I cannot imagine anything we need less than an opera in Irish'

SENIOR MANAGERS in the new station did appreciate that the original schedule was weak on home-produced variety, Barry believing that the pool of native variety talent was small and 'quite inadequate' to maintain a weekly programme. Top artists had theatre commitments and could be expensive; but an even 'more vexed' question than cost was 'the challenge of commissioning good written material'. The budget would be 'worth straining for' if Telefís Éireann could obtain the 'necessary sketches, turns and so on in the required quantity'. The BBC had taken 'many years and considerable investment' before the writers were found to maintain Tony Hancock, Eric Sykes and Jimmy Edwards. And Barry alluded to 'the tragedy' that had befallen Hancock when the link between comedian and scriptwriter had been severed. In Ireland Barry reckoned that the key problem was 'a matter of written material which simply does not exist'. Nor was there sufficient appreciation of the medium's 'hungry demands'.[17]

And this was in a context where top variety shows could be bought in at a fraction of the cost of home production. Comparable television services elsewhere had made the same discovery. In Australia *The Danny Kaye Show* – 'glossy, clever and wholesome' – had become 'a weekly demonstration of how far home-made variety programmes had to go if they were to compete on even terms with the best imports'.[18] There was a further barrier to good variety: performers, and especially comedians, could be wary of using material in a once-off television appearance when the same routine could fill a theatre for a season. If one adds in the 'below the line' costs of facilities and personnel, the attraction to the schedulers of imported variety programmes proved decisive, given the many other demands on budgets and production resources.

In just this context, Niall Sheridan had no difficulty in advising the director-general on how best to respond to one programme suggestion from Irish-language enthusiasts as the station faced into its second year of broadcasting. Sheridan forwarded to Roth a translation of a letter received in Irish, with a covering note: 'I think this specific proposal has no interest for us, as I cannot imagine anything we need less than an opera in Irish.'[19]

But just as variety itself was a broad umbrella – so too was television. The exact configuration of programme departments was

The Danny Kaye Show proved a worldwide success as a top variety show. Given the exceptional challenge and cost of attempting to compete in this field, Telefís Éireann was not alone in finding it difficult to resist.

---

17 Barry to Sheridan, 9 March 1963, on his note of 4 March re *Curtain Up*.
18 Inglis, *ABC*, 206.
19 Sheridan to Roth, 25 January 1963, File, Sheridan correspondence with director-general; January 1963 – November 1964, RTÉWA.

with
Brendan O'Reilly.

11.10 THE LATE LATE SHOW

A programme for late viewing featuring among others
Danny Cummins,
Liam O Briain
and
Verona Mullen,
Your host is
Gay Byrne
and, in lighthearted fashion, he sets the ball of conversation rolling.
Produced by
Burt Budin.
Transmission ends at 12.10 approx.

Just another programme in the *RTV Guide* listing, 6 July 1962.

not always easy to agree: turf wars were endemic. One solution to this dilemma – although it may not have been explicitly thought through at the time – was to develop programme formats capable of including variety along with debate. Thus did *The Late Late Show* begin in the summer of 1962. Originally scheduled as a filler to run for thirteen weeks, it is still flourishing half a century later – the longest-running chat show in the world – probably because it did not confine itself to light entertainment. Some of the most significant controversies of the twentieth century in Ireland took place on this programme and were witnessed by the largest audiences in Ireland since de Valera's radio broadcast replying to Churchill in May 1945 or Daniel O'Connell's monster meetings in the mid-nineteenth century.

The initial success of the programme relied on its presenter, Gay Byrne, and its first producer Tom McGrath. Despite the lack of experience of so many of the recently recruited staff, the fledgling station was so challenged by the ambition of its schedule that it became a forcing house for many whose talents had not yet been recognised, even by themselves. McGrath provides an example. Recruited from Canada as a budget control officer and 'serving his turn ably enough', Barry faulted him for an inclination 'to make heavy weather' of his tasks: but once tested with programme responsibility, 'he blossomed into a different individual'. He was able 'to get things done with small means in a field where the best performers cost more money than we can afford'. In effect McGrath fashioned *The Late Late Show* as the ideal vehicle to carry variety. It was leavening for the chat dimension, and could readily include major stars visiting Ireland, even if the price was plugging their Irish schedule. Barry reckoned that McGrath's Canadian experience was an advantage. Although his modernism left him somewhat 'exposed to attack', he looked 'ahead rather than back to the traditional Irish song and dance'. *The Late Late Show* also proved a vehicle for the emergence of one of Ireland's most accomplished broadcasters, Gay Byrne.

Recruited as an administrator, Tom McGrath (left) 'blossomed into a different individual', once entrusted with programme responsibility. With Gay Byrne he launched *The Late Late Show* in July 1962.

'television is such a universal art form – at its best – that it is hard to despise it'

MICHAEL BARRY had come to the new service as an internationally acclaimed pioneer of television drama. Although now with more general responsibilities as programme controller, his judgement in drama would have been among the most widely respected in the television world. He believed that the infant station had 'got away to a good start'. And this was despite the lack of appropriate studio space for a major production. Barry wrote of the production of *The Well of the Saints* that it was 'so startlingly good, in spite of limited resources', that he was confident that the new service could provide an internationally acceptable series of Irish drama.[20]

Many professional writers considered television to be an important new opportunity to practice their craft and worked on adaptations of stage plays. Eugene McCabe was among the aspiring dramatists who – while open to all offers of work – also had an interest in reaching the mass audience that an original one-off television play could command. McCabe advised Edwards that he would be 'watching all productions very carefully'. Already he thought that what he termed 'the faint aura of absurdity (Radio Éireann Drama)' had begun to disperse: he hoped that it would 'be replaced by an aura of achievement! Gate-Abbey Blend No.1 (Corny! But you know what I mean).'[21]

An early production of J.M.Synge's *The Well of the Saints*. Despite 'limited resources', it was, wrote Barry, 'startlingly good'. Set design, 1962.

McCabe was fascinated by the challenge of writing for the new medium. He informed Edwards that he 'very badly' wanted to write and could not go on 'stealing cow time to keep doing so (ploughing has already started).'[22] And he hoped Edwards 'might be able to outline suggestions, snags, opportunities or speak hopefully about "later on perhaps".' McCabe was also interested in testing the boundaries. When forwarding one script, he alerted Edwards that it 'might just send a few over-earnest "Knights of St Columbanus" marching on your office – if considered.'[23] The celebrated Abbey playwright M.J.Molloy expressed a related concern. He advised Edwards to appoint a Roman Catholic to a particular vacancy in the drama department – not in order 'to keep you people from heresy' – but rather to save 'you from being too cautious in the opposite direction', as he believed had happened in the Abbey Theatre under Ernest Blythe, a Presbyterian. Molloy reckoned that Blythe had found

20 Barry to Basil Thornton, National Educational Television and Radio Center, New York, 16 February 1962, Barry papers, RTÉWA.
21 McCabe to Edwards, 29 March 1962, Edwards papers, RTÉWA.
22 *ibid.*, 26 March 1962.
23 *ibid.*, c27 January 1962.

'the Catholic mind' to be such 'a smoke-screened minefield', that he would accept nothing for the Abbey stage 'which might disturb a Reverend Mother' who had been sheltered from the world since entering the convent at sixteen, 'in the last year of Queen Victoria'.[24]

Molloy, an established writer – and also a farmer – was conscious of the need to be properly remunerated. He was not impressed by the contract he was offered for an adaptation of his stage play *The King of Friday's Men*. And he predicted 'serious trouble' with playwrights at what he saw as the gratuitous limitations which Edwards's television contract placed on stage and radio versions of the same work. Such an approach constituted a 'serious threat to our livelihoods'. Between amateur productions and radio work, 'a man has been averaging at least a couple of hundred a year from his play' and was now being asked to give this up for television's 'modest fee'. Moreover, Molloy reckoned that RTÉ's precluding stage performances of the work for three years had 'only a nuisance value, which will incense the playwrights. And it will establish a tendency not to send one's plays to Irish Television until one has knocked the last ha'penny out of it on all other media around the world.' Molloy thought it 'most unlikely' that the BBC Third Programme, or Radio Éireann or the Abbey would be doing this play again within three years, but he could not guarantee this without writing to ask them 'to surrender their rights to you; and this would be biting the hands that fed me'.[25]

After much haggling over rights and fee – and the proposed duration of the production – Molloy informed Edwards that he wanted to avoid the proposed twenty-six-minute version. His intention was to first attempt a longer version and try it out 'on yourselves, the BBC, ITV, UTV, or Radio Peking, if they pay better'. *Friday's Men* had been a considerable success on radio and he was prepared to 'put an amount of work' into ensuring that its television version would be as good as his 'waning powers' could manage. 'Count Tolstoy wouldn't approve of such a waste of creative time; but television is such a universal art form – at its best – that it is hard to despise it.'[26]

Opinion could be fickle on how the station was performing in its first months on air as is demonstrated by the letters of Brian O'Nolan/Myles na gCopaleen/Flann O'Brien to Hilton Edwards. In February 1962 he wrote that he thought the station was 'doing unexpectedly well...'. But a mere nine months later he was wondering 'how long more TE will continue to be the most contemptible TV station in Europe.' Some few days later in a further letter he expressed his sympathy to Edwards 'for being a Montrosean at all.'

Based on O'Nolan to Edwards, 5 February, c. 10 November and 15 November 1962, Hilton Edwards papers, RTÉWA.

---

24 Molloy to Edwards, 5 April 1962, *ibid*.
25 Molloy to Fachtna Ó hAnnracháin, 18 January 1962, *ibid*.
26 Molloy to Edwards, 5 April 1962, *ibid*.

There were many slings and arrows aimed at the new station. George Roche wrote an article, 'Why Telefís is a flop' in *Hibernia* in November 1962, complaining of the station's 'rather disgusting slavery to the Tam rating' and suggesting that a monster had been created which would 'destroy us culturally'. It also mentioned that the first controller of programmes, Michael Barry, 'had tossed in a mysterious resignation'. The article prompted a comment from Barry to Sheridan, head of public relations.

> Is this not, I ask, intended deliberately as a *mandat provocateur*, a broad, blind-swiping discharge of shot into the air to catch the passing game? Who are the 'everybody' of the second sentence? Has the blunderbuss been more widely loaded than in one corner of a literary bar over a fine fume of 'Paddy' and polemic? If this suspicion of tendentiousness has any basis and since as the challenged we have not in any case the choice of weapons already decided – should we not request the choice of time. That is to say let the ferment boil and then come in last with our written comment. One point of incidental interest that I find myself asking is how much television does a writer of this sort find time to see. Much time that is not occupied in the considerable task of writing for a living must wisely be spent in meeting, talking and drinking with other folk of similar intellectual tastes and an overall personal acquaintance with programmes may be purely superficial or chosen to prove a point. Television is of its nature so multifarious that of course nearly any point can be proven by a choice of viewing.

In the following edition of *Hibernia* there was a robust defence of the new station by C. Mack Kyle, M.D. of Royds advertising agency and he also asked 'who George Roche might be'?

Michael Barry to Niall Sheridan, 20 November 1962, RTÉWA; *Hibernia*, November, December 1962.

'the opus minimum': rejection would have done O'Casey 'a great personal favour'

IN HIS TRAWL OF IRISH WRITERS to enquire if they might be interested in writing for television, Edwards had omitted Seán O'Casey. He had been in exile for over thirty years and was so embittered about Ireland that he would not give permission for professional productions of his work. Nevertheless Roth wrote to O'Casey. This could have been a solo run or it might have been prompted by Edwards, who had such a poor relationship with O'Casey that he could confidently have anticipated that any direct approach would have been met with a refusal, or silence. Whatever the truth, O'Casey can only have seen Roth's letter as a cold call.

Roth's first letter suggested that the two men simply meet in Devon. O'Casey responded with puzzlement. He could not 'think of any reason' why Roth should wish to see him and the letter itself had given 'neither cue nor clue'. Totnes in Devon was a long way to come for any meeting 'without a good reason'.[27] But O'Casey's curiosity had been aroused. He would be in London in two weeks to see an eye specialist and he suggested that himself

O'Casey agreed to meet Roth 'for the sake of the Stars and Stripes'.

---

27 O'Casey to Roth, 3 May 1962, Seán O'Casey – E. J. Roth correspondence, NLI, Ms. 38, 092.

A scene from the Telefís Éireann production of *The Moon Shines on Kylenamoe*, the only example of O'Casey's later plays to be seen in Ireland during his lifetime. [Left to right], Kevin McHugh as the Boy, Aideen O'Kelly as the Girl, Dermot Kelly as Seán, Paul Farrell as Lord Leslison and Harry Brogan as the Guard. The Authority, accepting that the play was 'a slight one', hoped that its production might 'persuade O'Casey to release the rest of his more important work for television'.

and Roth 'might arrange a meeting'. Roth now declared his agenda and made a number of proposals: that O'Casey would participate in a television self-portrait; or write 'an original drama' for Telefís Éireann; or, at least, exempt the station from the ban that he had placed on any Irish productions of his work. And if each of these was rejected, they could always just talk 'about Ireland'.[28]

The response which this letter received would have elicited dismay had it come from any writer other than O'Casey. From him, it must have seemed as if the door was being kept ajar. It was, he wrote, 'no go' to get him to write for television: he 'simply wouldn't know how to do it.' But to talk about Ireland, he would 'be glad to see you for the sake of the Stars and Stripes'.[29] When they met, O'Casey liked Roth and he agreed to the station adapting a recent stage play. Perhaps his curiosity was aroused to see how his work would be received in this new setting of television. Whatever his motivation, O'Casey had relented, his biographer, Murray, ascribing RTÉ's success to Roth's persistence.[30] And O'Casey confided to his grand-niece in Dublin that he had indeed given permission for Roth's sake because he had 'proved to be a very charming American'.[31]

The play *The Moon Shines on Kylenamoe* was broadcast on 4 November 1962. This was O'Casey's final play. It was 'a happy one-act farce set in a rural railway station'. Although 'written as filler material, and of little consequence as social commentary', it showed 'an easy-going O'Casey, content with life's absurdities and yet compassionate towards life's fools'.[32] The Telefís Éireann broadcast made it the only example of his later plays to be seen in Ireland during his lifetime. His grand-niece in Dublin wrote approvingly and O'Casey expressed his satisfaction that she had 'liked the little play' on television.[33] But this production did not meet with universal acclaim. Among its critics was Brian O'Nolan, who had, a decade earlier, described O'Casey's *The Silver Tassie* as loathsome, offensive, phoney, bunkum and drool.[34] O'Nolan – who knew of Edwards's

28 Roth to O'Casey, 15 May 1962, *ibid.*
29 O'Casey to Roth, 21 May 1962, *ibid.*
30 'The reason SOC allowed it' was because of Roth's visit. Christopher Murray, *Seán O'Casey: Writer at Work* (Dublin, 2006), p.531, note 50.; hereafter, Murray, *O'Casey.*
31 O'Casey to Lorraine Beaver, 5 December 1962, David Krause (ed.), *The Letters of Seán O'Casey, 1959-64, iv* (Washington, 1992), pp.340-41; hereafter, Krause, *O'Casey Letters.*
32 Murray, *O'Casey*, 413.
33 O'Casey to Beaver, 5 December 1962, Krause, *O'Casey Letters*, 340-41.
34 Murray, *O'Casey*, 514, note 55; see also 271, 335, 360 for O'Nolan's deteriorating relationship with O'Casey.

dislike of the *Kylenamoe* script – wrote to him with the complaint that one could 'only mutter HOLY GOD', and wonder for how long more the station would be 'the most contemptible' in Europe.[35] Edwards admitted that he had 'hated, loathed and despised' the script from the start – and although it was 'even treacherous to write this on this headed paper'– he could not resist giving his truthful verdict to O'Nolan 'under the strictest confidence!' He was, moreover, 'clinging' to his initial written assessment of the play which, he flattered himself, even O'Nolan 'would commend as a piece of vituperative rhetoric...'. However – in a clear reference to Roth – Edwards explained that 'high policy ordained that it must be done and as a law-abiding Englishman (!!!) there was but to do or die; well I am dead, I tell you this because I value your opinion too much to remain silent about this.'[36]

Some days later Edwards returned to the theme of what he called 'the O'Casey opus minimum.' Rejection would have been a kindness. 'Here was a genuine case of where refusing to take a work submitted was to do the author a great personal favour.' Edwards believed that from his letters to the paper and his comments to reporters, it was manifestly obvious that O'Casey was 'doting'. He might like to like to think of himself as another Shaw but he had not learnt 'the GBS trick of dealing with the great black oxen'.[37]

In January 1965 Séamus Ó Braonáin (former director of radio broadcasting) marked his letter to John Irvine, 'Personal – very'. He had been driven to writing by another 'vain effort to "enjoy" *Tolka Row*' but complained that 'the whole bloody lot' in *Tolka Row* were 'in continuous misfortunes of their own making. There is really no relief and the over-done Dublin "blas" puts the tin hat on it. For heaven's sake ... try and get them to wind it up.' The following year he had a different complaint, reporting his wife's dissatisfaction with the summer schedule: 'Mrs B. has a terrible grievance' because every single programme she liked had been dropped, including *Tolka Row*.

Ó Braonáin to Irvine, 15 January 1965 and 20 July 1966, Irvine papers, RTÉWA. One of the script editors on *Tolka Row*, Carolyn Swift, was bemused by the volume of complaints concerning the Dublin accents in the serial: 'Do we really wish Oliver Feeney to talk like a BBC announcer or Queenie Butler like a BEA hostess?' *RTÉ Guide*, 10 November 1967.

Edwards discovered he was 'not a white collar worker'

AT THE END OF ONLY TWO YEARS as head of drama, Hilton Edwards declared himself 'bored'[38] and he quit. Michael Barry's verdict on his tenure was kind. Referring to the station's failure to fulfil its original over-ambitious aspirations, Barry still claimed that the output of the department during its first year, 'when viewed against any comparable station', had been 'exceptional in quality.' But whereas Barry credits Edwards with 'an ebullient curiosity' concerning the new medium,[39] Edwards himself consistently emphasised his limitations, while

---

35 O'Nolan to Edwards, c. 10 November 1962, Edwards papers, RTÉWA.
36 Edwards to O'Nolan, 12 November 1962, *ibid*.
37 A reference to the passing years, based on Yeats's line, 'The years like great black oxen tread the world...'. O'Nolan to Edwards, 15 November 1962, *ibid*.
38 Edwards, *Aquarius* 104-09.
39 Barry memo for director-general, January 1963, Edwards papers, RTÉWA.

Hilton Edwards, Telefís Éireann's first Head of Drama. He used his many contacts with writers for the theatre to trawl widely for television scripts. But he remained insecure – and even innocent – concerning the medium of television. Photographed during the filming of *Hilton Edwards and Mícheál Mac Liammóir in conversation with Niall Sheridan*, broadcast. 27 December 1968.

Although Barry's verdict on Edwards was kind, there is no evidence that they were close colleagues, despite their shared interest in televised drama. Edwards confided to Denis Johnston in April 1962 that he found Barry 'very strange indeed', sought advice on 'how to handle him' and asked was Barry 'just passively nervous, unsure or Machiavellian?' He further enquired – betraying an extraordinary ignorance of Barry's BBC reputation – 'Is MB a good TV director? Judging from temperament I'll eat my hat if you say yes.' The reality was that Barry's reputation was world-class, whereas Edwards had accepted the job, did not know how to do it and was disinclined to learn.

Edwards to Johnston, 5 April 1962, Denis Johnston papers, TCD Manuscripts Department, 100066/287/1157.

demonstrating little embarrassment at his failure to tackle them. Indeed he explained that were he to take a course in television technique and 'make an ass' of himself, he could not sustain his dignity as head of department. On the other hand, if he did not know the job, he could not hold his position 'with any authority'.

He was also on record as admitting that, whereas good drama was possible on television, he did not think television to be 'the medium for it'.[40] Edwards manifestly thought television a poor relation to the theatre and TV serials a poor relation to the one-off television play. Always sceptical of big organisations, he left RTÉ with, it appears, few regrets. He confided to Johnston that his sojourn as a television executive had led to the self-discovery that he was essentially 'a labouring man not a white collar worker.' He knew that he 'should have retired years ago but after all, look at Melba.'[41] He had found that less work was required of him than he had expected: 'so eventually we drew back and drew back.' He was given a one-year contract as a consultant and was twice asked for his advice. 'On both occasions it was disregarded, and a good time was had by all, so that I drifted out of the television picture.'[42]

40 Edwards, *Aquarius*, 105.
41 Edwards to Johnston, 20 February 1963. His reference to Melba is a comment on the Australian soprano, Dame Nellie Melba, and her notoriety for repetitive 'farewell' performances.
42 Edwards, *Aquarius*, 105-06.

5

'a cynical, anti-everything approach' … an attitude entirely 'unsuited for broadcasting'

THE HISTORY of television in Western democracies is replete with government complaints that the medium held a peculiar attraction to left-wingers and radicals of all persuasions. Ireland was no exception. John Horgan, in his history of news and current affairs on RTÉ, writes of the left-wing recruits who envisaged the television service as a platform from which they would right the wrongs of society. He suggests that this new generation of broadcasters 'had more than a touch' of P.G.Wodehouse's journalistic hero, Psmith, about them. And he quotes Psmith's celebrated commitment to transform society through his makeover of the somewhat unlikely vehicle, *Cosy Moments*. His idea was that the publication 'should become red-hot stuff', with the public wondering 'why we do not print it on asbestos'. It would be both guardian of the people's rights and a searchlight into those dark corners where it would 'detect the wrong-doer, and deliver him such a series of resentful biffs,' that he would 'abandon his little games and become a model citizen'.[1]

Todd Andrews, as second chairman of the Authority, manifestly believed that Psmith and many fellow evangelicals had managed to infiltrate the production staff in RTÉ, where they saw themselves as the 'creative' people. Their hallmark, according to Andrews, was that they had temperament and expressed themselves as being concerned.

> Some were idealists prepared to go to the scaffold to eliminate the injustices of society. Some were dissatisfied because their jobs did not give them the power and influence they felt capable of exercising on contemporary events. Some were parlour pinks enjoying the social cachet attached to radical chic in pubs and suburban drawing-rooms.

Janet Moody, who joined as a researcher when the *Seven Days* team was being recruited, described it as 'a great place to work … we wanted to sail as close to the wind as possible.'

Savage, *Loss*, 139.

---

1   Horgan, *Broadcasting and Public Life*, 213-14.

To Andrews they seemed convinced that Irish society was 'rotten to the core', and in need of their zealous efforts 'to change it through the use of television'. He likened them to medieval knights riding forth 'on crusading expeditions'. His only puzzlement was 'how they expected so rotten a society to provide them with the expensive and complicated facilities of a television network' and, moreover, to pay them 'while they rushed into the fray to establish the new Jerusalem'.[2]

Horgan notes that because the Labour Party in the 1960s had made a decision not to consider coalition, this made the new television station all the more attractive to left-wing activists. And aside from party affiliation, many of those attracted to television saw their role as challenging whatever government was in power. One researcher, Janet Moody, described the *Seven Days* current affairs programme as 'a great place to work, we could do anything we wanted.' Not fearful of upsetting the establishment, 'we wanted to sail as close to the wind as possible, that is the nature of that type of journalism...to see how far you can go.'[3]

Fianna Fáil – which seemed to be the natural party of government at the time – certainly recognised this picture. Childers was among those who articulated it most often. 'There was a cynical, anti-everything, angry-young-man nihilistic approach to human life and destiny everywhere,' he complained. Childers found this attitude negative and 'entirely unsuited for broadcasting'.[4] While some saw this phenomenon as a case of infiltration and hidden agendas, it was also in the very nature of television that it tended to attract ideologues – and most of them well-intentioned ideologues, it must be allowed – intent on convincing the viewers of the righteousness of their case. Helena Sheehan, author of many academic studies of the station's drama output, concluded that working in RTÉ, 'some in relatively influential positions, were a significant number of people of progressive and even radical views. Although their work never expressed the full force of their convictions, they nevertheless put up a formidable fight to secularise and to liberalise programme output.' Her conclusion was that 'their struggles were not without success', although in 'their edging forward, they had to contend with the counterweight of forces striving to push them backward every step of the way.'[5]

2   C.S.Andrews, *Man of No Property* (Cork, 1982), p.275; hereafter, Andrews, *Man of No Property*.
3   Savage, *Loss*, 139.
4   *Irish Press*, 2 November 1967.
5   Helena Sheehan, *Irish Television Drama: A Society and its Stories* (republished in a revised edition on CD-ROM, 2004); hereafter, Sheehan, *Irish Television Drama*, revised 2004 edition. This CD-ROM enclosed in Sheehan, *The Continuing Story of Irish Drama: Tracking the Tiger* (Dublin, 2004).

Sir, You report Jim Fitzgerald as congratulating "Leftist Catholics" for promoting progress in Irish television. I protest, on behalf of right-thinking Protestants. (There are very few of us Left.) Wesley Burrowes.

Letter to the editor, *Irish Times*, 23 October 1968; cutting found in John Irvine's papers, RTÉWA.

Telefís Éireann 'should take the whine out of their voice'

AFTER ONE YEAR of the new station, Lemass, speaking to the television professionals themselves at the inaugural Jacobs Television Awards, took the opportunity to instruct the broadcasters on the government's expectations of the television service: it must be 'free from suspicion of bias' and also be 'in complete harmony' with the national interest. Responsibility may have been devolved to the RE Authority but the government did not regard itself as released from its own 'overriding responsibility'. When it had initially decided not to exercise 'direct control', it appreciated the 'calculated risk' involved and here Lemass confided that the government had been divided on the issue. Lemass was very aware of the audience he was addressing. He characterised the first year of television broadcasting as 'a period of experimentation, a period in which mistakes were bound to be made and a period in which the television service was perfecting its procedures by trial and error.' He expected continuous improvement 'so that all reasonable grounds for complaint and criticism' would be 'greatly reduced'.[6]

In private, Lemass's views were more robust. Among civil servants and government colleagues he made no secret of his unhappiness with the independent voice with which the new station was speaking. The secretary in Posts and Telegraphs, O' Broin, noted that Hilliard 'seemed frightened whenever the Taoiseach called him on the phone'. He had left Hilliard 'without words' when complaining that the Authority's notion of its independence 'was being pushed to an intolerable extent.' Ó Broin summarised the Lemass line as expecting the television service 'to be wholly supportive' of government policy, even threatening to change the legislation or the Authority to ensure compliance. Ó Broin – himself a distinguished historian – tellingly likened this approach to the era when the Department of Education had presumed that Irish history would 'be employed as an instrument of edification'.[7]

To Lemass, criticism from Telefís Éireann was an irritant: that it so often went unanswered was worse.

Minister for Posts and Telegraphs, Michael Hilliard. His department secretary, Leon Ó Broin, noted that Hilliard 'seemed frightened whenever the Taoiseach called him on the phone'.

Lemass did not waste his opportunity at the initial Jacobs Television Awards. In his speech he was attempting to rein in the new station's sense of its own independence. Here he presents news reader Charles Mitchel with one of the first awards.

---

6 Seán Lemass, 4 December 1962, typescript of address at inaugural ceremony for Jacobs Television Awards. Text in Irvine papers, RTÉWA; this reads like a transcript of a partly impromptu speech. Since Lemass is nuanced concerning his attitude to RTÉ, it seems probable that Irvine requested this transcription to establish exactly what he had put on the record at the dinner.
7 Ó Broin, *Yesterday*, 211-12.

Lemass would have welcomed the *Time* cover story on Ireland in July 1963: 'New Spirit in the Ould Sod'. But he would have disliked the leprechaun on the cover, and some of the commentary. *Time* quotes him as dismissing the 'image of the boozy, belligerent Irishman' as 'sheer hostile propaganda'. The magazine describes him as being 'passionately convinced that Ireland's timorous protectionism could only lead to national extinction.' The article also reports that television was 'a perennial assault on Gaelic puritanism. Ireland's own station competes with programs beamed from Britain that seem incredibly risqué to Irish viewers.'

Time, 12 July 1963.

His immediate response to a programme which he found unfair was to seek what he termed 'a make-good' programme: he saw this not as an opportunity to attempt a rebuttal but as essentially a programme that would correct what he reckoned was the error in the original.

When the Second Programme for Economic Expansion was published, Lemass took special exception to the broadcast verdict of Trinity economist J.B.Ruane which he described as 'misleading, shallow and unconstructive'. How did the Authority intend to correct these misrepresentations? 'Their function in this matter should be primarily to support the Programme rather than to facilitate criticism, and certainly criticism must not be allowed to go unanswered. If there is any resistance on the part of the Authority, let me know and I will deal with it.'[8] Telefís Éireann responded that the programme had been '90% favourable' and discouraged any attempt at a rebuttal programme, because if Lemass 'were to call for it, it would be all over Radio Éireann and outside' that it had been broadcast only because of government pressure.[9]

It was invariably a perceived lack of balance in programmes dealing with the economy which irritated Lemass most. And, like many of his contemporaries, he was especially sensitive on the subject of emigration. In January 1963 he complained about one such programme, describing it as 'thoroughly bad and depressing': it represented 'exactly the approach to serious national problems that Telefís Éireann should not adopt.' The station, he wrote, should 'take the whine out of their voice.'[10]

---

8   Lemass to Secretary, Department of the Taoiseach, 10 July 1964, NAI, DT S3532 D/95.
9   Secretary, Department of the Taoiseach, to Lemass, 14 July 1964, *ibid.*
10 Lemass to Ó hAnrachain, 4 January 1963, NAI, DT S3532 C/63.

P.P.O'Reilly, editor of *Broadsheet*, Telefís Éireann's first current affairs programme. Although taking the form of an early evening magazine programme broadcast Monday to Friday, *Broadsheet* managed to upset the establishment. Eamonn Andrews complained to Ernest Blythe that, because of the programme, he had had to endure criticism from the church, from political interests and now from Blythe himself. 'In all cases, the programme has been dubbed as suspect.' This might mean the programme was 'a very bad one' or perhaps 'a very virile one, but possibly headstrong, or striving for some measure of independence within the framework of the organisation.'

Andrews to Blythe, 6 December 1962,
Blythe papers, UCDAD, P24/1186.

NOTHING BETTER CAPTURES the establishment's discomfiture at the new station's presumption of editorial independence than the meeting between Seán Lemass and Archbishops Thomas Morris of Cashel and John Charles McQuaid of Dublin. Lemass, Morris and McQuaid were all dissatisfied with the new television station. The bishops named three broadcasters, Jack White, Proinsias MacAonghusa and Shelah Richards, complaining to Lemass about what they considered to be their subversive influence. Lemass later asked the head of the Government Information Bureau, Padraig Ó hAnrachain, what he knew about the three. Ó hAnrachain responded with what Horgan terms 'the unguarded and somewhat salty candour of a close political associate', his comments providing 'a rare insight into the political culture within which television was struggling to find its authentic voice'.[11]

Indeed, Ó hAnrachain reported back to Lemass in terms which tell more about his own narrow outlook than they do about White, whom he described as an individual with no 'firm beliefs about anything in particular', and with 'no national outlook in the broadest sense of the term'. White, he surmised, would 'think of Ireland as a place where those, like himself, who are "liberal" in outlook must suffer as best they may.'[12] McQuaid – although not on the Hierarchy's television committee – was probably responsible for the black list which was now the subject of these exchanges. That was his style. A control freak, he had a particular interest in the media and cultivated spies everywhere. His intelligence sources within RTÉ seemed to demonstrate insider information and suggest that it was not only leftist secularists who were working within the station. In March 1961, some ten months before television began, Dermot O'Flynn, Supreme Knight of the Knights of Columbanus, had elicited detailed information on the recently recruited producer corps. He complained that of the sixteen appointments, only four were Catholics, of whom one was separated and another divorced. The last was Richards, described as 'a divorced actress who has been associated with numerous left-wing groups for many years.'[13]

Ó hAnrachain's impression of MacAonghusa was that he was 'a complete opportunist, a very slick operator with considerable talent' and of the three mentioned he was 'undoubtedly the most undesirable generally' and 'capable of doing the greater amount of damage'. He did not think there was 'anything that MacAonghusa

Jack White was not, it appears, the sort of Irishman whom the bishops and some others wanted in the new station. In the preface to his book on southern protestants, *Minority Report*, White offers readers – lest they see it as relevant – a note on his own background. He was born a Protestant in Ireland. 'I am Irish, in a sense, by choice: both my parents happened to be English, but I have never thought of myself, from the age of fourteen, as anything but an Irishman.' In this photograph White is holding the 'Silver Dove' Ondas Award won by RTÉ for its production of *The Last Eleven*, based on White's play concerning the decline in the population of southern protestants.

Jack White, *Minority Report: The Anatomy of the Southern Irish Protestant* (Dublin, 1975), pp.7-8.

---

11 Horgan, *Lemass*, 317.
12 Ó hAnrachain to Lemass, 5 October 1962, Lemass papers, *ibid.*
13 O'Flynn to McQuaid, 7 March 1962, McQuaid papers, DDA, AB/8/B/xxvi.

Proinnsias MacAonghusa enjoyed a lengthy career as a broadcaster, despite courting antagonism from successive governments and RTÉ management. At a lunch with the minister in September 1963, director-general Kevin McCourt told Hilliard that he had determined the previous Monday that MacAonghusa – who was then chair of the Labour Party in Dublin – had crossed the line. McCourt had decided not to renew his contract but might retain him for a less political programme. Hilliard expressed himself as 'very relieved' that McCourt was proposing to resolve the issue. McCourt insisted that his decision was based on his own assessment of MacAonghusa's work and his 'own judgement of political infiltration.' MacAonghusa continued to embrace a socialist and republican agenda, especially in his journalism, books and political life. His television career was a distinguished one, but remained complicated by his inability to always convince management that he was obeying the guidelines concerning staff involvement in politics. He stood twice unsuccessfuly for the Dáil, for Labour in Louth in 1965 and as an independent in 1969 in Dun Laoghaire-Rathdown. He concluded his career as editor of the long-running current affairs programme *Féach*. When he died in 2003, Bob Collins described him as 'one of the most significant broadcasters in Irish', his flagship programme *Iris* 'was innovative, imaginative and way ahead of its time'. Cathal Goan said that he had 'set the standard for Irish language broadcasting – one which has not been surpassed.'

would not exploit to his own advantage.' Ó hAnrachain concluded that he reckoned it 'amazing indeed that such a rare crew as those mentioned – and some others – could get such a toe-hold in T.E. in so short a time.' Their activities were, 'undoubtedly menacing' and he believed 'the root cause of much of the present troubles in T.E.'[14] Childers – interested in media – presumed that this left-wing bias, while needing to be resisted, was also inevitable. His government colleagues were not so understanding. As Horgan notes, their initial attitude to any broadcast criticism of government policy was 'bafflement, tinged with querulousness. How dare they!'

14 Ó hAnracháin to Lemass, 5 October 1962, Lemass papers, quoted Horgan, *Lemass*, 317-18.

Concerning Shelah Richards, Padraigh Ó hAnrachain had heard that her selection as the producer of the *Recollection* series had been 'the subject of divisive comment' within and without the station; he himself believed it 'incredible' that a practising Roman Catholic had not been chosen as producer for such a religious programme. She is photographed with Hilton Edwards, with whom she had worked over many years in the theatre. She was one of many recruits to the new station who came from a theatrical background.

a tale of red herrings, sacred cows, cloud cuckoos, muskrats and coyotes

THE GAA HEADQUARTERS was assiduous in its attempts to control how the organisation was portrayed in the media. Believing that Gaelic games were 'entitled to preferential treatment' from the national broadcaster,[15] the GAA remained dissatisfied with much of RTÉ's coverage of its affairs, one complaint being that some broadcasters treated the association as a 'permanent cockshot for sniping jokes'.[16] The issue that elicited most controversy concerning the GAA was the association's ban on its members playing or watching what the GAA considered to be 'foreign games' which had been introduced by the British to Ireland: rugby, cricket, hockey and soccer.

Many senior figures wanted to close down this debate; and they were certainly critical of the issue being discussed outside the confines of the association, where it had become a litmus test of modernisation. Internally at the annual Easter congress, the modernisers argued that the rule should be deleted. Their leading spokesman, Tom Woulfe, suggested that the ban was no longer necessary for the well-being of the association. In the exchanges that followed, Woulfe came in for some harsh criticism. His defenders insisted that it was not he who had dragged in 'irrelevant red herrings'; nor had he called his opponents 'muskrats and coyotes.' The traditionalists 'should descend from cloud cuckoo land.' The Ban had become a 'sacred cow'.[17]

Pádraig Ó Caoimh, General Secretary GAA, 1929-64. Television producers 'usually look for the crank to put something across. We want to prevent that type of thing.'

It was not only in discussions of this Ban that the GAA establishment wished to control the airwaves. It was also concerned about who appeared on television in any GAA context. In the first year of the new service, the general secretary, Pádraig Ó Caoimh – who had guided the association in this post since 1929 – expressed concern about television appearances by GAA members. The issue uppermost in his mind was 'suitability'. There was no general prohibition, but the GAA leadership 'should like to have some control over the various showings' and approve of those who did appear. Such caution was in anticipation of the broadcasters approaching members and players. 'They usually look for the crank to put something across. We want to prevent that type of thing.'[18]

The GAA had traditionally been sensitive concerning how their games were portrayed in the media. When MGM made a short film simply called *Hurling* in 1936, a deputation of GAA officials sought out the Irish film censor 'and attempted to have scenes cut from the film which they deemed objectionable'. And there were objections to how hurling was portrayed in John Ford's 1956 film *The Rising of the Moon*. Nor was censorship absent from Michael O'Hehir's celebrated running commentaries on Gaelic games. In the event of the referee dismissing any player from the field, O'Hehir declined to name him, contenting himself with a statement that his team was now reduced to fourteen men. Not surprisingly, this idiosyncrasy did not survive the coming of television.

Mike Cronin, Mark Duncan and Paul Rouse, *The GAA: A People's History* (Cork, 2009), p.195.

15 GAA Archives, CC/1/30, 1967 volume.
16 *ibid.*, CC/1/27, 1964 volume.
17 *ibid.*, CC/1/28, 1965 volume.
18 *ibid.*, CC/1/25, 1962 volume.

the Irish language should be disassociated 'from all rancour, dogmatism and make-believe'

COMHDHÁIL NÁISIÚNTA NA GAEILGE had been established in 1943 by the government as a coordinating advisory body representing many voluntary Irish language organisations. Some months before the television station opened, Comhdháil – which had made no secret of its dissatisfaction with Roth's public statements on Irish – wrote to Eamonn Andrews requesting a formal meeting with the Authority. Andrews declined, suggesting instead that Comhdháil submit recommendations. Comhdháil replied with a twelve-part submission calling for urgent consideration of its 'minimum principles'. It sought reassurance that television would be used to serve the cause of the language 'in spite of the many signs, at present, to the contrary'. The language had already suffered, Comhdháil argued, because of the lack of a progressive policy 'in the cinema, theatre, press and other mass media of entertainment and communication'. It also reminded the Authority of Hilliard's promise in the Dáil that the role of broadcasting had to be one 'of active assistance in the restoration of the language'.

The tone of the submission was that Comhdháil should share in determining broadcasting policy and that there should be considerable Irish-language programming during peaktime viewing. Comhdháil specifically objected to a remark by Andrews that it was not the intention of the Authority 'to ram the language down the throats, eyes or ears of the viewers'. The document concluded that unless the RE Authority adopted 'an enthusiastic, positive policy', the new television service would cause 'irreparable damage' to the language. Subsequently Comhdháil wrote to Roth complaining that all job advertisements did not specify Irish language proficiency. Roth, in his reply, felt it necessary to remind Comhdháil that Telefís Éireann had not been set up to restore the language: it also had an obligation to attract audiences on a sufficient scale to ensure its financial viability. It did not interpret its obligations to the language as 'over-riding its general obligations'.

In March when the station had been on the air for ten weeks, a Comhdháil delegation finally met a group representing the Authority and station management: Roth himself, John Irvine, head of management, and James Fanning representing the Authority, a known sceptic on the language agenda. The meeting was chaired by the Trinity historian T.W.Moody, himself an Authority heavyweight. Representing Comhdháil were its president Liam Ó Luanaigh, Dónal Ó Móráin, director of Gael Linn, and David Greene, professor of Irish at Trinity College. There was no meeting of minds. The Comhdháil

Gael Linn caused alarm in government ranks by including an article by Dónal Ó Móráin with their weekly mailshot to participants in their football pools competition. The circulation was 200,000 and Ó Móráin called for the rejection of a television schedule so bereft of Irish material: while 'prepared to pay for something distinctively Irish and worthwhile', why should Irish viewers 'help pay for a service' which ITV could give them without cost? This initiative caused alarm within the government since it construed it as possibly a call to a civil disobedience campaign involving the non-payment of the TV licence. When the summer schedule included even more American material – with Barry saving his home production capacity for the autumn – Ó Móráin returned to the attack. In a public speech he claimed that the new service had 'acquired a shape which, if left undisturbed', would earn it the reputation 'of being the greatest depravers of public taste and cultural values in the history of the country.'

Ó Móráin quotations from Savage, *Loss*, 270-71, 275.

delegation believed that the most important function of the new television service was to help reverse language decline: Irvine told the delegation that the government had never intended that television should be used as a means of Gaelicising the people.[19]

In their ongoing relationship, Andrews found it necessary to remind Comhdháil that it was 'an outside body'. The Authority must 'carry out its duty to the language with tact and moderation'. Determining 'the timing, duration and type' of items to be televised in Irish, it must ensure that viewers were not 'wantonly driven away from Telefís Éireann and into hostility to Irish.' He also rebuked Comhdháil for its failure to maintain confidentiality in its dealings with the Authority, observing 'with regret' that individual members of Comhdháil had 'not respected the spirit of these negotiations'. The resulting publicity had been damaging to the station, had inflamed extremist opinion on all sides, had unsettled the staff and had created apprehension among viewers that the service was being turned into 'an instrument of propaganda'. He told Comhdháil that the Authority was convinced that 'the best hope of contributing to the restoration of the language through Telefís Éireann' lay in using Irish 'attractively, persuasively and realistically, and in disassociating it from all rancour, dogmatism and make-believe.'[20]

19 Meeting of Authority with Comhdháil Náisiúnta delegation, 10 March 1962, NAI, Department of Communications, TW 11292.
20 'The Place of Irish in the Television Service', 19 September 1962, *ibid*.

Another trenchant critic of Roth and Barry on the language issue came from within the gates, from Ernest Blythe, who was a member of the First Authority and relentless in his scrutiny of the new station's performance. Invited to comment on an Irvine draft of the Authority's first annual report, he took exception to the comments on the language policy, finding them 'most annoying'. Concerning the bilingual programme *Siopa an Bhreathnaigh*, he thought the introduction of French tended to make a cod of it' and indicated only 'hostility to the idea of doing something for Irish which is what we are interested in, not in bi-lingualism as such.' Blythe's response reveals a widening gulf between one faction in the Authority and the station's leadership on the language question. Blythe especially objected to the draft's phrasing that the Authority 'would wish to give a reasonable show to Irish'. There was also a comment concerning Irish-language programming which manifestly reflects one of Blythe's own complaints. But how it was worded in the draft did not appeal to Blythe. It can scarcely have been that it was too euphemistic since the draft suggested, that although the Authority had been 'thwarted heretofore by the hostility and stonewalling of the establishment' – this is a reference to Telefís Éireann senior management! – it was believed 'that when the Authority loses its patience and gets really angry, passive resistance will cease and proper attention will be given to Irish.'

Blythe listed further complaints. He did not believe the Authority could claim to 'have done fairly well'. Promises from *Broadsheet* to have an item in Irish had not been kept: 'Very little has been done since and some of the alleged items were mere apologies – songs, which might be compared to the songs in Spanish which have also been heard on *Broadsheet*.' Blythe expressed himself as not in favour of 'excessive quantities' of Irish but found himself 'forced to the conclusion that on this question we are up against obstruction by the establishment and that makes me object more than I otherwise would to paragraphs in the report which could not fail to encourage continuance of the passive resistance.'[21]

Some months later two of those 'passive resisters' exchanged comments on another Blythe communication, Barry telling Roth that he considered some of Blythe's criticisms 'nonsense'. Management's aim had been 'to walk the tightrope' between the needs of a national television service 'and the exigencies as I have been given to understand them of commercial survival'.[22] This letter was passed on to Blythe, whose papers also include

'Not only must all the programmes be Irish and the artists, technicians, engineers, writers, films and plays, but also, Mr. Roth, we insist that even the interference must be Irish.'
Dublin Opinion, June 1961.

---

21 Blythe to Irvine, 27 August 1962, Blythe papers, UCDAD, P24/1183.
22 Barry, memo to director-general re Blythe letter of 1 October 1962, *ibid.*, P24/1185.

a communication from the chairman, in which Andrews suggested that the Authority should attempt to 'coax rather than compel'. After all, such an approach was the basis of overall policy 'and perhaps we should use it internally as well'.[23] Later still, Andrews rejects Blythe's assertion that staff were 'flouting or subverting the wishes of the Authority'. In the long term it was the hope of Andrews that television would 'do far more for the language than has ever been done before by any organisation'.[24]

'a muddled and puzzled people' who had no need to 'learn from a Yank'

ALTHOUGH CONSIDERATION was given to a one-year extension or a consultancy, Roth's contract was not renewed and he left the new station not long after the builders had completed the television studio block.[25] After what must have been two of the most frustrating, challenging – and productive – years of his career, Roth was disappointed not to be offered a new contract with better terms. There was some speculation that he might be retained for another year or encouraged to take on the commercial challenge of making the Ardmore Film Studios profitable but, in the event, an offer from the Independent television sector in London decided the issue. Savage plausibly makes a case that Roth has been neglected by Irish historians. He ranks him 'one of Ireland's modernisers', who had withstood a great deal of criticism and who, despite difficult circumstances, had managed as 'an able diplomat' and technocrat to launch the new television service. And given the 'daunting task' that initially confronted him, his legacy was a viable service that had developed 'a foothold that others would try to expand, improve and develop'.[26]

As Roth departed from Ireland, he could have taken some comfort from his continuing correspondence with Seán O'Casey who now commiserated with him because of all the battles he had had to fight. In a possible reference to Blythe or Edwards, O'Casey wrote that he understood that Roth had handed in his gun 'without using it on ... one fat, fatuous, fool ... of a pinchback Buddha having power enough (because those around are on their knees) to order many

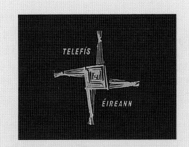

Seán O'Casey commented to Roth on both the name and the symbol of Telefís Éireann. 'What a name! Sounds as if it were a kinda coelacanth, a prehistoric fish hooked up out of the deeper oceans off the coasts of Cork or Kerry'. Later he told him he disliked the station's symbol, St. Bridget's Cross: 'looks like a fading starfish dissolving out its last days on a lonely seashore; but it will serve, for oddly enough, it also has a faint look of modern abstract design about it'.

O'Casey to Roth, 21 May, 10 August 1962, Krause, *O'Casey Letters*, 312, 323.

23 Andrews to Blythe, 6 December 1962, *ibid.*, P24/1186.
24 Andrews to Blythe, *ibid.*, P24/1187.
25 NAI DT S16922B, *passim*.
26 Savage, *Loss*, 45-48.

Gearóid Ó Tuathaigh, historian of the language policy, wrote pessimistically in 1979 in terms of retreat, failure, despondency and state neglect, 'or, more charitably, the inadequacy or inappropriateness of such initiatives in economic and social development as the state did undertake.' Three decades later he would fault the state for neglecting the use of Irish in parliament, courts and the public service, even in Gaeltacht areas. 'The corrosive effect of these contradictions – leading to cynicism or charges of hypocrisy, opportunism, tokenism – sapped the language policy of much goodwill, an asset which it could not afford to lose or seriously deplete. This would become increasingly apparent from the 1950s.'

Gearóid Ó Tuathaigh, 'Language, literature and culture in Ireland since the war', in Joe Lee, (ed.), *Ireland: 1945-70* (Dublin, 1979), p.112. Gearóid Ó Tuathaigh, 'The State and the Irish Language: an Historical Perspective in (eds), Caoilfhionn Nic Pháidín and Seán O Cearnaigh, *A New View of the Irish Language* (Dublin, 2008), p.32.

more intelligent Irish to plod along roads they should never travel.'[27] Later he assured Roth that the Irish were a 'muddled and a puzzled people' who believed that they had no need 'to learn from a Yank'. Nothing had changed. All was as it had been: '...the backbiting, the envy, the same uncertainty, the same disputes by the fireside and in the pub.'[28]

Roth cannot but have found his two Dublin years a learning experience, albeit a painful one. He had had such a bruising time at the hands of the church and language interests that he probably had forgotten by this stage the extent to which he had played the Catholic card when applying for the job or how he had impressed Andrews with his 'unprompted statement' that he favoured a revival of the Irish language.[29] Whatever about the language, he had now good reason to be circumspect about its champions and he had told the Comhdháil representatives at their first meeting that since coming to Ireland he had noted 'a great resistance to the Irish language'.[30] He now confided to O'Casey that while the challenge of setting up the new Irish station had proved one that he would not want to repeat, 'yet we are all much better for having had it...and we wouldn't have missed it for the world.' And then, in contrast to the pitch he had made when seeking the job and had claimed 'a considerable depth of insight to the Irish people',[31] he now shared with O'Casey 'a sad admission': he did not understand the Irish any more than he did when he first accepted the post and 'left the sunny shores of Mexico'.[32]

---

27 O'Casey to Roth, 3 October 1962, quoted Savage, *Loss*, 43.
28 O'Casey to Roth, 2 July 1963, Roth correspondence, NLI, Ms. 38,092.
29 RE Authority, minutes, 22 August 1960.
30 Meeting of Authority with Comhdháil Náisiúnta delegation, 10 March 1962, NAI, Department of Communications, TW 11292.
31 Roth to Administration Officer [Irvine], 9 July 1960, RTÉWA.
32 Roth to O'Casey, 3 July 1963, Roth correspondence, NLI, Ms. 38,092.

John B.Keane's *Kerryman* column on television is a reminder that muffled, intermittent, extraneous sounds – sometimes scarcely audible but always unmistakable – were still to be heard on Telefís Éireann transmissions more than a year after the station went on air. In his column, 'Televiewing' for 11 March 1963, Keane sympathised with the unnamed priest who had been given 'no chance at all' by the Montrose gremlins, some of whom could now be identified. 'Every time this poor man attempted to achieve sequence there was a prolonged hammering, which although it did not completely unnerve the speaker, very definitely left him rattled. You can identify these gremlins for yourself, when I tell you that they wear overalls, have nails in their mouths and hammers in their hands. It starts with a "c".'

John B. Keane papers, TCD MD Ms 10403/643.

6

if an "egg-head", the director-general should understand what interests the 'man in the street'

THE YOUNG TELEVISION SERVICE had very high expectations of Roth's successor. An undated, unsigned document, probably drawn up by Irvine, 'Director-General: job requirements', gives some indication of the qualities preferred in whomever would succeed to the job. The first requirement specified that 'he [*sic*] must have a good, solid, but liberal national outlook and be an Irish national.' Moreover, he must be 'modern and progressive in outlook', should be hard-working, an expansionist and an inventive, intuitive leader – this was 'a seven-day week job'. When it came to programme decision-making, the director-general would need to be 'impersonal and dispassionate'. His own tastes and opinions 'should never be allowed to obtrude'. As for temperament, he 'must be cool. He will have to withstand much public criticism and not let it interfere with his judgement. An impulsive or capricious director-general would be a disaster.' He must show courage, discretion and diplomacy; a delegator, he must be – and be seen to be – 'above politics'. Finally, he 'should not be an "egg-head" or if he is, he should understand what interests the ordinary man in the street.'[1]

Wanted: inventive, intuitive director-general, 'must be cool, will have to withstand much public criticism.' Kevin McCourt, RTÉ's second Director-General.

There is no indication that Kevin McCourt, a leading Irish businessman with experience in Ireland and internationally, was invited to tick all these boxes: but he was recruited to become Roth's successor, Eamonn Andrews making the approach at the prompting of Seán Lemass. McCourt met Andrews intermittently in London: 'It was all secret and I do not think I appeared in any Irish running list until close to end of the year.'[2] The first task facing the second director-general was one of consolidation: Roth's two-year term was short in such circumstances, much of it predating the launch of the new service. Moreover, since Michael Barry was also leaving, only Andrews of the three leaders who had brought the station through its first year

---

1   'Director-General: job requirements', An undated, unsigned document, (probably written by Irvine), Irvine papers, RTÉWA.
2   McCourt memo to Joe Dunn [n.d. but January 1996], McCourt papers.

offered any continuity. Some few years later – when Andrews himself resigned – McCourt confided to him that, although he had been keen to get back to Ireland, he was in no hurry, and broadcasting itself 'although immediately attractive' once mooted, would not have been the preferred vehicle of his return. It was Andrews's experience and commitment to the new service which persuaded McCourt to accept: 'the premium attaching to your invitation was the fact that you were chairman and my conviction after several meetings that I could develop a rapport officially and personally with you which would give me the security, support and professional guidance essential to my making at least some success of a difficult job.'[3]

The job was all the more difficult because of Barry's departure; one of McCourt's first duties was to recruit a successor as controller of programmes for television. At an early lunch with the Minister, Michael Hilliard, who was accompanied by his departmental secretary Ó Broin, the latter was curious about progress on the recruitment. McCourt was not giving much away with a reply which suggested there were as many as eight to ten possible candidates in Britain, a few on the Continent and another eight in the United States. But he insisted on the importance of making the right decision, although the choice 'might be even more "expensive" than myself'. McCourt had a hint of complaint in his note as he chronicled Ó Broin expounding 'at length' about his own many influential roles in broadcasting and on the need for a close relationship between the Radio Éireann Authority and the Department of Posts and Telegraphs. Hilliard reassured McCourt that the purpose of their first meeting was that the two men would get to know one another and to assure McCourt that he was 'whole-heartedly' behind him. McCourt noted that the atmosphere had been 'easy and informal', with a general emphasis on a better flow of information 'from us to them'. Even this did not sound to McCourt 'either like a direction or a major issue but might perhaps be described as a sort of preliminary brain-washing'.[4]

Lemass told Eamonn Andrews 'to get the bishops off my back'

AS MCCOURT BEGAN HIS TERM as director-general, he was surprised to learn that 'the biggest "blip"' that was preoccupying Andrews was Catholic religious programmes and the well-signalled intention of the Hierarchy – and especially McQuaid – 'to have that element of the new service under their direction and control'. This

---

3   McCourt to Andrews, 30 May 1966, McCourt papers.
4   McCourt, note of lunch with Hilliard and Ó Broin, 11 February 1963, RTÉWA.

When RTÉ failed to select him as clerical adviser, Fr Joseph Dunn returned to his leadership of the *Radharc* documentary unit. Years later when both men were in retirement, McCourt complimented him on how fortunate he had been that his career as a film-maker had resumed. 'How wise you were, Joe. You are a creator, not a show booth pugilist!'

they hoped to achieve through the Catholic Television Interim Committee (CTIC) which they had unilaterally established in advance of the new television service. The Hierarchy was hoping to replicate what the Roman Catholic church enjoyed in its relationship with the BBC where Fr Agnellus Andrew was both a BBC employee and religious adviser. But Andrew himself did not think the model suited the quite different Irish context and fully supported Andrews in his attempts to keep the Hierarchy at bay.

From his own early experience in his Dublin career, Andrews considered McQuaid guilty of arbitrary and uncharitable conduct towards the chaplain to Dublin's theatrical community. And he was all too aware of McQuaid's legendary reputation in all settings for presuming that his every wish would meet with acquiescence. There had been a power-play between the station and the bishops during Roth's period and a stand-off had followed. The television authorities were willing to employ a priest whom they could *consult* when necessary: McQuaid wanted his choice of priest as a station employee who could *determine* editorial policy on Catholic religious programming. To resolve the issue, McQuaid advocated a confrontational approach, while Archbishop Thomas Morris of Cashel, chair of the CTIC, believed more formal procedures were appropriate. An impatient McQuaid considered such a policy to be 'dilatory, timorous and piecemeal'.[5]

McCourt later recalled how, in Eamonn Andrews's house in London, he, along with Andrews and Fr Agnellus Andrew, had 'spent many hours, the three of us analysing, planning against giving the Hierarchy collectively or singly, any voice in control of programme-making.' McQuaid was also plotting. Thoroughly annoyed with how he had failed to resolve this issue with Roth, he had decided to use other avenues. McCourt learned that the archbishop 'had been talking with Dev (in Aras) who had been talking with Lemass', who had complained about the bishops to Andrews: '"This is your problem, get them off my back."'

'The shadow of John C[harles McQuaid] was over-hanging and Dodd was in – subject to an Authority meeting.' Along with his qualifications to be religious adviser, it was the fact that Fr Romuald Dodd was a Dominican which appealed to McCourt, Andrews and the Authority. Being a Dominican meant that Dodd was beyond McQuaid's reach.

5   Savage, *Loss*, 185

Was Fr Joseph Dunn, who was widely expected to be appointed as the hierarchy's clerical adviser to RTÉ, double-crossed by Archbishop Thomas Morris? Would Morris have wanted a man – 'chained and trained by McQuaid', as Morris himself described Dunn – in such a position? Nor can Morris (above) have been disappointed when McQuaid was so thoroughly outmanoeuvred: can he even take some of the credit? For the rest of his term as director-general, McCourt found Morris 'a tower of practical understanding and good advising.'

Kevin McCourt as a 16-year-old schoolboy playing rugby at Blackrock College.

Meanwhile McCourt had himself concluded that he 'must have an in-house staff priest' and that he should be recruited through the RTÉ Authority. McCourt discussed this with Morris, who told him that the CTIC 'was of the same intention, except that they would choose the incumbent'. Adding that McQuaid was also intent on making the final choice, Morris promised that he would ensure there would be no conflict arising from that particular ambition. Morris was then 'taken aback' when McCourt informed him that neither McQuaid nor the CTIC would have the final say but that he himself and the Authority would be making the appointment and the Morris Committee could help 'with possible candidates'. To underline his argument. McCourt added that he 'would advertise the job widely' if he 'could not succeed by head-hunting'. McCourt's recollections then reveal that Andrews went to the length of bringing a Dominican priest, Fr Romuald Dodd, to London where the whole issue was discussed and where he met his fellow Dominican Agnellus Andrew.

> There was conspiring, plotting – but, it could be argued, chairman's prerogative in circumstances in which I was still unproven, so to speak, in an environment new to me. And I knew how frustrated EA was by his having a new DG – not from broadcasting background – while he was locked into London and I was being devoured by the antipathetic voracious in Dublin.

McCourt later wondered 'how on earth' Dodd's name appeared as the third of three on the committee's short-list. McCourt concludes – since he did not then know his way 'through that labyrinth' – that Andrews took charge and consulted his Dominican friend Andrew who may have found Dodd who was a fellow-Dominican. Thus did McCourt surmise some thirty years after the event at the instigation of Fr Joe Dunn, the priest who had been selected by McQuaid as his preferred candidate and who had indeed been told that his appointment was a formality. McCourt was now helping with the 'loser's' memoir covering this turning point in Dunn's life. Manifestly there was now trust and openness between them. Besides, both men knew that Dunn – although presumed at the time to have lost the coveted prize – well appreciated, in retrospect, what a poisoned chalice it would have been and how fortunate he was not to have been chosen.[6] Dodd in later years liked to recall how he was appointed within hours of being approached with all contracts duly expedited.[7] But there is considerable evidence adduced above of a much more complex story. Was it really a fluke that a Dominican was included as an 'also-ran' in the list of three names put forward by Morris through

6 McCourt note for Dunn, January 1996, McCourt papers.
7 Brian Lynch interview with Fr Romuald Dodd.

I learned, too, that John Charles had been talking with Dev (in Áras) who had been talking with Lemass, who had told E.A. "this is your problem, get 'them off my back"

Archbishop McQuaid thought the new station did not know its place and he went so far as to lobby de Valera to persuade Lemass to take his side in the stand-off. McCourt's note recalls that Lemass's response had been to call on Eamonn Andrews to get the bishops off his back.

McCourt note for Dunn, January 1996, McCourt papers.

the CTIC? And that he was then chosen as the religious adviser?

Whatever the differences between Morris and the station, both seem to have been agreed that, such was McQuaid's temperament, it would be better to keep his nominee out. Years later McCourt recalled that Morris had advised him against accepting Dunn, commenting that since he was 'chained and trained by McQuaid, you'd have McQuaid himself there if you had Dunn'.[8] There is evidence that Morris had an antipathy to McQuaid and to his presumption that he should determine policy, while often – as in this case – staying off the committees which did the work. So Dodd was selected and McCourt wrote formally to the CTIC and announced the appointment. Some days later he received 'a chilling letter' from McQuaid, reminding him of a bishop's authority in his own diocese. But McQuaid had been outplayed and Andrews and the Authority were now satisfied 'that the shadow of John C. had retreated and that the feared omnipotence of the C[ommittee] was aborted'.[9]

As already noted, Dunn had a lucky escape. Instead of being caught in a career of interminable politicking between RTÉ and McQuaid, he returned to his much more productive work as a talented documentary film-maker with the *Radharc* team of Dublin diocesan priests. In his career he would make almost 400 films throughout the world. The *Radharc* films were RTÉ's first independent productions, enjoyed considerable popularity, won many awards, and even had the merit of confusing those who thought that only pagan secularists were making programmes for the national broadcaster.

McQuaid never forgave McCourt and although he corresponded with him intermittently to attempt to exert some influence, their relationship was never much more than minimal functional cooperation. It may be added that McCourt already had reason never to forgive McQuaid for his failure to support him some thirty years before during a personal crisis when he was a sixteen year old schoolboy in Blackrock College. McQuaid was headmaster at the time and although McCourt declined to reveal the details he confided to the author that it was only when he was in his twenties that he came to recognise McQuaid's intervention as selfish and lacking in headmasterly care for a vulnerable student. McCourt never forgave him.[10]

On the last occasion when they 'met', at a reception in the old Nunciature, McCourt saluted him: "Your Grace". McQuaid turned to McCourt 'said not a word, swept past me with almost a disdaining swoosh of his elegant robe. And I never spoke with him again, and I still regret that.'

Author interview with McCourt.

8   John Horgan interview with Kevin McCourt.
9   McCourt note for Dunn, January 1996, McCourt papers.
10 Author interview with Kevin McCourt.

'A few people in the cabinet who would never be satisfied.'
Michael Hilliard did not have Brian Lenihan (left) in mind.

A file entitled 'Broadcasting policy on ministerial statements, 1963-65' is instructive. Two young ministers in the Lemass government believed they had reason to complain about how their press releases had been reported on RTÉ News. In July 1963 McCourt wrote to Charles Haughey following a complaint from the minister. He sent him scripts of news reports: 'As you will see, the version of your statement is not garbled. If anything, it made clear a statement which, appropriate for newspaper coverage, would not have held the interest of radio listeners.' The following day Haughey telephoned: 'I mean if you quote us you must quote us, or not at all.' He was adamantly opposed to any rewriting of a minister's words and told McCourt he would bring the matter to cabinet. McCourt said he would be unhappy 'if you went in and said – that this louser up there says he will do what the hell he likes...'. Both men agreed they were 'deadlocked'.

Some months later at a lunch with Posts and Telegraphs minister, Michael Hilliard, McCourt raised the issue again but their conversation 'rather fizzled out with some vague references to a few people in the cabinet who would never be satisfied but complete understanding from the great majority.' In fact, Hilliard wrote to Haughey after this lunch suggesting that RTÉ had acted 'very fairly' with him, and agreeing with McCourt's line that a paraphrase was permissible and that most ministers would welcome it. Haughey was not impressed. McCourt was writing 'arrant nonsense' and Haughey also challenged McCourt's claim of a 'history of almost complaint-free broadcasting over the last three years.' He judged McCourt to be naive and instanced the numerous occasions on which different ministers had 'been enraged' by the manner in which RE/TE had dealt with various political matters.

In June 1965 Haughey's successor as Justice minister, Brian Lenihan, wrote to McCourt complaining that a statement of his had been 'gutted' in news broadcasts. McCourt replied that a rewrite was justified: the goal of RTÉ was to tell the news with 'veracity, clarity and brevity'. Some weeks later McCourt talked to Lenihan when he was in studio on another matter. Lenihan said he understood the RTÉ position 'and I should not give it another thought'.

McCourt, Haughey and Hilliard, exchange of letters, notes of telephone calls, July-October 1963; Lenihan letter and note, June 1965, 'Post and Telegraphs: Broadcasting policy on ministerial statements 1963-65', RTÉWA.

'The parochialism of just a few years earlier was peeling away.'

PRESIDENT JOHN F. KENNEDY was considered 'a perfect performer for television'. This was because of his charisma, presence, statesmanship and an 'ability to combine humour and seriousness'. A public relations team, in Ireland in advance of his visit in June 1963, 'strongly expressed' their preference for the welcoming ceremonies to be out of doors to optimise the media coverage.[11] Moreover, Kennedy wanted all public engagements on his Irish visit to be televised live. The Americans combined this approach with

---

11 Ian McCabe, 'JFK in Ireland', *History Ireland*, Winter 1993, 38-42.

This screen grab from the television transmission was among the most memorable images of the Kennedy visit. Basil Payne wrote that at Arbour Hill the Telefís Éireann cameras 'in a sustained close-up of President Kennedy's face, distilled the sense of serious endeavour which in his few years of office he has manifested so forcibly.'

Irish Times, 4 July 1963.

insisting that his itinerary remain secret until shortly before his visit. When McCourt complained to Kennedy's press secretary, Pierre Salinger, he was handed a copy of the itinerary, inviting him to 'take whatever notes you want'.[12]

Kennedy's visit and the fact that it was available to the whole nation through television made an enormous impact, not least on the then thirteen-year-old Gene Kerrigan. He could recall years later how his mother and aunt were watching the plane's arrival on television but – living close to the airport – they went to the front door to see if they could see the plane approaching. 'They saw a plane, which may or may not have been Kennedy's, heading in towards the airport. I stayed inside, partly out of annoyance that this Kennedy prat was responsible for me missing some of my favourite TV shows; partly because I was reluctantly fascinated by the novelty of being able to watch the event on live television.'[13]

T.G. Scanner, who wrote regularly for the *Irish Independent* and who specialised in the technical detail of television, seemed unaware of the scale of the engineering challenge to the young station which followed from the Americans' request for saturation coverage. This would have been impossible without pooling the resources of neighbouring broadcasters and RTÉ had enlisted the help

RTÉ through the US Embassy in Dublin made a presentation of the television coverage of Kennedy's visit to the Kennedy Library in Boston. In July 1964 Kevin McCourt received a letter of thanks from the President's widow, Jacqueline Kennedy, part of which is reproduced below.

As you know, the President had a very special place in his heart for Ireland, and for that reason this film will have particular meaning to the Library, and serve as a reminder -- to all the people who visit there -- of the wonderful welcome he received on his trip to your country.

You can be assured that the President's family and I are most appreciative of your thoughtfulness and generosity, and that we will never forget your wish to make this contribution to the Library.

With best wishes,

Sincerely,

Jacqueline Kennedy

12 Eugene McCague, *My Dear Mr McCourt* (Dublin, 2009); hereafter, McCague, *McCourt*.
13 Gene Kerrigan, *Another Country: Growing Up in '50s Ireland* (Dublin, 1998), p.188.

This RTÉ photograph gives some indication of the warmth of the reception accorded to President Kennedy on his arrival in O'Connell Street in Dublin in June 1963. A short five months later on 23 November 1963, Brian O'Nolan, wrote to his fellow-writer and television producer James Plunkett informing him that he was 'thinking of attempting a serious script on ASSASSINATION.' This was written the day following the assassination of President Kennedy in Dallas on 22 November 1963. 'Everybody is hind-sightedly marvelling at the foolhardiness of poor Kennedy. There was so much anti-Kennedy money kicking about that the deed might very easily have been staged in Dublin. I may give you a buzz on this.'

O'Nolan to Plunkett, 23 November 1963, James Plunkett papers, NLI, Ms Dept, Ms. 40,791.

In April 1964, the Galway Fine Gael TD, Fintan Coogan Snr., referred to the visit to the Dáil the previous year of President Kennedy.

When he came to address us here, we had the cameras beamed on the benches opposite, like big gun emplacements prior to battle. We, on this side of the House, took note of things. I went up to one of these gentlemen and I asked him: 'What side of the House are you going to film? The government side only? Is that right?' The poor man seemed to be very embarrassed. He seemed to have got his instructions.

Dáil Debates, vol.209, col.709, 29 April 1964.

of the BBC, UTV and Welsh stations and even then were at full stretch.[14] Scanner could still complain that the President was invisible between the airport and his arrival in O'Connell Street. He innocently added that a 'camera or two at intermediate points would have done much to maintain continuity'. Some crews were already de-rigging once one Kennedy event was complete and setting out to rig up and prepare for a later one.

'The impact of the Kennedy visit, and his dramatic death so shortly afterwards, had something to do with us realising how big the world was and, yet, how things were connected and how we all, even in little Ireland, were wired into something bigger. The parochialism of just a few years earlier was peeling away.'[15] This was especially the case because Telstar, an early orbiting satellite, offered some live pictures for the first time from Europe. Three major US networks, NBC, CBS and ABC, estimated the audience in North America as seventy million.[16]

---

14 *Irish Independent*, 20 June 1963.
15 Gene Kerrigan, *Another Country: Growing Up in '50s Ireland* (Dublin, 1998), p.189.
16 Ian McCabe, 'JFK in Ireland', *History Ireland*, Winter 1993, 38-42.

WINDOW AND MIRROR

7

'a dull colourless group' shaped by a Dáil which was 'tame, ordered and structured'

WITHIN THE FIRST YEAR the station had lost both its director-general and its controller of programmes: Roth had spent more of his two-year contract setting up the station than running it; Barry's resignation after only one year remains as unexplained as was his sudden arrival from the BBC twelve months before. Both John Irvine and Padraic Ó Raghallaigh – the latter brought in from radio as assistant controller – reckoned that Barry would have stayed had he known that Roth's contract was not to be renewed.[1] All the evidence points to Barry relishing his leadership role in an ambitious start-up station, walking 'the tightrope between the needs of a national service and the exigencies... of commercial survival.' But that, he believed, was challenge enough without being expected to endure what he saw as the nonsensical criticisms from Irish language lobbyists.[2] After Barry's resignation, Ó Raghallaigh wrote to him from Boston University – where he was on a television training programme – expressing satisfaction at having escaped 'from the awful unhappiness that had pervaded TE and the intrigue that accompanied it'.[3] Barry may well have disliked the intrigue. He was a highly talented, innovative television pioneer who had established a world-class reputation at BBC drama where he was revered by his colleagues. But his relationship with Roth was not good: indeed the suspicion could be entertained that Roth delayed recruiting a controller the better to impose his own American imprint on the schedule.

Nonetheless both men – whatever their differences – must be credited with establishing a viable, resourceful and professional television service very quickly. Fortunately for RTÉ, their successors proved more compatible: Kevin McCourt as director-general brought

Bunny Carr, in his memoir, recalled the 'searing energy' of Gunnar Rugheimer (below) when he took over as controller of programmes in 1963. He was attentive to programmes as they were transmitted and he circulated his verdicts on green-coloured memos. 'For some reason my efforts found his favour. Congratulatory greens were scarce but I collected them regularly. It was like being back at school and getting a star on your copybook from a tough teacher.'

Bunny Carr, *The Instant Tree* (Dublin, 1975), pp.53-54.

1   Savage, *Loss*, 50, note 42.
2   Barry, memo to Roth, re Blythe letter of 1 October 1962, Blythe papers, UCDAD, P24/1185.
3   Ó Raghallaigh to Barry, 25 November 1964, Barry papers, RTÉWA.

outstanding management skills and Gunnar Rugheimer as controller was a seasoned and ambitious television professional. Together they were ideally suited to consolidate what had initially been achieved by Roth and Barry. It is central to the argument made here that it was in the early years that the template for public service broadcasting was established. Rugheimer had no doubt that current affairs 'should be the fulcrum of the entire programming activity'. For him it was simply 'the thumping heart-beat' of the station.[4] He pursued the politicians of all parties to drop their defences and embrace 'a more detailed treatment, on an adult level, of the political affairs of the nation'. He showed no patience with their timidity in engaging with current affairs television. Lemass wanted to approve the chair of any televised debate between rival politicians and wanted the parties to control which TDs appeared. Manifestly he lacked confidence in the ability of many of his own TDs to be 'good on the box'. In this he showed insight. Rugheimer insisted that the producer must have full editorial control and – at a time when politicians preferred to engage only under the rules governing party political broadcasts – he managed in the autumn of 1966 to launch two new current affairs programmes: *Division* and *Seven Days*.[5] It seems probable that the newspapers were subjected to some political spin by the party whips as to the rules of engagement, but Rugheimer was quick with a robust and courteous correction: he insisted that the new programmes would represent 'an important step towards greater freedom and maturity in political broadcasting'.[6] Muiris Mac Conghail, presently to become the most controversial and radical current affairs editor, recalled that the main determination of the party whips was to so shape political programming that 'the politicians would not embarrass themselves.' Many TDs were simply not suited to the cut and thrust of broadcast debate. Some few were gifted but for the most part Mac Conghail found himself dealing with 'a dull colourless group', whose speaking skills had been shaped by a Dáil which was 'tame, ordered and structured'.[7]

On 22 December 1968 7 *Days* broadcast a controversial programme concerning a Fianna Fáil proposal to hold a constitutional referendum on the electoral system. The proposal was to abolish PR and the multi-seat constituencies and substitute the first-past-the-post system with single-member constituencies. On the programme two Trinity political scientists, Basil Chubb and David Thornley, projected that this would result in Fianna Fáil winning 65 per cent of the seats on 40 per cent of the vote. Their seat prediction at that time was Fianna Fáil 93, Fine Gael 44, Labour 8 and others 9. Given Fianna Fáil's traditional support base – from 1932 to 1965 they had always exceeded 42 per cent of first preference votes – most commentators reckoned that under the proposed change Fianna Fáil would retain power indefinitely by winning at least ninety seats. The then Fianna Fáil leader and Taoiseach, Jack Lynch, confirmed to the author that it was this 7 *Days* forecast which 'with certainty killed our aspirations about the change in the system.'

Lynch, interview with author, June 1978.

---

4 Rugheimer, 'Irish television in trouble', *Irish Times*, 20 October 1969.
5 Rugheimer to Michael Carty, 3 June 1966, NAI DT 98/6/83.
6 Letter to editor, *Irish Times*, 16 September 1966.
7 Savage, *Loss*, 76.

'tales of Micheal Ruadh ... were giving way to those of Kit Carson and Bat Masterson'

ACCORDING TO ONE HISTORICAL SURVEY, television had taken over 'the role of the cinema in promoting the Los Angelisation of Ireland. When it was not showing American films, it was showing American situation comedy, crime, or cowboy series.'[8] In this regard Ireland was not unique. In post-war Europe, American popular culture enjoyed a special appeal, especially among the young. This elicited a countervailing strand of anti-Americanism: Seán O'Faolain accused such critics of 'mean-mindedness', of being afraid of 'cultural colonisation by American films, entertainment, comics and literature'.[9] His successor as editor of *The Bell*, Peadar O'Donnell – and they were usually of one mind – disagreed with O'Faolain. He now warned that the firesides of rural Ireland were 'being overrun by television and that tales of Micheal Ruadh and Big Willie Boyle were giving way to those of Kit Carson, Vint Bonner and Bat Masterson.'[10]

Robert Young, as Jim Anderson, tries to take himself and his family back to nature in *Jim The Farmer*, to-night's episode in the *Father Knows Best* series. It can be seen at 6.10 T.E.

But despite their shallow plots and formulaic endings – or perhaps because of them – American programmes were popular. Nor can it be presumed that had Telefís Éireann boycotted them, their devotees would not have found similar programming on other channels. And some voices were raised in support. Fr Charles A. Scahill, opening the fourth annual Glenamaddy Drama Festival, had praise for RTÉ's choice of American series, finding many had 'a definite moral'. In particular he thought Irish viewers could benefit more from *Bachelor Father* or *Father Knows Best* than from some home-produced programmes: he was hoping for more of the latter while recommending 'a strict censorship'.[11]

Father Knows Best was an American sit-com which appealed to some because of its emphasis on American family values. It had run from 1954 to 1960 on US television.

According to one estimate in the 1960s RTÉ could afford to spend only approximately ten per cent of the BBC budget on home-produced programmes. At a time when it was costing the BBC £2,500 per hour to make programmes, the RTÉ figure was £214. Meanwhile the Irish rights of American series were available for a mere £20 per hour. Morash concludes: 'To put it simply, without American television, there would have been no

'*Even the interference seems to have a certain amount of American influence.*' – Dublin Opinion, January 1962

---

8   Cathcart, 'Mass Media', 694.
9   Seán O'Faolain, 'Autoantiamericanism', *The Bell*, vol.16, no.6, March 1951, 7-18.
10 Sheehan, *Irish Television Drama*, 138.
11 *Tuam Herald*, 9 March 1963.

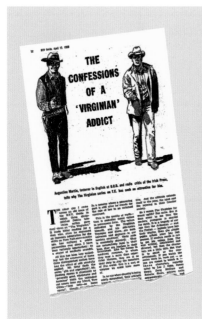

Irish television'.[12] The Irish television rights to feature films originally made for the cinema were similarly inexpensive, about £40 per hour in the 1960s. At a briefing for the RTÉ Authority in March 1966, Rugheimer outlined how nearly all the major distributors would sell only 'on a library basis', ensuring that the purchaser took 'usually not less than fifty but more often 100 films and upward'. This was to get some return for films with a lesser public appeal. Rugheimer added that RTÉ's position was complicated by the fact that BBC, UTV and Welsh TV broadcast two feature films every week into the Irish multi-channel area. This made it 'exceedingly difficult to buy groups of feature films of quality which have not been seen before on television in at least a multi-channel area'. He added that it was possible now to purchase more recent material but this had 'tended to become more violent and daring', resulting in many post-1948 films not having passed the Irish censor. 'For this reason, we must look very carefully at any post-1948 group of films to see that the individual titles are actually transmittable here.'[13]

That RTÉ executives were embarrassed by this over-dependence on American material seems probable from an internal document by

At an Authority meeting, McCourt intended mentioning *The Lucy Show* but hoped not to have to admit that the station had purchased as many as 84 episodes. He was 'not happy' concerning such commitments.

12 Christopher Morash, *A History of the Media in Ireland* (Cambridge, 2010), p.175; hereafter, Morash, *Media in Ireland*.
13 Rugheimer to McCourt, 24 March 1966; circulated to Authority.

In an article in the *RTÉ Guide*, Gus Martin of the English department at UCD complained of the 'subtle persecution' he had been obliged to endure ever since he had expressed his 'innocent admiration' of *The Virginian* some months previously. Clearly the series was 'not intellectually respectable' and the prudent thing would have been 'to sit at home on Friday evenings and practice it as a secret vice – even though it is watched, I'll go bail, by an underground army of bishops, monsignori, cabinet ministers and managing directors.' Martin found the values of Judge Garth and his sidekicks, Trampas and Steve, to be 'both universal and germane to our modern condition'. Far from being violent, they fought only if their chivalric code was threatened. 'Like the heroes in mediaeval romance, to whom they bear a more than superficial likeness, they see it as their duty to slay the monsters of this world: this is the sort of violence we could have more of.'

RTV Guide, 15 April 1966.

McCourt in advance of an Authority meeting where he would be invited to discuss the issue. McCourt wanted to put the emphasis on other quality programmes and admitted he was 'not happy' concerning the commitments 'made to 180 episodes of *The Virginian*, 58 of *The Monkees*, 84 of *The Lucy Show* and 86 of *Get Smart*'. He would use an extant list 'of titles, duration, description, country of origin', while hoping that it 'might not be necessary to mention the number of episodes we have purchased'.[14] But McCourt could have emphasised that this material was available only in such large quantities. Rugheimer's overall estimate was that RTÉ needed such material to support a television service which in terms of hours of output was greater than countries with three times Ireland's population. He could admit that the need to fill 'the yawning span of broadcasting hours' had led to programming fare which was 'often trivial and sometimes tawdry' but – unlike other young stations elsewhere – Telefís Éireann needed a full evening's schedule because of the proximity and availability to so many Irish viewers of rival British stations. These American series cross-subsidised other more valuable programming and of one matter he was certain: 'the Irish national broadcasting service was not conceived to become a national juke-box.'[15]

James Dillon TD was not impressed by RTÉ's choice of old American movies, a subject on which – he advised the Dáil – he had been expert as a younger man.

14 McCourt to Maloney, 27 September 1967, RTÉWA.
15 Gunnar Rugheimer, 'Irish television in trouble', *Irish Times*, 20 October 1969.

James Dillon, former Minister for Agriculture and Fine Gael leader from 1959 to 1965, was critical of RTÉ's choice of old films when he spoke in the Dáil in February 1966. He accepted that a station with a schedule as long as RTÉ's must use films. What astonished him was that they used films which by his reckoning were so old and so idiotic.

> I used to be a most ardent cinema fan for 30 years of my life. For many years, I am sure I went to the cinema twice a week. I loved the cinema as an art medium. But, glory be, some of the films I see trotted out today, which admittedly are 20 and 30 years old, are not only venerable and whiskered but the most idiotic examples of the period when they were made. When I think of the great actresses who adorned the screen of 30 years ago and see the films that are put on television today, I am absolutely aghast.... Probably we can get the rubbish in bargain lots at a very low figure but I do not believe that the difference in the cost of getting 30-year-old films which feature great artistes of the day and getting 30-year-old films which contain the rubbish of the past can be so great. Just imagine poor old Paulette Goddard thumping around and trying to look romantic in these days when she did not look romantic in the 'thirties and just imagine trying to get us all to swoon about her now – why, you might as well ask us to fall in love with a two-hundredweight sack of flour.

Dáil Debates, vol.220, cols.562-3, 1 February 1966.

I mean him to be possessed of stature and character, dedication without indifference to the factors of organisation, able to contribute by imagination and integrity to good programming. Be assured I will not settle for a second-rater nor will I be influenced by false economy in what he might cost.

Yours sincerely,

(Kevin C. McCourt)
Director-General.

It had been decided to establish a senior position, editor of Irish language programmes, to liaise with Rugheimer – and doubtless to cover for his lack of Irish. McCourt reassured Blythe that he was seeking an outstanding candidate.

did not want a policy 'to silence agitators or buy off critics'

Francis MacManus, novelist and broadcaster. As a senior commissioning editor in Radio Éireann (1948-65) an encourager of talent.

CONTROVERSY OVER the station's treatment of the Irish language did not end with Roth's departure. His successor McCourt in October 1963 tried to disabuse Blythe of his belief that there had been sabotage or at least antipathy to Irish from within the organisation. McCourt expressed satisfaction that this was 'not the case', adding that the station could not achieve all its goals in two years 'of dramatic and often tumultuous growth'.[16] A week later he was reassuring Blythe that he would give thought to shaping a policy which would reconcile the station's 'several responsibilities' – a clear reference to its other duty to be popular and economically viable.[17] The following month McCourt insisted that any deficiency in policy on Irish had been due to 'lack of identification and direction rather than malice or antipathy'.[18] Blythe was not alone in his scepticism. Contemporaneously, the American academic and lobbyist, Eoin McKiernan, believed that the state had been 'so slow, so awkward, and so timid' on Irish language policy that the charge of 'sit-down sabotage' had several times been made against it. McKiernan believed that Telefís Éireann in its opening years had 'shown no particular appreciation of the language revival as a proclaimed goal of the nation.' And it was to him 'all too obvious' that television might yet 'become an insurmountable obstacle to the restoration of the national tongue'.[19]

The station's leadership must also have felt under pressure when they were sent the same message in an early draft report of the Commission on the Restoration of the Irish Language. They were

16 McCourt to Blythe, 15 October 1963, Blythe papers, UCDAD, P24/1188.
17 *ibid.*, 21 October 1963. P24/1189.
18 *ibid.*, 18 November 1963, P24/1190.
19 Eoin McKiernan, *The will of a nation: Ireland's crisis*, (St. Paul Minnesota, 1964), p.10.

WINDOW AND MIRROR

Liam Ó Murchú was appointed Irish language editor in 1964. Before taking up the post, he sought advice from his friend and mentor Francis MacManus, novelist and head of features in Radio Éireann. MacManus was concerned. He advised that the television campus – radio had yet to move to the Donnybrook site – was akin to 'a snake-pit'. And as for the Irish language, 'no-one in authority wants it. They'll pretend they do and pay lip-service and make all sorts of public statements, but in the end they'll do nothing.' He advised that Ó Murchú's position would be impossible. 'One crowd will devour you if you don't do something, the other crowd will devour you if you do.' Ó Murchú next sought advice from Dónal Ó Móráin whom he found 'most intelligent and perceptive' and not 'at all the draconian manipulator' which some thought him. Ó Móráin advised that – on his own, Ó Murchú 'might not be able to achieve very much' – this because of 'the background, composition, personnel and financial strictures' of RTÉ; but aided and abetted 'by appropriate pressure from outside', he might achieve 'a great deal indeed'. Ó Murchú was to become assistant director-general and was presenter of the award-winning bilingual talk-show *Trom agus Éadrom*.

Liam Ó Murchú, *A Time to Love?* (Dublin, 1986), pp.96-99.

told that they could 'do more to promote, or to hinder, the revival of Irish than any other body'. The Commission approved of the fact that *An Nuacht* had been the last bulletin at night and – in a revealing comment – they regretted the change whereby it was then followed by a later news bulletin in English. They believed that the change had 'cancelled out almost completely every advantage to *An Nuacht* of the previous arrangement', which they wanted restored. They also called for items in Irish 'each complete within itself' to be included in the main News bulletin at 9pm and recommended that the Authority 'should henceforth demand competence in Irish as an essential qualification' for producers and broadcasters. A broadcaster without proficiency in Irish was 'a hindrance to the extension of the use of Irish' in the television schedule.[20]

McCourt was also pro-active on the language issue. He was supportive of one of Blythe's proposals, the recruitment of an Irish language officer. He assured him that the individual would be

---

20 RTÉ translation of broadcasting sections of a draft of forthcoming report of the Commission on the Restoration of the Irish Language, RTÉWA.

Ernest Blythe did not hesitate to express himself bluntly on Irish language matters. In a letter to John Irvine in August 1962, he commented on an initial draft of the first annual report to cover the new television service. Blythe wrote that the account of the opening night of television was 'a trifle too lyrical for an annual report'. The section on the Irish language, he found 'most annoying' and he would not like these sections to be included 'in anything like their present form'.

Blythe to Irvine, 27 August 1962, Blythe papers, UCDAD P24/1183.

'possessed of stature and character, dedication without indifference to the factors of organisation' and would be able to contribute 'by imagination and integrity to good programming.' Blythe could feel assured that McCourt would 'not settle for a second-rater', nor would he be deterred by cost.[21] This was the post to which Liam Ó Murchú was recruited.

But none of this assuaged Blythe's anger at how he thought the language had fared in the station's initial years. In November 1964 he complained to McCourt that the station had not done enough after three years on the air. He was particularly incensed by what he termed 'scraps of greeting and the like', whose use often indicated 'varying types of indifference or contempt', being mostly what he had previously described as 'incestuous or ghetto-minded or non-adult'. He did not want a policy based on an occasional item 'to silence agitators or buy off critics'. Blythe excoriated the station's record: he wrote in terms of a 'stingy minimum' and of 'miserly rationing'; and he reckoned refresher televised courses in the Irish language merely 'a delusion and a snare'. He believed that Irish language items should be on *The Late Late Show* ten or twelve time a year and called for 'drive, attentiveness, care and attention, willingness to explore and experiment and a sense of direction and purpose.'[22] McCourt replied promptly, promising 'to encourage, persuade, facilitate and seek every opportunity' to bring appropriate Irish language programmes to air.[23]

---

21 McCourt to Blythe, 18 November 1963, Blythe papers, UCDAD, P24/1190.
22 Blythe to McCourt, 6 November 1964, *ibid.*, P24/1191.
23 McCourt to Blythe, 7 November 1964, *ibid.*, P24/1192.

Agricultural programmes were a very important part of RTÉ television's initial schedule. Even *The Riordans* had as its initial purpose the inclusion of various sub-themes focussed on modernising Irish farming; hence the storyline based on Benjy as a graduate from agricultural college being impatient with the old ways of his father, Tom Riordan's. Later, Justin Keating, with *Telefís Feirme,* would break new ground with direct agricultural instruction to farmers, many of them viewing in group settings with agricultural instructors to lead a discussion based on the programme. This pioneering format was copied in many other countries.

Joe Murray

Joe Murray, who worked as a reporter, producer and later head of agricultural programmes, recalled how farmers were initially in awe of the arrival of a television crew; he found them 'a bit shy' and fearful of 'what this gang was going to do'? The farmyard would have been whitewashed as if the bishop was coming: 'A man would have spent days doing this.' Murray remembers going to one particular farm in east Galway to film a local farmer 'doing dredge'. Murray was completing a programme about drainage and the farmer – when they arrived – 'was in his drain working exactly the way we wanted him to be working'. There was only one problem. 'He had his Sunday suit on. It didn't look quite authentic. Yet he had decided that he wanted to look good on television and his wife – who had probably really made the decision – had decided that she wasn't going to have him disgraced.' Murray admitted that he 'couldn't think what to do'. Then a neighbour arrived, 'just out of curiosity and interest; he had been laying blocks and he had ravelled the front of his pullover'. Murray could still remember the garment. 'It was kind of a light blue pullover and the neighbour came over, and he says: "Ah Pat, you don't look right at all. What are you doing in the Sunday suit? Sure you can't wear that!" The neighbour then 'pulled off the pullover and he handed it to the man. Our man put on the pullover and he went on with his drain and he looked grand, like a man in his working clothes.' The filming was completed and transmitted. 'How his wife dealt with him subsequently, when she saw him on television, I don't exactly know.'

'*I've a few suggestions for your Image of the Irish Farmer!*'
– *Dublin Opinion,* June 1965

Not an 'interpretive or analytical' approach, but an 'idealistic and emotional' one

Michael Garvey shared with Louis Lentin the production and direction of the highly acclaimed *Insurrection* series which was Telefís Éireann's main contribution to the Easter Week commemoration in 1966.

EVEN ALLOWING FOR THE FACT that the national consensus on the Easter Rising was more settled on the fiftieth anniversary than it has been since, it is somewhat alarming to read that the Authority and the senior editorial team charged with producing the commemorative programmes seem to have settled well in advance on a uniform approach. There was not much leeway for different voices. In this regard RTÉ was not alone: in publishers' lists and newspaper coverage a not dissimilar line was taken. But in 1966 it was surely unduly prescriptive for RTÉ to insist that 1916 be portrayed 'as a nationalist and not as a socialist rising': might there not be more than one viewpoint on such a question? What most shocks, however, is the decision that the overall approach to programming should be 'idealistic and emotional' rather than 'interpretive and analytical'.[24] Can T.W.Moody, the most experienced member of the Authority – and a life-long advocate of independent thinking by Irish historians – really have signed off on this? And what of Kevin B. Nowlan, historical consultant to the *Insurrection* series, which attempted in eight episodes to re-enact the events of Easter 1916 with nightly reports as if television news had been present fifty years before.

This innovative programme produced and directed by Michael Garvey and Louis Lentin, and written by Hugh Leonard, won wide

---

24 Meeting of 1916 programmes committee, including Rugheimer, Garvey and O Gallchoir, 22 July 1965, following the RTÉ Authority meeting of 21 July 1965, RTÉWA.

In advance of the fiftieth anniversary, Telefís Éireann advertised in the press seeking the participation in their commemorative programmes of those with direct knowledge of the Easter Rising and its leaders.

RADIO ÉIREANN/TELEFÍS ÉIREANN

MAR chuid de chláracha cuimhneacháin Éirí Amach na Cásca tá sé beartaithe ag Telefís Éireann sraith sheacht gclár a chraoladh ar na fir a shínigh forógra na Cásca : Tomás Ó Cléirigh, Sean Mac Diarmada, Tomás Mac Donncha, Pádraic Mac Piarais, Éamonn Ceannt, Séamas Ó Conghaile, Seosamh Pluincéad.
Cuirfear mórchuid na gclár i dtoll a chéile ó chuimhní cinn na ndaoine a raibh aithne acu orthu agus dá bhrí sin táimid ag cur amach an achainí phoiblí seo chucu siúd a bhfuil ar a gcumas cabhair a thabhairt dúinn.
Aon ábhar a chuirtear chugainn, bhéarfar aire dó agus cuirfear thar n-ais é.
Féadfar litreacha a chur chuig :
Ceannasaí na gClár, TELEFÍS ÉIREANN, Domhnach Broc, ÁTH CLIATH 4.

acclaim from critics and viewers. Nowlan clearly did assert himself on some aspects of the initial script. In November 1965 he was reassured by Rugheimer that 'historical accuracy is of key importance in the *Insurrection* series. However desirable something may be from the dramatic point of view, it should not be accepted unless it corresponds with the facts as they are known.' Where unknown, the dramatist had 'some freedom' as long as the line taken was consistent 'with the weight of the historical evidence'.[25]

In a preview of the programme before transmission, the Authority expressed its general satisfaction. But Ruari Brugha – himself son of the Republican leader Cathal Brugha – alerted his fellow members to expect criticism that de Valera had not been featured in the *Insurrection* series while Collins had been featured six times. Given that de Valera's role was such that he had been initially sentenced to death and that Collins had yet to emerge as a major figure, this criticism seems fair. But McCourt explained de Valera's omission on grounds of sensitivity at casting a living person.[26] The series won wide critical acclaim. Tom O'Dea suggested that the station had not only been impartial but, just as important, it had shown the men of 1916 'not as the remote colourless idols' commonly conjured up in classrooms and elsewhere 'but as men of flesh and blood, with all the imperfections, passions, virtues, insights and blind spots that creatures of flesh and blood have.' Had the station done nothing else that week but 'take the 1916 leaders down off their pedestals and set

> 'Only so many of the original places, involved in the fighting remain to-day as they were then... in fact, all too few; if only they could have waited until next year to rebuild Liberty Hall... if only there weren't so many television aerials.'
>
> Louis Lentin, 'The making of *Insurrection*', *RTV Guide*, 8 April 1966.

Cólm O Lochlainn, publisher, printer, typeface designer and political activist, in response to the press advertisement, informs Liam Ó Murchú of his credentials to speak of 1916. His postcard to Ó Murchú [left] and Ó Murchú's translation for Rugheimer emphasises that he is 'not just a musicianer!'

---

25 Rugheimer to Kevin B. Nowlan, 15 November 1965, 1916 programme file, RTÉWA.
26 RTÉ Authority, minutes, 30 March 1966.

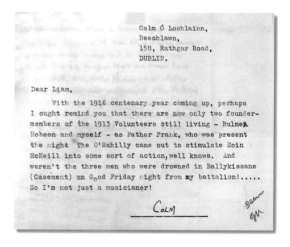

Scenes from *Insurrection*. Above: Patrick Pearse – played by Eoin ÓSúilleabháin – with the Proclamation of Independence.

Louis Lentin, producer-director – with Michael Garvey – of *Insurrection*, recalled their first filming foray into O'Connell Street in Dublin to film a re-enactment of the charge of the mounted British Lancers. Their filming stint 'brought forth a crowd of thousands', including one old Dubliner who could claim that it reminded him of the original mounted charge fifty years before, on Easter Monday 1916. Lentin recalled that throughout the filming, there were invariably many onlookers, 'all well meaning, who were certain it didn't happen like that at all, and said so.' Note the 1960s motor cars in Parnell Square. It is some measure of Garvey and Lentin's skill that the film was directed and edited to exclude all such unwelcome non-period detail.

RTV Guide, 8 April 1966.

them firmly on the earth, the element that even heroes inhabit', it would have done a service to the country.[27] Brian Devenney had praise for Hugh Leonard's script which 'bore the imprint of the master craftsman both in the economical use of dialogue and incident, and also, in the quick-fire cutting to the studio desk, where Ray MacAnally kept up the illusion that TV cameras were out in 1916.'[28] Sheehan attests that *Insurrection* was very much 'the communal talking point for days to come' and described it as one of 'the best remembered and well received productions in the whole history of RTÉ.'[29]

27 *Irish Press*, 16 April 1966.
28 *Irish Independent*, 16 April 1966.
29 Sheehan, *Irish Television Drama* (2004 revised edition), 59-60.

Insurrection was transmitted in many countries. The Norwegian newspaper, *Verdens Gang*, wrote that it was 'a masterpiece which could serve as a model for Norwegian and other TV stations planning similar programmes'. It was highly informative on an episode in European history that was 'very little known' in Norway.

RTÉ Guide, 12 April 1968.

8

'the wish to have what is desirable is not being related to what is either possible or acceptable'

IN OCTOBER 1965 a group of producers voiced their dissent to the Authority concerning Rugheimer's management style; and some made no secret of their dislike at being managed by a foreigner. McCourt, for his part, admired Rugheimer's blunt speaking, finding him 'tough, strong and intellectual', and adding, mischievously, that his only weakness was intolerance of sectional interests 'like the hierarchy, politicians and the Irish language people, roughly in that order.'[1] Rugheimer did manage to make enemies – enough eventually to cost him the prospect of a contract renewal – but in his custodianship of the schedule during its formative years he had proved to be not only combative, but also innovative, energetic, experimental and highly successful.

His tenure became insecure after the nomination of a new interim Authority, appointed for one year only and without Lemass consulting Andrews as to its composition. It included Dónal O Móráin of Gael Linn, who had been a scourge of the government's television policy for the best part of the previous decade. And in its general composition it was clear that O Móráin would have more supporters on this Authority than he would have had on its predecessor. Was the government hoping to appease O Móráin? On learning of the composition of this Authority, Andrews had been 'distraught', but had agreed to try to make it work. Along with McCourt he wanted to retain Rugheimer as controller, and indeed favoured a further five-year contract. The evidence points to Rugheimer's future role in the station as being the currency of the power-play which now ensued. As his contract was about to expire, the Authority decided that the post should be advertised. Andrews and McCourt both hoped that Rugheimer would survive on

Kevin McCourt (right) would presently fail to persuade the Authority to keep Gunnar Rugheimer (left) as controller; and Rugheimer's exit precipitated the resignation of Eamonn Andrews as chairman. In the background at this EBU summit in Dublin is a future director-general, George Waters.

---

1 McCague, *McCourt*, 79-80.

The RTÉ Authority, 1965 which did not renew Rugheimer's contract. (*front row*) James Fanning, Eamonn Andrews, Phillis Bean Uí Cheallaigh, Ed B. MacManus, (*back row*) Michael Noonan, Dónal Ó Móráin, Fintan Kennedy, Dr T.W. Moody and Ruairi Brugha.

grounds of being indispensable to the management team.

There were as many as 62 applicants, including twelve members of staff. McCourt travelled to New York, Toronto and London to interview some of them without finding any individual he regarded as suitable. Andrews was manifestly frustrated with what he saw as the power of the Anybody But Rugheimer faction on the Authority.[2] And when what he termed 'the expensive and arduous' search for an Irish controller of programmes from outside the organisation failed to yield any suitable candidate, Andrews believed that 'the refusal to make a last minute effort to retain Rugheimer was tantamount to saying we would accept second best.' It also ignored the fact that Rugheimer 'had succeeded in understanding our needs so well', initiating education, history and farming programmes, 'not to mention our 1916 celebration features'.[3] Andrews believed this to be a litmus test of the station's seriousness and concluded that it had failed that test. In April 1966 he sent his letter of resignation to Lemass, informing him that the Authority was 'too susceptible to outside pressures,

Before the station opened, Michael Barry called in all the producers for a review of progress. Most of them were still trainees but they still had programmes to produce for the inaugural schedule. Jim Fitzgerald stood up to make the complaint that as far as he was concerned the Irish producers, like himself, had been given the lesser tasks, 'the left-overs', while the best programmes 'had been allocated to the foreigners'. Michael Barry interrupted: 'Please remember that in art there is no such thing as a foreigner.' This silenced the room.

Author interview with Micheal Johnston.

2 RTÉ Authority, minutes, 16 February, 9 March 1966.
3 *ibid.*, minutes, 11 May 1966.

WINDOW AND MIRROR

principally on the score of the Irish language.' This was a reference to the policy statement *Irish on television* which had been drafted by O Móráin and which had won Authority approval. It had been widely circulated in the station and signalled an expectation that there would be a significant increase in Irish on television where it was to be presented in 'a sympathetic and imaginative way'.

In his resignation letter Andrews told Lemass that he had 'tried to compromise' but honesty compelled him to state that he believed that the change in policy, if pursued, would bring the television service 'so far ahead of public acceptance' that it would 'lose the Irish viewer to cross channel services as happened in radio'. Irish language advocates were sincere but were pressing 'an unrealistic policy' which Andrews believed would have 'both artistic and financial repercussions of an unfortunate kind'. He allowed that idealism was the inspiration but unfortunately 'the wish to have what is desirable is not being related to what is either possible or acceptable.'[4] And in a letter to the responsible minister he added that he 'had longed to give to the country a strong, virile, and national television service', but it was now just 'not possible'.[5] Rugheimer for his part found that the Irish

Eamonn Andrews 'was a prime broadcaster, but not then or ever a good hands-on businessman. He had no experience of the politicking of business, its power struggles, its inherent resentments, ambitions, unkindness, selfishness, its cunning and manoeuvring.'

McCourt memo to Joe Dunn, January 1996, McCourt papers.

---

4 Andrews to Lemass, 25 April 1966, copy in McCourt papers.
5 Andrews to Joseph Brennan [Minister for Posts and Telegraphs], 25 April 1966, *ibid.*

The letter which follows is from Edward J.Roth to his successor as director-general, Kevin McCourt. It is dated 6 February 1966.

I do not know at this stage whether or not the position of Programme Controller of Telefís Éireann has been filled but I have learned from a friend in the United States that Denis Johnston is very interested in being considered for the post. Away back in the very early days, before we went on the air, I recall speaking to Denis about the position but he was tied up at the time with his position as Head of Drama at Smith College, Massachusetts.

It is quite possible you know him. My impression of him was extremely high for he has a vast amount of experience in television, radio and, of course, the theatre as an executive, writer, producer and playwright. What's more, he's Irish. If you feel there is any merit in following this up, do let me know and I will do all I can to help. Unfortunately, I do not know his present address which, in any event, is no doubt available from his many friends in Dublin.

For what it is worth I would greatly support his candidacy for the job.

That this letter survives in Denis Johnston's papers suggests that there may have been some collusion between Roth and Johnston that Roth would recommend Johnston for the controller's job to succeed Rugheimer. It may be a draft for Johnston's consideration. It seems probable that Roth knew Johnston's address since this copy of the letter is in his papers. Whether the idea came from Roth or Johnston is unclear. The most plausible explanation to the author is that this was Johnston's ploy to test whether RTÉ had an interest in considering him for the job without the embarrassment of a rebuff had he made a direct approach. There is no mention of his ambition for this post or of him being considered for it in Bernard Adams, *Denis Johnston: A Life* (Dublin, 2002).

Roth to McCourt, 6 February 1966, Denis Johnston papers, TCD, Ms. 10066/290/2518.

Eamonn Andrews was featured on an Irish stamp in 1994 in a series, 'Impact of the Irish Abroad: the Irish in Britain'. Two distinguished Irish persons were featured. The other was Edmund Burke, statesman and writer. Incidentally in his memoir, Andrews writes that during one broadcasting crisis he was relieved 'to get a chuckle' when Kevin McCourt sent him a quotation from Edmund Burke. 'Those who would carry on great public schemes must be proof against the worst fatiguing delays, the most mortifying disappointments, the most shocking insults and, worst of all, the presumptuous judgment of the ignorant upon their designs.'

Eamonn Andrews, *This is my life* (London, 1963), p.239.

C.S. 'Todd' Andrews, chairman RTÉ Authority, 1966-70.

language lobbyists on the Authority 'were completely unreasonable'; they wanted to operate on a basis 'that everybody spoke Irish, and that the appropriate thing to do would be to sprinkle Irish throughout the programming: this was complete rubbish.' And he believed Andrews had been treated in an 'unreasonable and unfair' manner: 'this is why he resigned'.[6]

Two months later Andrews was writing from County Kerry to McCourt, both men still preoccupied with the need to find a programme controller, but Andrews believing that 'frankly ... all the ideas we've come up with between us are long shots.' Andrews was still nursing some hopes to retain Rugheimer but if McCourt felt that the situation had 'deteriorated even more to make G.R. an impossible consideration', then McCourt should think of 'looking again, if needs be to the USA, for a highly paid freelance.' Andrews also expressed the hope, 'despite all the stupidity and shortsightedness', that McCourt himself would 'not be lost to broadcasting' since his 'feel for and knowledge' of television was 'remarkable'.[7]

In September the Authority announced the appointment of the first Irish controller of programmes, Michael Garvey. A highly gifted producer, his contemporaries saw him as unsuited to 'the highly stressful and confrontational world of current affairs broadcasting.'[8]

'no particular interest' in television or 'what influence it might have'

C.S. 'TODD' ANDREWS was on the point of retiring from CIE when he read an evening paper headline at Paris Airport that he was to replace Eamonn Andrews. In his memoir he wrote that he had 'no notion' that the government was going to offer him the job. But he does not tell his readers that he had so coveted it that he had asked de Valera to intercede on his behalf. His account is at least confusing since it seems open to a plausible reading that the government appointed him without even consulting him. In fact Lemass had already met him 'at the end of May and offered him the position'.[9] Given the known misgivings of Lemass concerning the new service, Todd Andrews must have held exceptional appeal. Whereas Eamonn Andrews could be relied on to be a broadcaster's broadcaster in any differences with the government, Todd Andrews, after a lifetime of service in the semi-state

---

6   Rugheimer interview with John Horgan.
7   Andrews to McCourt, 25 June 1966, McCourt papers.
8   Savage, *Loss*, 102.
9   *ibid.*, 304.

sector, envisaged the provision of a television service – much as Lemass himself viewed it – as yet another example of the state setting up a public utility. His own memoirs confirm this. On the Lemass claim that RTÉ should be an instrument of public policy, Andrews writes that this 'was even more strongly held by me' because of earlier experience with semi-state bodies and civil servants.

And he acknowledged that he had 'no particular interest' in television 'in the sense of speculating on what influence it might have on the Irish character and culture'. But he was interested in the semi-state sector and had watched RTÉ emerge 'with more than casual attention'. He believed – and no public servant had more experience than he of so many state enterprises – that no semi-state company had 'got off the ground more quickly and with so few teething troubles...'. It was his impression that Lemass 'expressed very little interest in RTÉ except to say that some of the staff seemed to be "losing the run of themselves" in thinking that the government had no function in relation to the National Broadcasting Authority, a point of view that no government could accept.'[10]

Lemass was surprised, sometimes bewildered, by the presumed independence of the broadcasters

LEMASS HAD MANY SKIRMISHES with RTÉ as we have seen: his most celebrated was in 1966 shortly before he retired from political life and it arose in the context of how RTÉ felt it should best cover an long-standing dispute between the National Farmers Association and the Minister for Agriculture, Charles Haughey. The difficulty was undoubtedly exacerbated by RTÉ's ambitious plans for current affairs in its autumn schedule. These plans were driven by Rugheimer, ousted perhaps, but still determined to spend his final months incrementally expanding the settings in which politicians would appear on television. Up to this point, aside from news interviews, they had debated with other elected representatives only in programmes agreed with the party whips and classified as party political broadcasts. And just as a new code of practice for such broadcasts was being agreed with the politicians in September 1966, RTÉ was also launching two new

In June 1968 a discussion arose at an RTÉ Authority meeting concerning on-screen bad manners. This led to the following proposal from the chairman, C.S. Andrews, as recorded in the Authority's official minutes.

The Chairman stated that he did not think it was correct to encourage bad manners on television. Dr Moody vehemently agreed. Arising from the Chairman's reference, there was considerable support among Authority members for a programme or programme series on good manners for young people. This would be a programme which would deal with the reason for good manners, what good manners consist of and which would deal also with formal manners. The Chairman said that he thought that as a nation we were deficient in this field and that, to mount a programme of the type mentioned, would represent a good social use of television.

RTÉ Authority minutes, 7 June 1968, RTÉ Authority papers. It may be noted that in his interview with Padraigh O Raghaillaigh in the RTÉ Sound Archives, Andrews lists among the achievements of the Christian Brothers their success in teaching their pupils good manners.

10 Andrews, *Man of No Property*, 269-70.

current affairs programmes, *Seven Days* and *Division*, the latter to concentrate on legislative, political and parliamentary affairs. Its producer was Muiris Mac Conghail, with David Thornley and Patrick Gallagher as presenters. The *Division* programme had the declared ambition to coax the politicians into the studios with invitations to participate being issued as the requirements of the programme demanded.

Meanwhile a march organised by the National Farmers Association had set out from Bantry in west Cork on 7 October demanding a summit meeting with the agriculture minister. On the television news a statement by Haughey was juxtaposed with one from the farmers leader, Rickard Deasy. Haughey complained and Pearse Kelly, head of news, instructed the staff to drop the Deasy statement from subsequent bulletins. The journalists involved, through their union, publicly protested and the matter reached the floor of Dáil Éireann.[11] Since it was the minister's refusal to meet the farmers which formed a substantial part of the controversy, *Division*'s proposed television debate between both parties seemed optimistic. Fianna Fáil duly decided not to participate and – given the rules requiring impartiality – hoped thereby to prevent the item being broadcast at all. *Division* in turn nominated Ted Nealon to delineate Haughey's publicly known policy on the dispute. Because of the provenance of this programme, there was ample room for misunderstandings between the broadcasters and the politicians.[12]

That Haughey was the politician who disputed the ground rules in this major stand-off was scarcely surprising: he had never hidden the particular disdain he reserved for RTÉ. He disliked being questioned on anything other than his own terms and was one of those ministers whom his colleague Hilliard had admitted to McCourt 'would never be satisfied'.[13] He could prove a whinger about anything to do with RTÉ: the commentator on the Kennedy visit had overlooked his presence; he had repeatedly challenged current affairs broadcasters on what he saw as their self-appointed judgmental role; and McCourt was writing 'arrant nonsense' in defending the newsroom's right to paraphrase his statements.[14] Disgruntled at its presumption of editorial independence, Haughey's default attitude towards the station seemed to be one of truculent irascibility.

Lemass's most celebrated definition of RTÉ's role was made against this background. The Fianna Fáil government believed that

Lemass was so impatient to modernise the economy that he expected support rather than sceptical assessment from the national broadcaster. He was surprised, sometimes bewildered, by the presumed independence of the broadcasters.

11 For background, see Horgan, *Broadcasting and Public Life*, 40-42; and Savage, *Loss*, 78-84.
12 See 'Tighter Party Machines' Control over T.E. Political Telecasts?', *Irish Times*, 15 September and Rugheimer's riposte, *ibid.*, 16 September 1966.
13 McCourt memo, re lunch with Hilliard, 13 September 1963, McCourt papers, RTÉWA.
14 Haughey to Hilliard, 19 October 1963, copy to McCourt, *ibid.*

the National Farmers Association was directly challenging the government's authority. Two years before in the Dáil, Lemass had accused them of setting the country on the road to anarchy with their rates strike. Horgan also suggests – with the advantage of being his biographer – that the approach by Lemass on this occasion should be considered in the context of his awareness of his pending retirement 'and the difficulties the farmers' protest created for him as he tried to control the timetable leading up to the succession.' Questioned about ministerial protests to RTÉ in the Dáil, Lemass was prepared to stand over any actions any of his ministers had taken. Moreover, he emphasised,

> Radio Telefís Éireann was set up by legislation as an instrument of public policy and as such is responsible to the Government. The Government have over-all responsibility for its conduct and especially the obligation to ensure that its programmes do not offend against the public interest or conflict with national policy as defined in legislation. To this extent the Government reject the view that RTÉ should be, either generally or in regard to its current affairs and news programmes, completely independent of Government supervision.[15]

Charles Haughey, TD, Minister for Agriculture (1964-66): it was his confrontation with the National Farmers Association which prompted Seán Lemass to reveal how he perceived the role of the young television station.

Horgan credits Lemass with care in his use of language. This was not the hallmark of many subsequent commentators on this controversy: for some – Liam O Murchu, for instance – *public* policy was casually translated as *government* policy;[16] the authors of *Sit Down and Be Counted* state that Lemass had called the station 'an instrument of government';[17] another broadcaster, Bunny Carr, even accused Lemass of having described RTÉ as a 'tool of government';[18] and some thirty years later Eddie Holt ascribed to Lemass the opinion that RTÉ was 'an arm of government'.[19] *Seven Days* responded with a number of programmes focused on freedom of expression in broadcasting and recruited, among others, Grace Wyndham Goldie and Walter Cronkite to participate. Horgan suggests that Lemass's approach to RTÉ could be portrayed with hindsight as 'overbearing or unduly sensitive'. But it would also be possible to read it – given his party's expectations at that time – as 'less lethal than might have been expected'.[20]

'It's the Minister. He says that, while he objects to the item, and will raise hell if it's included, he is in no sense to be taken as bringing any pressure to bear

Dublin Opinion, November 1966

15 Dáil Debates, vol. 224, cols. 1045-8, 12 October 1966.
16 Liam Ó Murchú, *A Time to Love?* (Dublin, 1986), p.100.
17 Doolan, *et al.*, *Sit Down and Be Counted*, 91.
18 Bunny Carr, *The Instant Tree* (Dublin, 1975), p.54.
19 *Irish Times*, 9 May 1998.
20 Horgan, *Lemass*, 321.

'It's high, but it's not high enough to be above politics.'

Dublin Opinion, November 1966

It can also be said that this was all spelt out by Lemass – conscious of his imminent retirement from public life – as his definition of the relationship between government and broadcasting. Preoccupied by the need to modernise the country, and all too aware of his short period at the top, he had often shown impatience with RTÉ when it seemed to give disproportionate attention to the views of sceptics. But despite the general disappointment of Lemass at television's assumed role of independent scrutineer, Lee believes that this was ultimately to the Taoiseach's advantage. After all, television's impact on modernising Irish society chimed with the agenda being espoused by Lemass himself. Television was widening 'the opportunity to adopt a more searching attitude towards the serene wisdom of old age'. De Valera's Ireland was under scrutiny and had been found wanting. Television programmes 'took viewers on voyages of discovery of Irish society. Many did not like what they saw. But they now had to exert themselves to even more heroic self-deception to pretend it did not exist.'[21]

The mind of the Authority was now 'very clearly one rather more of directive than guidance'

WITHIN A YEAR of the resignation of Eamonn Andrews because the Authority was pursuing 'an unrealistic policy' on the Irish language, there is evidence that the successor Authority chaired by his namesake Todd Andrews was insisting on an even more ambitious policy on Irish. In February 1967, following an Authority discussion of the issue, a memorandum on the use of Irish on television was sent by McCourt to the new controller, Michael Garvey. Whereas they accepted that there had been 'considerable improvements' in Irish language policy, they sought further changes in presenting the language 'imaginatively and sympathetically' and wanted this attitude to 'percolate through to the very core of the organisation'. McCourt reminded Garvey that the broadcasting service was not neutral on this question and so 'must not be used as a platform from which to attack the Irish language'.

In any programmes discussing language policy 'tendentiousness should be avoided and the organisational viewpoint should favour the language'.[22] This was clearly a reference to the Language Freedom Movement [LFM], a lobby that was then challenging the state's emphasis on compulsory Irish in the educational curriculum. There

---

21 Lee, *Ireland*, 405.
22 McCourt to Garvey, memo re 'The use of the Irish language in television programmes', 16 February 1967, RTÉWA,

had been a highly controversial meeting organised by the LFM in Dublin's Mansion House the previous September which was gate-crashed by language supporters, among them Ó Móráin, who had calmed a fractious meeting by insisting that he did not care how anti-Irish any speaker was, he would 'defend his right to speak as long as the other spokesmen for those who represent my viewpoint are allowed an opinion'. Thus the LFM, having organised the meeting and booked the hall, were now having their right to free speech at their own meeting championed by a gate-crasher! And it will be noted that in the new policy being advocated within RTÉ – again Ó Móráin was the instigator – he was not adopting the Voltaire maxim.[23]

But here was an issue where RTÉ had arguably conflicting 'duties': firstly, to be supportive to the language as prescribed in the broadcasting legislation; but, secondly, to the requirement of free speech for a lobby which was representative of a significant section of public opinion. McCourt relayed the Authority's views quite explicitly to Garvey: RTÉ 'could not provide a platform for a body inimical to the Irish language or inimical to the Government-approved methods for its revival to ventilate contrary views.'[24] This directive could also be interpreted as inhibiting any repeat of a highly controversial debate on *The Late Late Show* a year before which had occasioned a bitter post-mortem in Seanad Éireann.[25]

Erskine Childers: 'The day criticism ends RTÉ will be lifeless.'

More generally McCourt called for greater use of 'passages or phrases in Irish in a natural and uncontrived fashion' in programmes such as *The Late Late Show*, *Quicksilver* and *The Riordans*. He told Garvey that at the Authority meeting there had been 'severe criticism' of the failure of the sports department 'to make any significant use of the Irish language'. However the Authority did not want exclusive use of Irish in all-Ireland finals 'because of the significant proportion of the community' who would be alienated. But the sports department had 'not received the message' and this required 'to be corrected'. McCourt concluded by suggesting to Garvey that he appoint an individual whose special responsibility it would be to be a mentor, 'to woo and persuade' programme-makers towards such a policy without creating antipathy. He informed him that the Authority's original statement of January 1966 was 'a document of guidance'. The mind of the Authority was now 'very clearly one rather more of directive than guidance'; their requirements were 'explicit'. He invited Garvey to meet him when he had considered how all this could be implemented.[26]

---

23 See national newspapers, late September 1966 for extensive coverage of this meeting.
24 McCourt to Garvey, memo, 16 February 1967, RTÉWA.
25 Seanad Debates, vol. 60, cols. 1499-1503, 17 February 1966.
26 McCourt to Garvey, memo, 16 February 1967, RTÉWA.

an entertainment organisation 'seething with gossip and rumours'

LEON O BROIN, AS SECRETARY in Posts and Telegraphs, had enough experience of Erskine Childers as minister in de Valera's government of 1951 to 1954 to be dismayed to see him return to that portfolio as minister in 1966 just as Ó Broin himself was contemplating retirement. Ó Broin's portrait of Childers is not reassuring: when he had first worked with him in 1951, he found him 'impetuous', his first thoughts on any subject invariably 'went down on paper' and he was 'endlessly writing memoranda'.[27] Childers's official biographer paints a different picture of a minister with 'no intention of merely acting as a rubber stamp', confident that he was 'fully capable of judging departmental issues' and expecting 'compliance and efficiency from his staff at all times'.[28] But his biographer misses many character traits which were manifest to those working closely with Childers. He was a poor delegator within his department and was an explorer beyond it with a penchant for solo runs. Ó Broin now found Childers 'much more assertive', and presently the minutes and memoranda landed 'in a flood' on the secretary's desk.[29]

In the aftermath of the 'instrument of public policy' line from Lemass, Childers provides a useful second opinion in calibrating how Fianna Fáil saw the relationship with RTÉ just five years after the station had opened. Childers shared his opinion with cabinet colleagues in a lengthy – and indeed long-winded and repetitive – memorandum for government, 'Political Broadcasting'. Firstly, RTÉ had an obligation to give adequate coverage 'to all important

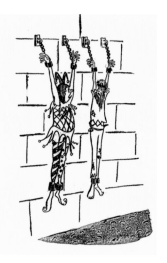

Photocopy of unidentified cartoon found in John Irvine's papers.

"I guess they're not ready for political satire yet."

---

27 Ó Broin, *Yesterday*, 179.
28 John N. Young, *Erskine H. Childers, President of Ireland: A Biography* (Gerrards Cross, Bucks., 1985), p.109.
29 Ó Broin, *Yesterday*, 215.

Childers told his colleagues that RTÉ was 'seething with gossip and rumours'. If ministers were to telephone the station, Childers advised that they should speak only to McCourt or Irvine.

government decisions'. When such decisions were announced there could be 'no vociferous, direct retort in the negative by interested parties at the time of the announcement'. Nor should ministers be confronted 'with sharp-shooting critics when announcing policy'. The government's policy as passed by the Dáil 'can be discussed and debated in a constructive manner, all interests having fair representation'. This, he believed, was 'universally accepted all over the free world'. It may be stated that much of this is obvious: in no democracy could a serious television channel not, in the first instance, announce the main details of a government initiative. It would be the critical evaluation of that policy which would provide the test of a station's independence.

Childers also reminded his colleagues that RTÉ was 'an entertainment organisation seething with gossip and rumours.' For a minister to interfere directly was cumbersome but he could 'criticise privately and ask for re-balance'. Ideally such contact should be channelled through Childers's office but if that proved impossible, ministers should confine themselves to contacting McCourt or Irvine. Fianna Fáil would 'gain nothing' for it to be known that interference was 'fairly constant'. Childers claimed 'with absolute certainty' that all party leaders would continue to criticise RTÉ, as would 'every minority, every vested interest'. The day the critics fell silent, RTÉ would be 'lifeless'. Pointing out that political programmes drew significant audiences – above the numbers for comparable countries – he asked when would politicians be obliged 'to be reasonably articulate and good TV personalities?' He also recommended the recruitment of a full-time party press officer who could assist ministers in their television presentation. He added his belief that if all parties would agree that RTÉ 'would discharge a fair proportion of the cost' of sending one representative from each party abroad for what Childers termed 'indoctrination and experience.'

He noted that Todd Andrews had informed him that between the Authority and the staff the idea that there was not sufficient support for Fianna Fáil in RTÉ was 'without foundation'. McCourt also had conflicts with Fine Gael and Labour. Childers's estimate was that the government's viewpoint enjoyed a ratio of advantage of about 5-1, due to 'the inevitable influence of Ministers, their frequent appearances,

In September 1963, the director-general Kevin McCourt had lunch with the broadcasting minister, Michael Hilliard. McCourt notes that when he asked for Hilliard's own opinion of the new station, he replied 'that great progress is being made in television broadcasting, he hears very good reports of atmosphere within the organisation, believes that it is being handled in the right way and has no real worries about the occasional complaint of which he recognises there must always be some continuing quantity.'

In February 1966, Hilliard's successor, Fianna Fáil Minister for Posts and Telegraphs, Joseph Brennan, told Dáil Éireann:

> There have been criticisms of the programmes on various grounds and from different quarters but this is only to be expected, and is indeed the experience of broadcasting organisations all over the world. It is impossible to please everybody all of the time but, on the whole, I think Telefís Éireann and Radio Éireann have given general satisfaction. I believe the Authority is to be congratulated on its achievements since it was established and I, therefore, confidently recommend this Bill to the House.

McCourt, memo re lunch with Hilliard, 13 September 1963, RTÉWA; Dáil Éireann, vol.220, cols.536-37, 1 February 1966.

their command of any discussion if they are well briefed.' But he also allowed that throughout the free world governments were 'at some disadvantage on radio and television'. It was the nature of the medium that their response to criticism was invariably 'a defensive one'.[30]

In evaluating Childers as a witness to the relationship between the station and the government, it would be salutary also to bear Todd Andrews's testimony. Andrews recounts a pattern of ministerial grouses about broadcasting being regularly relayed to him by Childers after cabinet meetings; but these 'were so many and so trivial' that Andrews came to the conclusion that some of his colleagues 'were, for the most part, pulling his leg'. Childers, who had 'not much sense of humour or sense of proportion', often approached Andrews after cabinet meetings 'in great distress'. Andrews advised him to tell his colleagues 'to go to hell'.[31]

---

30 [Erskine Childers], Memorandum for the Government, 'Political Broadcasting', 11 January 1967, Aiken Papers, UCDAD, P104/7135.
31 Andrews, *Man of No Property*, 286.

The exceptional success of *Amuigh Faoin Spéir* as a natural history programme tells much about the work culture of the young station. Because of shoestring budgets the original programme – despite its title! – was studio-based with Éamonn de Buitléar (left) bringing the animals into the TV studio. So chaotic was this that de Buitléar believes that a rerun now of archive footage would vie for top ratings in comedy. It was a newly arrived American producer, Don Lennox, who decided that some film footage of real wildlife in its natural habitat was needed if the series was to develop. Since there were no natural history cameramen or women in Ireland in those years, de Buitléar decided he would learn the craft himself. 'This immediately created a situation we had not at all expected. The taking of pictures by outsiders who were regarded by some of the RTÉ staff as pure amateurs was not looked upon too kindly and our plan was objected to in no uncertain terms, especially by one news cameraman.'

The film sequence required was of house sparrows, for an edition featuring birds of the city. It was suggested that 'the objecting gentleman' might like to film the sequence for us himself and he was given two days to deliver the film. De Buitléar insists that the first essential for any wildlife film-maker is to be a good naturalist. 'That this newsman had no knowledge whatsoever of our kind of wildlife was to be a distinct disadvantage when he would go on that particular safari.' It would never be known how many hours he spent, 'throwing breadcrumbs at the sparrows as he crawled on his tummy under the park seats in St. Stephen's Green, but we were to hear graphic descriptions from onlookers for months afterwards.' No pictures were delivered 'but there were no further objections as we began to take our first steps in becoming real wildlife film-makers.'

Eamonn de Buitlear, 'The independent film-maker', *The RTÉ Book* (Dublin, 1989), pp.152-53.

9

'the television camera is a very crude instrument'

ON THE RETIREMENT OF Seán Lemass, Fianna Fáil elected Jack Lynch as party leader and Taoiseach. An early test of his government's attitude to RTÉ came when the new head of news, Jim McGuinness, proposed sending a camera crew to North Vietnam. RTÉ's coverage of the Vietnam war at the time was largely based on what was available from international agencies, themselves biased towards an American interpretation. And there is copious evidence of the extent to which US war correspondents felt constrained by their reporting conditions: Barnouw reports one as complaining of being fed lies, half-truths and misleading information; another found the working atmosphere 'one of the most rancid' in thirty years' experience; a third complained to his news editor that the 'brass' wanted him 'to get on the team', while he thought his job was 'to find out what the score is'.[1]

McGuinness, himself a critic of the pro-American bias from the international wire services, was probably announcing a new broom in the newsroom. He had robust opinions on the limitations of the western news agencies' coverage of the Vietnam war. But it was Irish foreign policy – in so far as that could be ascertained on Vietnam – which prevailed. Whatever interests were in play between Frank Aiken and the State Department, it was clear that Lynch was following a pro-American policy which he had inherited from Lemass. This was based on a belief that no intervention by Ireland would have any effect and that Irish interests would be best served by a concentration on those bilateral issues which were then salient: resisting all State Department attempts to enable American airlines to bypass Shannon and land directly in Dublin; and encouraging foreign direct investment by American multi-nationals. Lynch avoided grand-standing on the Vietnam issue. The Johnson

Frank Aiken, TD. Served as Minister for External Affairs under de Valera, Lemass and Lynch (1951-54; 1957-69). Expected RTÉ reporters overseas to do nothing that might embarrass his department.

---

1   Barnouw, *Tube of Plenty*, 377.

While the controversy continued, Lynch took the opportunity of a television interview on *The Person in Question* in April 1967 to state that while Ireland was opposed to the bombing of North Vietnam, it did not believe that its cessation 'would necessarily result in bringing the parties to the conference table.'

Keogh, *Lynch*, 134

administration, for its part, appreciated Dublin's relatively quiescent line on Vietnam.[2]

Although the powers under Section 31 were not invoked, they were available to the government and Andrews as chairman later regretted that RTÉ had not insisted on them being formally used when the proposed visit was cancelled. What RTÉ did insist on was a statement which pinned responsibility for the cancellation on the Lynch government. The statement from Andrews read that the Taoiseach had informed him that 'in the opinion of the government, the best interests of the nation would not be served by sending a news team to Vietnam and that it would be an embarrassment to the government in relation to its foreign policy. In view of this the Authority decided to abandon the project.'[3]

Aiken spoke patronisingly about the proposed assignment. Vietnam was only one of the trouble-spots in the world: if RTÉ was to go there, Aiken's department would, he believed, be pressed to arrange that they would go to other areas in all parts of the world and it would not be believed if we said we had not promoted the visit to Vietnam by this semi-state body. He also had little faith in RTÉ's ability to usefully explain 'a very complicated situation', believing the reporting team would be working under the constraint of 'a conducted and protected tour', organised by North Vietnamese propagandists.[4]

In retrospect, the affair appeared 'staggeringly mishandled'[5] but many western foreign ministries thought similarly to Aiken at that

2 Dermot Keogh, *Jack Lynch: A Biography* (Dublin, 2008), pp.133-35; Hereafter, Keogh, *Lynch*.
3 C.S. Andrews papers, UCDAD, P91/70(11).
4 Dáil Debates, vol. 227, col. 1662-63, 13 April 1967.
5 Robert McNamara, 'Irish perspectives on the Vietnam war', *Irish Studies in International Affairs*, vol.14, 2003, pp.75-94.

'Films and television programmes are very entertaining. I think, however, it will be admitted that the television camera is a very crude instrument with which to describe or illustrate very highly complicated political social troubles.'

Aiken's speaking note for the Dáil debate on the Vietnam war.

Aiken papers, UCDAD, P104/7140.

What Aiken said in the Dáil debate.

Dáil Debates, vol.227, col.1662, 13 April 1967.

time.[6] A postscript to this came in a contribution to a Senate debate from a future foreign minister. Garret FitzGerald characterised as 'dangerous' the line taken by Aiken that RTÉ 'was going outside its normal functions in reporting wars in foreign countries' and that Aiken considered he had a right to insist that they should have sought permission. 'The reporting of affairs outside Ireland is important and we must challenge this principle.'[7]

McCourt was chastised for treating his reporters 'as if they were a group of small boys being deprived of an outing'

A FURTHER CONTROVERSY arose early in 1968 when a *7 Days* team negotiated seats on a special media flight into the embattled breakaway province of Biafra in eastern Nigeria. This was at the height of the Nigerian civil war, when access to Biafra was as coveted by the western media as was its presence there by the Biafran rebels: they well knew how important television footage was to their prospects of international recognition. Concerning the *Seven Days* expedition, there was – and remains – some confusion over who knew what when. Andrews's account asserts that the *Seven Days* team had not told Garvey or McCourt of their plans. His 'strong advice' to McCourt was to recall them from Lisbon.[8] Savage asserts that the fact that neither the controller of programmes nor the director-general was aware of the crew travelling to Biafra embarrassed McCourt and undermined Garvey.[9] Horgan suggests that Garvey had 'been informed in advance and had agreed' and that McCourt had also been informed.[10]

How can these different interpretations and testimonies be reconciled? It may be that none of these accounts is correct. In a memorandum for the director-general, Jack White outlined what happened. He had initially been contacted the previous December by the flight organisers – working for the Biafran government – who mooted the possibility of some RTÉ seats on a flight to Biafra. White, without making any commitment, told the organisers that RTÉ would be interested in considering an invitation. Then at about 6:30 on 17 January the organisers telephoned from California to say his plane 'was leaving Lisbon one week later and he had three seats for

Historian Joe Lee believed that the controversies between the government and the television service have received disproportionate attention: 'The clashes on specific issues or particular programmes have been largely nine-day wonders, lashed into a frenzy of almost auto-erotic excitement by a narcissistic media.'

Joe Lee, *RTÉ Guide*, 2 January 1987.

---

6 For Australian examples alone, see Inglis, *ABC*, 233-36; 247-48, 251-53.
7 Seanad Debates, vol.66, col. 323, 15 January 1969.
8 Andrews, *Man of No Property*, 278.
9 Savage, *Loss*, 119.
10 Horgan, *Broadcasting and Public Life*, 54-55.

McCourt – while he insisted that he would be making his own decision – telephoned the secretary of the Department of External Affairs, Hugh McCann, asking if there was anything about Biafra which he should know. The two men were at least acquaintances: here they are two years earlier talking informally at a European Broadcasting Union conference in Dublin.

RTÉ.' White asked him 'to hold the invitation open for 24 hours'. Two hours later White was hit by a temperature of 102. Appreciating that he would not be at work on the following day, he had telephoned Garvey and had given him 'all the information about the offer'. But when White eventually returned to the office on 23 January, he learned that the *7 Days* team was already in Lisbon, expecting to fly to Biafra next morning. And it was not until the following day that he learnt that the director-general knew nothing of the matter until after the team had left Dublin. Later that night he was telephoned by Garvey 'to say that he had recalled the team'.[11] Andrews, in his memoirs, asserts that as far as he knew the government was 'completely unaware of the incident'.[12] In this he was mistaken. The External Affairs archives reveal McCourt telephoning the department secretary, Hugh McCann, asking if there was anything about Biafra which he should know. He was told that the Biafran government was not recognised by Ireland, that Irish nationals living in Nigeria could be endangered, and that the whole exercise would certainly be used by the Biafrans for propaganda. McCourt informed McCann that on the basis of that information, he would make his own decision to recall the programme team. He spelt out to McCann that he was not consulting the government nor seeking their advice as to his course of action. He also naively expressed the hope that the controversy when it broke would not be misconstrued as government interference. He phoned McCann later that evening to tell him that, having spoken to Andrews, his chairman, the team had been recalled from Lisbon where they had been awaiting the flight to Biafra. McCann in turn informed McCourt that he had mentioned the matter to Aiken, who approved of McCourt's actions.[13]

The picture painted by Aiken to the Dáil was one of pro-Biafran international lobbyists who had spent money on an aircraft and who had 'hooked up as many television teams in Europe as they could' to go to Biafra and who had also 'nobbled' RTÉ.[14] One of the main lobbyists for Irish seats on the media plane, in an angry letter to McCourt, chastised him for treating his reporting team 'as if they were a group of small boys being deprived of an outing'. He also told him of detailed negotiations in Dublin with Mac Conghail and White to secure scarce seats on the plane. Indeed, he found it difficult to

11 Jack White memo, re timeline on Biafran proposal, 20 February 1968, RTÉWA.
12 Andrews, *Man of No Property*, 278.
13 [Hugh McCann], memo, 25 January 1968, NAI DFA 98/2/28.
14 Aiken, by then a backbencher, in exchanges with Conor Cruise O'Brien, who himself had reported from Biafra for *The Observer*, Dáil Debates, vol.241, col.1937, 28 October 1969.

If Fianna Fáil governments in the 1960s expected the fledgling station to be sensitive to the government's foreign policy, they were not the only politicians who held this expectation. Histories of broadcasting in western democracies are replete with comparable examples. In Australia, *Four Corners*, the noted ABC current affairs programme, was inhibited from travelling to some of those corners, the Australian government declaring Indonesia and China off limits. And when it had been announced that an Australian documentary team intended investigating how dominant the United States was in Canadian life, Canberra grounded the broadcasters by invoking an arcane regulation by which nobody could travel abroad at the expense of the Commonwealth of Australia without the approval of the Prime Minister!

In the case of Britain, there are numerous examples of Foreign Office expectations that the BBC would broadly reflect British foreign policy, one diplomat complaining of 'sinister extreme-left influences' at the BBC, making it 'high time one or two patriots' were put into key positions. And the BBC's very charter expected it to 'project Britain'; moreover, it was the recipient of government support for its World Service. One expert committee had a preference that BBC broadcasts 'should be used as *an instrument of Government policy...*'. In Australia similar language was invoked: when it came to travelling abroad to make ABC reports, the government reckoned it 'undesirable that an *instrumentality* identified in the public mind and internationally with the Government of Australia', should make itself responsible for television films 'relating to matters of great international delicacy'.

Inglis, *ABC*, 247-48; Asa Briggs, *The History of Broadcasting in the United Kingdom: Competition; v, 1955-1974* (Oxford 1995), pp.102-37 *passim*. Emphasis added.

explain what freedom of speech or independent broadcasting meant in Ireland when he had to account for the peremptory abandonment of the venture to the flight organizers.[15]

Meanwhile, Brian Cleeve, who would have been the reporter had the crew continued on their journey, scripted what Mac Conghail outlined as an analytical programme based on a Granada *World in Action* report and UPI material. He informed White that *7 Days* could independently assess the situation but he did not intend the programme to embarrass the director-general or to be seen 'as a way of revenge'.[16] But White – within hours of transmission – saw the script, which he found 'had a degree of emotional identification with Biafra which had not been forecast' in Mac Conghail's brief. Later, when he viewed the programme on transmission, he found it to be 'even more overcharged emotionally'.[17] McCourt was also unimpressed and thought the production in the circumstances amounted to 'an insolent gesture'.[18]

---

15 Fr Raymond Kennedy to McCourt, 19 February 1968, RTÉWA.
16 Muiris Mac Conghail to Jack White, 2 February 1968, RTÉWA.
17 Jack White memo, re timeline on Biafran proposal, 20 February 1968, RTÉWA.
18 Savage, *Loss*, 121.

At this juncture it came to the attention of Andrews that *7 Days* was shooting a film on the Garda Special Branch. Insisting on a preview by the Authority, Andrews declared it 'trivial and lightweight' and unsuitable for transmission. It was becoming evident to senior managers that their lines of communication with programme-makers were seriously wanting. Moreover, Andrews believed that the *7 Days* team 'despised the management and held the Authority in contempt' and given Mac Conghail's determination to test all boundaries, management was now losing faith in Garvey's ability as a line manager.[19]

McCourt, who was within weeks of his exit from the director-general's role, decided on 'an immediate organisational change' and – while intending to keep the *7 Days* team intact – switched the programme from Garvey's programmes division to the newsroom under Jim McGuinness. When posted on the notice-board, some staff opposed the move 'apparently on the grounds that it was being made in spite of the opposition' of Garvey, but McCourt had in fact obtained his prior consent but, 'at the last moment', Garvey had told him he had 'changed his mind'.[20] Not all personnel in *7 Days* accepted the move. Mac Conghail did and flourished under the more robust editorial relationship with McGuinness. Some commentators thought the programme never recovered its old verve. But it was presently to annoy the government even more than it had ever done with its controversial investigation into money-lending in Dublin.

---

19 Andrews, *Man of No Property*, 278-79.
20 Andrews, note from the RTÉ Authority meeting, 16 February 1968, Andrews papers, UCDAD, P91/70(12).

Fr Peter Lemass reporting from Biafra

Later in 1968, *Radharc* travelled to Biafra to make a documentary *Night Flight to Uli* and there was some media speculation that the programme would not be broadcast by RTÉ. This proved false: it was considered a major success for *Radharc* and was later given a private screening at the House of Commons at Westminster.

Savage, *Loss*, 134; Peter Kelly, 'Africa in *Radharc* documentaries, 1966 to 1993', MA dissertation, DCU.

10

'as a conductor magnificent' but otherwise 'a mental age of sixteen'

I
N ANY ASSESSMENT of the role which classical music played on television, one must remember that for many practitioners, there remained a suspicion of all new media. Sir Thomas Beecham believed that the innovations of the twentieth century had resulted in 'every imaginable sin' being committed against music and none worse than the broadcasting of it on such a 'ludicrous contrivance' as a radio receiver: he concluded that 'if the wireless authorities' were permitted 'to carry on their devilish work', it would take a mere decade to empty the concert halls.[1]

The composer Gerard Victory – himself part of the brain drain of radio producers, newly recruited to the television service – reassured

Tibor Paul, principal conductor of the Radio Éireann Symphony Orchestra (1963-67) in Studio 1, television block, 1963. Gerard Victory had a very high opinion of Paul as a conductor – 'magnificent'.

1   Paddy Scannell and David Cardiff, *A Social History of British Broadcasting: vol.i, 1922-1939* (Oxford, 1991), p.205.

Gerard Victory, composer, television producer, deputy director of music under Tibor Paul and his successor as director of music, 1967-82. Victory confided to McCourt that in anything not directly concerned with music, Paul had 'a mental age of sixteen'.

readers of the *RTV Guide* that music would have its place in the television schedules. He cited the significant recent advances in interference-free television sound. 'There was a time when music was regarded very much as the Cinderella of television.' He enthused about the 'incomparable' West German standards of producing music for television.[2] One year into the television service, when there was a need to trim all department budgets, Barry alerted the director-general to the relative costs of home-produced music compared to other sources. Symphonic music by a world orchestra could be bought in at one quarter the cost of the RTESO. The argument, he admitted, was academic, if the national broadcaster had to assume 'the burden' of maintaining a national orchestra, 'but the figures cut so sharply across the arithmetic of any normal television practice that they cannot be ignored.'[3] Roth appointed Tibor Paul as principal conductor and director of music. Richard Pine writes that 'the schizophrenic nature of the dual mandate' was captured by the *Irish Times* critic Charles Acton, who wrote that there was 'much evidence that the great improvement made by the conductor was very greatly retarded by the music director.'[4]

It can be presumed that Roth – given his background – had higher hopes for the television potential of the orchestras than had the existing music department, historically rooted as it was in the radio service. Roth commissioned a report from a BBC expert on the potential of both orchestras which – in considering a then current debate about a possible relocation of the Light Orchestra to Cork – instanced 'the needs of television' as a sufficient reason why it should stay in Dublin.[5] So far as the future of the two orchestras was concerned, and 'specifically with regard to their work for television', it recommended that two specialist heads be appointed, one for 'serious' music, another for 'light'.[6] It should be remembered that at this juncture RTÉ's attitude towards the orchestras – in Irvine's words – was 'one of reluctant ownership and responsibility'.[7] Roth, it can be added, expressed himself ambivalently on this subject: he confided to Acton that it was not worthwhile keeping the symphony orchestra in being 'because "only" 30,000 people listened to its [radio] broadcasts.'[8] Yet in another interview he boasted of the 'significant contributions' made by Telefís Éireann in bringing 'classical

2 Gerard Victory, 'Music and the television viewer', *RTV Guide*, 15 December 1961.
3 Barry to director-general, 13 March 1963, RTÉWA. The relative costs are expressed as a percentage since the real figures are difficult to evaluate at this distance. Barry's comparative figures were £6k, compared with £23.5k.
4 *Irish Times*, 30 November 1966.
5 Richard Pine, *Music and Broadcasting in Ireland* (Dublin, 2005) pp.422-24; hereafter, Pine, *Music and Broadcasting*.
6 ibid., 424.
7 ibid., 442-23.
8 *Irish Times*, 21 March 1974.

music into the homes of many thousands of people who previously had no knowledge of, or interest in, symphonic music.'[9] Paul made a similar claim in his annual report for 1962-63.[10] He portrayed himself as a pioneer availing of television to bring serious music to a new audience. This was a conceit. Overall his television policy was disappointing, Pine's verdict being that he had done 'little or nothing' to harness the potential of the new medium. With the exception of A.J.Potter's opera *Patrick*, the presentation of music on television had 'evaded Paul's imagination'. Pine concludes that although Paul organised some symphony concerts and chamber music on television, his relations with television administrators 'were frosty, and with individual producers ranged from tentative to offensive'. Acton confirms this picture of mutual antipathy between Paul's music department and those in charge of the television schedule who wanted 'to have nothing to do with the orchestra if they could help it.'[11]

The fault lay with Paul's personality and his authoritarian bullying of orchestral players. Senior insiders in the music department described him variously as 'a horror', incapable of taking 'a single tiny word of criticism' and, when conducting, a browbeater who had reduced the orchestra to 'a very unhappy' group of musicians, some of them 'destroyed as sensitive artists', others 'tortured for retaining artistic sensitivity'.[12] Paul, it must also be said, was credited with ambition and with improving standards. But his deficits outweighed these achievements. McCourt listened to the evidence and cannot be faulted for not renewing Paul's contract. In Paul's personnel file, Victory is forthright in the advice he gave confidentially to McCourt who needed, in the summer of 1968, to withstand pressure coming from a naive Lynch cabinet, who were lending credence to Paul's claim that he had been blackballed in Europe following his exit from RTÉ. Childers, pleading that Paul be given some work, claimed that he was by now 'practically destitute or to use the exact phrase "on his uppers".'[13] Victory advised that Paul was a born intriguer and, although he had 'a very high opinion of Paul as a conductor' – regarding him as 'magnificent' – it had to be admitted that in anything not directly concerned with music he had 'an intellect which is a mental age of sixteen.'[14]

Although sufficient evidence may have been adduced to explain why Paul failed to exploit television's potential to showcase the orchestra, it

Tibor Paul's behaviour towards some players shocked others in the orchestra. He was 'a browbeater', 'a horror'. If anyone wished to complain, they could do so; but to the director of music, who during Paul's time as conductor was Paul himself! It was Roth who had given Paul the dual responsibility. McCourt resolved the issue as quickly as contractual obligations permitted.

9   Roth in Irish supplement to *Television Mail*, reported in *Evening Press*, 22 January 1963.
10 Pine, *Music and Broadcasting*, 431.
11 *ibid.*, pp.428-29.
12 The verdicts of concerts manager Leo Donnelly, violinist Janos Furst and trumpeter Thomas Lisenbee; the last resigned in protest against Paul's ill-mannered humiliation of his fellow players; *ibid.*, pp.444, 454.
13 Childers to C.S. Andrews, 31 July 1968, RTÉWA.
14 McCourt, memorandum of telephone call to Victory, 16 August 1968, RTÉWA.

may also be noted that he had little financial incentive to do so. During television's first year of transmission, he had had a comprehensive meeting with Irvine, with one agenda item being listed as 'Supplementary fees for television concerts': Paul was advised 'that his contract did not provide for extra payments for these'. Incidentally, all the problems that would exacerbate Paul's future relations with RTÉ form the agenda for this early meeting: haggling over fees, income, budget and expenses; his poor relations with the orchestral players; and his propensity to bypass all rules and protocols when dealing with third parties, thereby embarrassing, if not compromising, his employer.[15]

Pine concludes that Paul 'with his forceful personality' could possibly have pushed 'the door to television more effectively open' and that there might have evolved in these vital formative years, 'a genre of televisual treatment of orchestral concerts, opera and chamber music'. Yet on the few occasions when such music was included in the television schedule, Paul's personality proved to be 'an obstacle and an irritant to the pursuit of sensible programming'.[16] This was all the more regrettable since Paul would have related in turn to three very different controllers of programmes, Barry, Rugheimer and Garvey. With none of them did he succeed: Barry was remembered in the BBC's drama department as an experimental, courageous and sensitive innovator;[17] Rugheimer – although a very different individual – was also an innovator and eagerly embraced all challenges; and Garvey was deeply interested in music. That Paul developed a television policy with none of them validates Charles Acton's conclusion that there was mutual antipathy between Paul's music department and those in charge of the television schedule, who wanted 'to have nothing to do with the orchestra if they could help it'.[18]

---

15 Irvine, 'Discussion with Mr. Tibor Paul at his request', 19 October 1962, RTÉWA.
16 Pine, *Music and Broadcasting*, 430.
17 Oliver Wake, *Michael Barry*, British Television Drama website, accessed 10 January 2010.
18 Pine, *Music and Broadcasting*, 428-29.

'A concert at London's Royal Festival Hall on 30 November 1966 was part of the Royal Philharmonic Society's 1966-67 season and it exposed the RTÉ Symphony Orchestra to the international limelight. It was an historic occasion which gave the Orchestra an added boost to its morale. Autocratic, charismatic, egotistical, energetic and even tyrannical as Paul may have been, and while he may have promoted himself as much as the RTESO, this Royal Festival concert and another one the following day for BBC TV at the Fairfield Hall in Croydon established the Orchestra abroad as Ireland's major music force.'

Pat O'Kelly, *The National Symphony Orchestra of Ireland: 1948-1998*, a selected history (Dublin, 1998) [no pagination, 'Concerts in the UK' section].

Paul Russell attempts to interview The Beatles for *The Showband Show*, Dublin, November 1963. Left to right: Paul McCartney, John Lennon, Paul Russell, Ringo Starr, George Harrison. Lennon has attempted to interrupt the interview by hanging a camera case around Russell's neck.

One of the most popular programmes in the early years of Telefís Éireann was *The Showband Show*. But it did not please all viewers, although some of the displeased continued to watch even while they expressed loathing for the performances. In May 1966, Séamus Ó Braonáin, writing to his old friend John Irvine, included an undated clipping from the *Evening Herald* in which a letter-writer complains of the 'shambling, shuddering' dancers responding with 'monotonous, joyless convulsions' to the overpaid singers who 'moan, groan and caterwaul their way to success'.Ó Braonáin agreed with the sentiments in the *Herald* letter and asked Irvine: 'Any chance that Mr. Gunnheimer [*sic*] or whoever is responsible, would spare us from the surfeit of Dicky Rock, Butch Moore etc.etc. There is nothing musical about their vocal efforts and the words, if they had any sense, are drowned by the band. We had a couple of girls on the *Late Late* and they were awful. One of them just mimed. That type of stuff is not worthy of T.E. Brendan Bowyer – probably the best of them – with his two cheer-leaders behind him doing gymnastics, was beyond me. Have we no budding McCormacks to whom we could give a show?' Irvine replied on 15 May 1966: 'Like yourself, I can't stand the wailing and frenetic acrobats presented as musical performances in the *Showband Show,* and elsewhere. God save Ireland. If not, I suppose a desert island or at least the North Bull is the only escape!' Irvine copied this reply to Gary Redmond, head of PR, with the comment: 'How not to function in PR!' But Redmond returned the copy letter, marked: 'Noted with acclamation.'

Ó Braonáin to Irvine, 11 May and his reply 15 May 1966, Irvine papers, RTÉ Written Archives.

everything retrieved and broadcast 'now enters the traditional music bloodstream and will never be lost'

Television cameras no longer create 'any particular stir in the countryside'.

Ciaran MacMathuna, *RTÉ Guide*, 17 June 1977.

ALTHOUGH THERE ARE SOME recordings from other sources, Irish traditional music on television is essentially the story of how RTÉ covered it from 1962. In the decade before the television service was inaugurated, Radio Éireann – exploiting its new capacity for mobile in-the-field recording – had harvested thousands of recordings by amateur musicians which remain of inestimable historic importance.

The highly successful series *Come West Along the Road* had the advantage of being based on the holdings of the Irish Traditional Music Archive at whose headquarters in Merrion Square, Dublin it was launched in September 1994; photographed above are (left to right) Nicholas Carolan, Niall Mathews, Cathal Goan and Tony MacMahon.

In 1966 some of RTÉ's television producers 'refused to have any further dealings with Seán Ó Riada, claiming they were tired of his working methods.' Ó Riada came to Dublin and walked into Rugheimer's office without an appointment and they spent more than an hour in discussion, although Rugheimer had originally said that he could not spare him five minutes. 'Rugheimer was excited by their meeting and exclaimed, "Why haven't I met this Ó Riada before now?!" Unlike the television producers, their boss did not see a problem working with Seán and Ó Riada resumed his duties on television.'

Tomas Ó Canainn, *Seán Ó Riada: His Life and Work* (Cork, 2003), pp.178-79.

Although television would capture an extra dimension of performance, Nicholas Carolan notes – and nobody has surely seen as much of the archive footage as he – that television in general seemed 'to squash and flatten and reduce reality, and put it in a box'. He also believed that insufficient resources had been allocated by RTÉ to 'adequately convey the realities of Irish traditional music'.[19]

But whereas greater resources could have provided a more artistic television treatment, it is also the case that television, because of its very methods of production, inevitably delimits the spontaneity of the musician's performance. Where radio had some chance of authentically capturing a succession of traditional musicians performing impromptu for one another, television was more likely to involve auditions and rehearsals before the musicians had to perform in what amounted to a studio setting. For some performers this may well have provided an opportunity to practise and present themselves at their best, but for many others

---

19 Nicholas Carolan, 'Televising Irish Traditional Music, 1961-1990', paper read at the University of Limerick, 9 October 1997.

the experience would have inhibited their natural spontaneity.

The most successful programme in recent years has been the long-running series *Come West Along the Road*. Carolan – who researched and presented, with Tony MacMahon as producer – recalled that initially 'it was to last for a season or two', but so popular did it prove that when MacMahon retired after the third series, Carolan also produced the programme and the many series which followed. Being 'an educator at core', he found it 'very compatible' with his job as director of the Irish Traditional Music Archive. Because of extensive off-air recording, everything retrieved and broadcast 'now enters the traditional music bloodstream and will never be lost, as it was in the past'. Moreover, its reach is extended by re-presentation in Irish on TG4, by DVD publication, and by being globally available through the TG4 website, the RTÉ Player and YouTube.[20] One indication of that reach: as of early 2011, the YouTube performance labelled 'Seamus Ennis, god of uilleann pipes' had been shared by over 360,000 viewers.

Two of the great collectors of traditional music, Seamus Ennis and Ciaran MacMathuna, here participating in RTÉ television's *The Humours of Donnybrook* in 1978.

why does the girl speaking Irish try 'to appear sexy?'

THERE WAS NOT ONLY persistent acrimony over Irish-language policy, there was also considerable division about the role which the television service could play in Irish-language instruction. Ernest Blythe, who was the champion of the language lobby on the First Authority, must have seemed to senior station executives a vacillator on this question. A letter from McCourt in October 1963 reminds him that he had once liked McCourt's idea of televised Irish lessons but had then reversed his endorsement 'with cogent reasoning'. McCourt also noted that the Authority, 'in effect, directed we should not introduce lessons in Irish unless they would be high-quality entertainment rather than educational or didactic'. McCourt himself favoured a programme for the estimated two million viewers who had learned Irish at school but were no longer fluent; he wished to offer them 'access to competent, adult, specially designed, refresher lessons once or twice a week on television'.[21]

Blythe dismissed refresher courses as 'a delusion and a snare' and declared them to be 'no part of the business' of RTÉ. For the station 'to run long series of lessons would be to waste time, money and energy' since they would prove to be ineffective and 'would amount,

20 Carolan to author, 14 April 2011.
21 McCourt to Blythe, 15 October 1963, Blythe papers, UCDAD, P24/1188.

Buntús Cainte presenters, Máire O'Neill and Aileen Geoghegan, press launch, September 1967. 'One viewer, a civil servant, asked: "Is there any particular reason why the girl speaking English is straight-laced and the girl speaking Irish tries to appear sexy?"'

in the end, to little more than a piece of whitewashing humbug'.[22] Rugheimer, who listed Blythe among the 'completely unreasonable' Authority members on these issues, described as 'complete rubbish' Blythe's preference for an incremental expansion of bilingualism throughout the schedule. 'Instead of this we had *Buntús Cainte*.'[23]

Buntús Cainte won immediate support from the coordinating body for language organisations, Comhdháil Náisiúnta na Gaeilge which was impressed 'with the whole effort behind the production'.[24] Within weeks of the series beginning, the Minister for Education Donough O'Malley, told the Dáil that he was 'well satisfied' with the programme which had been received 'with the greatest enthusiasm'. The booklet was then in its fifth printing, having sold 218,000 copies.[25]

However, RTÉ's panel of respondents found that the programme in its first six months had 'hardly matched up to the expectations of those who were informed of its coming and of its character and intention.' Goodwill towards the programme remained and it was considered useful to children learning the language. But it was also reported 'that boredom set in as it went on', and this factor together with 'the small proportion' who were prepared to say that they had learnt much had to be taken into consideration.[26] The series was broadcast for two years but its influence outlasted its broadcasting lifespan. Many consider it the most successful of all Irish-language courses; it has remained available in various formats for many years; it is again 'in print' in book form, with accompanying CDs from Foras na Gaeilge, and it can also be downloaded to iPod, iPhone or iPad.

22 Blythe to McCourt, 6 November 1964, Blythe papers, UCDAD, P24/1191.
23 Horgan, *Broadcasting and Public Life*, 319-20.
24 Colonel Eoghan O'Neill to McCourt, 7 September 1967, RTÉWA.
25 Dáil Debates, vol.230, col.2082, 8 November 1967.
26 RTÉ Audience Research Service: *Buntús Cainte*, a general report on the recent series, 17 May 1968.

11

'*I didn't know that guy was such a mensch*'

IN DECEMBER 1967 the Authority noted the resignation of McCourt and decided that the advertisement for a successor would specify Irish nationality.[1] In due course T.P.Hardiman became RTÉ's third director-general and the first staff member and career professional to be promoted to the position. Hardiman's was to be a turbulent period in the country's and in RTÉ's history: he was not to know this on his appointment save that on the matter of the station's relationship with the government there were any number of indications that Fianna Fáil was becoming increasingly hostile to RTÉ's presumed sense of independence. Andrews hosted a dinner to introduce Hardiman to the minister. On this occasion Childers produced a list of subversives who, he asserted, were dangerous fellow-travellers, if not communists. This was clearly a black list which it was hoped would be a guide to Hardiman in his role as editor-in-chief. Childers was willing to wound. But he would not disclose the source of his list. Manifestly to Andrews it had the fingerprints of the special branch, who forty years before had attempted to blight his own career in the aftermath of the civil war. Andrews declared his suspicions to Childers and told him he would pay no attention to the list nor would it be kept by RTÉ for the record. And he later wrote a 'rather violent' letter of protest to Childers asking him to inform Jack Lynch of the incident.[2]

Antipathy to RTÉ was not uniform within the cabinet: but with one minister in particular it appeared to mark most of his dealings with the station. Some few days after taking up his new post, Hardiman received a telephone call from RTÉ's political correspondent, Joe Fahy, to alert him to expect an important phone call. This duly came from a civil servant in Finance to tell him that the Minister, Charles Haughey, wished to see him. Hardiman asked what it might be about?

T.P.Hardiman on the day of his appointment as RTÉ's third director-general, 15 March 1968. Todd Andrews later wrote that Hardiman 'knew everyone of consequence on the staff of RTÉ, their ambitions, capabilities and peculiarities'. He found Hardiman 'polite and unassuming. He neither smoked nor drank alcohol. He was a devoted family man.' Indeed, Andrews believed that Hardiman had 'all the qualities of a perfect prig.' But he was far from that: his 'sense of humour and evident success in retaining the respect and goodwill of his colleagues' ensured that 'any such characterisation' was undeserved.

Andrews, *Man of No Property*, 281.

---

1   Andrews notes of Authority meeting, 8 December 1967, Andrews papers, UCDAD, P91/71(1).
2   Andrews, *Man of No Property*, 286-87.

He was told that there was no need for any agenda, 'if the boss wanted to see him, one didn't ask why'. Hardiman declined, suggesting that the minister be told that it would look very bad 'if he came running' just a couple of days after becoming director-general. Some time afterwards he was asked by Todd Andrews: 'What the hell was going on?' Hardiman reassured Andrews that he knew what he was doing. He then got another call from Fahy telling him that Haughey would be at a reception in Dublin Castle in a few days time, as would Hardiman. They could meet on that occasion. At the reception Hardiman recalls putting himself 'rather ostentatiously' in Haughey's path a couple of times but nothing materialised. Then as he was leaving he was informed that the Minister was waiting to see him in the room off the great hall. Hardiman found Haughey 'standing at the end of the room, back to the fire, surrounded by various flunkies'. First there were introductions, then some small talk. Haughey offered him congratulations on becoming DG; then told him that all the people wanted from RTÉ was entertainment, 'not this current affairs stuff'. Haughey warmed to his theme about the current affairs broadcasters 'who didn't know what they were talking about and he got more obstreperous'. Then Hardiman, sensing Haughey's agenda, grabbed him by the lapels of his jacket, and told him: 'Now listen to me, I'm a Christian Brothers boy like yourself and there's a Broadcasting Act, and an Authority, and as far as I'm concerned, I've a job to do and I will do it under the Act and the Authority.' Then he pulled back and disengaged; the room had fallen dead silent, all eyes on Haughey. Hardiman recalls apologising immediately: 'That was unpardonable discourtesy. I must apologise unreservedly for what I have done to a duly elected minister of the government.' As Hardiman was leaving Dublin Castle after this confrontation, he was followed out by a friend from college days, a fellow engineer and a member of Fianna Fáil, Noel Mulcahy. He had overheard Haughey's response: 'I didn't know that guy was such a mensch'. Hardiman was not familiar with the word and checked to find that it was Yiddish slang for a person of integrity and honour. He never had any trouble with Haughey thereafter.[3]

Meanwhile many individual ministers complained about programmes. Such complaints, according to Andrews, 'were frequent and extremely irritating'. Hardiman dealt with them 'by overwhelming the complainants with words. He enjoyed arguing and was never willing to let his bone go with the dog'.[4] The job was among the most challenging in Irish public life. John Irvine – whom some thought of

3 Author interview with Tom Hardiman, 2011; confidential source.
4 Andrews, *Man of No Property*, 286.

as a possible director-general – believed that there were 'so many qualities and virtues' which the chief executive was expected to have that the situation was unreal. RTÉ television had become for many 'a sort of hate symbol', something they were prepared to knock, akin to 'an Aunt Sally's cat'. At the same time, in contradiction to all that, the television service held a 'possessive sway over the populace', who were prepared to quite an extent to 'give themselves up to it.'[5]

'a bloated and swelling corpse', feeding an 'increasing number of parasites'

SOME READERS of Bob Quinn's letter might conclude that it would tell them more about Quinn than about RTÉ. Quinn had written an open letter from Clare Island in May 1969 to his producer colleagues, stating that he was 'snagging turnips and conceiving [*sic*] my first son' and working with a camera crew which he had 'hi-jacked' from RTÉ.[6] He felt he had to challenge the 'Factory' – as he described the station – which had become 'a bloated and swelling corpse', feeding an 'increasing number of parasites.'[7] If this was intended as an incendiary device, it achieved its purpose. The RTÉ campus could be likened to that of a university where the students were staging a sit-in questioning the establishment. Todd Andrews, who observed it all from the chairman's office, wrote later of the 'creative people' – for whom he reserved a particular disdain – generating 'a ferment in which meetings of small groups took place all day long, the "philosophy" of television was discussed in memoranda, teach-ins and seminars.' Hardiman advised him that resignations were threatened. The advice from Andrews was to keep pen and paper to hand to confirm the resignations. He appreciated that such a 'hardline' approach was inimical to Hardiman but eventually this was the route taken.[8]

It was taken with reluctance by Hardiman – especially in the case of Lelia Doolan, for whom he had a high regard – but in the course of the widespread press coverage of the ongoing troubles in RTÉ, she had accused management of 'hypocrisy, lack of candour, lack of trust, and trivialising prevarication'. Since, as head of Light Entertainment, she was herself part of senior management, Hardiman felt he had no choice but to instruct her to end what he reckoned was a public campaign of dissent. Doolan promptly resigned, complaining that the

Sit Down and Be Counted: critics saw it variously as 'most stimulating' or 'another skirmish – though a substantial one'.

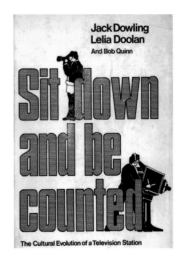

5   Irvine to O Ó Braonáin, 12 February 1968, Irvine papers, RTÉWA
6   Horgan, *Broadcasting and Public Life*, 68.
7   'Bob Quinn's letter', 14 May 1969, from *Sit Down and Be Counted*, xxxiv-v.
8   Andrews, *Man of No Property*, 281-82.

RTÉ management agonised on how the book, *Sit Down and Be Counted*, which followed the resignations of Doolan, Dowling and Quinn, should be handled by the station. Here Jack White (nearest camera) and Michael Garvey join in a discussion on *The Late Late Show* with Doolan, Quinn and Dowling, 8 November 1969.

It would appear that Jack White, for one, was not much influenced by the central thesis of *Sit Down and Be Counted*. A decade later, addressing the RTÉ Authority he allowed himself a risky metaphor, given that the book had characterised RTÉ as a factory. White insisted that broadcasting presented 'something new – an artefact made by an industrial machine'. Every programme 'however lowly, contains some creative element. But this infinite range of products is produced from a machine which must be kept running with industrial efficiency if the reasonable demands of good management are to be satisfied.' All programme decisions involved choices: of air-time, facilities and budgets.

Jack White, 'A digest of my remarks at RTÉ Authority, 9 July 1979', RTÉWA.

material being produced by RTÉ was 'dangerously and increasingly trivial, emasculated and contrary to the national cultural spirit'. Jack Dowling, producer of *Home Truths*, a consumer programme which had controversially challenged many claims by RTÉ's own advertisers, also resigned. It was Quinn's belief that the station had become a 'vehicle for the frustrated fantasies of ad-men, the megalomania of insane technocrats and the sanctification of the acts of conservative government.'[9]

Some few months later, Dowling, Doolan and Quinn published a book which reopened their campaign for soul-searching within RTÉ. Their title came from their critique that the station was preoccupied with TAM ratings: *Sit Down and Be Counted*. The book divided the critics. Fergal Tobin reckoned it 'part apologia, part broadside, part cultural inquiry' and found it 'one of the most stimulating books written in Ireland in the 1960s, an impassioned plea for the principles of quality public-service broadcasting and against the debilitating pap – most of it imported – which choked the airwaves in circumstances where commercial criteria were permitted an excessive influence in determination of programme content.'[10] From the sidelines, Rugheimer, in a review of the book, acknowledged that the need to fill 'the yawning span of broadcasting hours' had indeed led to schedules which were 'often trivial and sometimes tawdry.' But he saw the three authors as taking the course of 'self-immolation'.[11]

9   *Sit Down and Be Counted*, xxxiv-v.
10 Fergal Tobin, *The Best of Decades: Ireland in the Nineteen Sixties* (Dublin, 1984), pp.211-12.
11 Gunnar Rugheimer, 'Irish television in trouble', *Irish Times*, 20 October 1969.

Lelia Doolan was by far the greatest loss to Irish television of those who resigned. She was immensely talented and – typical of the pioneering generation of broadcasters – excelled in many fields. She transformed *The Riordans* with her superb skills as a director. She is credited with an outstanding television production of O'Casey's *The Plough and the Stars*. Sent on a study tour to America by Rugheimer, she returned to be a major pioneer in current affairs broadcasting: she 'worried, gnawed, scratched, pushed, cajoled, comforted and studied a disparate collection of individualists into the team that became *7 Days*.' And she was a head of department, Light Entertainment, with *The Late Late Show* as part of her responsibilities, when she resigned. As Savage notes, some believed 'she would eventually become director-general.' That she was also a feminist and member of the Irish Women's Liberation Movement could only have accelerated the push for gender equality in RTÉ. She never returned to television. She is pictured here in an even earlier role, as actress and singer in *Down at Flannery's*, an RTÉ light entertainment production in the summer of 1963 which combined ballad singing and traditional music with the day-to-day happenings in a fictional Irish village. Doolan was later artistic director of the Abbey Theatre, Dublin (1971-73); director of the Galway Film Fleadh; and chairperson of the Irish Film Board, 1993-96.

Christopher Fitz-Simon, letter to the editor, *Irish Times*, 24 February 1998; Anon., 'Unscientific Assessment', *Sit Down and Be Counted* (Dublin, 1969), xxi; Savage, *Loss*, 126-28;

Andrews agreed believing that those who left were 'highly intelligent, well informed and animated by the best of sociological and national convictions'. But they were not prepared 'to bear the yoke of discipline that membership of any organisation demands. They suffered considerable financial loss and preferred to immolate their careers in pursuit of principle.'[12]

Horgan suggests that the speed with which the controversy intensified 'backed both protagonists into their respective corners. Threatened in public, management moved into a defensive, uncompromising mode.' He adds that the book's thesis was 'elaborated in language which on occasion fought communication to a standstill.' But it managed to generate considerable controversy. 'The image of RTÉ producers as tireless seekers after truth and justice who were being continually frustrated by an obsequious or cowardly station management was stereotypical and over-simplified, and for that reason easily mediated to a large and non-specialist audience.' Taking a longer view, Horgan concludes that it was not so much 'a defining moment in the history of the organisation than as yet another skirmish – though a substantial one – in the perennial struggle for control of audio-visual content, a struggle which was as often waged between producers themselves as between producers and management, or between management and government'.[13]

* * *

The *Western People*, commenting on the attacks on R.T.E. in the book "Sit Down and be Counted", says: "the strongest impression retained from the book is that the Donnybrook studios must house a collection of the most prickly and difficult people it would be possible to collect together in any one place."

Cutting found in John Irvine's papers. Probably from Backbencher's column in the *Irish Times*. The worst kept secret in Irish journalism was that 'Backbencher' was John Healy. He was probably, in this instance, quoting his own column in the *Western People*!

12 Andrews, *Man of No Property*, 282.
13 Horgan, *Broadcasting and Public Life*, 70.

Justice Minister, Micheál Ó Móráin, summed up his criticism of the 7 *Days* programme: '(1) The allegation that strong-arm methods are being used by unlicensed moneylenders is, in the opinion of the Garda Síochána, without any foundation in fact. (2) While the gardaí know that some unlicensed moneylenders operate, their number or scale of operations is nothing like that suggested by the programme. (3) The statements purporting to be confessions by moneylenders about moneylending and strong-arm methods can be dismissed as wholly valueless.'

Dáil Debates, vol. 242, cols.1867-68, 26 November 1969.

Peter Feeney believed that the 7 *Days* Tribunal proved a watershed; the years which followed were 'more cautious, more self-censorial'.

THE 7 *DAYS* money-lending programme was controversial. The gardaí and the department of justice took it as an affront to their professionalism that loan sharks could be operating in Dublin in such numbers and employing such a level of intimidation. Justice minister Micheál Ó Móráin told the Dáil that some of the programme's evidence was 'wholly valueless'.[14] Jack Lynch believed that the programme had 'exaggerated the situation out of all proportion'.[15] The government's response had been to set up a tribunal of enquiry, not into money-lending but into the television programme itself and how it had been produced. The tribunal would sit for 51 days and cost a quarter of a million pounds.

Maurice Gorham, former director of Radio Éireann, reckoned that the tribunal exercise was 'ridiculous' and was seen to be that. He expressed his sympathy privately to Irvine: 'A whole pack of Senior Counsel, with the benevolent encouragement of the chairman, harrying reporters and producers day after day, labouring the ethics of hidden microphones and naming names, without any regard to the terms of reference, which heaven knows were searching enough; and all for no reason of public interest, as everybody knows.' He was pleased to see the RTÉ witnesses rebutting 'the bland assertions of the Gardaí.' Anyway, Gorham believed that the tribunal had 'shown its bias so clearly', that if it did eventually condemn RTÉ, nobody would be impressed and if it did not, it would prove to be 'a sweeping victory'. He hoped that 'the farce' would soon be over.[16]

The tribunal found that the conclusions of the 7 *Days* programme had been exaggerated, although earlier claims that participants had been bribed with alcohol to respond to questions in a certain manner were found to be untrue. Whatever the merits of the programme, Peter Feeney has suggested that many broadcasters regarded the tribunal 'as a watershed', arguing that in the years which followed programmes were 'more cautious, more self-censorial, and more likely to heed the attitude of politicians than before. The politicians, in the view of the broadcasters, had reasserted their control.'[17]

Although RTÉ publicly defended the programme there is some

---

14 Dáil Debates, vol. 242, cols.1867-68, 26 November 1969.
15 Lynch on *Lifting the veil: the politics of television*, RTÉ, 16 November 1983, quoted in Peter Feeney, 'Government and broadcasting: maintaining a balance', in Tom Garvin, Maurice Manning and Richard Sinnott (eds) *Dissecting Irish politics: Essays in Honour of Brian Farrell* (Dublin, 2004), p.237; hereafter, Feeney, 'Government and broadcasting'.
16 Gorham to Irvine, 10 February 1970, 7 *Days* file, Irvine papers, RTÉWA.
17 Feeney, 'Government and broadcasting', 237.

evidence that privately they felt more culpable and vulnerable. Oliver Maloney, as secretary to the Authority, had kept a watching brief at the tribunal. In 1977, as director-general, he would describe this period as 'one of tumult' because of the *Sit Down and Be Counted* debate followed by this tribunal, in which he thought 'the credibility of RTÉ's editorial processes' had been 'torn to shreds'.[18]

RTÉ cameraman Gay O'Brien 'changed the course of Irish history'

TELEVISION DISTORTS what it comes to report. The presence of the camera changes the event which it has been sent to chronicle. Many in Ireland did not yet understand this until the events of 5 October 1968 in the streets of Derry. And although the organizers of yet another Northern Ireland civil rights march on a Saturday afternoon well understood the importance of the camera's role, they could scarcely have anticipated the global impact which the television footage of that day would trigger. It was the worldwide reach of television news which gave 1968 its global character: activists in Paris and in California already knew that the media had an insatiable need for 'spectacle, novelty, and progression'.[19] One insider later recalled 'a sense of being hurled ... from

18 Oliver Maloney, 'Strictly private and confidential': Keynote paper for Authority meeting of 4/5 February 1977, RTÉWA.
19 Simon Prince, 'The Global Revolt of 1968 and Northern Ireland', *The Historical Journal*, 49, 3 (2006), pp.851-75.

Fianna Fáil backbencher Flor Crowley: 'Would the minister not also agree that producers and researchers in Telefís Éireann should declare beforehand their views, whether they are Leftist, Maoist, Trotskyites or Communists...'
A Deputy: 'Or Fianna Fáil.'

Dáil Debates, vol. 242, col.1266, 19 November 1969.

A planned civil rights march in Derry on 5 October 1968 was banned by the Stormont government. When the civil rights march organisers defied the ban and sought to enter Protestant areas, 'the RUC took them on with a will. But it calculated on this occasion without the nefarious influence of television. Their performance of taigue-bashing was suddenly exposed to an incredulous audience, much to RUC indignation at this intrusion on their privacy.'

Lee, *Ireland*, 421.

event to event without the time to learn from experience.' Derry's main international activist, Eamonn McCann, concurred that careful planning was impossible under such conditions: 'we became involved willy-nilly, just surfing along on it and really making things up as we went along'.[20]

The Northern Ireland civil rights movement was aware of this context. Inspired by Martin Luther King's tactics in the United States, the movement had held earlier marches that summer without making much impact. It was the police response on this occasion and the fact that it had been captured by television which made the difference.[21] Most especially it was the news film taken by Gay O'Brien of RTÉ which proved most dramatic, 'capturing the chaos and the fury of the baton charge close up'.[22] It was the circulation and worldwide impact of this film footage which dramatised for millions of television viewers across the world 'that something was very wrong in Northern Ireland'. It showed members of the RUC 'charging into the midst of peaceful marchers, cracking skulls with their batons, dragging some demonstrators roughly to police vans, battering others with high-powered water cannon. Unbeknownst to the constables, the whole world was watching.'[23]

RTÉ cameraman Gay O'Brien with sound recordist Eamon Hayes (centre foreground above) at the civil rights march in Duke Street, Derry, 5 October 1968. This was just before what historian Alvin Jackson described as the scenes of 'mayhem', accompanied by television images 'of baton-wielding policemen'. It was such images – as caught in a screen-grab (below) from O'Brien's footage showing the working conditions of a fellow-cameraman – which engaged British sympathies: 'it looked as if Prague or Paris or the American South had come to the backdoor of the United Kingdom.'

Alvin Jackson, *Ireland: 1798-1998* (Oxford, 1999), p.370.

Many diverse observers recognised a tipping point: Hennessy wrote of the 'profound impact' of the television images;[24] the Cameron Report spoke of 'very damaging pictures of police violence';[25] the House of Commons heard of 'the brutalities which we witnessed on television';[26] and Cathcart believed it was television which had 'provoked strong reactions against the unionist regime, most significantly in the British government'.[27] A young university lecturer at Queen's University, Seamus Heaney,

20 *ibid.*
21 'The Camera Cannot Lie', editorial, *Irish News*, 8 October 1968.
22 Morash, *Media in Ireland*, 160-65.
23 Neil Hickey, 'The Battle for Northern Ireland: How TV Tips the Balance', *TV Guide*, 26 September 1981, quoted Savage, *Loss*, 351.
24 Thomas Hennessey, *A History of Northern Ireland: 1920-1996* (Dublin, 1997), p.142.
25 *Cameron Report, Disturbances in Northern Ireland* (Belfast, 1969), 4:55.
26 Kevin McNamara, Labour MP, House of Commons Debates, vol. 770, col. 882-85, 21 October 1968.
27 Cathcart, 'Mass Media', 704.

witnessed the effect on the student population: he found many 'shattered ivory towers among educated and articulate people who had opted out of political affairs from embarrassment or disillusion.' In a contemporary essay in *The Listener*, he wrote that television had revealed 'the zeal of the police' and the 'bland indifference' of William Craig – the minister responsible for their behaviour – who 'refused to believe his eyes'.[28]

Craig's prime minister, Terence O'Neill, did believe his eyes. A week later he informed his cabinet that television had 'dramatically altered' the situation, to the 'great disadvantage' of the Ulster Unionists. Whether the coverage was fair or otherwise was 'immaterial': Northern Ireland had now become 'a focus of world opinion'. Moreover, it was an embarrassment to the British embassy in Washington, by then 'under intense pressure' from the American media.[29] Increasingly as the O'Brien footage was re-run in current affairs programmes, it was not the images themselves but the awareness by the political establishment in London that others were watching – 'in silent judgement' – which became the salient factor.[30] Heaney witnessed another response, the formation of the student-based People's Democracy which was ratcheting up the pressure on the O'Neill government with a promised civil rights march from Belfast to Derry. The 'main body of the march was made up of embarrassed, indignant young Ulstermen and women whose deep-grained conservatism of behaviour' had now been 'outweighed by a reluctant recognition of injustice.' Heaney added that the 'northern obstinacy' which had founded the Unionist state was 'beginning to tell against it'.[31]

'This IS happening in Britain [*sic*] you know,' Geoffrey Gilbert, UTV's controller of programmes would later say. 'We are not a foreign country. Imagine the coverage if this sort of situation was happening in an area of similar population in England, like Kent.'[32] RTÉ's head of news, Jim McGuinness, described the key scenes in the news report as one hundred seconds of film 'which ended a regime'.[33] Historian Paul Bew concurred: it was this civil-rights demonstration in Derry 'which opened up the modern Ulster crisis. The television coverage – especially the work of the RTÉ cameraman Gay O'Brien – changed the course of Irish history.'[34]

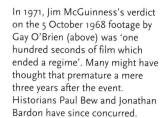

In 1971, Jim McGuinness's verdict on the 5 October 1968 footage by Gay O'Brien (above) was 'one hundred seconds of film which ended a regime'. Many might have thought that premature a mere three years after the event. Historians Paul Bew and Jonathan Bardon have since concurred.

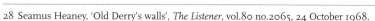

28 Seamus Heaney, 'Old Derry's walls', *The Listener*, vol.80 no.2065, 24 October 1968.
29 Memorandum by the prime minister, 14 October 1968, PRONI /4/1406.
30 Morash, *Media in Ireland*, 160-65.
31 *The Listener*, 24 October 1968.
32 Malcolm Stuart, 'Riot through the Eyes of the TV Men in No-Man's Land', *TV Times* (1968); reprint in Linenhall Library, P1126, n.p.
33 Author interview with McGuinness, 1971.
34 Paul Bew, *Ireland: the Politics of Enmity: 1789-2006* (Oxford, 2007), p.489.

RTÉ granted Sinn Féin's statements 'quite disproportionate publicity' – T.K.Whitaker

T.K.Whitaker advised Lynch to avoid opportunism and emotionalism. He believed that watching RTÉ's coverage 'an outsider would be misled into thinking' that Sinn Féin was the government party 'or at least the Opposition'.

Whitaker to Lynch [draft], 15 August 1969, Whitaker papers, UCDAD, P175

Screen grab from Jack Lynch's 'idly by' address to the nation, 13 August 1969. As the original video attests, Lynch did not use the word 'idly' on the broadcast. The words Lynch did use of his government – that they 'can no longer stand by' – has been described by historian Joe Lee as 'an exquisite choice of phrase which excluded no interpretation that the variety of viewers wished to impute to it.'

Lee, *Ireland*, 461.

AT THE HEIGHT of the rioting in Derry on 13 August 1969 Jack Lynch's televised promise that the South would not stand 'idly by' was intended for many audiences: it was to reassure the Northern nationalists that they were not forgotten in the Republic; to inform the British that the Irish government had a vital interest in what happened on the other side of the border; and it was to reassure the hawks in Fianna Fáil – and especially those in the cabinet – that the party's historic espousal of Irish unity counted for something.

The previous day the annual Apprentice Boys march had proved a flashpoint and Derry on 13 August witnessed rioting on a scale not seen before in the Troubles. The death toll then stood at three – all within the previous month. On the day of Lynch's broadcast over 100 had been injured and CS gas had been used against the rioters for the first time. Harold Wilson, in his memoirs, acknowledged that the scenes of violence 'dramatically shown on the television screens' were evidence that 'law and order had totally broken down'. It was on the following day that the British army was deployed on the streets, itself seen at the time as a civil rights victory, since they were initially acceptable in nationalist areas where the RUC – and especially their reservists, the B Specials – were not.[35]

It was against this background that Lynch made his televised address. It had many authors. It followed a cabinet meeting which had been deeply divisive – divisions which would later be reflected in the Arms crisis of May 1970. The first two drafts were dismissed as 'mere civil service talk' by Neil Blaney, Charles Haughey and Kevin Boland. Terms such as tough, hawkish, militant, emotional are among those used by Lynch's biographer, Dermot Keogh, in his reconstruction of the cabinet meeting. He reports 'wild talk about cross-border intervention', this to bring an international dimension to the crisis and involve the UN.[36]

Lynch was also being offered other counsel. Ken Whitaker – who would have worked closely with him when he was Finance minister – consistently advised him during this period to strike a pluralist, inclusive note in any references to Irish unity. He cautioned Lynch to avoid the 'terrible temptation to be opportunist' and to 'cash in on political emotionalism', warning him that the Irish government 'should not be driven before the emotional winds fanned by utterly unrepresentative and irresponsible organisations such as Sinn Féin'.

---

35 Harold Wilson, *The Labour Government: 1964-1970, A Personal Record* (London, 1971), pp.692-3.
36 Boland to Lynch, 27 June 1969, Lynch papers, UCC, Keogh, *Lynch*, 158.

Whitaker specifically faulted RTÉ for granting Sinn Féin's statements 'quite disproportionate publicity'.[37]

When, that evening, Lynch arrived at the RTÉ television studios for his address to the nation, the senior news editor on duty was Desmond Fisher, himself a Derry nationalist. He could not help noticing that Lynch's script was badly typed, 'with corrections in ink scrawled all over it' and advised against going into studio with such a disadvantage. He persuaded Lynch to allow it to be re-typed in a large font with adequate spacing to make it more comfortable to read. Lynch asked for a private telephone and Fisher overheard him talking to his wife, Mairin, 'to consult her on changes he proposed to make'. At one point Lynch asked Fisher what he thought would happen if he 'were to order the Army into the North as some of his advisers counselled'. Fisher replied that he thought the Irish troops 'would get about 20 miles into Down or Derry before they would be massacred in a fight with the British'. He records Lynch as smiling 'wanly at my answer and said he had come to the same conclusion himself'.[38]

Lynch had no shortage of advice: his problem was that it was contradictory. He was obliged to walk a tightrope between the competing demands of hawks and doves. Nor were there just two factions to satisfy. And he appreciated that as well as being written for the Fianna Fáil faithful, the speech must have a message for the London establishment, for the beleaguered Northern nationalists and for the paranoid Ulster unionists. One of his moderate ministers, Padraig Faulkner, in his memoirs wrote that in all the circumstances it was 'just as well the speech was somewhat tough'.[39] Eamonn Gallagher, one of the Department of External Affairs experts on the North, writing a month later, expressed the opinion that Lynch's promise 'not to stand idly by' had been necessary to avoid 'a massacre by B Specials'. He thought it certain that this had been 'a real possibility' and he believed 'the verdict of historians' would probably be that the Lynch broadcast of 13 August had 'helped to prevent its happening'.[40]

Kevin Boland, an irascible hawk in Lynch's government during the 1969-70 period. He signalled his considerable disaffection from Lynch's line on Northern Ireland in his letter to Lynch: 'You know also that I am not in agreement with the approach to Partition and to the stationing of troops outside the country in present circumstances.' Boland also attacked what he called 'RTÉ's planned sabotage of our nationality'. Dermot Keogh reckons this as Boland's wish to see RTÉ play 'a more constructive and patriotic role' vis-à-vis the North. On the day of the 'idly by' broadcast, Boland had stormed out of the cabinet meeting, shouting of treachery and betrayal; he would later resign from government when Lynch sacked Haughey and Blaney in May 1970. He is photographed here at the Fianna Fáil Ard Fheis, 18 January 1970, which fell between the 'idly by' speech and the Arms crisis of May 1970.

Boland to Lynch, 27 June 1969, Jack Lynch papers, UCC; Keogh, *Lynch*, 159;

---

37 Whitaker to Lynch [draft], 15 August 1969, Whitaker papers, UCDAD, P175(1).
38 Desmond Fisher, 'An Irishman's diary', *Irish Times*, 25 October 1999.
39 Padraig Faulkner, *As I Saw It* (Dublin, 2005), pp.90-91.
40 Eamonn Gallagher report, 25 September 1969, NAI, DT 2000/6/659.

Robin Day believed that the arrival of television to Northern Ireland had helped 'stir a challenge to blinkered bigotry and traditional intolerance'; and it had given 'impetus to the civil rights movement, and to the policy of building bridges between the two religious communities'. But television was then 'faced with a new responsibility when serious violence exploded.' Would television reporting of such violence 'tend to spread that violence in a country which was largely peaceful and so distort and inflame the situation?'

Robin Day, 'Troubled reflections of a TV journalist', *Encounter*, May 1970, 78-88.

the government 'regarded this as direct defiance' and had dismissed the Authority

In the 1960s Joe Foyle established a cyclostyled *Guide* which published anonymous reviews of RTÉ television programmes to consider how they related to 'moral/religious beliefs'. In October 1971, Foyle wrote to Archbishop John Charles McQuaid with an oblique request for financial support: whether the service 'would be financially feasible in the suggested recast form remains to be seen'. He was trying 'to interest people in London. It would help if similar interest were displayed here. I await word from you, in relation to my request for an appointment to discuss matters...'. Two months later, he wrote again to McQuaid expressing how 'deeply grateful' he was for the archbishop's 'generous gift' which would enable him 'to try out radically different methods' in the future. In an earlier exchange when Foyle wrote to McQuaid telling him that the Dublin diocesan area 'would appear to be a particularly valuable one for such a Receiving-End piece of dual research', McQuaid's note to his secretary included the comment: 'This television language is very complex.'

Guide, no. 32, 27 May 1969; Foyle to McQuaid, 9 May 1970, 11 October and 16 December 1971, DDA, McQuaid papers, Joe Foyle correspondence.

WHEN JACK LYNCH formed his second government in the summer of 1969, he did not know that in the lifetime of that 19th Dáil, the death toll in the Northern Troubles would number 737. It was at zero as the Dáil first assembled but during the remainder of that year sixteen died. In 1970, 24 deaths were recorded; in 1971, that had risen to 170; in 1972, to 472; and in the first two months of 1973 alone – before Fianna Fáil lost power to the Fine Gael-Labour Coalition – 55 died.[41] The period was punctuated by continuing violence and instability: there was a campaign of civil disobedience; the introduction onto the streets of the British Army; internment; the escalation of the IRA bombing campaign; the Arms Crisis and Arms Trial which split Fianna Fáil; the Bloody Sunday massacre in Derry at the end of January 1972 and the subsequent burning of the British embassy in Dublin; the proroguement of Stormont and the beginnings of the search by the British government and the Northern parties for some political way forward.

Throughout this time, Lynch's diplomatic efforts were focused on persuading the British authorities that the Irish government had an important contribution to make to any political solution.[42] The British, while not willing to concede to Dublin any rights at the negotiating table, did acknowledge that there was what came to be known as the 'Irish Dimension'. This need to persuade the British that Dublin had a constructive role to play needs to be borne in mind in any assessment of the government's relationship with RTÉ during this period. Above all, the Irish diplomatic effort was focused on disabusing London of its favoured analysis: that the IRA was predominantly based south of the border and was using the Republic as a safe haven from which to sustain its campaign of terror within Northern Ireland. For those in London and Belfast insisting on this latter analysis, what better evidence had there been than that apologists for Provisional and Official Sinn Féin had enjoyed the 'freedom of the airwaves' on RTÉ? To journalists, such interviews followed from the routine application of news values but others believed that they encouraged violence. And the greater the atrocity committed by their respective wings of the IRA, the more did their spokesmen enjoy 'the oxygen of publicity'.

---

41 Tabulated from Malcolm Sutton, *An Index of Deaths from the Conflict in Ireland: 1969-1993* (1994, Belfast), p.206.
42 John Peck [UK Ambassador, Dublin], note of conversation with Lynch, 23 October 1972, NAUK, FCO 87/28.

It was when RTÉ proceeded with the broadcasting of interviews with the leaders of both the Provisional and the Official IRA – despite a government request to cancel – that Gerry Collins, Minister for Posts and Telegraphs, in October 1971 resorted to the Broadcasting Act. He issued a directive under Section 31 ordering RTÉ to 'refrain from broadcasting any matter that could be calculated to promote the aims and activities of any organisation which engages in, promotes, encourages or advocates the attainment of any particular objective by violent means.' The RTÉ Authority complained that the order was imprecise but promised a balanced, comprehensive broadcasting service that would operate within its constraints. The minister for his part refused all requests to clarify his wording, claiming that it spoke for itself. RTÉ's coverage of the Northern Troubles continued to spark controversy. But it was the lengthy delineation of the opinions of Seán MacStiofáin, the leader of the Provisional IRA, in a radio broadcast on 19 November 1972 which triggered the gravest crisis in government-RTÉ relations. Although Mac Stiofáin's voice was not broadcast, it was the duration and detail of his opinions as read by Kevin O'Kelly which so offended the government. Manifestly it seemed to them a blatant attempt to circumvent section 31 by reading aloud what was to the listener a lengthy question-and-answer format interview. Given the challenges that the government was facing – and not least its need to win a hearing in London as honest brokers in the search for peace – its decision to sack the Authority cannot be considered surprising.

It may also be stated that politically the timing must have seemed singularly fortuitous for Lynch. In Britain for a long-standing engagement at an Oxford Union debate, he had accepted a dinner invitation to Downing Street from Edward Heath. The British agenda for this meeting was to underline their disappointment in cross-border security. The Foreign and Commonwealth Office had prepared a dossier termed 'the Great Summary of Border incidents to surpass all Summaries.'[43] In such circumstances the government's dismissal of the Authority must have been seen by Lynch as a fortuitous trump card. He impressed Heath – and the foreign secretary Alec Douglas-Home – with his account of how the RTÉ Authority had been asked to explain why the station had broadcast the Mac Stiofáin interview 'in defiance of a direction given to them by the Government that they should not publicise the views of those who sought to achieve their ends by violence.' The government, having found the Authority's unsatisfactory, reckoned the broadcast to be 'direct defiance' and had decided that very day to dismiss the

Following on Kevin O'Kelly's broadcast of the opinions of Seán Mac Stiofáin (his voice was not used but O'Kelly read a verbatim transcription of the interview), Gerry Collins proposed in government that he should ask the RTÉ Authority for its opinion in writing. But Lynch thought this too anodyne and insisted on asking for 'an indication, in writing, of the action the Authority proposes to take'. And it was informally agreed that, if RTÉ did not take action on the matter 'to comply with the Minister's direction, all members – or all such members as do not publicly disassociate themselves from such a stand by RTÉ – would immediately be removed from office.'

---

43 W.K.K.White [RofI desk] FCO, 13 November 1972, NAUK, FCO 87/28.

Kevin O'Kelly never expected to find himself making the news. It was the lengthy broadcast in which he read aloud a verbatim transcription of his taped interview with MacStiofáin which gave the government the impression that this was a provocative testing of the limits of Section 31. Hitherto, other reporters had paraphrased and quoted Provisional IRA and Sinn Féin sources in their regular reporting.

Authority. This would be announced along with the membership of the new Authority at 9:30 in Dublin that very evening.[44]

The sacking of the Authority was an awesome moment in broadcasting's history: but Lynch – given his responsibilities and difficulties – was obliged to take a wider perspective. And that he did so can be gleaned from an exchange he had shortly afterwards with his occasional confidante, Ulick O'Connor. When questioned by O'Connor as to whether his government was not now vulnerable to critics who might accuse it of restrictions on freedom of speech, the usually mild-mannered Lynch replied: 'Fuck them!'[45]

Professor T.W. Moody, (front row right) who had been a member of all Authorities since the station had begun broadcasting, claimed that they had acted 'under a strong sense of responsibility and according to their judgment and conscience'. They had been obliged to give due weight to two conflicting claims: 'on the one hand the freedom of public expression and debate, on the other the protection of society and the State against subversion.' Their dismissal, he concluded, was the logical outcome not of any refusal to carry out the direction, but of the Minister's refusal to explain what the direction meant. It had 'imprecise and omnibus terms' but when they sought clarification from the minister, none was forthcoming. 'So either there was to be a total blackout on all reference to the IRA or the Authority was to be left to discover by a process of trial and error how much liberty remained to broadcasting.'

Quoted in Leon Ó Broin, 'The Dismissal of the Irish Broadcasting Authority', *E.B.U. Review*, March 1973, 24-28.

44 Robert Armstrong, note of Heath-Lynch dinner, Downing Street, 24 November 1972, NAUK, FCO 87/28.
45 Ulick O'Connor, *The Ulick O'Connor Diaries: 1970-1981* (London, 2001), p.126.

'probably no part of the world' where news reporting was 'not at all an abstract matter'

AT THE CONCLUSION OF RTÉ television's first decade of broadcasting, the Broadcasting Review Committee was established to evaluate the station's performance. When its report was published in 1974, it was highly critical of RTÉ's coverage of the early stages of the Northern Troubles. It did not believe that the station had 'conformed to an adequate standard of objectivity and impartiality'. Rather had its reporting exemplified all the dangers potentially inherent in the medium: 'lack of detail, bias, distortion, sensationalism, the crowding out of moderate by extreme opinions and the tempta¬tion to select items for television news for their visual excitement, or because film of them was available, rather than because of their real news value.'[46]

Screen grab of Kevin Myers reporting from Belfast, 21 July 1972, when a series of Provisional IRA bombs – without adequate warnings – killed nine and injured over 100 in Belfast city centre. This became known as Bloody Friday. Two months later Myers protested against Section 31 because in his experience of reporting from the North, it had steadily eroded RTÉ's credibility. 'We feel we have been journalistically compromised'.

Horgan, *Broadcasting and Public Life*, 108-09.

Jim McGuinness anticipated this line of criticism – he may well have had an advance copy – and on its day of publication he circulated to his staff a robust defence, especially against the charge of bias or partiality. He complained that the report implied that his staff had been 'for a protracted and vital period, acting in a professionally reprehensible manner'. McGuinness was all too aware that the same bulletin was capable of causing offence to all sides and he was especially aware of the criticism of RTÉ's coverage which came from nationalists north of the border. Sometimes these were 'people of fairness and perception who were trying to keep the peace in the Catholic ghettoes and sustain people who were the daily victims of violence.' They wanted RTÉ to be their allies, 'even if this meant, or so it seemed to us, tacitly suspending correct journalistic standards'. McGuinness believed that 'the greatest aid and comfort' which RTÉ could bring 'all the people' was, as far as was possible, 'to report accurately and truthfully all that happened.'[47]

But who would define accurate? Who would determine truth in the context of Northern Ireland coverage? Anthony Smith believed that there was 'probably no part of the world' where the effects of what was transmitted was 'not at all an abstract matter'. What was objective or impartial in British – i.e. English, Scottish and Welsh – terms was 'not necessarily so in Irish terms', there being 'no shared frame of reference on the question of Ireland, no generally agreed centre of intellectual or political gravity.' And throughout Ireland there was certainly no such

46 Horgan's summary, *Broadcasting and Public Life*, 126-27.
47 *ibid.*, 127-28.

A Republican wall mural, painted on the gable end of a house on Rockmore Road in West Belfast, in October 1982. Its subject is the demand of Republican inmates in the H-block prisons for political status. The mural reads: 'Break Thatchers Back: Status Now'. The photograph was taken for use in RTÉ News bulletins.

Fr Edward Daly, on *7 Days*, 31 January 1972, the day following Bloody Sunday when 13 civilians were killed by the Parachute Regiment in Derry. A witness to the events, his leading of a group of civilians carrying the mortally wounded Jackie Duddy, while Fr Daly waved a blood-stained white handkerchief became one of the iconic images of the Troubles. The testimony he gave that night on *7 Days* was manifestly compelling: it took the British authorities the best part of four decades and some hundreds of millions of pounds to come to the same conclusions and to apologise.

shared frame of reference. And was there one among RTE broadcasters?

This is but one reason why it is well beyond the scope of this volume to adequately chronicle the role which RTÉ television played – or failed to play – in covering the Northern Troubles. But what is manifestly the case is that the eye of the beholder ought to be taken into account when attempting any adjudication on the question of bias in RTÉ's coverage. Where T.K.Whitaker could charge in August 1969 that RTÉ was granting Sinn Féin 'quite disproportionate publicity',[48] others could hear only the unionist viewpoint being favoured.

There was the further complication that spin doctors would take on the role of choreographer as they anticipated how television would be obliged to cover hunger strikes, invariably accompanied by protest marches, protracted negotiations, distraught relatives, international attention – and always with the possibility of a succession of emotional funerals. That the hunger strikers could be nominated as abstentionist candidates in electoral contests only multiplied the opportunities for news management. Broadcasters could see that for Provisional Sinn Féin this all had an element of political theatre, with a shrewd press office brilliantly exploiting its television potential. It is scarcely surprising that some broadcasters felt caught between the demands of news values and a reluctance to be drawn into playing a supporting role in somebody else's well-honed television drama.

There is no western democracy whose television stations have not attracted recruits who are highly political. Talking about the intake of new talent in 1991, the chairman of the Authority, Jim Culliton allowed that 'some of these young people were excellent – the problem might be that they had very radical views.'[49] And such recruits were invariably a generation younger than the politicians and civil servants whose policy-making they would be scrutinizing. Indeed some of the latter could even qualify as game-keepers, having once been among the ranks of the broadcasters. What would Muiris Mac Conghail, who was handling the Irish government's media relations at the Sunningdale talks of December 1973, have thought of the *7 Days* coverage had it included an invitation to both wings of the IRA to pass judgment on the Cosgrave government's efforts to deliver power-sharing in Northern Ireland? Of course, by 1973, Section 31 precluded such interviews. But had Mac Conghail's former colleagues in *7 Days* not – a mere two years before – invited the chiefs of staff of both wings of the IRA to pass judgment on Jack Lynch as he returned from his first

48 Anthony Smith, 'Television coverage of Northern Ireland', Bill Rolston, David Miller (eds), *War and Words: the Northern Ireland Media Reader* (Belfast, 1996), p.24.
49 RTE Authority, minutes, 29 November 1991.

trilateral talks with Edward Heath and Brian Faulkner?[50] In fact those talks laid some of the early foundations for power-sharing: just as that invitation to Cathal Goulding and Seán MacStiofáin led eventually to the invocation of Section 31 to prevent such IRA appearances.

Just as in other western democracies, RTÉ recruited its share of politically motivated broadcasters. And they were of all political persuasions, but mainly liberal and left-of-centre. While this was to be expected there was one party which had more deliberative designs: the Workers Party had set up a secret branch in RTÉ, and its members 'formed a fierce, brilliant caucus', with a 'militantly anti-nationalist agenda'.[51] Gerry Gregg, when a *Today Tonight* producer, believed that his work on the programme was 'a matter of opposing a "looming" civil war being whipped up by the Provisionals'. When management moved him to children's programmes, he 'brought a Marxist perspective to kids' programmes'.[52] The charismatic broadcaster and WUI trade union activist, who was the main inspirational figure for this Workers Party faction, was Eoghan Harris. He was a highly gifted producer who had many remarkable programmes to his credit, including *The Greening of America* with John Kelleher. That he had won an early Jacobs Award – for *Féach* in 1970 – and declined to accept it, added to the enigma. But he was also manifestly breaking the rules about engaging in party politics and inflicting damage on his current affairs colleagues by lending plausibility to the charges from the Dail parties – and Fianna Fail in particular – that RTÉ broadcasters were biased.

According to McCafferty, Harris characterised as 'hush puppies' those of his colleagues who in his opinion 'did not totally condemn Sinn Féin and/or the IRA.' McCafferty believed that most broadcasters were against the Provisionals, 'but were trying to fulfill the station's commitment to objectivity in political reportage' and her impression was that there was 'a great deal of fearful self-censorship in RTÉ'.[53] Mary McAleese claimed that 'there was a definite and tangible anti-nationalist, anti-Catholic and anti-intellectual atmosphere' in RTÉ when she joined the station in 1979.[54] Wesley Boyd for his part believed that the influence of the Workers Party was much exaggerated by commentators. And it must be emphasised that one factor is constantly overlooked in this debate. Antipathy to the Provisionals' campaign was not a Workers Party copyright: it was shared by all the Dáil parties, by the SDLP and by all shades of Ulster unionism – and, it might be added, by democrats in general.

Mary McAleese, recruited to *The Politics Programme* as studio presenter she was later a reporter with *Today Tonight*. She faulted the programme for bias on the hunger strikes. Moreover, she found it difficult to make an alternative case 'without people getting shirty, pompous or downright nasty'.

McAleese diary [n.d.] Mac Manais, *The Road from Ardoyne* (Dingle, 2004), p.181.

---

50 *7 Days*, 28 September 1971; see Horgan, *Broadcasting and Public Life*, 98-99.
51 Nell McCafferty, *Nell* (Dublin, 2004), p.373; hereafter, McCafferty, *Nell*.
52 Brian Hanley and Scott Millar, *The lost revolution: the story of the official IRA and the Workers' Party* (London, 2009), p.430; hereafter, Hanley, *Lost Revolution*.
53 McCafferty, *Nell*, 373.
54 Ray Mac Manais, *The Road from Ardoyne: The making of the president* (Dingle, 2004), p.173.

A poem for Liam Hourican

Liam Hourican was northern Editor of RTÉ News at the height of the Troubles in the early 1970s. In 1974 the *Irish Press* published this poem, 'Tribute to a reporter in Belfast' by Paul Durcan, in its 'New Irish Writing' page, edited by David Marcus.

Poets, is not this solitary man's own uniquely
utilitarian technique of truth-telling,
this finely apparent effort of his
to split the atom of a noun and reach truth through language,
to chip-carve each word and report
as if language itself were the very conscience of reality –
a poetry more than poetry is?
Tonight once more he has done his work with words
and fish roots and echoes of all manner and kind
did flower up out of an ocean-floor resonance
so rapidly but with such clarity
that you were made to look out of the eye of another
even as the other shot you dead in the back,
out of the eyes of a catholic republican
whose grandparents were quakers in Norwich,
but likewise out of the eyes
of a seventeenth-century Norfolkman in Virginia
sailing a copper knife through the soft pink air
of an Indian's open mouth...

Gratias for the verbal honesty of Liam Hourican
in a country where words also have died an unnatural death
or else have been used on all sides for unnatural ends
and by poets as much as by gunmen or churchmen.
Day and night his integrity of words has sustained us.

Paul Durcan has made some minor changes to this poem since it first appeared in 'New Irish Writing', *Irish Press*, 20 July 1974.

12

a vortex of interests, demands, preferences, vetoes, misunderstandings – and 'Nelsonic eye' understandings

BRITISH CIVIL SERVANTS were bemused by what they manifestly saw as the innocence of the Broadcasting Review Committee in Ireland as it considered how the second Irish television channel should be exploited. On reading one of the committee's reports, one diplomat commented that the Irish seemed to believe that they had 'a right to play finders keepers' with any TV signal which may chance 'to fall like manna upon the wilderness of Irish broadcasting.' And the suggestion was even mooted that perhaps the BBC and the Independent Broadcating Authority should have this drawn to their attention.[1] It was in the nature of broadcasting signals that to ensure quality reception throughout their host territory, they invariably overspilled to contiguous areas. This was natural overspill: but if such signals were further boosted and sold on to cable subscribers in the other jurisdiction, did this not amount to rebroadcasting? Did it not breach the intellectual property rights of the original programme-makers? Should they not be compensated? There could be other knock-on consequences for the original broadcasting organisation. Would the contractual agreements – usually drawn up with provision for further payments if the programme is sold abroad – not apply? The broadcasting unions thought so and especially those representing actors and musicians. And the Irish branches of these same unions were not slow to point out that such rebroadcasting in the Irish case limited the work opportunities of their Irish members. And if this was not sufficiently complicated, there was the further consideration that the boosting of a BBC signal within the Republic of Ireland could unravel a complex contract which the BBC had already struck for the UK-only rights to back catalogues of old Hollywood movies!

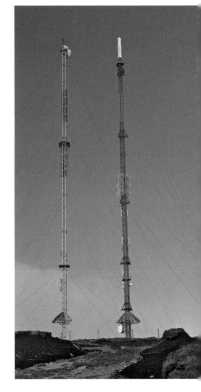

A pair of RTÉ television transmitters. To secure good reception throughout the state, their signal would cross the border? But how far?

---

1   Thorpe to Moore, 12 March 1973 enclosing report from *Irish Times* on Broadcasting Review Committee re second channel; 'Open Broadcasting between Northern Ireland and Republic of Ireland', NAUK, FCO 87/196.

There were also town planning issues: was there not a strong cost-benefit argument for communal aerials which would discourage the proliferation of domestic aerials in parts of the Republic where marginal reception of British signals was possible? The view of a street in the north inner city of Dublin in 1969.

It was little wonder that some civil servants charged with the duty of advising politicians in this sector suggested that it was 'a legal no-man's land.'[2] With the advent of satellite and cable systems, many of these controversies are now redundant, but they were complicating factors at this earlier period. Indeed British ministers, when explaining why the Republic could not extend its broadcasting reach into Northern Ireland, were constantly advised not to rely on technical explanations because, over time, they had 'a habit of being solved.'[3]

There were also town planning issues: was there not a strong cost-benefit argument for communal aerials which would discourage the proliferation of domestic aerials in parts of the Republic where marginal reception of British signals was already feasible? And if communal aerials were to be permitted, how could the map be agreed to define the areas of 'natural' overspill? It was noted in London that in the past, British stations had turned a 'blind-eye' to much of this; but now that it was being widely considered, the BBC and ITA might review the situation.[4] And if Dublin was within the range of Northern Irish transmitters why should not RTÉ's transmitters be so configured as to bring Belfast within RTÉ's range? That there was a serious demand for RTÉ among Northern nationalists was manifest. There was no better testimony to this expectation than the dismay and chagrin expressed at successive annual conferences of the GAA. Speakers in 1961 when the new station was within months of being launched feared that any failure to broadcast throughout the North would make the border 'really permanent'. Nor was the Ulster chairman impressed by talk of obligations to respect international boundaries: he wanted to know 'where diplomacy ends and subservience begins.'[5] Ten years later the grievance remained: in 1971 the Easter Congress in Belfast was told that 'apparently the great god

2   J.M.Lyon to Howard Drake, 25 August 1971, NAUK, CJ 4/2421.
3   T.U. Meyer to D.E. Baptiste, 23 December 1970, NAUK, HO 256/626, 'Irish Republic: Broadcasting by RTÉ from Carlingford into Ulster [sic]'.
4   F.J.C.Evans to R. Dane, 28 March 1973, 'Open Broadcasting between Northern Ireland and Republic of Ireland', NAUK FCO 87/196.
5   P. MacFloinn, Ulster Chairman, GAA archives CC/1/24, 1961 volume.

status quo continues to be worshipped, in Montrose, and elsewhere.'[6]

The cultural case for all-Ireland broadcasting which was championed by the nationalist community of Northern Ireland was formidable. This was a community which had been discriminated against methodically and systematically. Their cultural interests, including Gaelic games, had been historically marginalised by the Unionist establishment. BBC radio's record was not impressive. It even – at the request of the Northern Ireland prime minister, Lord Craigavon – declined to broadcast the results of GAA matches, it being explained that since the games had taken place on the Sabbath, the broadcasts would hurt 'the feelings of the large majority of people in Northern Ireland'.[7] Those Unionists who remained hostile to all efforts to improve RTÉ television's access to the North would have been under no obligation to watch the channel themselves. What they seemed determined on was that others would be denied that access, including those nationalists who felt that their indigenous cultural interests in sport, language, traditional music and history would be better served if they could include RTÉ television among their choice of channels.

But unionists saw RTÉ as a Trojan horse and councillors at local level – who might have policy on communal aerials in their remit – remained so opposed that the British government, in rejecting Dublin's arguments, found themselves somewhat embarrassed and, in the case of the Foreign and Commonwealth Office (FCO), even ashamed. The FCO complained that it was being invited to deny a minority access to RTÉ just because 'another substantial part of a population' might object. They asserted that they 'would not accept this argument from other countries about the BBC's services', and they did not think it was the sort of censorship in which they should become involved.[8]

This was more than a cultural issue. There was also a commercial dimension. If UTV enjoyed an advertising bonus through geographic proximity to greater Dublin, why should not the same argument work in reverse? UTV was meticulous in not making any explicit claims to its advertisers – in its rate card, for instance – that its signal could reach Dublin. But its advertisers knew this to be the case and took it into consideration in allocating their budgets, as one can presume UTV did in pitching their advertising rates. It was also the case that UTV had an explicit legal commitment from the UK government, having already 'in effect bought the advertising monopoly' for

In an earlier exchange when Jack Lynch had suggested building 'an especially powerful' TV mast at Carlingford, one British diplomat – aware of the legal, commercial and copyright difficulties – wondered whether the Irish could achieve 'all they desire, or most of it' by simply building to X feet and transmitting on Y strength.

W.K.K.White to R.A.Burroughs, 15 December 1970, NAUK, HO 256/626.

---

6   GAA archives CC/1/34, 1971 volume.
7   Gillian McIntosh, *The Force of Culture: Unionist Identities in Twentieth-Century Ireland* (Cork, 1999), pp.82-83.
8   W.K.K.White to J. Drumgoole, [MPT], 5 November 1973, NAUK, FCO 87/196.

Northern Ireland.[9] This was an important factor whenever the Irish government requested permission to boost RTÉ's signal to win better reception north of the border.

Into this vortex of interests, demands, preferences, vetoes, misunderstandings – and 'Nelsonic eye' understandings – came the new minister Conor Cruise O'Brien with his proposal for all-Ireland broadcasting: specifically that the second Irish channel should be dedicated to the rebroadcasting of BBC 1 and that RTÉ should reciprocally be accessible throughout Northern Ireland.

'a worthwhile gain in the propaganda war – a war which will continue long after the shooting has stopped'

Before his summit with Edward Heath at Downing Street in July 1973, Taoiseach Liam Cosgrave received a briefing note from Conor Cruise O'Brien. O'Brien, acknowledging that it was 'notoriously difficult' to give expression to the Irish dimension, reminded Cosgrave that securing RTÉ television access to Northern Ireland was 'surely one way in which an important minority aspiration' could be met without encroaching on majority rights. Unionists had three channels and 'need not watch RTÉ at all if they don't want to do so'. He added that if they did watch it, RTÉ would 'generally tend to have a calming rather than an incendiary effect, and tend to better mutual understanding, especially when combined with the reciprocal aspect of the open broadcasting proposals – which present no political difficulties, though they do present a lot of other difficulties.'

Cruise O'Brien to Cosgrave, 21 June 1973, NAI DT 2004/21/452.

INITIALLY CRUISE O'BRIEN'S all-Ireland broadcasting proposal won wide approval. A 'wonderful benefit' was the verdict of his predecessor, the outgoing Fianna Fáil minister, Gerry Collins. The *Irish Press* also argued that such an initiative 'could only lead to greater understanding all over this island'.[10] In the North it received the endorsement of the *Belfast Telegraph*, the New Ulster Movement and the Unionist politician, Roy Bradford, who asserted that television coverage 'in both directions' was already 'de facto but an extension of this and its formalisation would not only have solid and positive social advantages' but also, he believed, political advantages.[11]

The Foreign and Commonwealth Office also liked O'Brien's idea as they had for a long time been asking the Irish to come up with 'some sensible proposals' for a possible Council of Ireland, which would form part of a comprehensive Northern settlement. They now saw the working out of reciprocal broadcasting arrangements as a possible challenge for such a North-South body. If Dublin's first serious proposal were to be rejected, the British believed they would have difficulty in offering 'something of equal value to them' to put in its place. And 'whatever the faults of the BBC', it was less likely 'to sell the IRA propaganda line' than was RTÉ. London believed that any increase in BBC influence in the Republic at RTÉ's expense 'must be regarded as a worthwhile gain in the propaganda war – a war which will continue long after the shooting has stopped.'[12]

---

9   W.K.K.White to R.A. Burroughs, 15 December 1970, NAUK, HO 256/626, 'Irish Republic: Broadcasting by RTÉ from Carlingford into Ulster [sic]'.
10 *This Week*, RTÉ Radio, 13 May 1973; *Irish Press*, 14 May 1973.
11 Roy Bradford to Sir Stewart Crawford (Chairman, Committee on Broadcasting Coverage), 22 October 1973, NAUK, HO 237/211.
12 Adrian Thorpe to White, 16 May 1973, NAUK, FCO 87/196.

O'Brien, for his part, promised that there would be 'no question of special propaganda programmes' being beamed into Northern Ireland.[13]

The British ambassador in Dublin, Arthur Galsworthy, believed that O'Brien would only abandon the idea if 'it could be demonstrated to him that there were overriding legal, financial or technical obstacles'.[14] But it was just such obstacles which were to accumulate in the months which followed: the BBC emphasised the complexity of copyright when an entire channel's output was under consideration; the British also pointed to a constitutional difficulty whereby any station officially broadcasting in Northern Ireland would need Westminster's approval through new legislation; and the Northern Ireland Office was in despair over the proposal because of its fears that it would be misread by unionists whose support was needed for a devolved power-sharing executive.[15]

O'Brien's opposite number in the British government, John Eden, at one point queried the 'public acceptability' of distributing RTÉ programmes in Northern Ireland.[16] O'Brien had drafted a tart reply in which he argued that it was surely 'questionable whether the opposition of people who do not themselves wish to receive a certain service' – which in any case they could ignore or boycott – 'should be allowed to outweigh the known demand of a substantial part of the population'.[17] O'Brien did not send this reply but sought the advice of Gilchrist, thereby ensuring that its sentiments were conveyed to the appropriate authorities. And he did win the support of the FCO for his point. They deplored any consideration of how many Northern viewers wanted RTÉ, because it invited in return the question 'whether we support that section of the population of Northern Ireland that loathes all things Southern' and claims the right to over-rule other sections that either want RTÉ, or as Bradford puts it 'do not object'. The FCO reserved a particular disdain for such arguments which they considered 'a form of censorship.'[18]

Although he may have won that round, his proposal thereafter made little headway, even when – through his adviser Nicholas Simms – he signalled that BBC 1 access to the south could come as a first phase with reciprocal access for RTÉ to follow. Simms confided 'succinctly if cynically' that the real basis of policy was that 'voters in Cork and

The Northern Ireland Office view 'to begin with at least, was that Garret FitzGerald having got good publicity exposure by making a thorough nuisance of himself in Northern Ireland, O'Brien thought it was time he did likewise.'

Thorpe to Blatherwick, 23 May 1973, NAUK, FCO 87/196.

Foreign Secretary Alec Douglas-Home wrote that the British recognised that Conor Cruise O'Brien's initiative was 'in part a publicity stunt', but that did not mean the proposals were 'not worthy of serious consideration'. But the Irish must accept that 'they do not help their case by insisting in negotiating through the newspapers'. David Blatherwick – a future British ambassador to Ireland and then at the political desk in Dublin – thought this analysis too cynical. The embassy was 'fairly sure' that the 'apparent rudeness' in the arrangements had been simply due 'to muddle, inefficiency and carelessness'. The Irish, he added, were 'quite good at this'.

Douglas-Home to Galsworthy, 16 May 1973; Blatherwick to Donnelly, 17 May 1973, NAUK, FCO 87/196.

---

13 Fortnam [Private Secretary to Sir John Eden], Minute of meeting between Eden and Cruise O'Brien, 14 May 1973, *ibid.*
14 Galsworthy to Thorpe, 12 July 1973, *ibid.*
15 Thorpe to Blatherwick , 23 May 1973, *ibid.*
16 Eden to O'Brien, 19 October 1973, *ibid.*
17 Cruise O'Brien draft reply to Eden, October 1973 [not sent but copy given to Galsworthy], *ibid.*
18 White to Drumgoole, 5 November 1973, *ibid.*

Charles Curran [above] the then director-general of the BBC, and himself a Dubliner, had taken advantage of a visit to Dublin by paying a courtesy call on Cruise O'Brien. Galsworthy had heard from O'Brien that Curran 'had expressed himself as being generally in favour of the minister's ideas for an open broadcasting area, providing the technical, legal and financial problems could be satisfactorily resolved.' They had discussed only the legal and financial dimensions and Curran had 'tentatively suggested' that it might work if – based on viewership numbers – the Irish were to pay an agreed proportionate share of artists' fees and performing rights. O'Brien liked this since it 'would prove less expensive than the Irish had originally thought'. Galsworthy – in reporting this to London – noted that it had already been understood that any exploration of the financial, technical and legal dimensions of O'Brien's proposal should be government-to-government and should exclude the broadcasting organisations. A comment in the FCO file, handwritten in the margin of this paragraph, reads: 'How CCO'B reconciles agreement not to discuss with the BBC with little chats with the DG is beyond my comprehension.'

Galsworthy to Thorpe, 12 July 1973, NAUK, FCO 87/196.

Before the Baldonnel summit in September 1973, Heath had suggested that rather than attempt to negotiate the Council of Ireland in front of the Northern Ireland parties, it would be better for the British and Irish governments to agree its responsibilities in advance. Heath's visit to Ireland in September was the first by a serving British prime minister since independence. He was briefed by all three relevant British departments. The Foreign and Commonwealth Office emphasised that the O'Brien proposal would be popular in the Republic, although it was doubtful whether it had 'the full support' of RTÉ since the station was 'unlikely to welcome the competition'. He was advised by his Ministry of Posts and Telegraphs that the competition which would follow between UTV and RTÉ 'did not seem likely to provide any insuperable difficulty'. The Northern Ireland Office advised Heath that the people of Northern Ireland were sated with coverage of terrorism. There was a need to convince them that all was not 'bombs and bullets in their own country'. Should not 'a reasonable balance' be struck between 'the nice and the nasty'?

FCO brief, copy in NIO files, NAUK HO 237/197; MPT brief, NAUK FCO 87/196; NIO brief, September 1973, NAUK, HO 237/197.

Donegal' wanted British television. The reciprocal demand for RTÉ in Northern Ireland was 'more muted'.[19] The British appreciated that Simms was being realistic. By December O'Brien's proposal had galvanised more formidable opposition. This came from the trade unions and especially those unions representing actors and musicians who had members in both Britain and Ireland. Solidarity was invoked to defend the interests of Irish members who felt vulnerable that their work opportunities must suffer if BBC 1 were chosen as the second Irish channel. At a joint meeting in Dublin of Irish, British and international trade unions, such total opposition to O'Brien's proposal was expressed that its prospects of being delivered – irrespective of the level of public demand for it in Ireland – were seriously damaged.[20]

---

19 Thom to Simeon, 22 November 1973, NAUK, *ibid.*
20 Union joint statement from 9 December 1973, 'Open Broadcasting between Northern Ireland and Republic of Ireland', *ibid.*

'the insurmountable obstacles arise from the limitations of geography, the limitations of science, and the limitations of money'

AS O'BRIEN'S TENURE as minister began – indeed as he launched his Open Skies proposal – Hardiman had reminded him that the preference of the Broadcasting Review Committee was that RTÉ should be granted the second Irish channel, with a mandate to broadcast a selection of programmes from BBC, ITV and other sources and some which would be home-produced. Cruise O'Brien had already confided to the British ambassador, Arthur Galsworthy, that while this 'might be accepted in the country districts', it would be unpopular in the urban areas – he cited Cork, Waterford and Wexford – from where he was getting 'a clear message that what people wanted was to be in the same position as the people in Dublin': they wanted direct access to all British channels without having 'to get at them through an RTÉ filter.'[21] RTÉ drew the minister's attention to the Broadcasting Review Committee's observation that the demand might not so much represent an 'expression of conscious selectivity' of these British stations, as simply an insistence on equity with those parts of the Republic where – through an accident of geography – British channels were already accessible. A case of Dublin has it, why not Cork?

Parity with Dublin was a popular demand at meetings throughout the single-channel areas, and, as likely as not, the RTÉ spokesperson attempting to counter it came from Dublin and enjoyed the very choice which was so coveted by those attending these public debates. But it seems probable that the RTÉ case, as expounded by Louis McRedmond, would have brought some clarity as to what the real choices were. He told a meeting at Westport in County Mayo in August 1975 that the 'hard and brutal fact' was that Mayo could not have

> what we have in Dublin. RTÉ can't give it to you. The Minister can't give it to you. You can't get it for yourselves. It's not that anyone is trying to deprive you of what you want. The obstacles, the insurmountable obstacles, arise from the limitations of geography, the limitations of science, and the limitations of money.

He added that a new network was being constructed for a second channel which could either provide one of the British stations or a second RTÉ service. These were 'the options, the real possibilities', which the government was outlining. 'In these circumstances, in the

Hugh Gibbons Fianna Fáil TD for Roscommon-Leitrim told the Dáil in November 1975 that 'one of the most presumptuous arguments' made for BBC 1 by people in Limerick, Cork and Galway was that because people in his constituency had three channels, 'two of which we were not paying for', they should also receive British television at the taxpayers' expense. But such areas had centres of higher education, hospitals and railway services. Were the people in his area of Carrick-on-Shannon, Boyle and Drumshanbo, 'to demand from the government that we should have all those facilities or amenities just because the people of Galway and Cork and Limerick have them, we would be laughed out of existence and considered most unreasonable.' He also surmised that the whole issue of access to unavailable channels might, in time, solve itself. 'The years may prove that this cannot be prevented by virtue of the fact that so many more signals will be made available by satellite, and so on.'

Dáil Debates, vol. 285, cols.1034-35, 6 November 1975.

---

21   Note of meeting with Cruise O'Brien , Galsworthy to FCO, 12 July 1973, *ibid.*

Louis McRedmond dealt in 'hard and brutal' facts: the limitations of geography, science and money.

either-or situation of two options only, RTÉ says that the wiser choice is a second national channel.'[22]

Meanwhile Jack White was discussing how RTÉ might use the second channel. It should neither be so specialist in its programming that it would cover only the interests of cultural minorities: nor should it be a pop channel. The goal would be that at any time during peak hours, at least one programme of wide popular interest should be available. He added that programming in Irish would be 'more acceptable to the monolingual segment of the audience' if an alternative programme was available on the other RTÉ channel. He also acknowedged that one of the major demands of the single-channel audience was 'for access to British sport, in particular to top-grade soccer.' He expected a 'patient and complex negotiation' to secure the Irish rights, believing that 'a high price' might have to be paid. Nevertheless it was accepted that a second RTÉ channel 'would fail to satisfy its audience if it did not come up with the best available sports programming'.[23]

RTÉ's case turned on maximising complementary scheduling with all Irish viewers in mind. Were the second Irish channel simply plugged in to BBC1, complementarity would be much more difficult to achieve since RTÉ would be without any influence in shaping that channel. RTÉ schedulers were already aware of the challenge of maintaining a loyal and significant audience share while in competition in the multi-channel areas.

RTÉ needed as much flexibility as possible to schedule smartly. Many politicians had to be educated on this point. If Ireland had been allocated two television wavelengths, why should one broadcaster want both? It had not occurred to them that complementary scheduling by one overarching editorial team was more likely to give viewers a balanced service than two competitive channels which would only 'result in a fragmentation of scarce resources' and would tend to 'a Dutch-auction in programme standards'.[24] The point is most easily elucidated through sports coverage. How could RTÉ justify dedicating a channel to a major sports event like the Olympic Games or World Cups in rugby or soccer if it did not have RTÉ 1 to provide general programmes for those with little interest in sport. With two channels, it could justify comprehensive sports coverage to those most interested while offering an alternative to general viewers. RTÉ had to construct a strategic campaign to win the battle for public opinion – and it was eventually decided in just this arena, the government's final decision being based on an opinion poll which showed a two-to-one ratio in favour of RTÉ.

22 Verbatim transcription of McRedmond address, 27 August 1975 at Westport, Co. Mayo, published *The Kerryman*, 22 October 1978.
23 Jack White, memorandum on second channel, n.d. (c.April 1973), RTÉWA.
24 *ibid.*

13

what had been seen as a charter for interference was rendered into a safeguard

TOM HARDIMAN was the first director-general to have been promoted from within RTÉ. His seven-year term included some of the most turbulent episodes in the state's history, many of them presenting formidable challenges to the station and its editor-in-chief. When he first took up office, he had spoken of balance in broadcasting 'as something more than a measurement of the arguments for and against' on any particular issue. Rather, it should be 'a deliberate attempt to go beyond the presentation of two rehearsed sides' in pursuit of a comprehensive understanding which would be 'as near the truth as possible.' The essential point was that RTÉ, being a monopoly national broadcaster, had 'no editorial policy, no editorial opinion on current affairs'. Over a period of time it was committed to maintaining a balance between the various conflicting points of view on any topic.[1]

When he outlined this position in February 1969, Hardiman was not to know just how difficult this would prove in the context of the next six years. Hardiman's term as director-general would be fraught with unforeseen challenges – many of them arising from the fact that his period as director-general coincided with the worst of the Northern troubles. The first death was more than fifteen months away when he became director-general: before he left seven years later, no fewer than 1,239 had been killed.[2] He was also on record as insisting that a broadcasting service could not be impartial on all matters: it would not be 'impartial about crime or racial prejudice or religious intolerance'.[3] When he first made this point in early 1969, it seemed straightforward enough but as the Northern Troubles worsened, it would become more problematical: some saw the face on the television news as that of a major political leader, others saw a

Joe Murray, then head of agricultural programmes, was asked in 1971 for his most surprising moment in the first ten years of reporting agriculture. He recalled an interview in the west of Ireland with the proprietor of a small farm and a large household.

RTÉ: How many acres have you altogether?
Farmer: Twenty-six.
RTÉ: And how many in the family?
Farmer: I'm the father of fourteen children.
RTÉ: And what's your main problem here?
Farmer: Low fertility. There's low fertility in this area.

RTÉ Guide, 31 December 1971

---

1 *Irish Times*, 17 February 1969.
2 Tabulated from Malcolm Sutton, *An Index of Deaths from the Conflict in Ireland: 1969-1993* (Belfast, 1994).
3 *Irish Times*, 17 February 1969.

History is indebted to Liam Cosgrave, the incoming Taoiseach in 1973, for obliging the sports department in RTÉ to reveal its allocation of resources to different sports. Shortly after forming his government, Cosgrave wrote to his minister with broadcasting responsibilities, Conor Cruise O'Brien, complaining about the time devoted to horse-racing. It had been brought to his attention – he regularly attended race meetings – 'that football, golf, tennis and virtually every other sport' enjoyed far better coverage. He did not specify any football code. Cosgrave felt inclined to agree with the criticism and suggested to O'Brien that he make the 'appropriate approaches'. O'Brien replied that he had asked Tom Hardiman 'to consider the matter'. Hardiman's reply to O'Brien claimed that racing received 'more coverage than combined Gaelic games, golf and tennis.' There were 18 live outside broadcasts for Irish racing and another 15 such broadcasts of special interest to Irish viewers. This coverage was greater than the combined coverage of Gaelic football and hurling (eight events), golf (ten days) and tennis (six days). The balance favoured racing 'to a considerable extent' and moreover the sports department must take into account public reaction to any 'over-emphasis of one sport to the exclusion of others'.

Correspondence July 1973, in 'Broadcasting: Improvement of, and representations re, programmes', NAI DT/2009/135/9.

T.P.Hardiman speaking at his retirement presentation in December 1975. He had been succeeded as director-general by O.J.Maloney in April of that year.

religious bigot; for some, the hunger strikers were political prisoners, for others the actions which had led to their convictions were criminal.

Hardiman was punctilious concerning the broadcasting acts and expanded RTÉ's independence by insisting that any exercise of the government's reserved powers to intervene should be done in public. Todd Andrews, who worked alongside him in Hardiman's first years in the job, reckoned him 'fearless in the expression of his opinions and quite immune to outside pressures from the politicians or the special interest lobbies'. But he faulted him for his capacity to be 'garrulous to a point which often led to overstating his case'. Andrews believed that Hardiman had all the best qualities of a public servant while also being alert to the fact that RTÉ could not be thought of as yet another semi-state body, this because of its unique role as an important media player.[4]

Hardiman was host – not guest – when a new minister lunched with him. He dismissed all blandishments of 'black lists' from government or civil service. And he well appreciated how the public's expectation of an independent television service could be relied upon to stay the hand of those politicians who wished to interfere but who were shy of the publicity and opprobrium of doing so in public through the Broadcasting Act. Thus what had been seen by some as a charter for interference in the original legislation was rendered into a safeguard.

4   Andrews, *Man of No Property*, 281.

George Melly, the jazz singer and critic – the impact of whose own exotic suits and ties was lost on black and white television, could complain in 1969 about the 'self-induced hysteria' of media controllers when talking of the then imminent prospect of colour television. Melly even suggested that there might be a 'small resistance movement of middle-class intellectuals, the children of those who in the early fifties wouldn't have the telly at all' and who would equate black and white 'with high seriousness.'[1] At this same time at a meeting of the RTÉ Authority, Tom Hardiman reviewed colour development throughout European television and informed the Authority that RTÉ's major expenditure would not be in the transmission system but in the conversion of programme production facilities. The current equipment – in use since 1961 – would 'shortly be reaching the end of its economic life' and would be due for replacement in any event. The television industry was switching to colour and it was even 'becoming increasingly difficult to find satisfactory monochrome replacement equipment'. Besides, the cost of colour did 'not greatly exceed' monochrome. The transition would take three to four years.[2] All this reads now like prudent strategic planning. At the time it was the stuff of conspiracy theories, with a new left-wing staff magazine Feedback arguing that staff might be puzzled 'at the seemingly Houdini-style ability of RTÉ to venture into colour in the middle of a financial crisis'.

The Feedback writer believed it would be 'foolish to complain' were it the case that the station was being 'run by financial wizards. Let's hope we also have engineering elfs and managerial magicians with sufficient pride and expertise to do colour at its best', and asked: 'is this a vain hope?' Feedback added that one matter seemed 'for real': that colour television could well prove to be 'the obituary notice of quality in Irish broadcasting'.[3] That the Feedback group should have chosen to pick a fight on this agenda marks them off as naive, even Luddite. History was against them. Hardiman knew that colour was not an optional choice: without it, RTÉ would lose its market share in multi-channel areas and would find it impossible, in due course, to even purchase monochrome equipment. And on the positive side, he was all too aware of the transformation which colour would bring to all television but especially in sports broadcasting and in arts, food and natural history programmes.

1 Briggs, Competition, 862-63.
2 RTÉ Authority, minutes, 10 October 1969 and Hardiman memo, 3 October 1969, RTÉWA.
3 Anon. 'Colour Bar in RTÉ', Feedback [RTÉ workers magazine], vol.1, no.1, August 1970.

Horgan writes that Hardiman 'had to encourage the growth of innovative and independent broadcasting, while at the same time restraining – without crushing – the exuberance (and from time to time the exaggerated sense of self-importance) of an entirely new generation of broadcasters'. And he did this at a time when these broadcasters were attracting 'a degree of intrusive political attention that imperiled the independence in public service broadcasting' which Hardiman was attempting to create and protect. Horgan concludes that some of his qualities 'became more apparent to his critics in the years after he had left the station.'[5]

5   Horgan, Broadcasting and Public Life, 139.

RTÉ broadcasters and journalists outside Dáil Éireann, 22 January 1986, demonstrating against section 31 of the Broadcasting Act. Picketing (left to right) are: Cathal Mac Coille, Fintan Drury, Pádhraic Ó Ciardha, Charlie Bird, Jim Dougal, Seán Duignan and Seán O'Rourke. Among the placards: 'Section 31 is bad for broadcasting: Let the people hear'. This demonstration was organised by the Broadcasting Branch of the NUJ.

On 1 October 1971, Gerard Collins as minister with responsibility for broadcasting directed RTÉ, under Section 31 of the Broadcasting Authority Act, 1960, to refrain from broadcasting 'any matter that could be calculated to promote the aims or activities of any organisation which engages in, promotes, encourages or advocates the attaining of any particular objective by violent means.'[1] This wording became controversial: Wesley Boyd believed it 'ham-fisted'[2] but despite repeated requests the government declined to clarify its terms, claiming that its meaning was clear. Section 31 divided the broadcasters: most opposed it simply on grounds of free speech; some believed it amounted to a vote of no confidence in their own editorial judgement, among them Kevin Myers, who described it as 'intolerable oppression'.[3] Some others supported it as a plausible response by the government given the perceived threat and agenda of Sinn Féin and the IRA. Joe Mulholland believed that 'there possibly was a need for Section 31 at a particular time'. He had always had 'divided views' on it: there was the view that allowing 'people who kill and maim the freedom of the airwaves' was wrong but there was also the consideration that 'these people have, whether we like it or not, a certain amount of support, particularly in Northern Ireland, and you feel that in the interests of true reporting and objectivity their voice should be heard at least on occasion.... So one is torn between one's revulsion as an Irishman at what is done and one's profession as a journalist.'

But Mulholland was also critical of the wording, calling it, in 1990, 'far too blunt an instrument'.[4] Just over a decade later he reckoned that news and current affairs programmes had 'an immense contribution' to make to the peace process and needed section 31 gone.[5] When it was rescinded by Michael D. Higgins, the post Section 31 coverage was debated by the RTÉ Authority. William Attley suggested that 'RTÉ had never come to terms with the fact that Sinn Féin understood RTÉ's approach better than RTÉ understood it'. He did not accept that there was any pro-Sinn Féin conspiracy in RTÉ but any credence it had gained was attributable to the fact that the station 'had not been professional enough to know and understand what Sinn Féin's propaganda approach was'.[6]

1   The government following cabinet discussion issued the above statement on 1 October 1971.
2   Tom Manning and Seán Duignan,
4   'Forty Years of News', RTÉ 1, 19 December 2002.
3   ibid.
5   'Forty Years of News', RTÉ 1, 19 December 2002.
6   RTÉ Authority, minutes, 27 June 1997.

the history of the organisation was 'one of tumult'; the current problem was 'one of depression'

OLIVER MALONEY as incoming director-general, told all staff in April 1975 that he had 'no interest' in being the chief executive of 'a subdued, enfeebled and uncompetitive organisation'. If it was not possible to have harmony in RTÉ, they could at least have collaboration. Courage would be needed 'to face up to the unpleasant decisions as well as the pleasant ones.' Maloney – given that he would be director-general for only three years – was nothing if not ambitious concerning his reform agenda. He first detailed his plans to the Eighth Authority, chaired by Sheila Conroy at their first business meeting held over a lengthy weekend in County Wicklow in September 1976. He suggested that too many producers lacked a sense of accountability, especially since they could determine the 'content, style, accuracy and character' of their programmes. He complained that there had been a gradual drift in the direction of licence. If programme-makers were 'to get a free hand', they had to be responsive to the views of those who ultimately carried 'the responsibility for what *they* do'.

Maloney believed that there was inadequate leadership from the controllers, that money was being wasted and that 'small groups of strategically placed staff exercised inordinate influence'. He then won the Authority's agreement for a reform agenda.[6] It would be for a limited period and would mean assuming more direct control of programmes. The most significant announcement was that *7 Days* was to end. Control of current affairs was transferred to Dick Hill. Horgan is probably fair in his assumption that the previous Authority – chaired by Dónal O Móráin – 'might not have been as persuadable' to support this programme.[7] Tom O'Dea, in his *Irish Press* column, accused Maloney of 'springing the trap door on everyone but the Authority'.[8] Presently, Maloney was complaining to the Authority that he had been the subject of 'extremely damaging' press comment. He believed this to be orchestrated from within RTÉ and he was especially critical of O'Dea – known for his 'inside track' to key producers – and who now published a spate of columns hostile to Maloney:[9] staff were 'going about the compound looking stunned, keeping silent counsel, counting the minutes from nine to five'.[10]

Oliver J Maloney, director-general, 1975-78. As incoming director-general in April 1975, Maloney addressed the staff. RTÉ, he advised them, was not akin to a co-operative society. Rather, it was a place where there was 'competition and conflict' over access to air time and resources. And he would 'not have it otherwise, were I God, rather than being merely director-general.'

6 Maloney, memo for RTÉ Authority, September 1976.
7 Horgan, *Broadcasting and Public Life*, 148.
8 *ibid*, 18 September 1976.
9 See Tom O'Dea, television column each Saturday, *Irish Press*, August to December 1976, *passim*.
10 *Irish Press*, 11 September 1976.

The DG, the minister and the chairman, January 1976. (Left to right): Oliver Maloney, who was director-general, 1975-78; Conor Cruise O'Brien, who applied to be DG in 1968 and was not called for interview; and Dónal O Móráin, who before the station opened had offered to provide a television service without cost to the government, as one wag put it: 'Not only Gaelic but free as well!'

Some months after he had announced his sweeping changes, Maloney told the Authority that he had 'little doubt' that much of the subsequent press comment formed part of a systematic campaign. It had 'unsettled some of the staff to a considerable extent'. This was a reality which had to be faced. RTÉ had never been 'a very settled organisation', but, in recent months, the public impression had been given that it was 'in a state of disorder and disarray'.[11] Maloney then challenged O'Dea in the columns of the *Irish Press*. He advised him to canvass the views of 'the vast silent majority' of RTÉ staff who were 'hard-working, totally dedicated, perceptive, and consequently fed up with so much public attention being paid to that tiny minority of their colleagues who trade gossip with the newspapers'. Maloney had read of O'Dea's 'vivid tale of intrigue, plots and counter-plots, purges and axing' with 'wry amusement' and suggested that O'Dea would be 'uncomfortable to be labelled as the mouthpiece of the obscurantists'. RTÉ current affairs staff were 'not political eunuchs; neither were members of the RTÉ Authority'.[12] What Maloney termed a disaffected section of the staff was 'leaking information in a form best calculated to cause further confusion and unease'. All this should be put in the context of the previous decade: the history of the organisation was 'one of tumult'; the current problem was 'one of depression'.[13]

---

11 Maloney, Keynote paper for Authority meeting of 4-5 February 1977, RTÉWA.
12 Oliver J. Maloney, 'RTÉ: view from the man at the top', *Irish Press*, 10 January 1977.
13 Maloney, Keynote paper for Authority meeting of 4-5 February 1977, RTÉWA.

In his book, *Moral Monopoly: The Catholic Church in Modern Irish Society*, published in 1987, sociologist Tom Inglis (left) suggested that television had 'changed the face of Catholic Ireland because the practice and discourse of imported programmes was at variance with traditional Catholic principles'. Television had broken through 'the iron cage of censorship' and prompted a demand 'for a modern western lifestyle'. Moreover the church now found itself to be no longer 'above public criticism'. It was the media, and in particular television, which had 'brought an end to the long nineteenth century of Irish Catholicism'. It had introduced 'a constant advocacy for an individualist, consumerist, sexualised, urban lifestyle that broke the unquestioning "respect for the cloth", and has forced the Church into giving a public account off itself'.

Tom Inglis, *Moral Monopoly: The Catholic Church in Modern Irish Society* (Dublin, 1987, first edition), pp.91-94.

At the Authority's initial meeting, some few months before, Maloney had claimed that good management of a broadcasting station, if it was to be more than 'demoralising retrospective criticism', had to operate by a very delicate process of 'nudging and encouraging people rather than by diktat.'[14] But diktat would be how very many of those at the receiving end of Maloney's changes would characterise his approach. Some of them first heard of demotions, programme terminations and other major policy changes through the media.

---

14 Maloney, memo for RTÉ Authority, September 1976.

Michael Heney (left) undertook an investigation for *The Politics Programme* in 1978 into the illegal selling overseas of Irish Hospitals Sweepstakes tickets. 'We had the lists; we had the names; we had the addresses; we had the places; we had the events; we had the smuggling; we had the pay-backs, the kick-backs, the money paid to the hauliers; we had chapter and verse.' But the programme was postponed, then shelved after legal threats from the Hospitals Trust. John Horgan believed that the shelving of the Hospitals Sweepstakes programme represented 'a major failure of nerve at senior levels within the organisation.' Part of it was broadcast in a *Today Tonight Special* in 1992, by which time the Sweep has closed for five years.

Marie Coleman, *The Irish Sweep: A History of the Irish Hospitals Sweepstake: 1930-87* (Dublin, 2009), pp.182-83; Horgan, *Broadcasting and Public Life*, 153.

Horgan concludes that Maloney had come into the director-general's office with much goodwill 'and on a platform designed to reassure producers and reporters about his commitment to courageous and innovative programming', but his departure was now 'on a more subdued note'. His short time in charge served to underline 'the extreme difficulty' of introducing change in any 'large, highly talented and often quarrelsome organisation, especially when some of those who had been initially in favour of change found themselves at the receiving end of particular changes which were not to their liking'.[15]

he would favour 'building a moat around the news division'

ANOTHER PART OF Maloney's reform targets was to challenge what was seen as the failure of the newsroom to embrace television production values. There had been numerous attempts at reform, including an early self-assessment report from within the newsroom. Its verdict of shaggy jackets and poor diction combined with 'a lack of discipline, rehearsal and pride', had not proved popular.[16] In September 1976, Maloney set up a News Study Group to examine resources and output. The newsroom again proved defensive and, through the NUJ, refused the study group permission to have an observer sit in and assess working practices. To Sheila Conroy – as the incoming Authority chair and a trade unionist – this was 'frightening'. In talking to the Authority, Maloney was forthright about what he perceived as the newsroom's limitations. He had points to make 'which he didn't want to put on paper'. That might 'sound defeatist, but it was a view born of experience'. Manifestly, he believed anything on paper would find its way into Tom O'Dea's next *Irish Press* column. Maloney told the Authority that he would favour 'building a moat around the news division'; he also suggested that analysis and comment on current affairs should be concentrated in other programmes. There was a need to develop talent and he instanced Olivia O'Leary's emergence from a news reporting background as a current affairs presenter on television.[17]

There was a feeling that News had never quite integrated with the rest of the organisation. The Authority believed that in a twenty-minute bulletin, there should be concentration on 'style, presentation and authority'. It

Maloney instanced Olivia O'Leary as an example of how broadcasting talent could be developed: he approved of her career path from the Belfast newsroom, to radio's *This Week* to anchoring *The Politics Programme* on television.

---

15 Horgan, *Broadcasting and Public Life*, 153.
16 See above, pp.40-41.
17 RTÉ Authority, minutes, 1 April 1977.

had a virtually guaranteed audience and 'should be a showpiece for RTÉ'. Maloney confided that the 'more he investigated the area, the greater did it appear to be a jungle'. The problems in the News area were 'of a major kind' because of deeply embedded work practices, themselves derived from print journalism. Moreover, there was 'a lame ducks problem'. Maloney was satisfied with Wesley Boyd's editorial competence as Head of News but he believed that Boyd had 'inherited an intractable and very difficult situation'. There was still too much complacency in the newsroom: any additional resources should be contingent upon 'quality output and sustained excellence. He thought it important that the Head of News be brought to a realisation of the problem'.[18]

Maloney believed that Wesley Boyd (above) as Head of News had inherited 'an intractable and very difficult situation'.

why was it all right for a black woman to appear naked on Irish TV but not an Irish woman?

THE TAOISEACH'S postbag had no shortage of advice: *The Spike* was 'filth and dirt'; it was insulting. RTÉ's new series by Patrick Gilligan was set in a co-educational, post-primary school in a working-class area of Dublin. 'How do you allow RTÉ to drag our lovely country down to the level of the *News of the World*?' asked a mother of six. A nun pleaded with the Taoiseach to ensure that the programme would not be shown abroad: 'Whatever our defects – and we certainly have them – we are not as bad as this.'[19] Controversy followed the series. When *The Spike* transmitted a nude scene, there followed a national controversy. A young woman in the series who was lacking in confidence was encouraged to pose for the art students in the life class. This made tabloid headlines when the founder of the League of Decency, J.B.Murray, suffered a heart attack, which his family attributed to the stress he was caused by watching this episode. 'His wife told the papers that the family had tried to stop him watching it, but he insisted on doing so. He got very worked up at the nude scene and was phoning the newspapers to complain when he came to grief over the "filthy play".'[20]

The series quickly became a test case for the 'Clean up TV' campaigners. There were calls for the rest of the series to be deferred,

18 *ibid.*, 6 May 1977.
19 NAI DT/2009/135/9.
20 Sheehan, *Irish Television Drama*, 169.

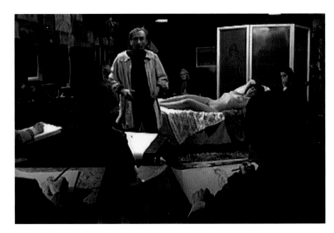

or dropped altogether. Muiris Mac Conghail – by now controller of programmes, having returned from his stint as press secretary to the Fine Gael-Labour coalition – wrote to Maloney advising against any deferment of the rest of the series. Such a move 'would have serious implications for future drama policy': it would be read as a victory for those critics who were 'provoked by prudish, or, indeed, illiberal and censorious considerations'. Much of the criticism of the series so far, Mac Conghail allowed, was 'well-founded' and had been expressed sensibly; but there was also 'a high "anti-porn" and slightly hysterical note' in the public controversy. Furthermore, there was a 'considerable class reaction to the series'. His advice to the director-general was to see the series through, then to review 'in a dignified and considered' manner the 'very many flaws which infest *The Spike*'. If taken off, he believed there would be 'little prospect of RTÉ ever undertaking a project like it again'.

This memorandum became public after Maloney had unilaterally decided to discontinue the series. The director-general could have been under no illusions about the depth of feeling of the programme's critics. The minister with responsibility for broadcasting, Padraig Faulkner, had telephoned him to complain and had also forwarded 'for appropriate consideration' the letters of complaint which had been received. In addition, an assistant secretary in his department had telephoned Maloney asserting that the series had been criticised for 'its unfair portrayal of the vocational education system, its unreality, moral tone, etc. and raised the question whether the remaining episodes should be dropped.' The director-general replied that he had already decided not to broadcast one particular episode but one other would be transmitted before the Authority next met when the future of the series would be discussed. However he then ignored Mac Conghail's advice and on 2 March deferred all remaining episodes. The minister told the Taoiseach that the department 'learned of this decision from reports in the newspapers'.[21]

There were widely varying responses to this outcome: television producers believed it could only lead 'to excessive self-censorship';[22] Murray – by now happily recovering from his coronary event – received news of the programme's demise 'with jubilation'; and actor Jim Fitzgerald, explaining a cut on his forehead, said that 'he had been thumped by a fat elderly lady' who, on learning that he was in *The Spike*, had assaulted him.[23] One week later, Lynch as guest speaker at the Jacobs Television Awards, sided with the director-general, expressing his approval of the decision taken.[24]

As drama, *The Spike* was criticised, Sheehan complaining of 'the clumsiness' of its treatment of the issues, 'the superficiality of the characterisation and the immaturity of the underlying point of view.' The legacy of the debacle which followed its axing was difficult to assess. The decision might have reinforced 'nervousness and timidity' and may have damaged efforts 'to open up drama to the terrain of dealing with the controversial growing points of contemporary society'. Maloney should perhaps have listened to his controller. Mac Conghail was aware of the *The Spike*'s failings, but he sensed there would be a higher cost in cancelling it. As he would say later, RTÉ made two mistakes with *The Spike*: the first was putting it on and the second was taking it off.[25]

Muiris Mac Conghail, controller of programmes, thought *The Spike* had many faults and some of the criticism was 'well-founded'. But there was also 'a high "anti-porn" and slightly hysterical note' in the public controversy.

21 Faulkner to Lynch, 31 March 1978, NAI, DT/2009/135/9.
22 *Irish Times*, 4 March 1978.
23 'RTÉ split as "Spike" is dropped', *Irish Times*, 3 March 1978.
24 Lynch, speech at Jacobs Television Awards, 11 March 1978, NAI, DT/2009/135/9.
25 Sheehan, *Irish Television Drama*, 162-77.

Noel O Briain, the producer of *The Spike*, asked: 'Why was it all right for an American or a black woman to appear naked on Irish television screens but not an Irish woman?' He believed the series was abandoned in mid-run because of its view of the educational system, rather than for any other reason.

Irish Times, 25 February 1978.

The message of the Pope was carried worldwide 'due to the miracle of the Irish television service'

George Waters, director-general, 1978-85; believed his biggest challenge was the visit of Pope John Paul II, 1979.

IF TOM HARDIMAN and Oliver Maloney had done much to secure the second television channel for RTÉ, it fell to George Waters as director-general to deliver it. Waters came from a single channel area himself and had considerable sympathy for viewers there. He believed that their attitudes were 'highly influenced' by programmes that irritated them most, rather than by those they liked best. He had 'no doubt' that in a single channel area each viewer would find one programme each night irritating 'to some extent' and what such viewers wanted was to press 'another button'. He did not really believe it was British television they wanted: 'what they required was choice'.[26] And it was during his tenure as director-general that the second station was launched, providing more hours of programming and wider choice for the viewers. Of course, the complaints department did not close but if the intention was to satisfy more of the people much of the time, then it could be argued that RTÉ – once the second channel was providing some choice – was consolidating in its second decade of operations what the pioneering generation had established in its first.

That two of the first five directors-general had been engineers underlines the central contribution which had been made by that department in this achievement. It was also true that the work of RTÉ

26 John Walsh, interview with George Waters, *RTÉ Guide*, 14 April 1978.

Vatican Radio was impressed by the RTÉ coverage. It had 'never found such efficient organisation for an event of this magnitude.'

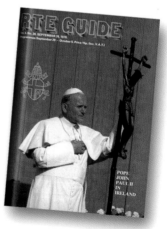

There has been an onus on RTÉ throughout its existence to accommodate itself to new technology and how it might impact on broadcasting. George Waters was director-general when the first small home computer, the ZX-81 or equivalent, was introduced by Clive Sinclair. Giving the opening address to the Educational Broadcasting Seminar in Dublin in November 1983, he told delegates that they would all be familiar with the new concept, the so-called 'Information Age'.

> Our children with frightening dexterity can solve mathematical problems without recourse to slide rule or log table. The computer keyboard has become the new attraction for the young – and, indeed, the not so young. Although the television set in the corner remains the centre of interest, it is not always for its purely entertainment value. Coupled to a Sinclair ZX-81 or equivalent it is now assisting many students in the pursuit of knowledge. I sometimes wonder if the interest is of a transitory nature and when the craze wears off we will see a return to the pen and pencil. I am reminded of the fate of the once popular spinning top or the marbles that we used to play on the footpaths.

engineers could go largely unacknowledged by the general public. By 1979 viewers took for granted that they would have access through RTÉ to Pope John Paul II's pastoral visit to Ireland. The television coverage won wide acclaim. Vatican Radio announced from Rome that if 'the voice, the image and the message of the Pope were carried everywhere in the world at a high technical level, this is due to the miracle operated by the Irish television service'.[27]

Shortly after Waters retired and when Vincent Finn had assumed the leadership of the station, television's twenty-fifth birthday prompted some retrospective evaluations. Among the contributors was historian Joe Lee. He concluded that few other Irish institutions, public or private, had 'so consistently to endure critical comment'. No doubt RTÉ could have done better in some respects but 'the acid comparison' had to be with the general level of national performance, not with 'some abstract ideal'. Allowing that in the Irish context this was an undemanding test, he still believed that RTÉ rated 'well above average'. He also reckoned that it was the 'relative tranquillity of relations' with the government of the day that was 'historically important, not the occasional storms in teacups', adding that RTÉ-government relations had been, by international standards, 'remarkably untroubled'.[28]

Outside broadcast units from neighbouring countries augmented RTÉ's own resources to cover the Papal visit, September 1979.

---

27 *Irish Broadcasting Review*, no.7 Spring, 1980, 51.
28 Joe Lee, *RTÉ Guide*, 2 January 1987.

After seven years presenting *Newsbeat*, it was decided to give Frank Hall a new programme more focused on his satirical gifts as an observer of the Irish scene. In June 1971 he told the *RTÉ Guide* that they were 'tentatively calling the programme *Hall's Pictorial Weekly, Incorporating the Provincial Vindicator* – and if you look at the mastheads of some provincial papers you'll find mastheads much more imposing than that.'

Eamon Morrissey played many characters in *Hall's Pictorial Weekly*. In 1977, he won a Jacobs Television Award for his portrayal of the then Taoiseach, Liam Cosgrave, as the Minister for Hardship. The show was set in a mythical town, Ballymagash. It divided local councillors throughout Ireland: some laughed, but many more passed resolutions complaining that it belittled their efforts.

management 'nervous enough', but they 'never intervened'

HELENA SHEEHAN believed that *Hall's Pictorial Weekly* in the 1970s 'went very close to the bone and it was to RTÉ's credit that it had sustained such a sharp production for so long'. One of its producers, Peter McEvoy, believed that RTÉ management was 'nervous enough' about what they were doing, 'but they never intervened and the programme always proceeded with a free hand.' There was also the consideration that were the politicians to complain, 'they would have placed themselves in a ridiculous situation, if it ever came to libel suits, in the act of identifying themselves with ludicrous fictional characters.'[29] Some critics believed that Hall 'only got away with it and rose to such glorious heights because to a great extent he was lampooning the worst aspects of parochial life: the rural councils with Ballymagash, the tacky-glam pubs with the Comanchero Bar, Grill and Art Gallery, provincial snobbery with the Cork Chapter of Mothers of Seven' and other such targets. After its demise there was a 'paucity of social and political satire' on RTÉ.[30]

Sheehan reckoned that Hall's programme was 'at its strongest' during the Fine Gael-Labour Coalition government from 1973 to 1977. So 'sharp and constant' was its satirical send up of the Coalition ministers, that it may have eroded their credibility when they next faced

---

29 Sheehan, *Irish Television Drama*, 181.
30 Michael Murphy, 'Funny Business', *In Dublin*, 6 February 1986, 16-17.

the electorate.[31] Historian John A. Murphy believed this to be so: he considered it to be 'a very politically damaging programme which arguably contributed to the fall of that government in the election of 1977.'[32] And from within that government's ranks, the Fine Gael chief whip, John Kelly TD, would later claim that 'week in and week out' they endured the lampooning from *Hall's Pictorial Weekly*. 'We endured; and enjoyed it.' He had often gone home from the Dáil and sat back and enjoyed 'the depictions of Deputy Liam Cosgrave and the Cruiser. I was able to laugh at my

colleagues and once or twice at myself.' But Kelly believed that Fianna Fáil – once back in power – were more thin-skinned. 'Once there was any talk about Judas Mac Sleeveen, that was the end of *Hall's Pictorial Weekly*. One might as easily get me to believe that the earth is flat as that the demise of that programme had no political content in its motivation.'[33]

far beyond the dreams of 1962

WHEN THE SECOND television channel was finally launched, on 2 November 1978, RTÉ decided that the Cork Opera House should be the venue. Cork had led the charge for total access to British channels. The Cork Multi-Channel lobby group had had one

Frank Hall found that as he worked on next week's script, his producer John Condon (above, directing *Hall's Pictorial Weekly*), had 'an uncanny knack of ringing up' to inquire about progress and 'would often spark off some idea or encourage me in something I wasn't sure of'.

31 Sheehan, *Irish Television Drama*, 180.
32 Seanad Debates, vol. 126, col. 725, 18 July 1990.
33 Dáil Debates, vol. 322, col. 2183, 26 June, 1980.

Taoiseach Jack Lynch at the opening of RTÉ 2 at the Cork Opera House, 2 November 1978. As a local TD, the demands of the Cork Multi-Channel lobby had presented him with challenges. Seated behind him, left to right, are: George Waters, RTÉ director-general, Brian Sloane, Lord Mayor of Cork, Sheila Conroy, chair of the Authority, and Padraig Faulkner, Minister for Posts and Telegraphs.

The Chieftains also performed at the opening concert. From left to right: Kevin Conneff on bodhrán, Michael Tubridy on flute, Seán Potts on tin whistle, Paddy Moloney on uilleann pipes, Seán Keane on fiddle, Martin Fay on fiddle and Derek Bell on harp.

Irish Ballet Company principals Kathleen McInerney and Richard Collins dance the *pas de deux* from *The Sleeping Princess*. They are accompanied by a corps from the Cork Ballet Company. This was a popular inclusion as Cork was justly proud of being the leading Irish centre for ballet.

fundamental demand: they wanted the same choice of stations as Dublin viewers enjoyed. And – as the Taoiseach Jack Lynch's postbag confirms – they expected support for this campaign from their local TDs. When Lynch pointed out to a correspondent that there were 'legal, financial and technical problems' involved, he was reminded of some reference he had made to the subject in his final election rally in Cork before the 1977 general election. His correspondent asked: 'Is it not time to get things straightened out a bit, and show that you are a true Corkman and will keep the promise you made to your electors that night. Jack, remember the cheer they gave you then just about thirty seconds before you finished your speech. Looking forward to hearing from you.'[34]

Conradh na Gaeilge declined the invitation to the opening of RTÉ 2. But fifteen members did picket the Opera House protesting about the content of the new service.

Jack White – who had been in at the beginning of television both as programme-maker and senior manager – did not underestimate the challenge facing the Controller of RTÉ 2, who 'had to create a new channel out of a production plant already designed to deliver at top pressure to meet the needs of RTÉ 1.' More broadcasting hours revived 'worries about cultural domination'; it re-created 'many ambitions in the field of home production' and thus added an extra spur for more

34 John G. O'Reilly to Jack Lynch, 13 December 1977, NAI DT/ 2009/135/322

John McColgan, producer of the RTÉ 2 launch, with vision mixer Una Crowley.

Mike Murphy, presenter of the launch, with guest Terry Wogan.

resources. It reminded RTÉ executives 'that we have unsolved problems on our plate – among them our service to Irish speakers, our service to education, and our service to minorities overall.' White reckoned that the initial two-channel schedule was 'a substantial achievement and far beyond the dreams of 1962.' He believed that, within months, RTÉ would be 'offering a genuine alternative to the former single channel viewers'. At the same time it was evident that RTÉ was still in the early stages of two-channel planning.[35]

It took much experimentation and audience research before the relationship between the two channels settled. Over the years that followed, the second channel underwent a variety of rebrandings and relaunches. All this was happening at a time when the television industry itself was being churned by new technology, the digital revolution and the increasing competition from satellite, cable and subscription channels. These were turbulent waters for RTÉ management to negotiate. And there were many parties hoping they would fail to maintain their substantial hold on the loyalty of the Irish audience. That they did so is no indication that this was inevitable. But the credit must go not only to RTÉ managers and broadcasters. There is also abundant evidence over the half-century of its existence that the viewers exercised their own strong preference for home-produced programmes.

Dick Hill, RTÉ 2's controller of programmes in November 1978 when RTÉ 2 was launched. In retirement he would say – and it must be a tribute to Waters, who was director-general during Hill's most senior management years – that he had 'never come across an organisation with such rigorous governance as RTÉ'. On the retirement of Waters, Hill applied for the director-general's post but was unsuccessful. He left RTÉ and became chief executive of the Cork Opera House. From 1990 he was chair of CoCo TV, pioneers in independent film-making.

35 Jack White, 'A digest of my remarks at RTÉ Authority, 9 July 1979', RTÉWA.

Letter of congratulations from Joyce's grandson, Stephen Joyce (above), when Ó Mórdha's documentary won the Emmy Award. Letter from consultant, Richard Ellmann (right), during production.

it would remain 'a most important record of Joyce so long as he is read'

Ellmann wrote to Ó Mórdha: 'No one but you, who had been soaked in the material all your life, and especially during the last two or three years, would have been able to bring it to such a splendid culmination.'

RTÉ invested heavily in the Joyce programme and it enjoyed worldwide sales.

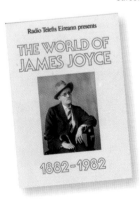

Radio Telefís Eireann presents

THE WORLD OF JAMES JOYCE

1882-1982

IN MAKING HIS award-winning documentary to mark the centenary of James Joyce's birth, *Is there one who understands me?*, Seán Ó Mórdha worked with Richard Ellmann, whose life of Joyce is considered one of the greatest literary biographies of the twentieth century.[36] In December 1981 having seen a rough-cut, Ellmann wrote to Ó Mórdha that his film on Joyce now had a theme: 'essentially the determination of Joyce to be an Irish writer and to write the moral history of Ireland and to combat the tyrannies of church and state and suggest what a more emancipated life should be like.'[37] Two months later, Ellmann viewed the completed film. He found that 'all the roughnesses and jerks which were necessarily present in the earlier version had been marvellously eliminated, so that it was extremely professional and I thought entertaining, unexpected, and very well constructed.'[38]

The documentary won critical acclaim in Ireland and beyond, justified RTÉ's initial investment and won a coveted Emmy award. This latter prompted a letter from Joyce's grandson, Stephen Joyce, who suggested that it 'must be very satisfactory indeed for all of you to have received such an award after the long months and work put into the "making" of the programme.' Stephen Joyce had insisted on travelling to Zurich – where Joyce is buried – for his interview with Ó Mórdha. He added that 'neither you nor your colleagues will ever know what that day in Zurich cost me, and I'm not talking about money!'[39] Ellmann's verdict was that Ó Mórdha's was a 'first-rate programme' and he believed it would remain 'a most important record of Joyce so long as he is read, which I assume is as long as this terrestrial ball persists in having people on it.'[40]

36 Nor was the indebtedness one-way. In his revised 1982 edition, Ellmann thanks Ó Mórdha 'for discovering some new leads in Dublin and elsewhere'; Richard Ellmann, *James Joyce* (Oxford, revised 1982 edition), p.xiv.
37 Ellmann to Ó Mórdha, 13 December 1981, Ó Mórdha papers.
38 *ibid.*, 11 February 1982, *ibid.*
39 Stephen J. Joyce to Ó Mórdha, 25 November 1982, *ibid.*
40 Ellmann to Ó Mórdha, 11 February 1982, *ibid.*

14

'without any precedent in the history of human culture'

IN SCALE ONE of the most historic changes in the latter half of the twentieth century was the access which the medium of television gave to dramatic performance. Raymond Williams argued that it was 'without any precedent in the history of human culture'.[1] Of course 'dramatic performance' in this context includes, not alone full-length television plays but also serials and series, sitcoms, made-for-television films, along with old movies purchased at bargain prices to fill the hungry television schedules. The Irish experience is no different from that of other modern societies. And in one regard it may be somewhat richer.

In the first instance it should be noted that the playwright in Ireland has traditionally been an influential figure. Vivian Mercier argued that the 'literary works most likely to have an impact on Irish society, especially after the introduction of television, were plays.' Noting the typically low sales of an Irish novel, he contrasts this with a playwright 'who captured the imagination of the Irish people', and who might thereby 'reach not merely the theatre audience in the cities and the broadcast audience, but also a remarkable number of people who attended performances by the amateur dramatic companies, over 300 of which competed each year in fourteen regional festivals and the national finals.' Mercier suggested that the audience for amateur drama was 'estimated at a quarter of a million people'. Hence, through the amateur drama movement and broadcast productions, a playwright might reach an Irish audience 'numbered in hundreds of thousands, as against tens of thousands for even the most successful novelist'.[2] John B. Keane provides a good example of this, relying on the theatre – including the amateur movement

Hilton Edwards's successor as Head of Drama was Chloe Gibson, a 'brilliant, wayward, and much-loved matriarch', according to Wesley Burrowes.

RTÉ Guide, 31 December 1971

---

1   Raymond Williams (ed. Ederyn Williams), *Television: Technology and Cultural Form* (London, 1990), p.59.
2   Mercier, 'Literature in English', 511-12.

– to reach his audience. From the start he largely ignored television. It was only weeks old when he gave his considered assessment of its probable impact. He believed it would 'not affect new plays, but revivals must suffer', especially if an adaptation had been televised. He saw a danger that it might attract 'budding playwrights who might become slaves of its technique', but predicted that dedicated writers for theatre would avoid such pitfalls. He had no fear that audiences for new plays would be affected. 'The glamour and excitement of a first night, the hush and the thrill as the curtain rises on a new work' was something with which television could not compete.[3]

a project such as Strumpet City could take 'up to five years from concept to screen'

WESLEY BURROWES, in an assessment of the output of the drama department in RTÉ's first decade, listed out an impressive run of original plays and television adaptations of some classics. 'Add to these the long-running serials, the roughage of tellydrama, represented by *Tolka Row*, *Southside*, and the ever-present *Riordans*, and we come up with the most surprising statistic of all: that in proportion to our viewing population, we have had easily the highest output of home-produced drama in Europe.' In terms of quantity, Burrowes argued,

---

3 *RTV Guide*, 26 January 1962.

Fionnula Flanagan as Tressa and Niall Toibin as Scobar MacAdam in Eugene McCabe's play *King of the Castle*. It had been written for the 1964 Dublin Theatre Festival where one critic predicted that it would never be shown on RTÉ television. Louis Lentin, who produced the television adaptation in 1977, believed it 'the best Irish play for a quarter of a century'.

RTÉ Guide, 3 October 1977.

King of the Castle caused considerable controversy when first televised. Leitrim viewers were especially outraged, one councillor claiming that it had 'made dirt of the women of Leitrim'. He asked why the playwright, Eugene McCabe, 'hadn't the guts' to locate the play in his own county of Monaghan. It might appeal to the 'so-called intelligentsia in Dublin' but people in rural Ireland were 'shocked, annoyed and appalled'.

Sheehan, *Irish Television Drama*, 209.

there could be no complaint. On quality he believed that RTÉ had 'attempted too much' but allowed that this might be better than lacking ambition. Answering those critical of the drama department for showing too many adaptations of stage plays, he believed that RTÉ had a 'special duty' to do so. 'How else but through television could the Irish rural dweller, with his proven appetite for the drama', have an opportunity of seeing the classics?

It had been an ambitious start. By the mid-sixties, there was on average a new home-produced play every fortnight, plus several series and serials. Of the 136 plays produced in the first ten years by RTÉ, 103 were by living writers, 81 of whom were Irish, 33 were classified as classics, two-thirds of them Irish. Over half of these began life as stage plays. There were also anthologies and serials. By the end of the decade, serialised drama represented more than half of RTÉ's drama output as measured in actual television running time. A sure indication of the ambition – and achievement – of the early drama department would be to compare its output with the dilatory and indifferent achievements in Australian television in its first decade.[4]

Alongside these achievements it must also be noted that the station remained over-reliant on imported series, mainly American, and, while acknowledging their popularity, Jack White also emphasised the preference for home-produced programmes. In particular it was felt that RTÉ had

> failed to come out and compete with the UK services in mainstream programmes – i.e. the type of entertainment or drama programme

John Kelleher, executive producer of *Strumpet City*, which he described as the adaptation 'by one Irishman of a novel by another, which is about Ireland and made there with Irish actors, and it has been entirely produced by Irish men and women.' Kelleher wrote that 'RTÉ *must* continue to embark on major drama series such as *Strumpet City*.' He believed it would be 'a sad waste if experience gained and lessons learned from that production were not to bear further fruit'. There were, he argued, 'compelling reasons to proceed: satisfaction for our viewers; enhanced creative fulfilment for production and technical staff; prestige for RTÉ internationally; sustained employment and income for actors and freelance technicians; and, of course, the possibilities of lucrative international sales which in turn could help to finance further production.'

Irish Broadcasting Review, No.7, Spring 1980, 52-55.

---

4   Inglis, *ABC*, 204-05.

Cyril Cusack as Fr Giffley and David Kelly as Rashers Tierney in a scene from the seven-part drama series *Strumpet City*, first broadcast in 1980. Set in Dublin between 1907 and 1914, it was adapted by one of the most accomplished television writers, Hugh Leonard, from the novel by James Plunkett and was produced and directed by Tony Barry. Helena Sheehan wrote that although RTÉ 'proceeded to produce more historical drama, some of it equally large-scale', she doubted if any such productions 'were as rigorously honest or as challengingly resonant in contemporary significance' as *Strumpet City*.

Sheehan, *Irish Television Drama*, 314.

The scene where the French enter Killala in *The Year of the French*, a six-part adaptation of Thomas Flanagan's novel. It was a co-production by RTÉ with Channel 4 in Britain and FR3 in France. Michael Garvey, its director, said that they went 'to great lengths to avoid paddywhackery', but perhaps made the mistake of making the production 'too reverential'. Cinematic values now prevailed in such series. They were films made for television rather than television drama. Some critics believed that the one-off TV play was now losing out to these costly film productions, which could be compromised by their need to win popularity with an international audience.

which will command the peak hour audience. We should attempt a policy of providing the 'main dish' of the evening, and not supplying simply the side dishes to someone else's joint.

More ambitious long-term programme planning was agreed, it being 'recognised that drama planning may take place a year before production, and up to two years before transmission of a programme.' A special project such as *Strumpet City* could take 'up to five years from concept to screen.'[5]

the locals watching the programme in the village pub would nod to each other and claim: 'I told him that.'

TELEVISION DRAMA DEPARTMENTS in newly established stations are traditionally staffed by refugees from the legitimate theatre. Not surprisingly, they think initially of commissioning one-off plays or of adapting novels, short stories or stage-plays for television. It was some time before the full potential of serials was discovered. Helena Sheehan, chronicler of Irish television drama, writes that 'most important in taking hold of the public imagination were the longer-running serials of the genre called soap opera, although those involved in making them invariably pleaded for a more dignified label.'[6]

---

5   Jack White, address to the RTÉ Authority, 9 July 1979, RTÉWA.
6   Sheehan, *Irish Television Drama* (revised 2004 CD-ROM edition), 66.

Christopher Fitz-Simon was asked by Rugheimer to 'think up' a rural counterpart to *Tolka Row*. He reckoned it 'a daunting assignment'. *The Riordans* was the result,

> the earliest drama serial in the world to be shot entirely on videotape. Technical facilities were primitive. All scenes had to be recorded in full; if you upset the milk-pail, or if the lowing kine outspoke the actors, you had to go back to the beginning and start again.[7]

Fitz-Simon remembered the initial series as presenting 'a somewhat bleak view' of farm life. And he praised the direction of Lelia Doolan and the 'warmly humorous' writing of Wesley Burrowes as winning for *The Riordans* 'a permanently high place in the charts'.[8] One of its aims when it was launched was to carry educational messages for farmers but, with the launch of *Telefís Feirme*, *The Riordans* was enabled to secure its own exceptionally popular place in the schedules. Its appeal was partly its topicality since it dealt with countless taboo subjects, helping to reshape Irish attitudes. Burrowes liked to emphasise how dependent he – an Ulster urban protestant – had been on the local community in Kells, Co. Kilkenny to where he went to live, the better to write the serial. He was especially indebted to the village pub where he would often join the locals in watching the programme on Sunday nights. They would nod to each other and claim: 'I told him that.'

The Riordans ended in 1979, to be followed by two six-part series, *Bracken*, a new challenge for Burrowes and one which he considered his best work: 'There was a beginning, a middle and an end.' *Bracken* also introduced Dinny and his son Miley, who would become such central characters in *Glenroe*. Through it all Burrowes has witnessed some extraordinary social changes in Irish society, incremental but also extraordinary. He points to the lack of controversy concerning what was a bigamous marriage of two of the characters in *Glenroe*. He even had the word 'bigamist' painted on the front wall of the house. 'And still the public didn't react.' For Burrowes this demonstrates how society has changed in Ireland since the outcry which followed in *The Riordans* when a priest advised a mother fearful of another pregnancy to use artificial contraception.[9] Historian Joe Lee suggests that perhaps 'the

The Riordans, with John Cowley as Tom Riordan, Tom Hickey as Benjy Riordan and Moira Deady as Mary Riordan. Burrowes praised Cowley for his capacity to improvise and ad lib, all-important since there was no editing facility when using videotape in the early years. If an aeroplane passed overhead, Tom Riordan might add in some remark about the noise nuisance upsetting the cattle. 'We could be shooting, and a passer-by could start up a conversation with John and we ended up filming it.' Burrowes praised Cowley as the best actor with whom he had ever worked.

---

7   Christopher Fitz-Simon, letter to editor, *Irish Times*, 24 February 1998.
8   *ibid.*
9   Eileen Battersby, 'Last of the soap: Thursday interview: Wesley Burrowes', *Irish Times*, 8 January 1998.

most pervasive influence of RTÉ on broad social issues' has come not only through chat shows but also through the popular serials like *The Riordans* and *Glenroe*, 'which have broached previously taboo topics in a manner which rouses the sympathy of many viewers who might not be regular clients of more cerebral programmes.'[10]

the cultural importance of the TV serial, an essentially new form

BURROWES DID COMPLAIN of a tendency, 'particularly among quasi-literary column-writing, smart-ass pub-poets' to denigrate the telly serial 'as "pap" and "pabulum".' While admitting to being an interested party, he argued persuasively that the function of the serial was 'the observation of a lifestyle *from within*', free from any 'theatrical necessity for stylishly contrived wrap-up endings'. He believed that serials 'better represented the proper aims of television drama than did the conventional television play.'[11] The one-off play had one major disadvantage for the television professionals involved: the first night was also the last. This can only have come as a shock to those who had spent their lives in the theatre, where the early weeks of a run would be spent ironing out the flaws identified in the opening night. One of Telefís Éireann's most versatile recruits as a producer-director, Burt Budin, had come from the American theatre, where a first night rarely represented the complete performance. 'That play may look completely different three weeks later. In television you have one shot – and that's the only one that counts. So that all your energy is expended for one show on one night.'[12]

A new serial, *Glenroe*, is announced in the *RTÉ Guide*, 9 September 1983. The photograph introduces Mick Lally as Miley, Joe Lynch as Dinny and Mary McEvoy as Biddy. *Glenroe* is 'all very real, there is nothing in this series that could not happen to real Irish people'. Joe Lynch. Glenroe would run until May 2001.

Fair City has been another highly successful serial: here, celebrating its twentieth birthday in 2009.

In contrast to the one-off TV play, actors for a television serial are contracted for a fixed period, a production team settled and then a number of writers can develop a storyline which gives professional satisfaction and some security to all involved. There is also the compensation that audiences watched in far greater numbers than for one-off plays. Treated with disdain by some critics, they have been popularly categorised as 'soaps', a term derived from the fact that the template was fashioned in America where serial drama was sponsored by soap manufacturers. 'Chronicle drama' would be Burrowes's preferred term and it would have the merit of greater accuracy. It would also draw attention to a very telling comparison: had not Dickens, Eliot, Scott and Thackeray transformed the

10 Joe Lee, '25 Years of Irish Television', *Comoradh, RTÉ Guide*, 2 January 1987.
11 Wesley Burrowes, 'Drama' [review of drama 1961-71] *RTÉ Guide*, 31 December 1971.
12 Burt Budin, *RTV Guide*, 23 February 1962.

popularity of the novel in the nineteenth century by publishing their latest works of fiction in just this fashion – in regular instalments in newspapers and periodicals? And in post-Famine Ireland, had not Kickham's *Knocknagow* introduced many readers to fiction – and some to literacy itself? Television soaps are, according to Burrowes, concerned with creating a form of reassurance. 'These people become our friends. Nothing too terrible can happen to them so the audience can be reassured by their continuing presence.... In real life, nobody "solves" their problems, their problems just become part of their history. In a soap, problems are solved.'[13]

One of the foremost commentators on popular culture, Raymond Williams, believed that televised serial fiction was a most promising field. Writing in 1969, he suggested that the 'most encouraging example' he knew, 'though unfortunately only from scripts' was RTÉ's *The Riordans*. It did not surprise Williams that millions of viewers turned away from so much else on television and preferred what the serial drama could offer: 'people regularly and connectedly known; the development of a life-situation; the experience of having to pick up and go on again through pressures which can't be resolved by any stylish cut-off.' If looked at that way round, and if serials were no longer despised, 'we may get to a position in which the facts of

Some of the cast members from the RTÉ Television drama series *The Riordans* and *Tolka Row*, in an exterior shot taken in late 1966/early 1967. Front row, from left to right: Catherine Gibson (Maggie Bonar, *Tolka Row*); Iris Lawler (Statia Nolan/Doyle, *Tolka Row*); Biddy White-Lennon (Maggie Nael, *The Riordans*); Brendan Mathews (Larry Guiney, *Tolka Row*); Laurie Morton (Peggy Nolan, *Tolka Row*); Pamela Mant (Mrs Howard, *The Riordans*); May Cluskey (Mrs Butler, *Tolka Row*) and Jim Bartley (Seán Nolan, *Tolka Row*).
Back row, from left to right: Frank O'Donovan (Batty Brennan, *The Riordans*); Anne D'Alton, wearing dark glasses (Minnie Brennan, *The Riordans*); May Ollis (Rita Nolan, *Tolka Row*); Tom Hickey (Benjy Riordan, *The Riordans*); Moira Deady (Mary Riordan, *The Riordans*); John Cowley (Tom Riordan, *The Riordans*); Des Perry (Jack Nolan, *Tolka Row*); Gerry Sullivan (Dr Howard, *The Riordans*); John McDarby (Gabby Doyle, *Tolka Row*) and David Kelly (Dancer Hanlon, *Tolka Row*).

---

13 Eileen Battersby, 'Last of the soap: Thursday interview: Wesley Burrowes', *Irish Times*, 8 January 1998.

connection and consequence would be written as experience rather than as plot-calculation, and there would be more to think about than a romantic era or the actors becoming household names.'[14] Elsewhere Williams wrote that the fact that detectives, ranchers and doctors were so often featured should not obscure 'the cultural importance of the serial, as an essentially new form'. And again he suggested that one of the more successful attempts to engage with the run of contemporary majority experience was Irish Television's *The Riordans*.'[15]

14 Raymond Williams, 'Most doctors recommend', *The Listener*, 27 November 1969.
15 Raymond Williams [ed. Ederyn Williams], *Television: Technology and Cultural Form* (London, 1990), pp.60-61.

Bob Collins at a meeting of the RTÉ Authority in May 1990 reassured the outgoing RTÉ Authority that a 'great deal of work' had been done on the new urban serial, *Fair City*: there had been 'a major investment in resources, people and time in bringing it on twice weekly and it was important that it would work.' The Chairman Jim Culliton said that the Authority regarded the urban drama serial 'as very much a challenge to the whole organisation' and he reckoned that thus far 'it had exceeded expectations'.

For her book in 2004, *The Continuing Story of Irish Television Drama*, Helena Sheehan asked a number of key figures in *Fair City* about the sort of picture of contemporary Ireland it portrayed. Kevin McHugh, script editor from 1995, suggested that it was 'dealing with the problems of ordinary people along the social spectrum ranging from the criminal to the yuppie'. Asked about restrictions, he replied that the only pressure was the pre-watershed slot. This had not kept it from dealing with AIDS, abortion, homosexuality.... He believed that "You can tell any story, if you tell it fully, properly, organically."' John Lynch, executive producer in the mid-1990s, said that it 'was a view of working-class people becoming less downtrodden and more aware of the world around them.' Niall Mathews, executive producer in 1991-92 and again after 1998, emphasised 'how much it had evolved. "It was like turning a tank around." In the beginning, there was an assumption that an urban serial meant lots of rows, so there were rows and rows, but they were based on nothing. There was no depth. Over the years, they built a pool of writers, added credibility to storylines, improved production values, increased the audience. About how it represented contemporary Ireland, he answered that he didn't 'directly set out to do that.' Bob Collins argued that *Fair City* 'had eventually claimed its space and reflected urban life at work and at home. It had tackled difficult issues, such as abortion, which had brought criticism, but it was the degree of acceptance that was more striking.'

RTÉ Authority Meeting, Minutes, 23 May 1990; Helena Sheehan, *The Continuing Story of Irish Television Drama: Tracking the Tiger* (Dublin, 2004), pp.56-57.

15

'she is the producer's memory – he probably would forget to eat if she didn't remind him...'

T HE STATUS OF WOMEN in Irish society has been transformed during the half-century covered by this book: television has witnessed and accelerated that transformation. The change is also reflected in the evolution of programming and departmental structures. When Telefís Éireann opened, there was a department dedicated to women's programmes. Its head, Edith Cusack, was rather patronisingly praised by the first controller, Michael Barry: her first year of programmes, although 'well carried out', tended too often 'towards the conventionality of Stillorgan Road and to miss the common touch' that would have widened their appeal.[1] This reference to Stillorgan Road – which forms part of the boundary to the RTÉ campus and runs between Donnybrook and Mount Merrion – can be taken to be an early reference to 'a Dublin 4' outlook before that term had gained currency. It was undoubtedly the conventional thinking – and probably correct for the 1960s – that women expected their own programmes. Barry also found that women could be vocal about the scheduled timing of these programmes: 'We have not at any time been ignorant of the breadth, depth and reach of the anger of the housewife militant. A later showing of women's programmes can invoke a similar if less briskly expressed reaction from her men folk.'[2]

RTÉ was conventional in another respect. It inherited the civil service rules concerning the employment of married women. Until 1972 all women in RTÉ had to resign on marriage. There were some exceptions for those with specialised roles but even when this rule was abolished – a year before it was

Doireann Ní Bhriain and Marian Finucane, presenters of *The Women's Programme* in October 1983

---

1 Barry, memorandum, n.d., but probably January 1963, Barry papers, RTÉWA.
2 Barry to Sheridan, 24 January 1963, RTÉWA.

abandoned in the civil service – women employees were still required, until 1977, to take three months unpaid maternity leave.[3]

The representation of women in television drama – both plays and serials – was, according to Helena Sheehan, 'extremely traditional'. The plays portrayed earth mothers 'sacrificing themselves to their husbands' appetites, spoiling their sons, shamed at their errant daughters, sorrowing over their emigrating offspring, sturdy and nurturing amidst domestic stress and setting a sound moral example to one and all.' These were stereotypical women who knew their place – 'home and hearth' – and also 'knew well enough not to reach beyond it'. Sheehan absolves television drama from creating such a stereotype since it represented reality.

> But it could perhaps be blamed for not representing it more sharply, for not digging into its roots in the sexual division of labour, as a historically contingent and not an eternally necessary condition. It could be faulted for not highlighting the exceptions more carefully, for not exposing the alternatives more credibly. Even in Ireland by the 1960s, there were a growing number of women reaching towards a more liberated way of life.[4]

That television accelerated that liberation cannot be gainsaid. Whether it should have done more, sooner is another question. And liberation, like so much else, is in the eye of the beholder. The women's lib agenda was certainly impatiently espoused by the all-female production teams which in the 1980s brought *Women Talking* to air – what Tom O'Dea called the 'the most remarkably real, uncontrived and down to earth programme' which he had seen 'in a long time'.[5] *The Women's Programme* followed. Listing out the production, editorial and presenting teams who were entirely female, Gene Kerrigan wrote in *Magill* that it would indeed be odd if

> all RTÉ programmes were made with such a predominance of the female sex. And if the political, financial and business worlds were similarly dominated by that sex. For a male it would be odd, unsettling, even intolerable. Just for a minute you get an idea of what women have been on about for the past fifteen years.[6]

The *Women's Programme* could be seen as an agenda-setting programme, appropriate for its time and an expression of positive

Clare Duignan, with Nuala O'Faolain, producer of *The Women's Programme* from 1982 to 1986. Since then she held various senior positions in Features, Current Affairs, Independent Productions before becoming Director of Programmes, Television. Since 2009 Managing Director, Radio.

3   See Savage, *Loss*, 135-36.
4   Sheehan, *Irish Televsion Drama* (revised 2004 CD-ROM edition), 54.
5   *Irish Press*, 17 July 1982.
6   Gene Kerrigan, 'The women's programme', *Magill*, November 1983.

discrimination which would achieve enough not to be the appropriate vehicle for future discussion of this agenda. There were two schools of thought – even among feminists – on such programmes. Some saw them as a temporary necessity to accelerate and broaden a cluster of issues of special interest to women; others thought that any such issues should compete for editorial attention in mainstream programmes. The latter view eventually prevailed. RTÉ was by this time unrecognisable from the station that had opened a generation before. On the eve of the opening, the *Irish Press* had published a television supplement which described the important role of a new category of worker: 'On the producer's right hand sits his [*sic*] assistant, a young woman known as a P.A. or production assistant. Her job is one that calls for stamina as she combines the functions of secretary with a hundred and one other duties. She is the producer's memory – he probably would forget to eat if she didn't remind him...'.[7]

'the people's very own jester who came right into the living room and seemed at home.'

IT WAS ONCE SAID of Mike Murphy that he was the man who became famous for not being able to sing and dance. Derek Dunne suggested that 'people related to that, not really sure if he was being serious or just codding us all the time.' The image of Murphy standing on the hilltop doing his famous dance reminded Dunne 'of the one person in the classroom who will stand up and act the clown just to entertain. The people's very own jester who came right into the living room and seemed at home.'[8] If Murphy made a virtue of his inability to dance, there was very little else that he could not do. His virtuosity and curiosity about the medium and its limits made him one of the most successful broadcasters of his generation. If variety was not a genre, the term would have had to be invented to describe the range of his output.

His sense of mischief was at its best in his candid camera routines – he managed to hoodwink both his parents! His producer, John Keogh, another versatile and accomplished broadcaster, enjoyed working with Murphy. The failure rate in the candid camera cameos was, he recalls, about twenty per cent. Keogh found most 'victims' to be remarkably tolerant.

Mike Murphy 'was always up for a challenge. For programmes, he parachuted out of an aeroplane, was thrown in judo by a twelve-year-old girl, went into a lion's cage with half a dozen lions, "two of whom had been in a major fight just before I went in. The one who was bleeding was the one that had to jump over my head." His failures included hang-gliding: "I resent the fact that I allowed myself to fail. I just lost my nerve. I just couldn't face going off that cliff."'

Deirdre Purcell, *Days We Remember* (Dublin, 2008), pp.137-53; hereafter, Purcell, *Days*.

---

7 'The Men on the Floor', *Irish Press* TV supplement, 29 December 1961.
8 Derek Dunne, 'Murphy's Law', *RTÉ Guide*, 14 October 1988.

Mike Murphy recalled a persistent letter writer to his morning radio programme: 'Funny letters. A lot of them.' The letter-writer was a Dublin school teacher 'who obviously wanted to be in showbiz'. With producer John Keogh, Murphy went to a performance of his in UCD where he was sending up Big Tom. After the show Murphy and Keogh asked him if he had any other characters: 'Yeah, I have this priest,' replied Dermot Morgan, 'I call him Father Trendy.'

Purcell, *Days*, 149-50.

Dermot Morgan's television career as a comedian began on *The Live Mike*. He is photographed above as Father Trendy in December 1980.

Television programmes in which a broadcaster uses secret filming while playing hoaxes on unsuspecting victims is an early form of reality TV and it has had many practitioners. Few could have equalled Mike Murphy's ability to cajole his subjects into considering the most outrageous propositions while delaying their recognition that it had to be a hoax. And could any others equal his record of including both his parents as his victims? And also (above), Gay Byrne.

'Once a man did stalk off' and came back with a policeman, 'who twigged it instantly. He was quite amused so long as we didn't put him in the act.'[9] Murphy's most unsuspecting victim was Gay Byrne, who had long known that he was a target but presumed himself to be immune. The successful deception involved John McColgan as producer scheduling an unsuspecting Byrne to film in Front Square in Trinity College Dublin for a documentary on which they were working. This was to be filmed on the eve of an Ireland-France rugby international. It was traditional for the French team to have a practice run on Trinity's rugby pitch on the eve of the match. Thus was the scene set for the most celebrated of all Murphy's Home Movies.

As Byrne prepared to record an into camera link for the programme, Murphy – disguised as a French supporter – was loitering behind him observing the filming. He then became increasingly disruptive, expressing support for the French team. Byrne was initially tolerant but as he was obliged to record retake after retake he became irascible and eventually asked the French supporter if he understood the words: 'Fuck off!'? As the accompanying grabs from the footage show, Byrne enjoyed the joke when he – eventually – was asked: 'How do you like being on television?'

9   John Walsh, 'Disguising Mike', *ibid.*, 9 January 1981.

RTÉ was 'to be destroyed and curbed' and Burke had been 'hand-picked for that job'

IN 1959 THE TOP EXECUTIVES in the BBC – privately asked for their comments on the draft broadcasting legislation by León Ó Broin – warned of an 'endless source of argument' if the minister of the day retained powers to determine the amount of permitted advertising.[10] It was just these powers that Charles Haughey's communications minister, Ray Burke, now proposed to use. His original intention had been to divert part of the licence fee to independent broadcasters but he had then decided to cap RTÉ's advertising instead. Jim Mitchell, for Fine Gael, claimed that never before in Irish broadcasting history had there been a minister 'so doggedly and visibly opposed to and angry with RTÉ'. He told the Dáil that, off-air, on the last election night at RTÉ, Burke had promised that in government Fianna Fáil would 'screw RTÉ'. He spoke of Burke's proposals in terms of folly, shambles, madness: the policy was the first example of a directive from a government minister to a state company 'to go out and fail'. Labour leader Dick Spring claimed that Burke was carrying out 'his master's bidding'. Haughey's motive seemed all the clearer to Spring since, despite Burke's successively taking on ministerial duties for Energy,

---

10 Ian Jacob to Hugh Carlton Greene, 2 October 1959, 'Ireland: Radio Éireann', EI/2092, BBCWA.

An Taoiseach Charles Haughey is shown around the Eurovision 'village', the site of the 1988 Eurovision Song Contest, in the Simmonscourt Pavilion at Dublin's RDS in April 1988. From left to right in the front row: Liam Miller, Eurovision executive producer for RTÉ, Charles Haughey and Minister for Communications, Ray Burke. Behind this group are RTÉ director-general Vincent Finn (left) and Bob Collins. Burke had already expressed himself as 'very impressed' at a Eurovision briefing in RTÉ the previous month. But Jim Culliton, chairman of the Authority, expressed 'some serious concerns' to their meeting on 22 March concerning the Eurovision banquet to be hosted by the minister but paid for by RTÉ. The Royal Hospital at Kilmainham could hold only six to seven hundred but the minister intended inviting 1,300. 'The Minister could not be dissuaded from taking this course.'

RTÉ Authority, minutes, 22 March 1988.

The minister comes to the RTÉ Authority's lunch, 11 June 1990. Minister for Communications, Ray Burke TD, being greeted by RTÉ director-general Vincent Finn. In the centre is former assistant director-general, John Sorohan, who had just been appointed chair of the incoming RTÉ Authority. A large group of RTÉ employees are protesting against the minister's recently announced cap on RTÉ's advertising revenue. Burke asked the RTÉ picketers if they had no work to go to. Two years before, he had told Jim Culliton, chair of the previous Authority, that 'all his cabinet colleagues comment to him on the staggering manning of RTÉ crews at press conferences'.

RTÉ Authority, minutes, 2 September 1988.

Protests continued against Ray Burke's proposed cap on RTÉ's advertising revenue. Here broadcaster Pat Kenny addresses a crowd of RTÉ workers outside Dáil Éireann, 20 June 1990. The Authority was divided on how RTÉ should respond. Gay Byrne wondered why the incoming chair, John Sorohan, 'would not speak out about this'. But Sorohan insisted that it would prove counter-productive and Des Maguire argued that were they to adopt 'a confrontational style, they would be seen to be a crowd of whingers'.

RTÉ Authority, minutes, 22 June 1990.

then Industry and Commerce and now Justice, he had throughout this period also remained Minister for Communications and saw it as his job 'to engage in a war of confrontation' with RTÉ. One of 'the unstated and secret items' on the Fianna Fáil agenda was that RTÉ was 'to be destroyed and curbed' and Burke had been 'hand-picked for that job'.[11]

Some days later, at the first meeting of the new RTÉ Authority, the chair John Sorohan revealed that the minister's plan would result in a reduction in RTÉ's income of £12 million in a full year. Sorohan admitted that he could not say 'that RTÉ was surprised'. Manifestly, the Fianna Fáil-Progressive Democrat government and its predecessor, the Fianna Fáil minority government 'had put their minds to independent broadcasting and that was now coming about. They intended that it would survive and the bulk of the population was with them on that front.' For RTÉ, it was 'the suddenness' of these decisions that was 'extremely difficult'. Sorohan predicted that if this legislation were to be passed, it would have 'a traumatic effect' on the station. Gay Byrne – an appointee to the Authority – suggested that they might 'come out a little bit more in a fighting mood'.

11 Dáil Debates, vol. 399, cols. 1574-1625 *passim*, 7 June 1990.

Later, when the minister joined the meeting for lunch, he assured them that no criticism was intended of RTÉ but it was 'vitally important in a democracy' that there be choice, especially in news and current affairs. If Burke had been embarrassed by the widespread publicity that had been given to his remarks on election night, about a Fianna Fáil government 'screwing the station', he did not now reveal it. He invited the RTÉ Authority to think of a blank sheet of paper. Would any government give all the licence fee and all the advertising pool to one broadcaster 'without doing some regulation'. He was convinced they would not: 'the days of monopoly were gone'.

Sorohan told the minister that the advertising which RTÉ was now refusing because of the minister's cap might well have scattered across the marketplace and outside the state before the putative new independent television station opened. Burke admitted that this was a risk 'and he was conscious of some of it'. Byrne suggested that the new television station would 'probably not get on the air' for twelve to eighteen months. His concern was that the cap 'would end up doing nothing for anybody insofar as most people involved in the advertising business were of the opinion that a lot would go to UTV and the satellite stations'. He did not believe that the cap on RTÉ would help independent radio broadcasters such as Century in the short term. Byrne suggested a moratorium on the cap 'until one saw how TV3 was progressing'. Otherwise the advertising budgets might be assigned to other media outside the state. Burke reported that the government's attitude was that they were 'prepared and determined' to take this risk. He did not accept that it would go to external channels. The government was not just in the business of saving Century as such, but in the business of ensuring space for an alternative broadcasting sector. Burke said he realised that there was 'a very comfortable working relationship' between RTÉ and the advertising industry. The latter would now have to think 'where they placed their client's money'.[12]

At a further meeting one week later, Finn explained to the Authority that the net effect would be that RTÉ's commercial income in 1991 would be capped at £46 to £47 million when they had been anticipating £58 million or more. Sorohan, while acknowledging the seriousness of the position, insisted that no purpose would be served by the RTÉ Authority 'going out and making statements about the Minister – they would be completely misunderstood'. He added that competition was inevitable and would benefit RTÉ. But he did not want an 'artificial straitjacket' where RTÉ could not develop. He claimed that RTÉ was 'the most cost-effective service in Europe', given Ireland's small, scattered population.

John Sorohan, chairman of the Twelfth Authority. He had been nominated by the Tenth Authority to be director-general in succession to George Waters, but this was rejected by the then minister, Jim Mitchell, in March 1985, on the grounds that he had already – pending a major review of RTÉ's structure and finances – requested the Authority to suspend the process of recruiting a new director-general. When Fred O'Donovan ignored this instruction, Mitchell declined that Authority's nomination of Sorohan. Some five years later Sorohan was appointed by the Fianna Fáil-Progressive Democrat government as the chair of the Twelfth Authority.

For partisan accounts of this episode, see Dáil debates of 12 and 13 March 1985, vol. 356, cols 2160-96; 2372-96.

---

12 RTÉ Authority, minutes, 11 June 1990, RTÉWA.

At the height of the controversy over Ray Burke's proposals to cap RTÉ's advertising revenue, Joe Mulholland, Director of News, gave an interview to *Magill* magazine. He argued that any organisation whose finances were 'frozen at a certain figure' would eventually 'wilt and die'. The interview continued:

Do you feel that you are being punished now?
Punished is possibly the wrong word. There has been deregulation in a lot of countries. It is the atmosphere of the times. What is not quite recognised is the complexity of the circumstances in which we have operated: the size of the country, the amount of revenue available to broadcasting, and what broadcasting costs. There is a rather simplistic notion that RTÉ is an arrogant, big, impersonal monopoly that is sometimes unfair in its broadcasting. None of that I accept.
Is Fianna Fáil getting its own back?
There is a lot of paranoia around in this organisation about the present government and about the minister [Ray Burke]. I'd prefer to avoid that paranoia and to presume that this legislation is based on the desire to open up the airwaves, nothing more. I don't agree with it because I don't think the revenue is there to do what has been begun, so something is going to have to go. Maybe RTÉ will have to go. If another organisation can provide the services which we have provided, then so be it.
Why is there unease about Fianna Fáil in RTÉ?
It is easy to understand – look at what is happening. Perhaps not paranoia but terrible disappointment and frustration and depression and anger, because it doesn't seem to matter what we do, or the efforts we make.

Michael Ross, 'Lights... Camera... Action... Cut!', interview with Joe Mulholland, *Magill*, June 1990.

'RTÉ would be strangled if the legislation were left as it was'

SINCE THE ESTABLISHMENT of the television service, various RTÉ Authorities had learned that the broadcasting policies of successive communications ministers could differ – and differ widely. Never was this more tellingly illustrated than in the case of Seamus Brennan, who succeeded his party colleague Ray Burke in 1991. At a meeting with the Authority in June, Brennan expressed his own 'deep admiration' for what RTÉ had achieved, given that it was up against such formidable international competition. He emphasised that it was 'his own very definite approach' to broadcasting to maintain RTÉ's strength. The government's policy was also to encourage 'competition and choice, and Irish choice if possible'. Concerning the Burke legislation, Brennan said that if it was not working, he would change it. His major objective was to allow for choice 'without damaging the fabric of RTÉ which had to remain strong. He thought that within a few months he would be able to make that judgement.'

Sorohan emphasised how RTÉ had wished to help the independent programme-making sector but because of the effect of Burke's capping of advertising revenue, had been obliged to cut back its support from £3.2 to £2.5 million. 'Frankly, RTÉ would like to have been increasing it' and could do so if the legislation was reconsidered. RTÉ's schedule 'would be greatly enhanced' by independent programming. Sorohan further emphasised the increasing competitiveness in the multi-channel television marketplace. There were now fifty television channels available in Dublin. He recorded that the Authority was 'delighted' with the minister's belief in a strong RTÉ. Niall Weldon added that the minister's approach had been 'most encouraging' and emphasised how the Burke legislation had been a constraint on RTÉ's aim 'to expand and develop and grow'.[13] The challenge posed by TV3 was discussed at the following meeting, with Bob Collins insisting that RTÉ had not radically altered its schedule in advance of the new station lest it reveal RTÉ's hand. It did not want to allow the new station 'to set the pace'.

Reporting discussions between the director-general and the department's secretary, the Authority was advised that any extra money that had accrued to RTÉ – because its advertising had exceeded Burke's cap – could not be retained. The department believed that the 'full rigour of the law would have to apply', which could prove to be 'a very painful process'.[14] Sorohan had told Brennan that 'RTÉ would be strangled if the legislation were left as it was'. Brennan had accepted this and had insisted that there was 'no pressure on him within Cabinet' to retain the Burke legislation.[15] The Authority complimented the chairman and director-general on 'a remarkable feat' of delivering a government 'U-turn on legislation in the course of a year or so'.[16]

Historians of Irish broadcasting have not been kind to Burke's tenure as minister. Cathcart suggests that the new station had 'proved successful both in its capacity to attain profitability and on the premise on which this had to be based': winning a high audience share. But neither of these achievements had protected RTÉ 'from the designs of unsympathetic, disaffected politicians, who were increasingly determined to provide directly competitive alternative commercial services'. And when these almost immediately proved non-viable, 'the

At a meeting with the RTÉ Authority in June 1991, the new minister, Seamus Brennan, 'expressed his own personal admiration for RTÉ' and was not saying that lightly. He had always had 'a deep admiration' for what RTÉ had achieved, given that it was up against such international competition.

RTÉ Authority, minutes, 21 June 1991.

13 RTÉ Authority minutes, 21 June 1991.
14 *ibid.*, 19 July 1991.
15 *ibid.*, 13 September 1991.
16 *ibid.*, 25 October 1991.

politicians moved once again to attack RTÉ by skimming off its profits to subsidise the rivals'. The rhetoric used to justify these political actions was that the new services would provide 'greater choice for viewers and listeners. The reality was that the politicians were set on the deliberate taming of public-service broadcasting.'[17] John Horgan writes that 'the popular wisdom' was that Fianna Fáil, now in a position 'to wreak its revenge, was deliberately curtailing RTÉ financing in order to force the station to cut back particularly on the kind of investigative programmes on which RTÉ in general, and *Today Tonight* in particular, had based its reputation.' In a telling understatee.nt, Horgan adds this advice in a footnote: 'An instructive source of documentation and information on the relationship between Mr Burke and RTÉ at this time can be found in the Tribunal of Inquiry into Certain Planning Matters, transcript of proceedings on 18 July 2000, no. 169'.[18]

17 Cathcart, 'Mass Media', 707.
18 Horgan, *Broadcasting and Public Life*, 192

A screen grab of Seán Doherty in January 1992 on *Nighthawks*, RTÉ 2's late night innovative talk-show. This interview is generally credited with bringing Charlie Haughey's career to a close. Doherty had been Haughey's controversial Justice Minister in the short-lived GUBU government of 1982. He had authorised the tapping of the telephones of two journalists, Geraldine Kennedy and Bruce Arnold, who he believed were publishing confidential details of cabinet meetings being leaked by Haughey's rivals in government. When the tapping was revealed in December 1982, Haughey, had immediately stated that he considered any such tapping an abuse of power and that he would not have countenanced it. Doherty, through a sense of loyalty, never corrected this claim.

A decade later, Doherty, disappointed at Haughey's lack of support for him in the intervening decade and frustrated that he was destined to be remembered as a disgraced failure, used the unlikely vehicle of *Nighthawks* to light the fuse, which led inexorably to Haughey's demise. On *Nighthawks*, he insisted that at cabinet level a decision had been taken to prevent the leaks. 'I, as Minister for Justice, had direct responsibility for doing that – I did that. I do feel that I was let down by the fact that people knew what I was doing.' Haughey persisted in proclaiming his innocence.

It may be that the *Nighthawks* broadcast hastened Haughey's demise; but it was not part of any wider conspiracy. The plan by Albert Reynolds to remove Haughey was already well in place, and, if anything, the Reynolds camp was thrown by Doherty's intervention. After his *Nighthawks* interview, Doherty had to alert the programme's presenter, Shay Healy, to the import of his statement. The author believes that the most plausible reconstruction is that Doherty, having recognised that Haughey's exit was imminent, felt his only chance of salving some historical reputation rested on playing the contrite sinner who had brought him down. Evidence of his consultations with Tom Savage and Terry Prone, his calling of a press conference at which he merely read his reconstruction of the events of 1982 and his refusal to ever answer questions arising from this statement would all be consistent with this interpretation.

Justin O'Brien, *The Modern Prince: Charles J.Haughey and the Quest for Power* (Dublin, 2002), pp.131-46; Steve Carson, *Haughey* (Mint productions, television series, RTÉ, June, July 2005); *Irish Times*, 22 January 1922.

RTÉ 'could be badly damaged from ignorance more than anything else'

WHEN ALBERT REYNOLDS succeeded Charles Haughey as Taoiseach, the Sorohan Authority had yet another change of minister, Brennan being replaced by Máire Geoghegan-Quinn. The new minister believed that two years after the Burke 1990 Act, there had been 'ample opportunity' to review its impact. Having taken soundings, she concluded that there had been 'massive frustration' in the broadcasting marketplace, and also with small and medium-sized enterprises needing access to television advertising. She had consulted widely: it would have been 'very easy' just to lift the cap and change the minutage. Instead, she was asking how all players would see broadcasting 'in ten years time'. All were agreed that the Burke cap should go. Geoghegan-Quinn herself reckoned that there was 'no room for a third television channel and she thought she would now accept that. The market was too small in Ireland and that had to be faced up to.' But competition still had to be provided for RTÉ.

Máire Geoghegan-Quinn was Minister for Tourism, Transport and Communications in 1992. She asked all the interested parties how they saw 'broadcasting in ten years time'.

The director-general emphasised that RTÉ, while acknowledging its defects, was an organisation that 'had a real role and place in Irish society'. It needed resources to enable it to compete and 'not be demolished by external services', some of them owned by 'very large multi-channel organisations.' It was mentioned that up to 75 per cent of viewers would have more than twenty channels in the future. 'Sky television was trying to become TV3 by the back door.' Niall Weldon cited the Lemass principle and expectation that semi-state agencies should be encouraged to operate commercially. The cap contradicted this.[19]

At an RTÉ Authority meeting in Galway, the outgoing director-general, Vincent Finn, said that since the Burke initiative of 1990, working with politicians had proved 'volatile'. It was imperative to get the legislation changed 'by every means' RTÉ knew how. He thought there was quite a risk that the national broadcasting organisation 'could be badly damaged from ignorance more than anything else'. At this stage there was a £16m surplus which had accrued in advertising above the cap's limit since it had been introduced. Finn thought it 'likely that the money would be taken from RTÉ'. Sorohan had had a meeting with Geoghegan-Quinn and felt 'there was a lot of trust on both sides'. But some members believed that the Authority did not seem to be as strong with the present minister as it had been with Brennan. Sorohan agreed, believing there was room for concern: it was possible that Geoghegan-Quinn 'could make serious errors of judgement'.[20]

---

19 RTÉ Authority, minutes, 10 July 1992.
20 RTÉ Authority, minutes, 30 October 1992.

Eoghan Harris, after a turbulent career in RTÉ since the 1960s in which, by his own admission, he consistently breached the rules concerning outside political involvement, finally left the station in 1990 in the wake of the presidential election which had been won by Mary Robinson. In the aftermath of the election he had given an interview to John Waters in the *Irish Times*, entitled 'The Robinson reconstruction: a message in new politics'. Harris was introduced in these terms: 'Former Workers Party political activist and RTÉ producer worked for Mary Robinson's campaign.' At no stage in a lengthy article did it state that Robinson and her team had used Harris's advice, or had given him any official position; but the thrust of the article was that his advice was original and useful in the strategic pitching of the Robinson campaign. Towards the end of the article Waters asked: what's in it for Harris? Harris replied that he did not 'work for six months' to put Robinson in the Park 'to do anything'; but he believed her presence in the Park was itself 'a political statement of enormous importance'.[1]

At the following meeting of the RTÉ Authority, Bob Collins told the members that since the early 1960s Harris had been a permanent and pensionable staff member and 'for some considerable time' RTÉ had been discussing early retirement with him. His public statements concerning the Workers Party earlier in the year had 'made his continuing employment in RTÉ more untenable and in recent times possible severance arrangements were being vigorously pursued with himself and subsequently with his legal adviser.' To compound matters, the article in the *Irish Times* had 'raised very serious questions for RTÉ'. In spite of Harris's statements that he was leaving RTÉ, 'no letter to this effect' had been received. The Director of Personnel had written to him immediately after the *Irish Times* article, informing him that he 'was being removed from the payroll'. Harris had not replied. Collins added that all the publicity surrounding Harris in recent weeks had 'wider implications for RTÉ' with regard to the perception among many politicians/political parties that some members of RTÉ staff could 'influence programmes to the benefit of certain political interests'. Collins concluded that this aspect of RTÉ's public relations strategy would 'now require top priority'.[2]

Collins added that RTÉ had been in discussion with a range of advisers 'for what seemed like an eternity' concerning a retirement exit package and this had just been concluded. Harris, he said, had been 'a particular embarrassment' between May and September – a reference to the peak of the presidential election campaign. The chairman said that 'the greatest damage' Harris had done 'was that he was boasting that he was a political activist in RTÉ for a number of years'. The RTÉ Authority should be happy that 'the position had been resolved'.[3]

In the 1997 presidential election, Eoghan Harris, by now retired from RTÉ, attacked the Fianna Fáil candidate Mary McAleese as 'a tribal time-bomb', predicting she could not win the presidency. Cartoonist Ian Knox shows Robinson calling at the Aras and commenting to President McAleese about 'that strange Mr Harris'.

Ian Knox, *Culture Vultures* (Belfast, 1999), p.62

1   John Waters, 'The Robinson reconstruction: a message in new politics', *Irish Times*, 9 November 1990.
2   [Collins] memo re Eoghan Harris for RTÉ Authority meeting, 30 November 1990.
3   RTÉ Authority, minutes, 30 November 1990.

'It was a deferred debt to the people of this country and an obligation for the future.'

IN FEBRUARY 1990 the director-general Vincent Finn had alerted the Authority that the issue of Teilifís na Gaeilge was now 'quite a major matter'. He said that 'the agitators' for the service were 'a small local group'. Meanwhile Bob Collins warned that RTÉ should be 'very slow' to accept financial support 'thinking that this was a pilot scheme'.[21] It was a 'very complex' issue with 'all sorts of political elements' involved and there was a considerable risk that whatever RTÉ recommended, 'the Government would say RTÉ should pay for it'.[22] Two years later at his last meeting of the Authority before his retirement, Finn again emphasised the 'enormous amount of money' which would be needed for the Irish language channel. Were RTÉ expected to subsidise any new station, it would transform £7-8 million surpluses into 'staggering losses'.[23]

By the summer of 1995 RTÉ had been drawn in, being expected to provide one hour per day programming at an annual cost of £6m. At Authority meetings, there was a wariness of assuming responsibilities for any new station: 'these things had a habit of growing'.[24] By December 1995 the Authority debated their options before a visit from yet another new minister, Labour's Michael D. Higgins who – like his predecessor – included the Connemara Gaeltacht in his constituency of Galway West. The Authority was concerned lest the viability of the whole organisation might be undermined by the burden of a cost commitment that it had been assured it would not have to bear. And there was considerable debate about what had been agreed or understood at an exploratory informal meeting of 3 October 1994 between RTÉ and the department. The Authority was now informed that it was Finance's opinion that the totality of the Irish language channel 'should be supported by the licence fee and the compromise in January 1995 was £10 million'. Higgins argued that if RTÉ was to be the national broadcaster, it had obligations. Concerning Teilifís na Gaeilge, 'historically it was not a good record for RTÉ'. The argument could be made that 'the national broadcaster' should have developed the new station rather than require his initiative: in that case his life 'would have been easier!' Higgins complained of RTÉ's accounts and how they were presented. Finance

Minister for Arts, Culture and the Gaeltacht, Michael D. Higgins, turning the sod for the Teilifís na Gaeilge studios in Baile na hAbhann, Connemara, Co. Galway on 12 January 1996. Standing from left to right are: Ceannasaí of TnaG, Cathal Goan, the Chairman of Comhairle Teilifís na Gaeilge, Brian MacAongusa, and RTÉ's then director-general, Joe Barry. A month earlier Higgins had told the RTÉ Authority: 'It would be there for better citizens in better times and their children and that was his function and that was the way it was going to be.'

RTÉ Authority, minutes, 15 December 1995.

21 RTÉ Authority, minutes, 23 February 1990.
22 *ibid.*, 30 March 1990.
23 *ibid.*, 30 October 1992.
24 *ibid.*, 28 July 1995.

believed that RTÉ was 'cash rich' and Higgins had told the previous
Authority to present accounts so that Finance 'could be disabused of
that notion'. He had a particular problem in arguing to his cabinet
colleagues that RTÉ was facing the imminent challenge of TV3, the
renewal of its own transmission network, increasing competition
from the satellite sector and an increase in the independent sector.
'He made those cases all the time.' Higgins told the meeting that 'the
bottom line' was that while Finance argued that RTÉ had £40 million
surplus, he had to argue that 'it could easily turn around into
£10 million deficit. He had resisted a raid on RTÉ's resources to
establish Teilifís na Gaeilge. That took a lot of effort on his part.' But
on one point he was adamant: 'that was that Teilifís na Gaeilge would
happen.' He emphasised that it was part of the national broadcasting
structure. 'It was a deferred debt to the people of this country and an
obligation for the future.' Higgins 'thought he had negotiated a
strategy' for starting TnaG 'which would not be an unfair burden on
RTÉ.' He had resisted taking about £13 million from RTÉ.

Garret FitzGerald – one of Higgins's appointees to the Authority –
stated that their 'major concern looking ahead was the gap between
expenditure and income'. Reserves would be 'used up fairly quickly'.
The Authority feared that within its lifetime RTÉ's 'very viability might
come into question'. Higgins was in favour of recommending a licence
fee increase; and he believed the politicians 'would have to carry that
flak'. He told the Authority that he had to convince not just Finance but
politicians of all parties concerning 'the true situation about the cash
reserves'. He told the Authority members that they had been selected
because they 'believed in public service broadcasting at a time when
that was not popular'. This was not a time for 'weak wills'. He insisted
that he had not initiated TnaG 'to punish RTÉ'. He saw it as part of the
national broadcasting system. 'He was not protecting it at the cost of
RTÉ – far from it. There should be a partnership approach with no weak
nerves involved and the project should take off in that direction.'

Higgins said he would not 'be undermined' in a decision to proceed
with TnaG which the government had taken in January 1995 after three
previous decisions by the previous government. 'Everyone would make
it happen and if they had to have butter instead of jam then butter they
would have!' He allowed that RTÉ was entitled to a licence increase
and indexation but he wished to avoid 'any linkage' in the public mind
that the licence increase was because of the new Irish language station:
that would 'kill off the new service'. He had emphasised to the previous
Authority that they should 'have the guts to make their case without
living off the back of a corpse'.[25]

25 Meeting with Michael D.Higgins, Tadgh Ó hÉalaithe, Michael Grant and Colm Ó Briain,
   RTÉ Authority minutes, 15 December 1995

16

remuneration figures 'bore no relation' to other RTÉ pay; they were 'quite astronomical'

IN 1962 AS TELEFIS EIREANN began its first year of programming, Gay Byrne had television engagements in Manchester, London and Dublin. But he was so keen to come back to Ireland that he 'jumped at Gunnar Rugheimer's offer' to host *The Late Late Show* 'without any attempt at bargaining'. He wrote of a former agent warning him that he accepted terms 'too hastily', selling himself 'too cheaply'. But over twenty years later – when facing a financial crisis having been defrauded by his accountant – he was considering an offer to work in the United States. He believed those in charge in RTÉ realised that he was serious and decided to offer him 'a real incentive to stay here'. The situation 'improved again' when commercial radio was introduced and by the time his 1989 memoir was published, he was in no doubt 'that RTÉ cherishes me!'[1] This was as much as his readers learned about top pay for RTÉ presenters. And it would be a decade before such details become public under Freedom of Information legislation.

In March 1992, the matter was still considered highly confidential and commercially sensitive when the director-general, Vincent Finn, circulated to the RTÉ Authority a secret list of the pay of RTÉ's best remunerated presenters. He reminded the Authority that RTÉ had always tried to estimate the commercial value of these broadcasters to RTÉ. He allowed that it was a 'very subjective business' but in the specific case of Gay Byrne he had asked 'RTÉ's commercial people to try to put a value on his personal contribution to RTÉ's income'. Their figures showed that Byrne's radio and television programmes brought in between seven and eight million pounds out of an RTÉ total of about £56 million 'and as to what the personal element was, the best they could do was that in their view it was certainly

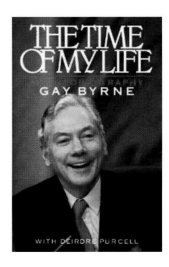

In his autobiography, published in 1989, Gay Byrne writes: 'I have been asked if I know my own worth to RTÉ. I probably do not – but which of us does? What my status is within RTÉ may be a very interesting question for the hedge-sitters and the "pundits", but very difficult for me to answer.'

Gay Byrne, *The Time of My Life* (Dublin, 1989), p.226.

---

1   Gay Byrne, *The Time of My Life* (Dublin, 1989), pp.227-28.

£1.5 million and could be over £2 million'. Finn reckoned these figures were 'probably reasonably right' and added that if it were not for the stars, RTÉ's income would be 'greatly reduced'. He appreciated that the remuneration figures 'bore no relation' to other RTÉ salaries and that they were 'very high'. Chairman John Sorohan thought them 'quite astronomical' and emphasised that there were no rival employers willing to match these fees.[2]

Four months later the Authority noted that the Joint Oireachtas Committee with responsibility for broadcasting had privately got information on the pay of top presenters and 'obviously it did pose some difficulties for RTÉ'.[3] By September the Authority was noting that the politicians did not 'buy these figures at all', reckoning that this was what RTÉ was doing with the licence money. Sorohan agreed with Finn that it would have to be emphasised that the Authority took this issue very seriously and it might 'dispense with existing contracts', even if the broadcasters concerned 'were prepared to settle on present terms'. Sorohan added that there was 'a serious problem on air': for example, Marian Finucane 'was asking questions about the high salaries some people were earning'. The meeting was reminded that on television, Byrne was unique and cited the 'striking example' of the audience figures for successive nights of the *Rose of Tralee* which averaged 1.2 million viewers. This was twice the audience of the best-watched programme at a comparable time in the following week.

One new factor was then alluded to: Pat Kenny's request to put his case for a pay rise directly to the Authority. He knew its workings

2   RTÉ Authority, minutes, 27 March 1992.
3   *ibid.*, 10 July 1992.

because he had recently served on the Eleventh Authority. To complicate matters, the traditional seat reserved for a practising broadcaster on the Authority was occupied by Byrne! But what was now being requested by Kenny was an Authority meeting with both broadcasters present, Byrne as a member and Kenny to argue his case for some level of pay, taking Byrne's remuneration into the equation. Finn explained that when he had told Kenny that a 3.5 per cent increase was the best that RTÉ could offer, Kenny had replied that 'he had more than an idea of what Gay Byrne earned'. Finn confided to the meeting that Kenny felt 'very very strongly about the Gay Byrne thing. He does not like being number two and in many ways he believes he is better than Gay Byrne and there was all that kind of under-current to his attitude.' The Authority minutes reflect a strong disinclination to find themselves hosting a Kenny-Byrne denouement.[4]

The director-general told the Authority that Pat Kenny (above) did not like being number two and in many ways thought he was better than Gay Byrne.

Some two years later the issue of Byrne's pay again came up for discussion. The director-general clarified the precise sums involved: in that current year Byrne was getting £200,000 for his radio work, £250,000 for television, plus £25,000 for his role as producer of *The Late Late Show*. There was a further £125,000 due to him from sales of *The Late Late Show* to Channel Four in Britain where an edited version was broadcast on Monday afternoons. Although the Authority's minutes are not recorded verbatim, it is clear from his many interventions over the lifetime of that Authority that its chair, John Sorohan, remained the most critical of Byrne's pay, which at this juncture totalled £600,000. It is worth pointing out that the total

---

4 *ibid.*, 11 September 1992.

In 2011, the incoming director-general, Noel Curran, declared RTÉ's goal as 'seeking to maintain the widest public services on the slimmest cost base'. Referring to the controversial subject of pay for leading presenters, he wrote that 'their dedication, their talents or their audience appeal' were not underestimated, but added that financial constraints dictated that by 2013 fee levels 'must reduce markedly' from those applying in earlier years. The intention would be that by the end of 2013 the payments total would 'have reduced by in excess of 30 per cent relative to the 2008 levels'.

Originally RTÉ had always resisted disclosing what its top presenters were paid on the grounds of commercial sensitivity and contractual obligation. Ever since the figures of individual presenters became public through a Freedom of Information ruling, it had triggered continuing controversy. This had especially been the case in the context of the banking crisis and attendant criticism of the remuneration packages of top bankers. These issues were often discussed in programmes presented by broadcasters whose own pay was controversial. The pay of politicians was also a matter of controversy. The then Minister for Social Protection, Éamon Ó Cuív, when questioned on *Morning Ireland* about the bonuses being paid to AIB traders, responded that there were 'horrendous amounts of money' being paid to RTÉ presenters in the context of the Irish economic situation. 'That was a fair point that had to be examined.' Ó Cuív claimed that presenter's pay could be five or six times that of a politician's salary, which was always being used as a comparative reference in the debate.

Irish Times, 10 June 2011.

could have been expressed differently: as £475,000 from RTÉ, with permission to accept a market-based fee from the sales of *The Late Late Show* to Channel Four – which also, incidentally, made a payment to RTÉ for the programme. The director-general then outlined pro-rata reductions totalling £150,000 in Byrne's RTÉ remuneration for the following year because he was reducing his workload. The chair reminded the Authority members that all of this arose in the context of competition for Byrne's services and negotiations with his agent. Barry's only alternative, he advised the meeting, was that he could have told Byrne that the Authority had 'never agreed' with the scale of his remuneration 'but he thought there would be a parting of the ways if this were to happen. He was happy that it was being handled in a very professional manner. Gay Byrne was extraordinarily important to the organisation.'[5]

---

5   *ibid.*, 22 July 1994.

Historian Joe Lee, summarising the first twenty-five years of RTÉ television, suggested that television exerted 'most impact on specific topics about which the public previously knew little'; they then relied heavily on RTÉ for their knowledge which could 'mobilise enormous support for the cause in question by tapping existing sympathies in the society'. He believed that the case of Niall O'Brien and the Negros Nine in the Philippines, 'a brilliant scoop for RTÉ', provided 'a classic example.' In his memoirs Charlie Bird (photographed left in his prison cell with Niall O'Brien) recounts how he first arrived with a bottle of whiskey to see prisoner 30856, Fr Niall O'Brien, who was awaiting trial on a trumped up charge of murder. 'It was a welcome gift. He later recounted our first introduction – "I thought it strange that an Irish reporter was called Bird, but when I woke up in prison in the morning and saw him perched at the end of the bed looking at me as if he were a bird, I thought it even more strange."' RTÉ's coverage certainly raised O'Brien's profile in Ireland and 'helped to get greater attention for the Negros Nine.' On 3 July 1984, Niall O'Brien was released from Bacolod prison. The charges had been dropped; international attention and diplomatic efforts had proved effective.

Joe Lee, '25 Years of Irish television', Comoradh, 1962-1987, *RTÉ Guide*; Charlie Bird with Kevin Rafter, *This is Charlie Bird* (Dublin, 2006), pp.44-45.

The history of televised sport is replete with technical innovations and experimental production techniques introduced the better to communicate to the viewers – and often to the marginally interested viewers – what is happening, why and how? One of the achievements of RTÉ Sports Department is the manner in which a major event central to a particular sport has been introduced to a wider public through innovative presentation. A breakthrough must have been the RTÉ coverage of Italia '90. It was also a vindication of RTÉ's case for winning the second channel. This enabled the station to dedicate that channel to the event and offer saturation coverage to those who were keen followers.

Bill O'Herlihy – who made access to the ordinary non-specialist viewer all the more possible – believed that Italia '90 was 'an outstanding example of the country coming together'. He attributes this to an RTÉ strategy to widen the appeal of the competition beyond the country's soccer fans. 'The mood of celebration and of people coming together was even bigger than when the Pope came

Having scored only two goals in four games, Ireland's fate at Italia '90 depended on a penalty shoot-out against Roumania. With both teams level at 4-4, Packie Bonner saved the ninth penalty and Dave O'Leary scored the tenth to put Ireland through to the quarter-finals. In studio there was hugging and dancing. The son of the floor manager had a supporter's hat which Bill O'Herlihy borrowed. The entire press corps covering a European Summit in Dublin Castle took time off to share the drama. John Healy (right) did not hide his emotions.

to Ireland. We walked tall and smiled a lot and the sense of community was terrific.' He was asked by many if he was disappointed not to be in Italy for the competition. He had no regrets: 'I wouldn't have missed being in Dublin under any circumstances.'

'You can't have an elephant and not have it do tricks in both rings in the circus'

THROUGHOUT THE 1990s there were persistent attempts to find a television vehicle suited to Gerry Ryan, who was making such an impact on radio. In May 1990 Bob Collins told the Authority that Ryan's 'moving to television would give the audience a different perspective of him to that on the radio'.[6] Three years later Liam Miller as Director of Television Programmes explained why Ryan's programme was not working: *Ryantown* 'suffered to some extent' because RTÉ was 'not putting enough into the development of

---

6   *ibid.*, 23 May 1990.

The Ryan Game

This *RTÉ Guide* interview with Gerry Ryan on 25 July 1997 was debated by the RTÉ Authority. Patricia Redlich disliked the 'implied criticism of past editorial people on his programmes'; chairman Farrell Corcoran described the interview as 'unfortunate'; Bob Collins thought it 'bizarre', insisting that RTÉ 'was quite unhappy that Gerry Ryan had spoken out – but "it was in the nature of the beast".'

RTÉ Authority, minutes, 25 July 1997.

entertainment strands'.[7] By 1997 Ryan's television performances were still a matter of controversy for Farrell Corcoran's Thirteenth Authority. At a meeting in July, Bob Quinn expressed his scepticism on learning that Ryan 'was suddenly being groomed for television', for which, in Quinn's opinion, 'he was totally unsuitable'.[8]

This was being debated in the context of his just having signed a new RTÉ contract which included a liability to present a television series but without any such entitlement. Ryan himself was all too aware of how unsatisfactory had been his attempts to find a successful television format. The chapter covering this in his memoir is entitled 'The longest audition in history' and he refers to a concern among his radio colleagues that his 'dismally short TV career' might damage his appeal to radio listeners.[9] For *Irish Independent* critic John Boland, one of 'the abiding mysteries' of RTÉ television was that it kept coming up with new formats for Gerry Ryan, 'the ultimate face for radio'. Boland had 'lost track' of Ryan's many programmes but he found his 'drooling over celebrities in *Ryan Confidential* was especially gruesome'.[10] At the July 1997 Authority meeting Patricia Redlich had called for another look 'at the whole notion that a brilliant talent on radio necessarily translated on to the screen. RTÉ should be disabusing presenters of the notion that they have not made it unless they are on television.' Ryan himself was on record that RTÉ management thought 'you can't have an elephant and not have it do tricks in both rings in the circus.'[11]

---

7 *ibid.*, 29 October 1993.
8 *ibid.*, 25 July 1997.
9 Gerry Ryan, *Would the real Gerry Ryan please stand up?* (Dublin, 2008), p.178; hereafter Ryan, *Ryan*.
10 John Boland, 'A TV Year', *Irish Independent*, 28 January 2011.
11 Ryan, *Ryan*, 179.

Many tributes were paid to Gerry Ryan when he died in April 2010.

Ryan Tubridy: 'The moment I set foot in RTÉ, he put his wing around me and said: "I like what you do. I like what you are. I'm going to look after you." From that moment, there was a protective, almost paternal outlook from him to me.' Gay Byrne: 'Apart from the broadcasting altogether, what Gerry represented to me was skit, fun and trick-acting, just for the sake of disgusting people.' Pat Kenny: 'Gerry Ryan was a true original. ... He is, for me, both personally and professionally, irreplaceable.'

The three men are photographed above on *The Late Late Show*, 30 April 2010. Gerry Ryan's death had been announced earlier that day.

Sunday Times, 2 May 2010; *RTÉ Guide*, 15 May 2010.

There are many indicators of how the television industry in Ireland has changed in the first half-century of RTÉ's life. One of the most stark is to be found in the international market-place where the Irish television rights of American TV series are negotiated. Compared to the shopping expeditions of director-general Edward Roth, who could report to the first Authority that Irish rights would cost somewhere between £20 and £40 per hour, today's market is unrecognisable and far more costly. Every year in May, immediately following the announcements of the US network's autumn schedules, the pilots of the new series are screened for about 1,200 international buyers who converge on Los Angeles. Since 1995 Dermot Horan has represented RTÉ in this marketplace. 'Why is it that just a few shows emerge to garner international success? Is it the theme? The casting? The timing?' In Horan's opinion, 'it is all of these things.' He cites one example from 1994 when *E.R.* was launched by Warner Bros in the same year as another medical series, *Chicago Hope*. Both these hospital-based series were set in Chicago and both had strong, well-produced pilots. 'However while *Chicago Hope* was produced in a conventional way, *E.R.* brought emergency medicine into your living room, with an intensity and pace never seen before in a television drama. Dialogue was fast and furious. Sometimes it was difficult to hear what the doctors were saying. This was deliberate.' *E.R.* proved to be a television phenomenon. 'It broke records for the amount broadcasters were willing to pay for it. It launched movie stars such as George Clooney, but the real star was the hospital and its emergency room.' For Horan, this was proof again that 'the audience wants something new, something different from the norm.'

Dermot Horan, 'Quality US TV – A Buyer's Perspective', 10 January 2010.

'a moment when past and present ignited a sense of the future'

RIVERDANCE WAS HAILED – when first seen as the interval act at the 1994 Eurovision Song Contest – as 'a far cry from the straitjacket' in which Irish dancing had languished for most of the twentieth century. As it stomped onto the Eurovision stage, its creators could scarcely have imagined 'that it would excite so much comment at home and abroad'. Jean Butler and Michael Flatley won international plaudits and had been 'generally credited with putting the sex back into Irish dancing'. What had been refreshing about the performance was 'the blend of dance influences from Ireland, Spain and classical ballet and the obvious exuberance with which the dancers strutted their stuff and looked at each other as they did so.' For many of the audience – those present and the hundreds of millions looking in – it had upstaged the very contest at which it was merely the interval act. Much of the credit for this went to Bill Whelan's music. *Riverdance*, with its 'triumphant joyfulness', showed that a culture that had the confidence 'to borrow and adapt from others', while valuing what was native to its own, could 'rise head and shoulders

Riverdance would later be voted the best interval act in half a century of the Eurovision Song Contest.

WINDOW AND MIRROR

above the bland Euro-American pap that was on offer the same evening.'[12]

Cultural historian Terence Brown found *Riverdance* 'a surprisingly convincing blend' of Irish traditional dancing 'with North American showbusiness panache, exuberantly resexualizing what had, since the nineteenth century, been overlaid with an inhibiting Victorian respectability'. In this verdict, he was including the phenomenally successful international dance show later developed by John McColgan and Moya Doherty. Brown's verdict was that the original televised version at the 1994 Eurovision Song Contest had had an 'electrifying' impact and immediate appeal to a mass television audience. 'It was simultaneously authentic and completely new, a moment when past and present ignited a sense of the future, in which Irish identity in process was a matter for celebration.'[13]

the Toy Show presented a 'very serious' question which transcended RTÉ's 'concern for its pockets'

TWENTY-FIVE YEARS AFTER the publication of *Sit Down and Be Counted*, one of its co-authors, Bob Quinn, was nominated to the Thirteenth RTÉ Authority by minister Michael D. Higgins. This news can only have been met with foreboding by senior management at the station, and indeed, when the Authority met for its first business meeting in September 1995, it was manifestly a case of 'As I was saying when I was rudely interrupted...'. Quinn opened with an attack on the advertising industry. He was especially concerned that it viewed children 'as objects of strategy', and he invited his colleagues on the Authority to support his suggested curbs on toy advertising in the weeks before Christmas. Des Geraghty thought it should all be considered in a broader context. He did not take lightly the loss of 'the best part' of £1 million to RTÉ and asked if the government could ensure that 'other people broadcasting into Ireland' would comply with any new code. Garret FitzGerald thought the suggested cancellation of toy ads before Christmas to be 'a very good one', but also thought it 'illogical' to cut advertising while continuing with the annual *Late Late Toy Show* itself. William Attley found the programme 'very repulsive', complaining that the children involved 'were well-heeled'; but he did not believe that RTÉ's potential losses – which he reckoned at £3 million – could be considered a matter 'of minor

Jean Butler performs *Riverdance* at the Eurovision Song Contest, 1994, wearing not the 'usual twee outfit' but 'this sexy black number'.

Bob Quinn believed television commercials were part of 'a rapacious consumer culture'.

---

12 Uinsionn Mac Dubhghaill, 'Putting the sex back into Irish dancing', *Irish Times*, 5 May 1994.
13 Terence Brown, *Ireland: A Social and Cultural History: 1922-2002* (London, 2004), p.400.

The then ten-year-old Jonathan Philbin Bowman on the *Toy Show*, 13 December 1980. He was reviewing and demonstrating an old Houdini trick from the Paul Daniel's Magic Kit. He also bet Gay Byrne that he would fail the same challenge and won three pounds from him.

GB: 'So this is the Paul Daniel's Magic Kit?'
JPB: 'Yes, the Paul Daniel's money-making kit.' [laughter].

The Late Late Show, 13 December 1980.

import'. He believed the advertising budgets would merely switch to UTV. He declined to 'take the high moral ground.' But that is exactly where Anne Tannahill believed RTÉ should be and where it would be best positioned to win leverage for a licence increase.

The director-general can only have been alarmed at this concerted attack on what was considered one of RTÉ's most popular annual programmes. He referred to the damage to existing contractual understandings with advertising agencies, and warned of a possible 'crisis of confidence' in the relationship. He said RTÉ had to deal with the industry fairly; if ads stopped immediately, it would prove 'disastrous'. If disengaging, RTÉ had to do it 'in an orderly way'. Geraghty called for a programme where value for money toys could be shown. Betty Purcell thought such coverage should form part of *The Late Late Toy Show* itself. Chairman, Farrell Corcoran proposed that that suggestion be agreed and it was. Quinn considered it all a 'very serious' question which transcended 'RTÉ's concern for its pockets' and called for a complete ban on advertising to children on the grounds that all such advertising 'exploited the credulity and belief system of children'.[14]

At the next Authority meeting in October, the assistant director-general, Robert Gahan, reported on the advertising agencies' negative reaction by to the controversy. Geraghty complained that the issue had been handled 'appallingly' and that the Authority had been 'weakened because of it'. He felt that they had been 'rushed into it'. Geraghty believed that RTÉ could not afford to embark 'on a moral crusade' at a time when 'powerful competition' was imminent. He was opposed to 'pre-emptive jumps into the public arena'. The director-general noted that 'the Authority could not cut out toy

14 RTÉ Authority, minutes, 15 September 1995.

Among the 'YouTube' moments on *The Late Late Show*. Also noted in media reviews of the programme's history.

'Pat Kenny showed just how seriously he takes his job when he called a prizewinner last November to tell her of the happy news that she had won a weekend in Dublin, two tickets for the *Toy Show*, and €10,000 to go shopping. Showing no trace of the expected delight at receiving a call from the host, Barbara Heavey from Cork said she was not particularly interested in going to the *Toy Show*. Without further ado, Kenny pulled the tickets from a breast pocket and ripped them up as he cradled the receiver. Clearly taken aback at the audacity of her acceptance of €10,000 and rejection of the coveted tickets, Kenny rather presciently mused: "I think I'll give up this job."'

Fiona McCann, 'A host of memorable moments', *Irish Times*, 23 May 2009

advertising prior to Christmas and he had had very abrasive meetings with advertising interests'. The controversy had precipitated 'a major crisis of confidence' in the sector: what had been especially unsettling was talk of this being 'the first step'. RTÉ's advertising revenue 'would collapse' if the station indicated that it would not provide 'a window space for advertisers'. Meanwhile Quinn had annoyed some of his colleagues by speaking publicly on RTÉ on the issue; Corcoran thought this 'was dangerous' but Quinn remained unrepentant,[15] although at the November meeting he did allow that a further interview in the *Sunday Business Post* 'was unfortunate' as the comments had been made 'in the heat of battle'.[16] But he had not modified his opinions. He believed that 'television commercials and a rapacious consumer culture were part of a "growth" mindset that actually intensified unemployment, emigration and the growing inequality in the distribution of wealth.'[17]

The *RTÉ Guide* gave a mere paragraph to *The Late Late Toy Show* in the wake of the Authority controversy. The transmitted programme showed no signs of being any different to other years. And the *Guide* quickly reverted to 'business as usual' with many cover features in the years which followed, as above, 27 November 2010.

7 Days, Today-Tonight, Prime Time

MUIRIS MAC CONGHAIL has argued that current affairs broadcasting never recovered from the sacking of the RTE Authority. 'News and current affairs are no longer the essential items to be protected in public-service broadcasting, and therefore editorial independence is no longer the backbone of public-service broadcasting.'[18] The archives of RTE television offer much contradictory evidence. Both *Today Tonight* and *Prime Time* – along with other current affairs programmes – have achievements to their credit which match that of Mac Conghail's pioneering programme *7 Days*.

One example: the Stardust fire, which claimed the lives of 48 young people who died in the early hours of Saturday morning when attending a St. Valentine's night disco in Artane in Dublin in 1981. By Monday night an extended edition of *Today Tonight* was broadcast which was comprehensive, analytical and forensic: it used the television camera to prove – by showing the intact paintwork in the door frames – that some firedoors had remained locked throughout the fire. Some twenty-five years later *Prime Time* revisited the official

The ruins of the Stardust Club in Artane in Dublin after the fire on St. Valentine's night, 14 February 1981.

---

15 *ibid.*, 20 October 1995.
16 *ibid.*, 17 November 1995.
17 *ibid.*, 15 September 1995.
18 Muiris Mac Conghail, 'David Thornley at RTÉ, 1966-69', in Yseult Thornley (ed.), *Unquiet Spirit: Essays in Memory of David Thornley* (Dublin, 2008), pp.114-25.

Brendan O'Brien was among the most formidable investigative reporters in RTÉ Current Affairs with a number of ground-breaking reports on the North to his credit. He also famously investigated the notorious Dublin criminal, Martin Cahill, known as 'The General'. He 'doorstepped' Cahill coming out of the dole office and spoke to him for more than an hour on a Dublin street for *Today Tonight*. Throughout the interview Cahill kept his hand over his face. When O'Brien confronted Cahill with a list of his crimes, Cahill said: 'It must be someone else.' He also claimed he was unemployed and was 'in Anco trying to get a job.' He later surprised – and amused – O'Brien by claiming that he was a private detective. 'Surely that's the joke of the century', was O'Brien's response.

YouTube has a ten-minute extract from this programme which has recorded 130,000 hits.

David Nally, initiator of some of the most influential *Prime Time Investigates* programmes.

inquiry into the Stardust fire and established major flaws in their findings, not least undermining their main conclusion that the cause of the fire was 'probable arson'. The programme was partly instrumental in obliging the Oireachtas to acknowledge that this Tribunal finding was hypothetical, there being no evidence on which to base it. Other *Prime Time* programmes, and especially the documentary series *Prime Time Investigates,* have repeatedly demonstrated the power of television to expose malpractice, investigate scandals and often oblige the Oireachtas to bring in legislative reform. There have been highly influential programmes on standards in nursing homes, on Accident and Emergency services, on mandatory breath-testing at collision scenes and on corruption in a variety of spheres – often exploiting undercover reporting with hidden cameras. Originally introduced by Noel Curran, and under the successive leadership of Eddie Doyle, Angela Daly, Tara Peterman, David Nally, Brian Pairceir and Ken O'Shea, *Prime Time Investigates* has won many awards and a formidable reputation for campaigning broadcast journalism.

Current affairs debates – as *The Late Late Show* throughout its history underlines – do not all occur in formal current affairs programmes. Nobody's career underlines this more than Pat Kenny's. Having worked with *Today Tonight*, he moved to *Kenny Live* and succeeded Gay Byrne as host of *The Late Late Show* in 1999. He is seen here on the occasion of his final programme a decade later, in May 2009. That September he anchored a new programme *The Frontline*. At the end of its first season Glen Killane spoke of Kenny's 'storming performance' on *The Frontline*. 'Pat is the most capable broadcaster in the country.'

Irish Times, 7 August 2010.

17

1961-2011: then and now, some comparisons: the interview; the television personality; television and elections; cookery and food; sport; the Eurovision Song Contest; investigative reporting; children and television; Gay Byrne and The Late Late Show

AS WAS EMPHASISED in the introduction, this book makes no claim to being a comprehensive history of RTÉ television's first fifty years. The paucity of original research and the fact that so many of the most important recent files are still closed under the thirty-year rule means that such a history will have to wait some considerable time before it is attempted. In the meantime, this can be considered as an interim report on some aspects of that history.

Television greatly accelerated changes in Irish society which were probably inevitable and it undoubtedly shaped those changes in many ways. And television itself was modernised out of all recognition during the half-century under review. Because so many of these changes were incremental, they went largely unnoticed by viewers who, properly, took them for granted. Much of what changed in society was also incremental. But younger readers who have no memory of black-and-white pictures with patchy and indifferent reception – and older readers who can recall what television was like half a century ago – will, I hope, appreciate the pages that now follow. A disparate selection has been made of quite different facets of Irish television's history to illustrate what has changed between the pioneering decade of the 1960s and the modern era. Ireland has been transformed in that half-century, with television being both window and mirror to that change. It is hoped that the examination of so many different aspects of television's history will provide insights into the broader societal change over the period.

Television's impact on politics and elections is considered along with lesser discussed topics, such as the history of the broadcast interview, and the rise of the television personality; also television's impact on food, sport and children's leisure; and TV's role as investigative reporter and the impact of *The Late Late Show*. All are among the topics considered in the following pages.

Even before the television service opened, the first director-general, Edward J. Roth, instructed the Radio Éireann newsroom to cease using female newsreaders on radio. He believed women lacked authority when reading the news.

RTÉ newsreaders Anne Doyle, Bryan Dobson, Sharon Ní Bheoláin and Eileen Dunne

origins of the interview: 'some humbug of a hack politician and another humbug of a reporter'

THAT RTÉ TELEVISION had been launched in the early 1960s was both an advantage and a challenge: the advantage was that many of the experiments in programme-making techniques had already been tried elsewhere; the challenge was the availability of British stations to so many Irish viewers, inviting comparison with some of the best television in the world.

In its infancy, the medium was competing to position itself in a political system which – like so much else at this time – was in a state of flux. It was creating a new interest in politics. While the parliamentarians remained 'trapped in their rigmaroles and conventions', their role in educating the public was being usurped by 'a handful of men in TV studios'. To the viewer and voter, television was 'comprehensible and very informal'. A competent television interviewer could 'put straight questions and get straight answers far more quickly and vividly than a parliamentary debater'.[1]

The unrehearsed, spontaneous exchanges, which are now the hallmark of the interview, were largely developed by television. Its previous characteristic – ever since its origins in American journalism in the mid-nineteenth century – was that it was contrived. *The Nation* complained in 1869 that the interview was 'generally the joint product of some humbug of a hack politician and another humbug of a reporter'.[2] Radio, which was well suited as a medium to develop the interview, had largely passed on this opportunity. In the 1950s 'interviews' on radio were rehearsed, sometimes even scripted.

But when television began, most interviews were studio-based, which meant they were live or recorded 'as live', not to be edited. Filmed interviews on location could be edited but those facilities were a scarce resource, resulting in a strong preference by producers for spontaneous interviews and discussions. In all this it should be remembered that live broadcast interviewing was then a recent innovation, 'a quite new kind of informal art'.[3] No longer acceptable was what one BBC executive described as the 'hesitating, ingratiating manner which was supposed to represent conversation'.[4] In

> The interview is now such a staple of all media that it is easily forgotten how underdeveloped it was half a century ago. In telling Edward J. Roth that he had declined an invitation to be interviewed by John Freeman on *Face to Face*, Seán O'Casey reported that the BBC 'wanted to send down a cohort of magic lantern men to take pictures while I answered questions'.
>
> Typescript by Eileen O'Casey of an O'Casey manuscript draft of letter to Roth, 10 August 1962.

---

1 Anthony Sampson, 'Time they let the monster in', *The Observer*, c. autumn 1963, undated clipping in Irvine papers, RTÉWA.
2 Daniel Boorstin, *The Image* (New York, 1971), p.15.
3 Briggs, *Sound and Vision*, 906-07.
4 *ibid.*, 606.

John O'Donoghue interviewing UN Secretary General, U Thant.

Patrick Gallagher, interviewing the former Taoiseach, Seán Lemass.

In November 1967 John O'Donoghue and Patrick Gallagher were presenters on the then leading current affairs programme, *7 Days*. In this memo to the programme's editor, Muiris Mac Conghail, an expenses claim for the use of taxis was queried by the then Assistant Controller of Programmes, Jack White.

'I attach a batch of taxi dockets in the name of John O'Donoghue and one docket in the name of Patrick Gallagher. I understand from Gallagher's docket that he was on a visit to James Larkin at Bray. I presume that owing to pressure of time he made use of a taxi instead of taking the Bray bus. Perhaps you could confirm these two assumptions. In the case of John O'Donoghue, there appear to be four journeys between the studios and his home at Shankill. There is no indication that these were made at unusual hours which would justify the use of a taxi. As you know, travel from home to the office and vice versa is not an expense which can be charged to RTÉ. Will you please instruct John O'Donoghue to send a remittance for the appropriate sum (£3.7.0.) immediately to Mr. Brian Pierce, Administrative Services Officer.'

Memo, Jack White to Muiris Mac Conghail, 20 November 1967, RTÉWA..

its place came a spontaneous, and ever more robust style of questioning. Audiences and broadcasters quickly appreciated how suited the new medium was to a snatched interview with a winning sports captain or a defeated candidate in an election broadcast. One of those pioneers quick to appreciate television's potential, Grace Wyndham Goldie, wrote, almost with a hint of surprise, that British cabinet ministers in the early 1960s 'became increasingly willing to be cross-examined by television interviewers who had no political standing, who had not been elected and who were simply freelance operators working on contract for broadcasting organisations'. She devotes a whole chapter in her book on broadcasting and politics to what she terms 'the rise of the interviewer', a broadcaster whom the

David Thornley and Muiris Mac Conghail on the set of *Division*, 1966. Mac Conghail has written of an acrimonious encounter with Charles Haughey when he had invited the two men to his home in Kinsealy after a programme. 'Haughey said we were insulting to him and in defiance of him, and who the hell were we to appoint ourselves to such a position of power without responsibility.'

Yseult Thornley, Unquiet Spirit: Essays in Memory of David Thornley (Dublin, 2008), p.120.

When Ryan Tubridy presented his first *Late Late Show* in September 2009, his first guest was the Taoiseach, Brian Cowen. Some forty-two years earlier in November 1967, Gay Byrne telephoned the Taoiseach's office requesting a meeting with Jack Lynch to discuss the possibility of ministers appearing on the programme. He hoped that politics might be discussed in a serious manner and had already approached three of Lynch's most senior ministers, Charles Haughey, George Colley and Donough O'Malley. Byrne intimated that O'Malley was available subject to Lynch's agreement. The matter was discussed at cabinet the following day, and Lynch told his secretary to tell Byrne that he did not approve of ministers going on *The Late Late Show* and that provision for political discussions on television had already been agreed. 'There wasn't therefore any need for Gay Byrne to call on him to discuss the matter.' The party whips were later assured that Byrne had been reprimanded in RTÉ for making the approach.

Lynch to secretary of department, 2 November 1967; Childers to Carty, 4 November 1967; note of meeting, 5 November 1967, NAI, DT 98/6/19.

public believes is 'informed, impartial' and asks the questions 'which the public wishes to have answered'. She adds that the arbitrary selection of these powerful players 'caused legitimate resentments among politicians and the public'.[5]

RTÉ 'was not anxious to promote the kingdom of God'

WHEN HE SERVED as Chairman of the RTÉ Authority, Todd Andrews disliked the emergence of what he termed the television personality, who achieved a status which bore 'no relation to his professional competence'. Acceptance of such criteria 'as a standard of value in the community' was, to Andrews, 'deplorable'. He also believed that some of those attracted to television had one of three motives: 'they have a point of view to evangelize; they want to earn money; or they appear for reasons of vanity and self-indulgence.'[6]

Andrews was not alone in his resentment. The assumption of roles of authority by broadcasters and journalists was sensed by others in the old establishment. In 1976 the Bishop of Limerick, Jeremiah Newman, wrote that journalists and broadcasters had become 'a new kind of expert', critics of society as they witnessed it, and 'imbued with an intellectual and political ambition'. He complained that the journalist had become commentator. And the same phenomenon was happening in the non-entertainment

---

5   Grace Wyndham Goldie, *Facing the Nation: Television and Politics: 1936-76* (London, 1977), p.197.
6   Andrews, *Man of No Property*, 276.

broadcast programmes where 'interpretations and personal attitudes' abounded. 'Far from being primarily recorders of events', they were 'very much communicators of ideas'.[7] And it was the ideas being communicated which upset Newman's colleague Archbishop McQuaid, who pronounced himself 'very tired' of the concentration by RTÉ on bishops and priests. He told his press secretary that he did

not understand why RTÉ did not pay attention to the army, the law, medicine 'and especially journalism'. All these would, McQuaid believed, prove 'fruitful fields for investigators'. And he concluded with this rebuke for the broadcasters: they were 'not anxious to promote the Kingdom of God'.[8]

Mary Kelly researched the first two decades of current affairs output. In summary, she suggested that the values articulated in these programmes had been predominantly 'liberal and progressive with a sufficient tinge of moral indignation to criticise existing entrenched elites, bureaucracies and what are seen as non-progressive conservative forces'. She also found that 'overwhelmingly those given time to express and elaborate these views, whether as presenters or as interviewees, have been male and middle-class'.[9]

Kelly reckoned that current affairs programming was 'a potentially dangerous arena' for any broadcasting organisation: programmes on the activities 'of political and other powerful elites, on conflicts between them, on ineptitudes and inefficiencies may easily fan the flames of a desire to contain and limit the independence of the broadcasting organisation'. She noted that, in a highly competitive environment, RTÉ current affairs programming had commanded significant audiences, with 'assiduous viewing by the political parties – a group who have never been slow to launch complaints'. She argued that the 'personality system of a small group of tried and trusted presenters' was one way in which the broadcasting organisation could

attempt to ensure that 'due care' is maintained. However, a well-established personality system characterised by professionalism and authoritativeness, may not only contribute to holding onto the relative independence of the broadcasting organisation but also, possibly, to slowly

Echoing Bishop Newman's point, Declan Lynch suggested that during Gay Byrne's era *The Late Late Show* had found a role offering solace 'to the devout, the unorthodox and the barking mad'. Lynch believed that religion had provided the programme with some of its most memorable moments. It had certainly revealed 'more mind-altering mayhem' than any other subject. 'Throughout this spiritual quest, the moral authority of Gay Byrne remained high in the hearts of the people and in him they trusted. And you know, in a way, they were right.' Cartoonist, Tom Halliday added his comment.

Declan Lynch, 'In Gay we have trusted', *Sunday Independent*, 16 May 1999.

Mary Kelly complained in the 1980s that overwhelmingly the current affairs presenters were male and middle-class. The *Today Tonight* team January 1987: [left to right] John Bowman, editor Eugene Murray, Brian Farrell and Pat Kenny.

7   Jeremiah Newman, *The State of Ireland* (Dublin, 1976), pp.99-100.
8   McQuaid to O.J.Dowling, 6 March 1970, DDA/AB8/xxxx/ic.
9   Mary Kelly, 'Twenty years of current affairs on RTÉ' in Martin McLoone and John McMahon (eds), *Television and Irish Society: 21 Years of Irish Television* (Dublin, 1984), p.98; hereafter, Kelly 'Twenty Years of Current Affairs'.

Brian Farrell and Miriam O'Callaghan in 1997.

'In current affairs, presenters can use the tendency of the audience to identify with them to bolster their own authority to speak for us the viewers, and to hold their own in the light of elite criticism.' – Mary Kelly

expanding the extent to which criticism of those in powerful positions is tolerated.

Kelly notes that this is an international phenomenon, 'endemic throughout television'. The presenter's 'familiarity, dependability and populism' was essential in forging this identification with viewers and it frequently integrated 'authoritative, populist and paternalistic elements'.[10]

10 Kelly, 'Twenty Years of Current Affairs', 103-4.

In 1963 the *Irish Independent,* in an editorial, argued that if the Dáil and its members were 'to retain their status and importance, surely the people outside Leinster House should have the chance to see and hear them at work.' The newspaper wanted access for TV cameras to the Dáil.: 'televising a few sessions will heighten rather than harm the role of the press in its constant reporting – and watching – of our parliament.' In 1966 the then minister with responsibility for broadcasting, Joseph Brennan, insisted that there was 'not the slightest hope of having television coverage of either House of the Oireachtas'. As far as he knew, this applied 'to every parliament in the world'. He assured the Seanad that the government was 'entirely opposed to it' and believed no party favoured it. He claimed that it 'would have the effect of making Deputies and Senators talk to the television and not to the debate'. There was not 'the remotest chance' of allowing the cameras in. When the cameras were admitted – just twenty-five years later, in January 1991 – politicians wondered what the fuss had been about. Maurice Manning, political scientist and sometime Fine Gael TD and senator, believed that television had raised general public awareness and 'allowed for coverage of the element of theatre that is an inescapable part of the life of all parliaments: the fall and appointment of governments, sackings, scandals, confrontations and party tensions.'

Irish Independent, 20 March 1963. Seanad Debates, vol.60, cols.1586-87, 17 February 1966. Maurice Manning, 'Houses of the Oireachtas: background and early development' in Muiris MacCarthaigh and Maurice Manning (eds), *The Houses of the Oireachtas: Parliament in Ireland* (Dublin, 2010), p.33.

electioneering: from mass rallies to major television debates

THE MAJOR EVE-OF-POLL RALLIES in central Dublin which had traditionally concluded Irish general elections survived only into television's first decade. Although these rallies attracted huge crowds, it was largely a case of party leaders preaching to the converted: in contrast, when the climax to the campaign shifted to the television studios, the politicians were invariably focused on influencing the 'Don't Knows'. Television's impact on Irish elections was pervasive but in no respect was it greater than in how election campaigns concluded. The first serious prospect of a head-to-head debate between the protagonists who would be Taoiseach came in 1981. Both Charles Haughey and Garret FitzGerald were asked at early press conferences if there would be such a televised debate. After two weeks negotiation the idea was abandoned by RTÉ because of the 'mutually irreconcilable' positions of the two parties. Haughey while 'prepared to debate with anyone, anywhere, anytime', insisted on a three-way debate including FitzGerald's putative coalition partner, Labour's Frank Cluskey. This was a masterly move. It depicted Haughey as fair-minded and – had it been acceptable to Fine Gael – would have allowed Fianna Fáil strategists to concentrate on the policy differences between the two parties promising an alternative government.[11] FitzGerald countered by offering two debates, one three-way and one head-to-head with Haughey whom he accused of being shy of the confrontation: RTÉ could not 'lasso him and drag him into the studio'.[12]

Given the failure to agree the terms of engagement, it was decided that each party leader would be interviewed by a panel of print journalists. This formula was by common consent – especially of the newspaper interlocutors themselves – not a success. But the possibility of a head-to-head debate between the two leaders who would be Taoiseach was now firmly on the agenda and was duly raised at the early press conferences of the snap election a mere eight months later in February 1982. The usual skirmishing followed, with party managers keen to achieve the optimum setting for any encounter without appearing publicly reluctant to participate. Labour again claimed the right to join the debate, but their new leader Michael O'Leary then accepted

Skirmishing about the rules of engagement in any leaders' debate is inevitable. In the first election where such a debate was even mooted in 1981, Fianna Fáil played a masterly card: Haughey would debate only if FitzGerald's putative coalition partner, Labour leader Frank Cluskey was also included. Martyn Turner's cartoon captures the point. After two weeks of negotiations, the debate format was abandoned in favour of interviews with both leaders.

Irish Times, 6 June 1981.

---

11 *Irish Times*, 4 June 1981.
12 *Irish Press*, 5 June 1981.

Before television, major rallies marked the end of general election campaigns. But on such occasions, politicians invariably found themselves speaking to the converted. Television debates, in contrast, were focussed on influencing the Don't Knows.

a separate interview. On this occasion both main parties found that they had more to lose by a refusal to engage and so, for the first time in Irish electoral history, it took place. Viewers were undecided whether FitzGerald's preoccupation with the small print of policy was a fault or a virtue. The consensus was that Haughey's accomplished performance was of greater benefit to him since his low rating in the polls ensured that he could only move up.

Ever since then, such a televised debate was the expected climax to a general election campaign, although there were occasions when it failed to materialise. Indeed in 2011 a new template emerged with a series of debates on different television channels. Enda Kenny, who would emerge as Taoiseach after that election, even survived unscathed when he refused to participate in the first proposed three-way debate between Fianna Fáil, Fine Gael and Labour. Scheduled by TV3 without his agreement once they had secured the acceptance of the other two party leaders, Kenny managed to avoid this debate by insisting that it should also include the leaders of the minor parties of Sinn Féin and the Greens. Such a five-way debate was indeed staged by RTÉ's *Frontline* during the campaign – which also included a leaders' debate in Irish on TG4 and concluded with a *Prime Time* three-way debate between the leaders of Fine Gael, Labour and Fianna Fáil.

One dimension has been consistently present since 1981: brinkmanship and gamesmanship has dominated the negotiation of these broadcasts. Given that the stakes are so high, it is inevitable that

'it came perilously close to being the yawn of the election.' – John Healy.

Charles Haughey shakes hands with Garret FitzGerald prior to the first leaders debate in an Irish general election, 16 February 1982. In the centre is Brian Farrell. In the November election of that same year, FitzGerald upstaged Haughey by not appearing for such a photo-call. His strategists, aware that Haughey's bitter personal attacks were winning sympathy for FitzGerald, wanted to avoid a handshake lest it appear as a gesture of conciliation. FitzGerald himself explained his absence from the photo-call on the grounds that he did not want the debate to resemble 'the beginning of a prize fight'.

Irish Independent, 24 November 1982.

ground rules will be the subject of complex negotiation. And there is usually some wriggle-room for a protagonist who does not wish to engage, to find grounds for declining. Any potential Taoiseach leading in the opinion polls inevitably negotiates from a position of self-interest: if ahead, why risk a gaffe in such a debate? It would always be the challenger who would be keenest for such an encounter. And party strategists – while never admitting as much – would also be weighing up the respective abilities of the protagonists to be 'good on the box'. But what the 1981-82 period did change was that such debates were expected by the voters to provide a major test of leadership in any election campaign and a price might be paid by any party which was perceived to be shy of such an encounter. It had first become a feature of Irish elections two decades after its inauguration in the 1960 US Presidential election. But it would take Britain five decades before what Robin Day had described as this 'most lamentable gap' in British elections was closed and televised debates between party leaders became a feature of the UK election in 2010.[13]

Fianna Fáil would not agree to a leaders debate in the snap election called by Charles Haughey in 1989. Instead there were individual interviews with the party leaders. Olivia O'Leary interviewed Charles Haughey on 13 June 1989. *The Star* published this cartoon by Gugi the following day.

---

13 Robin Day, *Day by Day: A Dose of My Own Hemlock* (London, 1975), pp.16-17. See also John Bowman, 'Media coverage of the Irish elections of 1981-82' in Howard Penniman and Brian Farrell (eds), *Ireland at the polls: 1981, 1982 and 1987* (Washington, 1987), 167-91.

Lenihan never recovered from his contradictory testimony

FROM A MINIMAL ROLE in 1966, television has come to play a central – and sometimes a decisive – role in presidential elections. In 1966, Eamon de Valera, as the incumbent, had decided to stand for re-election but without campaigning. De Valera's strategy was self-serving. He was eighty-three – and above the fray of party politics – and he had the fortuitous advantage that in the weeks preceding the election he was obliged to fulfil many presidential duties associated with the Golden Jubilee of the Easter Rising. By denying oxygen to the presidential campaign, Fianna Fáil at least ensured that television's impact was minimal which better suited the incumbent. De Valera won narrowly by 50.5 per cent of the vote to 49.5.[14]

Television would play little role in the outcome of presidential elections for some years since only one of the next four presidential terms was decided at the ballot box, three being uncontested. But the outcome of the 1990 election was decided on television. The clear leader in the opinion polls, Brian Lenihan, found his campaign unravelling from the time he appeared on *Questions and Answers* where he was challenged by Garret FitzGerald concerning controversial phone calls to President Hillery in February 1982. The calls were to invite the president to use his 'absolute discretion' to refuse FitzGerald's request to dissolve the Dáil: it could then be determined whether Charles Haughey might be able to win sufficient support to form a government without an election. Whereas Lenihan could have defended the phone calls as an appropriate request, he instead denied them and fell into a carefully laid ambush by Fine Gael which knew he had already made contradictory claims to an academic researcher. The editorial team on *Questions and Answers* were unaware of the Fine Gael ambush but had – scarcely

---

14 McCague, *McCourt*, 103-04.

Mary Robinson signs the declaration of office, 3 December 1990. Left to right; Taoiseach Charles Haughey, former President Patrick Hillery, former Taoisigh Liam Cosgrave, Jack Lynch, Garret FitzGerald, Chief Justice Thomas Finlay.

'Ms. McAleese, are you now or were you at any time guilty of being a nationalist?'

surprisingly – readily accepted FitzGerald as a substitute panellist when Jim Mitchell became 'unavailable' some few hours before the broadcast. Lenihan never recovered from his contradictory testimony: to the voters it seemed like 'a tangled web' and Mary Robinson was the beneficiary being elected president on transfers from Fine Gael's Austin Currie.

Seven years later Mary McAleese was elected in another controversial campaign in which her director of elections, Noel Dempsey, complained of media bias, including RTÉ's *Prime Time*, whose profile of her he reckoned 'tough but fair' until he saw the 'soft-focus Hello-type treatment' of her main rival, Fine Gael's Mary Banotti. He insisted on a meeting with RTÉ executives at which they accepted his complaint.[15] Dempsey was also annoyed at the pervasive coverage given to leaked documents of Department of Foreign Affairs intelligence notes on Northern nationalists. Initially the *Sunday Business Post* published a document suggesting that McAleese had Sinn Féin sympathies. This prompted another of the candidates, Derek Nally, to challenge on *Questions and Answers* whether McAleese was 'a proper person' to be president. The following evening in a Trinity debate with McAleese, Nally withdrew this charge but his director of elections, John Caden, persisted with an *Irish Times* article, 'Memo on McAleese by reputable civil servant rings true to any sensible reader'. McAleese ignored the pervasive media antipathy – including Eoghan Harris's characterisation of her as an unelectable 'tribal time-bomb' – ran a positive campaign and enjoyed a comfortable victory, inaugurating a two-term presidency which would rank among the most popular in the history of the office.

This cartoon by Ian Knox ran across six columns on the front page of the *Irish News*, 20 October 1997. It reflected the newspaper's anger at how McAleese was being subjected to what they believed were McCarthyite tactics in parts of the Republic's media. Knox's cartoon depicts her accusers;

Left to right:

John Caden, initially director of Derek Nally's presidential campaign, who insisted that the accusations against McAleese rang true even after Nally had accepted her denial;

Labour leader, Dick Spring, who called for a 'very critical examination' of McAleese's politics;

Derek Nally, who initially queried whether McAleese was 'a proper person' to be president;

Fine Gael leader, John Bruton, who exploited what he termed Sinn Féin's 'calculated endorsement' of McAleese, although this merely rested on Gerry Adams stating that if he had a vote he would prefer McAleese to the other candidates;

Eoghan Harris, who was McAleese's sternest critic throughout the campaign.

Paul Cullen, 'How Aras race turned into a bitter FF-FG battle', *Irish Times*, 18 October 1997.

15 Justine McCarthy, *Mary McAleese, the Outsider* (Belfast, 1999), p.194; RTÉ Authority, minutes, 31 October 1997.

Before RTÉ initiated day-long coverage of the election count in the 1965 election, the closest approximation to live media coverage was the 'scoreboard' on the *Irish Times* building in Westmoreland Street which was updated as the newsroom heard of seat gains by the parties. This photograph shows many passers-by looking upwards to read the state of the parties at lunchtime on count day, 5 February 1948, during that year's general election.

John O'Donoghue (above) was among the pioneers of current affairs programmes: he was presenter of *Broadsheet*, then of *64*, *65* and *66*, later of *7 Days*. And he anchored the inaugural election results marathon on the 1965 general election. By the 1969 election Brian Farrell had joined the presenting team. The photograph below shows (left to right) Basil Chubb, Ted Nealon, Brian Farrell and John O'Donoghue analysing the results in the 1969 general election.

Who governs next?

ONE OF THE CENTRAL RESPONSIBILITIES of a national broadcaster is to give the citizens the opportunity to communally experience great national events: the state visit of John F. Kennedy or Queen Elizabeth II or the pastoral visit of John Paul II; a state funeral or presidential inauguration; or great sporting moments. But from the beginning of the television service, the most significant event has been the results coverage in general elections. As in so many other spheres, it was the television service which initiated this coverage: before Telefís Éireann was launched, Radio Éireann had made no attempt at rolling coverage. The 1965 election results provided the first challenge to both services.

Election-results broadcasting provides an awesome moment in any democracy. Multi-seat constituencies and the proportional representation system of voting add considerably to the complexity and excitement of an Irish election count. For many younger citizens their first engagement with democracy is often kindled by the excitement generated by broadcast results coverage. It has also been acknowledged among academics that the communal involvement of the electorate during election night results programming is a significant event in most western democracies.[16]

---

16 See the comparative study of election night television coverage in 1968 and 2000 in Thomas E. Patterson, *Diminishing Returns*, (Kennedy School of Government, Harvard, 2003).

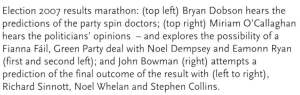

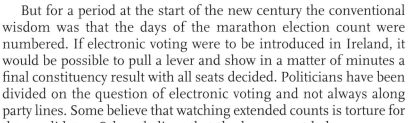

Election 2007 results marathon: (top left) Bryan Dobson hears the predictions of the party spin doctors; (top right) Miriam O'Callaghan hears the politicians' opinions – and explores the possibility of a Fianna Fáil, Green Party deal with Noel Dempsey and Eamonn Ryan (first and second left); and John Bowman (right) attempts a prediction of the final outcome of the result with (left to right), Richard Sinnott, Noel Whelan and Stephen Collins.

But for a period at the start of the new century the conventional wisdom was that the days of the marathon election count were numbered. If electronic voting were to be introduced in Ireland, it would be possible to pull a lever and show in a matter of minutes a final constituency result with all seats decided. Politicians have been divided on the question of electronic voting and not always along party lines. Some believe that watching extended counts is torture for the candidates. Others believe that the long count helps the electorate to learn about the complexities of proportional representation.

And it is the broadcasting of the results over many hours which has introduced vast numbers of them to how this can matter. This in turn better informs their voting strategy in future elections. Among the many letters of congratulations to the then director-general of RTÉ, George Waters, after the 1981 results coverage was one from the newly elected Fine Gael TD, Mary Flaherty. She suggested that 'interest in and information about the PR system must now be at its highest ever in Ireland and in no small measure due to RTÉ.'[17]

Dublin North was one of three constituencies where electronic voting was piloted in the 2002 general election. As polling closed, the computer could deliver the final result. Screen grab from the live election coverage shows Nora Owen's response on learning she has lost her seat. She is being comforted by Seán Ryan (right) and Trevor Sargent (left), both elected.

---

17 Flaherty to Waters, 26 June 1981, RTÉWA.

Ed Mulhall, Head of News and Current Affairs from 2002. He instanced RTÉ coverage of the financial scandals, the tribunals and the commentary on the economic downturn as impressive in terms of 'high audiences and challenging programmes'.

'Forty Years of News', RTÉ 1, 19 December 2002.

Wave after wave of new technology, the digital revolution, satellite links and the miniaturisation of equipment all enabled a more flexible approach to news-gathering – and, indeed, to the live transmission of news as it was happening. The capacity of the Newsroom to anchor a news bulletin by satellite link is now taken for granted. Here Bryan Dobson anchors the *Six-One News* from St Peter's Square in Vatican City covering the election of Pope Benedict XVI. As Eamonn Delaney wrote: 'Everything is placid and controlled' and especially when Bryan Dobson 'has decided to deliver the news from some foreign place'.

Irish Times, 2 December 2000.

politicians now preferred 'the pseudo-event, the sound-bite and the spin.'

NO DEPARTMENT IN RTÉ changed more than the Newsroom over the first fifty years. This is not to say that it embraced change. Indeed, there was no department in the station which resisted it more. The Newsroom had been complacent in the 1960s, believing that at least its workers knew their trade, whereas elsewhere in the organisation individuals from a variety of backgrounds were only learning theirs. But with a new medium of communications, such as television, those without preordained notions of how programmes should be made were arguably better positioned to become effective communicators. Note Michael Barry's 'heady exhilaration' enjoyed by the earlier BBC pioneers when television production was still 'a rough-hewn affair'.[18] What was needed was industriousness, curiosity and innovation: 'experience' – especially if accompanied by union-backed restrictive practices – could be a distinct disadvantage.

Moreover, the first three Heads of News, Pearse Kelly, Jim McGuinness and Wesley Boyd, were all from print journalism. It was their successors, Joe Mulholland and Ed Mulhall – both with a wealth of experience in current affairs – who finally modernised the newsroom and comprehensively brought television production values to its output. Mulholland was one of the most gifted producers of his generation and a broadcaster with exceptional qualities of leadership, as he had demonstrated in *Today Tonight*'s long run. He continued Boyd's policy of embracing new technology and made no secret of his view that 'it would make sense' with regard to resources, to amalgamate news and current affairs: with 'the proper structures' it would be possible 'to bring about rationalisation and still keep the integrity of each'.[19] This amalgamation was eventually achieved under the leadership of Ed Mulhall in 2002. Mulhall believed that the joint strength of both departments could better compete against the well-resourced multi-nationals.[20] Meanwhile, Horgan recognised a significant change in how politicians attempted to influence the news: 'the legislative hammer-blow, the ukase, and the intimidatory phone call' of the early days were no longer the weapons of choice. They now preferred 'the pseudo-event, the sound-bite and the spin'.[21]

---

18 See Barry quoted in Box on p.12 above.
19 Michael Ross, 'Lights, camera, action, cut!', *Magill*, June 1990.
20 Tom Manning and Seán Duignan, 'Forty Years of News', RTÉ 1, 19 December 2002.
21 Horgan, *Broadcasting and Public Life*, 215.

'mistakes were not the end of the world, just part of the game'

THE IMPACT OF TELEVISION on home cooking would be difficult to measure. Arguably the greatest impact could prove to have been through the television commercial. But over the past half-century, food and cookery programmes have proved increasingly popular. Telefís Éireann's first cook was Monica Sheridan, a natural screen performer 'with a subversive disregard' both for the rules of cookery and for how the Telefís Éireann establishment might respond to her 'unpredictable asides and irreverent sense of humour'. Her programmes – despite the limitations of black and white TV – were popular and influential throughout the 1960s. 'A companionable but authoritative voice gave her departures from the received kitchen etiquette a daring seal of approval: by famously licking her fingers she horrified traditionalists and delighted younger audiences.'[22] The great American TV cook, Julia Child, also caused offence: so much so that when her series *The French Chef* was first screened in Ireland, its run was curtailed. 'People complained she dropped things, licked her fingers, forgot to defrost chicken in time and had to axe it to death and – worst of all – spoke like the Titanic foghorn.'[23] But she returned to RTÉ screens where she demonstrated her passionate belief that her job was as an educator: competent cooks, if they followed the recipes, 'would find even complicated French dishes within their grasp. Mistakes were not the end of the world, just part of the game.'[24] Darina Allen was also a passionate educator, investing her teaching with a missionary zeal: 'You teach someone how to make a loaf of bread or a soup or a gravy, and it's actually something they're going to use, not like teaching them a theorem in maths.'[25] This would be an outlook shared by another of the great television teachers, Delia Smith, many of whose BBC series proved hugely popular on RTÉ. Irish viewers clearly found her, as *The Times* did, 'competent without being bossy, friendly without being familiar'.[26]

Meanwhile beyond the kitchen-based, 'how-to' programmes, food and cookery programmes with an emphasis on entertainment were

Monica Sheridan had 'no more eager fans' than the production team assigned to her programmes. The *RTV Guide* reported that her 'on the air' cooking was done for the studio crew. She had to cook for someone, she insisted. She could not cook for a cathode tube. 'It would be sacrilege to let such fine fare go to waste.' It never did as Paul Gleeson, Aidan Maguire and Eugene Barrington demonstrate at the end of a recording of *Monica Sheridan's Kitchen* in 1963.

RTV Guide, 19 March 1965.

---

22 Patrick Long, 'Monica Sheridan', *Dictionary of Irish Biography* (Dublin and Cambridge, 2009).
23 Elgie Gillespie, *Irish Times*, 31 January 1986.
24 Obituary, Julia Child, *New York Times*, 13 August 2004.
25 'Darina Allen talks to Deirdre Purcell', *The RTÉ Book* (Dublin, 1989), pp.24-25.
26 *The Times*, 15 March 1980.

Despite presenting many series of *The French Chef* on RTÉ, Julia Child never made the cover of the *RTÉ Guide*. But she was on the cover of *Time* magazine (25 November 1966) as an iconic figure in American popular culture. It all began when she was invited to discuss her book on French cooking on a Boston TV channel. She decided to whip up an omelette during the interview, which prompted an invitation to record 26 programmes at $50 each. It was called *The French Chef* because those three words would fit on any TV listing guide. She became a celebrity chef not through any promotional gimmicks but because patently she wanted to teach and the viewers appreciated this. She rejected many offers to switch channels but stayed with public television where her programme became the longest-running series ever.

Darina Allen has been one of Ireland's most influential broadcasters through her *Simply Delicious* series which ran on RTÉ from the late 1980s. Dedicated to basic skills, authentic produce and supporting local farmers and artisan producers, she is also interested in food history and forgotten skills. Her appeal to viewers is akin to that of Julia Child: viewers recognise a passionate teacher.

Richard Corrigan, a farmer's son from County Meath, owes his international career to his mother, whom he remembers as a brilliant cook: watching her bake bread or roast a pheasant, he knew his career would be in food. Successful restaurateur and writer, it was his enthusiasm as a broadcaster which made his series *Corrigan Knows Food* such a success.

Rachel Allen's RTÉ series have won international recognition. She believes the recession and the need to make economies in the household budget may bring some cooks back to the skills of baking. 'It really is a cheap way to treat yourself. Baking is a really simple thing that we can all afford to do.'

RTÉ Guide, 25 October 2008.

proving increasingly popular on television worldwide. There were many genres: travelogues, competitions and make-over programmes. It seemed that viewers could not get enough food programmes on television. Their appeal has been explained as offering 'vicarious pleasure for the armchair cook and the couch potato alike'. This is pleasure deferred: it epitomizes 'the culture of visual and psychological consumption: consumption of cooking, of tasting, of hunger, of passion, of the familiar and the exotic, and of the television viewer's willingness to be entertained by someone performing in the kitchen.'[27] While other channels indulge loutish presenters whose unique selling point seems to be their propensity to bully those around them, RTÉ has kept the emphasis on home-produced programmes imparting new skills and also encouraging curiosity, experimentation and aspiration. It is all a long way from the cookery book which, as television began in 1962, could advise its readers how to source garlic through the postal service.

27 Pauline Adema, 'Vicarious consumption: Food, television and the ambiguity of modernity', *Journal of American and Comparative Cultures*, 1 October 2000.

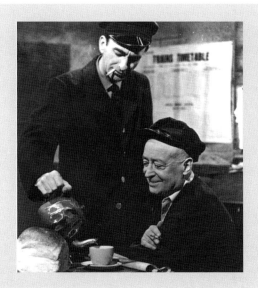

George Waters on becoming director-general in 1978, admitted that RTÉ had not been very successful with comedy. He identified the problem as a lack of good scripts. He looked back to the short comedy sketches, 'O'Dea's Your Man', from the station's early years with Jimmy O'Dea (right) and David Kelly, here seen in *The Signal Box* in 1963. The series was written by Myles na gCopaleen and directed by James Plunkett. This was 'very good comedy and very well received. We've never done anything on that level since then, I think.'

John Walsh, interview with George Waters, *RTÉ Guide*, 14 April 1978.

Podge and Rodge in their first RTÉ series, *A Scare at Bedtime*. They have maintained their popularity – and won many comedy awards – while being the flag-bearers for what has sometimes been called 'edgier and riskier' programming.

In December 2006, expressing his concern at what he termed a 'growing coarseness and aggression' in Irish society, the Roman Catholic primate, Archbishop Seán Brady asked: 'Do we want to have a culture of *Podge and Rodge*, or one of decency and respect?' His citing of the popular adult puppet show as his benchmark of coarseness is not surprising. *Podge and Rodge* – or to give them their full names, Padraig Judas O'Leprosy and Rodraig Spartacus O'Leprosy – graduated from children's television in 1997 in a series entitled *A Scare at Bedtime* which was a satire on *A Prayer at Bedtime*, a nightly religious interlude. Not everyone has been amused. Fionola Meredith allowed that sometimes the pair were 'worth a quick guffaw' but added that there were 'only so many times that saying "feck" can be funny.' She found herself siding with the bishop. 'But not because *Podge and Rodge* are rude – just that their rudeness is so dispiritingly one-dimensional.'

Patsy McGarry, 'Primate cites growing coarseness and aggression', *Irish Times*, 18 December 2006; Fionola Meredith, *Irish Times*, 6 January 2007.

*the 'native weaklings' rebuked by the GAA in 1955 for playing the game of
'the wily Saxon' were, by 2007, playing rugby in a rebuilt Croke Park*

HOW SPORT IS SHOWN on television has been transformed
during the past half-century. In 1962 the governing bodies in
Irish sport could only have been uncertain about the new
medium's possible impact. The rugby authorities, for instance,
could not have foreseen that it would be money from television
rights which would prove the catalyst to turn their game
professional. Nor could those with responsibility for soccer
foresee how the extraordinary fees that would be paid by satellite
broadcasters would transform their code into a multi-billion
dollar worldwide industry, with inevitable consequences for the
game in Ireland.

The GAA – given its achievement in remaining an amateur
association – provides yet another case history. Would television
pose a threat or an opportunity? The question is implicitly there
throughout the 1960s and 1970s in the minutes of the Central
Council. One faction in the association presumed that they were

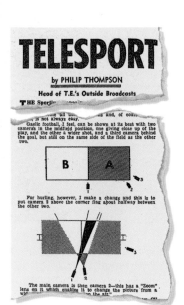

Hurling was, reputedly, the fastest field game in the world – so fast that Telefís Éireann's
internationally recruited TV sports directors wondered whether it was even possible to televise it
successfully. In an article in the *RTV Guide* (left), director Philip Thompson shared with readers
how he had determined the optimum placement of cameras to capture hurling on television.

At the GAA's Easter Congress in 1968 RTÉ received a compliment – rare at this gathering –
that the televising of GAA matches had been 'excellent and technically brilliant'. The sports
department's policy was one of constant innovation. This photograph shows TV cameraman
Phil Mulally with a mobile camera and a power-pack transmitter attached to his back. He is on
the pitch at Croke Park just before the start of the All-Ireland Senior Hurling Final between Cork
and Kilkenny on 7 September 1969.

John Boland, television critic of the *Irish Independent*, has acknowledged the extraordinary improvement in presentation of sport on television, 'an expertise that's only fully appreciated when we look at archive footage from the 1960s, 1970s or even 1980s.' He writes that RTÉ's sports coverage in the new century 'has generally been outstanding, whether of GAA fixtures, international football and rugby or the Olympics'. While other channels 'can be either superficial or cretinously fanzine', Ireland has been fortunate 'with punditry that's unusually intelligent and engaging'. He specifically praised Eamon Dunphy, John Giles and Liam Brady on soccer and George Hook, Brent Pope and Conor O'Shea on rugby: 'far more articulate and absorbing than their BBC or Sky counterparts'. Such forthrightness has been consciously encouraged by the RTÉ sports department for many years through the efforts of editors such as Tim O'Connor, Mike Horgan and Glen Killane. They have consciously reached out beyond the core supporters of a particular code and encouraged, in Killane's words, 'strong, independent editorial comment with which the Irish audience can identify'.

John Boland, 'A TV year', *Irish Independent*, 28 January 2011; Killane to author, 19 April 2011.

'entitled to preferential treatment' from the national broadcaster and should threaten a boycott were there any failure 'to preserve, protect and foster the culture and traditions of the Nation'. The more mainstream view was that television remained of such 'tremendous value as a propaganda vehicle' that it would be 'folly in the extreme' to boycott it. The 1973 records show that television continued to be a matter of dissatisfaction for many members. Despite the promise that Gaelic games would have 'pride of place' from the new head of sport, Fred Cogley, GAA delegates believed they could not relax their vigilance in relation to television: special recognition 'should be ours as a matter of right, as a thirty-two county, unashamedly national organisation, striving to maintain something of Ireland's traditions in these times.'

Specifically in the case of hurling, there was a hope that television coverage might especially widen its appeal. In the event, the telecast of the 1962 final – to which access had been accorded virtually without charge – did provide a significant stimulus to hurling, whose geographical concentration in the southern half of the island had been a perennial concern. The 1963 Annual Congress was reassured that no 'kind of propaganda would beat the real thing'. And it was through television that many viewers first witnessed hurling expertly played.[28] Decades later the claim would be made that television coverage had boosted interest – and attendances – among people 'who might otherwise not have been exposed to the great game'.[29] The GAA remained especially sensitive concerning television's analysis of foul play. It had been much more

The GAA president's address to Congress in 1955 was critical of the popularity of foreign games and he criticised 'the native weaklings' who played the game of 'the wily Saxon'.

Micheal Ó Donnchadha, presidential address, Annual Congress 1955, GAA archives, CC/1/18.

Whatever would he have made of this 'native weakling', Paul O'Connell, half a century later, in 2007, helping to defeat the 'wily Saxons' 43-13 in a rebuilt Croke Park?

---

28 GAA Archives, Central Council files, 1967 to 1979, CC/1/30-42, *passim*.
29 Seán Kilfeather, 'These are the "good old days" of hurling', *Irish Times*, 5 August 1997.

RTÉ Sport broadcasters with Noel Curran (Director of Television) and Director-General Cathal Goan, at the launch of RTÉ's 2007 GAA Championship coverage, in the Hogan Stand at Dublin's Croke Park on 2 May 2007. *Front row*, left to right, are: Michael Lyster, Noel Curran, Cathal Goan, Pat Spillane, Joanne Cantwell, Marty Morrissey and Evanne Ní Chuilinn. *Middle row*; Jim Carney, Siobhán Madigan, Kevin McStay, Bernard Flynn, Paul Curran, Tommy Lyons, Micheál Ó Muircheartaigh and Cyril Farrell. *Back row*: Con Murphy, Brian Carthy, Anthony Tohill, Tomás Mulcahy, Michael Duignan, Anthony Daly, Peter Finnerty, John Kenny and Dónal O'Grady.

comfortable in the O'Hehir era when he would use a euphemism such as a 'shemozzle'[30] and the cameras would duly avert their gaze. In contrast, the modern practice was to replay any infraction in slow motion and proceed to a television inquiry in that evening's programme as to who the guilty party might be and whether the referee had proved correct in his decisions.

Overall sport on television proved to be so popular that no code could afford not to embrace it and use it as a showcase for its most important events. Television, for its part, adapted new technology to bring many analytical insights which proved popular with viewers. And in some codes – rugby and cricket would be prime examples – the availability of television cameras with slow-motion replays even provided the means of determining what had hitherto been difficult and controversial calls by the referee.

---

30 Shemozzle is a Yiddish word meaning a muddle, quarrel or melee; many dictionaries of slang credit Michael O'Hehir's use of it in the context of hurling commentaries.

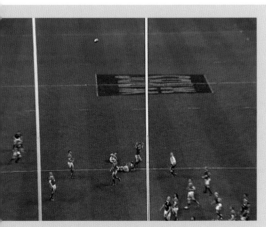

Spot the ball. It may be minuscule in this screen grab from the television coverage but 1.2 million viewers to RTÉ 2 had no difficulty seeing it bisect the posts to win the Grand Slam for Ireland after a sixty-year wait. The television audience had added over 200,000 viewers as the match reached its climax.

In the final moments of the 2009 Six Nations rugby tournament, Ronan O'Gara's winning drop goal against Wales in Cardiff brought to an end a sixty-year wait for an Irish Grand Slam. As Gerry Thornley wrote, it was O'Gara who 'ultimately needed the ice in his veins'. In an age of multi-channels and multi-media, there were fewer and fewer 'of what the Americans call water cooler moments, those seminal moments most of us witness together'. And it was through television that these become communal experiences. Thornley wrote:

Great sporting theatre, as seen in the Millennium Stadium on Saturday, is the purest form of reality television. No writer can script it in advance, no producer or director is directing its finale from behind a camera. Nobody is manipulated, because it is real. It came down to the last kick, in the last minute, of the last match of the tournament between its top two sides. Even if a producer had come up with the idea, they wouldn't even have bought it in Hollywood, and if they had, it wouldn't have been real anyhow.

Gerry Thornley, 'Honesty of effort, truth and integrity = Grand Slam', *Irish Times*, 24 March 2009.

In the 1960s there was constant debate about reception difficulties in various parts of the country. Piped and cable systems were in the future, satellite dishes unheard of. The *Western Mail* newspaper in Cardiff ran regular reports on how viewers in certain parts of Wales could receive Irish television signals better than others intended to cover their area. There were regular questions in the Dáil concerning local reception difficulties. Galway TD John Geoghegan claimed that in parts of his constituency 'two-thirds of the time we cannot get a picture, though we pay our licences just as they do beside the booster stations.' He thought this unfair and when he had asked the minister to lobby for a booster station 'on one of the Twelve Pins,' he got the answer that one was already 'being provided on Curraun Hill'. He wondered if the Minister realised 'how far away Curraun Hill is from my area, how the mountains and the lakes and the sea intervene', There were times when his constituents turned on Telefís Éireann and they received pictures of 'a bull fight from Spain'. When James Tully of Labour quipped: 'They should charge you an extra fiver for that', Geoghegan replied: 'Often it may be worth more than a fiver but if we are paying for Telefís Éireann, we should have reception from it.' During the course of the next half-century television reception would be transformed. In 1987, Vincent Finn could tell the World Federation of Advertisers General Assembly, in Killarney, of the relatively limited, muted impact of the new satellite broadcasters. RTÉ had been achieving its best multi-channel viewing figures in a decade, and this in 'one of the world's most competitive broadcasting environments'.

In 2010 Geraldine O'Leary, commercial director of RTÉ Television, argued that RTÉ had to see its role changing from being a broadcaster to a content provider. Individuals could now choose where and when to watch content: 'it might be mobile or the internet with RTÉ Player – it's about making sure it's available. Rather than say technology is working against television, it's the reverse, it's actually working for us.' The internet was not a threat to RTÉ. Rather, it was an asset, as international research had shown. TV was still needed 'to make a brand famous and give it credibility' and that was how she believed it would be 'for the forseeable future'.

Dáil Debates, vol.220, cols.607-08, 1 February 1966; Vincent Finn, address to World Federation of Advertisers General Assembly, Killarney, May 1987; *Marketing.ie*, April 2010.

the 'Eurovision': from Dana to Dustin

IN 1968 Séamus Ó Braonáin, having watched the preliminary heats to decide the Irish entry in that year's Eurovision Song Contest, wrote to his friend John Irvine. 'Now here's something to worry you. What the hell is that song business... supposed to achieve from an Irish point of view?' Ó Braonáin wondered whether singer or song was meant to be representative in any way of Ireland – 'our native music, native songs, our language, our nationality – any damn way?' Although admitting to his 'ignorance of music', he believed the contenders were not 'worth a dime... and Brendan O'Reilly said there were over 600 who had a go! Heaven help us.' Irvine did not dissent, admitting in his reply that the Eurovision Song Contest did nothing for 'the native cultures of small countries'; it had become 'an exercise in the international language of mass modern musical expression'.[31]

Yet it remained a staple of the television year and by far the event for which the European Broadcasting Union was most famous. Even those critical of what was termed the 'bubble-gum pop' style of music could still enjoy the vote which decided which song had won. In Ireland there was considerable pride when Dana won in 1970 and when Johnny Logan won twice in the 1980s. This was followed by four Irish wins in five years in the mid-1990s.

The convention that the national broadcaster of the winning country hosted the following year's event – and picked up the bill – was by now a serious concern for RTÉ. And it was discussed by the RTÉ Authority when it met in May 1996 after yet another Irish win. It was also appreciated that the national interest was involved with considerable benefits to Irish tourism. But should the station simply welcome the opportunity to again host the competition or should it use the issue as leverage in its ongoing request for an increase in the television licence fee? Authority members were divided on the question: Bob Quinn insisted that the song contest 'was a hymn to the banality of non-music and an absurd insult to the most important expression of human culture. It was completely contrary to the consciousness of young people interested in music in this country.' Joe Barry, as director-general, was hesitant about a quick announcement that RTÉ would 'pay £3 million to stage the event.' Chairman Farrell Corcoran thought RTÉ should limit itself to stating that it was 'well disposed' towards it. However, Patricia Redlich considered any such approach as 'suicide': the station had shown itself capable of a 'masterly effort' by RTÉ staff whose business it was 'to put on first-class shows'.[32]

Irish winners Dana 1970;
Johnny Logan 1980 and 1987
and Linda Martin 1992

31 Correspondence: Ó Braonáin and Irvine, 1968, Irvine papers, RTÉ Written Archives.
22 RTÉ Authority, minutes, 31 May 1996.

Labour Party Minister for Arts, Culture and the Gaeltacht, Michael D. Higgins (left) with the director-general, Joe Barry, at Eurovision 1994 when Ireland won the contest again. The headline in Mary Cummins's report read: 'Third consecutive Eurovision success almost too much for RTÉ's top brass'. Cummins reported that RTÉ's senior executives were 'obviously ill at ease with success....The Eurovision dream is obviously kept alive by a breed of ageing people. Looking down from the balcony, all you could see was a sea of balding/greying pates. Even the young people were old-looking, sounding and behaving like the nasal yuppies of the Eighties. ... Everybody talked about the interval act, which showed 24 Irish dancers hopping and lepping to a thumping African rhythm with a verve which will put set dancing back into the cupboard. "It's Irish ballay, dear", an American told her partner.' *Irish Times*, 2 May 1994.

Irish winners Niamh Kavanagh 1993; Paul Harrington and Charlie McGetigan 1994 and Eimear Quinn 1996

Dustin the Turkey, whose mock entry, *Irlande Douze Pointes*, did not amuse the Europeans in 2008.

In the years that followed, RTÉ was presented with no such difficulty. As the map of Central and Eastern Europe was redrawn, the 'centre of gravity' of the contest moved eastwards and Ireland was seen as a peripheral contestant with dwindling prospects. A decade after their run of success in the mid-1990s, they struggled, coming third last in 2004, failing to qualify in 2005, and, although in the top 10 in 2006, last in 2007. The following year the puppet Dustin the Turkey competed for the right to represent Ireland by popular vote. He won the support of Bob Geldof, who declared that it would be nothing short of 'rank poultryism' should one of Ireland's 'greatest talents' fail to win the right to represent his country. If the Eurovision Song Contest was known for anything at all, he added, it was for 'the vast number of turkeys' it produced each year.[33] In the event Dustin did win the telephone poll to represent Ireland.

The London *Times* reported that some of the nation's song-writers had 'suffered a sense of humour failure' over the matter.[34] The website eurovisiontimes reckoned Dustin's song a contender for the Worst Eurovision Song award and asked: 'Was it Ireland's revenge for their bad placings in the new millennium? Probably! Because Dustin's entry, "Irlande Douze Pointes", is a mock entry, making fun of the Eurovision Song Contest, with lyrics such as "Drag acts and bad acts and Terry Wogan's wig".'[35] In the event the Europeans did not see the joke.

---

33 Gigwise.com/news, 25 February 2008.
34 *The Times*, 6 February 2008.
35 website http://eurovisiontimes.wordpress.com/, accessed 15 January 2011.

'I think we cannot afford to lose this chance.' Sister M. de Montfort on an invitation to allow an RTÉ documentary on Industrial Schools, 1965. 'It might well be useful to lose it.' – Archbishop McQuaid

Brian Cleeve, a reporter with the *Discovery* programme, began researching a television documentary on industrial schools in 1965. Among the institutions from whom he sought permission to film were Goldenbridge and Artane. It would be thirty years before investigative television programmes would expose the physical and sexual abuse that took place in both these institutions. Initially Cleeve seemed to be making progress but his initiative foundered at the hand of Archbishop McQuaid. When Cleeve was told that neither institution would be participating, he was assured that the archbishop was 'in no way responsible'.

'GOLDENBRIDGE AND ARTANE have been chosen to show the work of Industrial Schools.' The television report – by Brian Cleeve in the *Discovery* series – would conclude 'with a description of a small home'. Thus wrote the nun running the small home in May 1965. She was writing for permission to accept an invitation from Brian Cleeve of the *Discovery* programme to participate in a documentary on the 'Displaced or Homeless Child'. Her superior had forwarded the request to archbishop's house. McQuaid comments in the margin: 'Is it meant to pit the "home" against the large Institution?' Sister de Montfort expressed a keenness to participate because it would awaken interest in the hostel, and make the order's work more widely known. 'I think we cannot afford to lose this chance.' McQuaid underlined this sentence and commented in the margin: 'It might well be useful to lose it.'[36] McQuaid was aware of many scandals in Artane. In 1962 he had received a scathing report from the chaplain, Fr Henry Moore, and eighteen years earlier in 1944 he himself had intervened to prevent Garda inquiries into allegations of abuse against two Christian Brothers on the staff there.[37]

It is obvious from the archives that McQuaid did not wish the initiative to prosper. He would rely on Monsignor Cecil J. Barrett to achieve this result. But initially Barrett was quite supportive, writing to McQuaid that, having consulted widely, 'all appear to think that the television people are approaching the subject from a sympathetic and helpful angle'. In such circumstances the programme 'could do good by disposing of some of the false ideas' current about industrial schools.[38] McQuaid manifestly had no such confidence and, by 4 June, Barrett – having presumably been alerted to the archbishop's preferred outcome – could inform him that Goldenbridge and Artane, would not now be participating. Barrett knew how to deliver McQuaid's result without McQuaid's fingerprints being visible to any of the players and Cleeve had been reassured on the telephone that the archbishop was 'in no way responsible'. McQuaid's draft reply notes that Barrett's answer to Cleeve was 'very accurate. I meant to leave whole affair in your hands. What you decide is right with me.

36 Sister M. De Montfort to Mother General, Monastery of Our Lady of Charity of Refuge, 24 May 1965, copy forwarded to McQuaid. DDA McQuaid papers, TV film, Radharc Box.
37 Cooney, *McQuaid*, 152.
38 Barrett to McQuaid, 1 June 1965.

I think we cannot afford to lose this chance., Mother.
First of all, it will make our Order known, and secondly it will
awaken interest in our hostel.

PAROCHIAL HOUSE,
BOOTERSTOWN,
Co. DUBLIN.

4 . vi .'65.

The nun may have thought her order should not 'lose this chance' of having her orphanage on television. McQuaid – as his marginal notes attest – wanted to keep the television cameras out.

Glad Artane is out.' He then added, enigmatically: 'Film, if edited, can correct many errors.'[39]

It would be naïve to presume that had *Discovery* gained access to Artane and Goldenbridge in 1965 the full extent of the abuse then being perpetrated in those institutions would have been exposed. McQuaid had been reassured at one point that the authorities in Artane were 'shrewd enough' and 'alive to the dangers' of cooperating with a television report: any agreed access would have been controlled and those interviewed would undoubtedly have been carefully chosen.

It remains an unanswered question how the media along with the gardaí, courts, medical profession and politicians – as well as the professional inspectorate of these institutions – somehow failed to bring such widespread abuse to public attention for so long. And might culpability not also be shared by non-abusers who were working in these institutions but who failed to pursue any suspicions? Who knew what when? The answer must be that many people were in a position where their suspicions should somehow have led to earlier revelations. Indeed, it is difficult to escape the conclusion that something of that fear of scandal – which so disgraced the hierarchy in its failure to act against abusers – must also be shared by some of the many professionals who blew no whistles on abuse now known to have been so widespread.

And RTÉ is not immune from this criticism. The station was part financiers of an independent drama documentary,

One of the most significant programmes was Louis Lentin's dramatised documentary *Dear Daughter* which was based on the experience of Christine Buckley who had been brought up in the Goldenbridge orphanage. In the programme some of those who had shared her experience returned as adults and re-enacted their daily routine, making rosary beads by hand. The children were expected to make a quota of sixty sets of beads each day.

---

39 Barrett to McQuaid, 4 June 1965, with McQuaid's comments dated 7 June 1965. These would have formed the basis of McQuaid's secretary's reply.

Mary Raftery, writer, producer and director of the RTÉ television series *States of Fear*, broadcast in April, May 1999. This won the Best Documentary in English category in the 1999 Irish Film and Television Academy awards. Raftery was also producer-director of *Prime Time: Cardinal Secrets* which won the IFTA Best Current Affairs award in 2003.

After the publication of the Ryan report, Michael O'Brien recounting on *Questions and Answers* (25 May 2009) how he had been brought from Clonmel Courthouse, aged eight, 'on a scut-truck' to Ferryhouse orphanage in Clonmel. Two nights later he was raped. His testimony was so telling that it drew a round of applause from the panel and was quickly available on YouTube where by the end of that year alone it had been viewed 100,000 times.

Our Boys, made by Cathal Black in 1980 detailing the trauma some pupils felt at the hands of the Christian Brothers. It was shelved for ten years before being broadcast. Black stated that 'there was a feeling in the society at the time that you couldn't say anything about it. I simply wanted to put the record straight. Mind you, if I knew how things were going to turn out, I really would have put the boot in.' Compared to what had emerged since, he believes that *Our Boys* 'was a veritable tea party'. At one point RTÉ agreed to show the film if the director would come onto *The Late Late Show* afterwards and discuss the issues with Christian Brothers representatives. But Black refused, believing he would have been 'torn apart, the sacrificial lamb ripped to shreds'.[40] Whether or not this was a missed opportunity on his part is for others to judge.

There is no doubting that television, because of the very impact of the medium, did eventually play an important role in exposing the scale of this issue. Jerry O'Callaghan's report on *Today Tonight* in 1989, Louis Lentin's dramatised documentary *Dear Daughter* and a series of programmes by Mary Raftery cumulatively brought the scale of the abuse to such public attention that it could no longer be ignored by the political establishment. Historian Tom Garvin has suggested that television documentaries had the effect of 'activating the collective memory, often covertly retained' by many powerless individuals who had been abused by clergy. 'Suddenly, hundreds of cases of sexual abuse, physical assault, effective imprisonment of young women and enslavement of children came to be researched and reported in the media.' Documentaries re-enacted the experiences 'of orphans, unmarried mothers and young delinquents who were ill-treated in clerically run and owned institutions.' What was revealed was not only the physical and sexual abuse but an institutional cover-up which had put the avoidance of scandal and its implications for those responsible above the interests of victims. This, of course, was the greater scandal. Garvin concludes that a 'conspiracy of silence which had protected the Church in the twentieth century came to a sudden and dramatic end.'

And whereas the response of the government some thirty years before to a television investigative report on money-lending in Dublin had been a tribunal of inquiry *into the television programme* – manifestly a case of shooting the messenger! – the government's response now was acceptance of the television evidence, apologies to the victims, redress boards to agree compensation and tribunals of inquiry into the offending institutions.

---

40 Cathal Black interviewed by Vincent Browne,
    http://www.iol.ie/~galfilm/filmwest/24cathal.htm, accessed 17 January 2011.

how used they keep themselves contented, before this monster was invented?

HOW WOULD TELEVISION affect children? Would it not turn them into juvenile delinquents? As television services opened across the developed world half a century ago, this question was widely debated. That they would become television addicts was presumed. In 1950 readers of the *Irish Monthly* learned how American children were responding to the new medium. No longer was it necessary for parents 'to call the children off the streets at bed-time'. Rather, the difficulty was 'to tear them away from that world of wonder that forever unfolds itself ... as they squat there right on the family hearth-rug.'[41] In 1967 the Catholic Television Committee suggested that primary school children should be warned against sitting 'goggle-eyed all night' before television programmes made for adults: it was 'just wrong; *it's waste of time.*'[42]

Wanderly Wagon on location in Powerscourt, Co. Wicklow in August 1977; Nora O'Mahony as Godmother, Judge the Dog and puppeteer Eugene Lambert as O'Brien. The programme ran from 1967 until 1982, entertaining generations of younger viewers.

While parental supervision was recommended, it was likewise presumed that there would be some evasion of the parental censor. Some even advised that television sets 'should have shutters and the parents have the key'.[43] The Church of England's submission to the Pilkington Committee on the future of broadcasting was concerned at the amount of violence and sex which had been included in programming in the 1950s in Britain. One bishop was even more fearful of other television values: 'money for jam, money for nothing, take it easy, it will all come if you are slick enough, cash prizes, nothing to pay'; all this 'candy floss', as he termed it, was 'a much more subversive influence than violence, or even, direct sex.'[44]

That Eamon de Valera had concerns on these matters was clear from his opening night address in December 1961. But some years earlier when Taoiseach in his last government, he clearly spoke of these issues when he met Ivone Kirkpatrick of Britain's Independent Television Authority. In October 1958 Kirkpatrick forwarded to him, as he had promised 'the other night', a copy of the ITA's 'recent report on the impact of television on children'. Kirkpatrick allowed that it was

---

41 Patrick Purcell, 'TV or not TV?', *Irish Monthly*, vol.lxxviii, December 1950, 573-79.
42 Catholic Television Committee, 'Notes for the clergy', issued for World Communications Day, 1967, Catholic Truth Society.
43 Andrew, 'Television and religion', 12-26.
44 The speaker was Dr F.A.Cockin, recently retired bishop of Bristol. Church of England, oral evidence to Pilkington Committee, NAUK, HO 244/261.

Bill Golding, who played Rory in *Wanderly Wagon*, here introduces a group of children to some of the puppets in the grounds of RTÉ in 1968. This formed part of a recording of *Wanderly Wagon* which was then attracting a large following after its launch in 1967.

There have been many pickets at RTÉ over the years. On this occasion the protesters won the argument. Children picketing at the station's entrance in December 1974 in protest at the proposed axing of *Wanderly Wagon*. The series was not cancelled and ran until 1982.

'not conclusive' since it was a survey confined to the opinions of parents and his 'old headmaster used to affirm that parents knew little or nothing about their children'. Because it was somewhat specialist, Kirkpatrick had marked the passages which seemed to him 'of the greatest general interest'.[45] Among these were the main findings: that most parents approved of their children watching television; claimed that it improved their minds and social conduct; that it tended to keep them at home, making 'family life happier and more interesting'; that the whole family watched television together 'much more often than not'; and that there was evidence of 'fairly extensive' parental guidance in the selection of programmes.[46]

Bob Collins spoke of 'a particular concern' in relation to programming for children. Increasingly, European public service broadcasters were withdrawing from children's programming, spending less, allocating fewer resources, making fewer programmes. And he called for resistance to what he termed 'a dangerous and sinister and insidious erosion' of what had been the traditional expectation that television would play a significant role in the lives of children. More and more use was being made of internationally produced material whose principal purpose was 'to allow the sell-through of other products rather than to provide a service for the children at whom they are broadcasting.' He suggested that if this trend were to continue, children would have 'a greater sense of American and Australian communities or pseudo-communities than they would of the communities from which they themselves come.'[47]

Helping generations of Irish children to have a sense of their own

---

45 Ivone Kirkpatrick to Eamon de Valera, 8 October 1958, NAI DT S14996A.
46 'Parents, Children and Television', Independent Television Authority, 1958.
47 Bob Collins, in Martin McLoone (ed.), *Culture, Identity and Broadcasting in Ireland*, (Belfast, 1991), pp.71-76.

community was the long-running *The Den*, and especially during Ray D'Arcy's tenure in the 1990s. Aimed at children, it also developed a cult following among older students. It introduced *Zig and Zag* and also *Podge and Rodge* – in their more innocent days – to Irish television screens. In 2010, a renewed emphasis on indigenous young people's programmes was promised by the incoming Managing Director television, Glen Killane. He believed that as a public service broadcaster it was essential for RTÉ 'to serve all ages'. Digital Terrestrial Television (DTT) would provide further opportunities and challenges on this front.[48]

Roald Dahl, who, it must be acknowledged, was an interested party – since his children's books sold in millions of copies – wondered what children did before television: 'How used they keep themselves contented, before this monster was invented?' And he answered his own question: 'Oh, books, what books they used to know, those children living long ago!' In the song, 'Television', the Oompa-Loompas offer this provocative advice to parents, who presumably were reading *Charlie and the Chocolate Factory* to their children.

The puppet Bosco, star of one of RTÉ's most popular children's programmes.

> So please, oh please, we beg, we pray,
> Go throw your TV set away,
> And in its place you can install
> A lovely bookshelf on the wall.
> Then fill the shelves with lots of books,
> Ignoring all the dirty looks,
> The screams and yells, the bites and kicks,
> And children hitting you with sticks.

Dahl then advised parents to hold their nerve because within 'about a week or two', finding they had little else to do, their children would turn to reading.

> And once they start — oh boy, oh boy!
> You watch the slowly growing joy
> That fills their hearts. They'll grow so keen
> They'll wonder what they'd ever seen
> In that ridiculous machine,
> That nauseating, foul, unclean,
> Repulsive television screen!
> And later, each and every kid
> Will love you more for what you did.[49]

Glen Killane, Managing Director, RTÉ Television: essential for RTÉ to serve all ages.

48 *Irish Times*, 7 August 2010.
49 Roald Dahl, 'Television', Song by the Oompa-Loompas from *Charlie and the Chocolate Factory*.

'perhaps the whole shebang is quite bananas'

At the Rose of Tralee, August 1985, Gay Byrne dancing with the South Carolina Rose, Kathleen McCarthy.

The Rose of Tralee festival predates the launch of Telefís Éireann by just two years. On the fiftieth anniversary of the Festival in 2009, RTÉ broadcast a documentary, *The Rise of the Roses*, 'a nostalgic hour featuring grainy archive of optimistic-looking girls with beehives, and lots of footage of small planes taking off and landing again'. For many decades live television coverage over two nights in late August has been amongst RTÉ's most popular broadcasts of the year, often recording double the highest rating programme of comparable nights in the same week.

On the fiftieth anniversary of the festival, one television critic seemed perplexed by the entire phenomenon: 'perhaps the whole shebang is quite bananas. Truly, The Rose of Tralee is the strangest, most wildly anachronistic gig one could hope to witness. Neither a beauty nor a talent contest, more a gala of congeniality, from Birmingham to Brittany, from Baltimore to Bally-I'm-losing-my-reason-here, the girls all bloom in highly individual directions, which admittedly makes a welcome change from the mass-produced, post-surgical chic of most televised gatherings of young women.' Hilary Fannin, *The Irish Times*, 29 August 2009.

to ensure that the client talks, reveals, spills the beans, performs

WHAT BEGAN AS a summertime filler in 1962 within months of the station opening, became RTÉ's most celebrated programme: *The Late Late Show*, described by Michael Parkinson as the 'best talk show I have ever been a guest on';[50] and by John Naughton as 'the Western world's best chat show'.[51] Although open to severe criticism in its early years, it became generally acknowledged that the programme's impact on its own society derived from the exceptional broadcasting skills of its first host, Gay Byrne, who steered it as presenter and producer for the first four decades of RTÉ television's history. Naughton also called it 'the only example in history of an intelligent chat-show with a large audience'.[52] Concerning the size of the audience, this is an understatement. Probably no society anywhere had such a high proportion of its population watching such a programme. That it achieved this over so many decades underscores its extraordinary reach.

The psychiatrist and broadcaster Anthony Clare saw Byrne as

50 Michael Parkinson, *Parky: My Autobiography* (London, 2008), p.133.
51 John Naughton, *The Observer*, 11 April 1993.
52 *The Observer*, 19 June 1988.

exuding self-control 'even when apparently taking risks'. He cites Byrne's often stated point that *The Late Late Show* reflected what Irish people were themselves 'ready to talk about'.[53] This emphasis on Byrne as facilitator rather than innovator is taken up by Diarmaid Ferriter:

> On the face of it this suggests generous self-deprecation on Byrne's part, but it could also have been defensive – Byrne always had to protect his various viewing constituencies, so the idea of him as 'host' and not 'instigator' was important. Rarely did his mask, or his professionalism, slip.[54]

Clare agreed with Byrne's own claim that his particular ability was to know when the boundaries were 'ready to be pushed out another half-inch'.[55] Younger readers may be surprised to learn just where that boundary line was when television started. Séamus Ó Braonáin spoke for many of his generation when the first programme of the 1968-69 season annoyed him: he admitted that he 'could have shrieked' at Byrne to stop 'when he continued pressing an ex-brother, who had blossomed into a comedian, to give a definitive opinion' on the papal encyclical on the Pill. This was a debate of which Ó Braonáin was tired. He believed that he would 'never get over the fact' that he was once Director of Radio Éireann and still felt 'a kind of let-down' when anyone on radio or television 'nears the danger line'. As far as he was concerned, religion 'should be "out".'[56] But Desmond Forristal, then a young priest,

Gay Byrne addresses the *Late Late* audience in the 1960s and on his last programme, 21 May 1999, of whom many were colleagues and friends.

Front row; right to left; Bob Collins; Avril McRory; Ronan and Suzy O'Byrne (GB's daughter); sixth from right is Gerry Lundberg;

Second row, right to left: Kevin Lenihan; Mary O'Sullivan; Sharon and Colman Hutchinson; David and Mary Orr (GB's sister); further on in this row are Tony Boland (eighth), Larry Gogan (tenth) and Marian Finucane (thirteenth).

Third row: third and fourth from right, Joe and Annie Mulholland; sixth in this row is Jim Jennings; 13th, Peter Feeney; third from left, John Masterson.

Fourth row includes the familiar figures of Mike Murphy and later Jimmy Magee; the woman seated next but one to Magee (black top with grey scarf) is a special guest on this last night of Gay Byrne's last *Late Late Show*, Pat McGrath, widow of the programme's first producer, Tom McGrath with their daughter, Nita, to the left of her. (see p.46, above).

53 Anthony Clare, 'The man who nobody knows', *Sunday Tribune*, 1 October 1989.
54 Ferriter, *Occasions of Sin*, 375.
55 Anthony Clare, 'The man who nobody knows', *Sunday Tribune*, 1 October 1989.
56 Ó Braonáin to Irßvine, 8 October 1968, Irvine papers, RTÉWA.

Tom Garvin has written that when Dr Tom Ryan, the bishop of Clonfert, 'denounced a married woman for saying on television that she had worn only perfume on her wedding night', he was 'promptly drowned out in a national wave of collective laughter', a dimension of the episode which 'rarely got into the history books'. But the contemporary record suggests that the bishop's strictures on *The Late Late Show* were taken more seriously. The *Irish Times* did not join in any collective laughter. The newspaper allowed that the bishop was 'killing a fly with a sledgehammer', but adjudged RTÉ to be guilty of 'a lapse of taste' rather than 'an outrage to morals'. McQuaid was wise enough to confine his disapproval to a private note to McCourt. He regretted that the offending section of the programme was 'really unworthy'. The discussion with Mrs. Fox was 'vulgar, even coarse and suggestive. You have not been fairly treated; for this type of thing is quite unlike what you have been so warmly thanked for.' At the next RTÉ Authority meeting the minutes referred discreetly to the 'incident' which had given rise 'to public controversy and public condemnation of the programme by the Bishop of Clonfert'. McCourt faulted Gay Byrne for 'an error of judgement', reminding the Authority that it was 'the first such mishap on the show during its five-year run'. The Authority solemnly concurred, adding that 'there was no cause for official chastisement of the producer'. However, they hoped that Byrne would have full regard in future 'to uphold the standards of Irish taste' in presenting the programme and hoped that 'a similar deviation' would not recur. Ó Móráin questioned whether Byrne 'should have spoken in an official capacity to the press immediately after the programme'. McCourt insisted that the apology should come from Byrne: were it to come from a higher level, 'the question of continuing Mr Byrne's services on the programme could have arisen'.

Fr Joseph Dunn adds a postscript to this celebrated controversy. It all proved to be 'a traumatic experience' for the bishop 'from which he never fully recovered. He felt himself the laughing stock of the country, which to some extent, unfortunately, he was. It became the only thing people knew about the Bishop of Clonfert. I don't know what he could ever have done about it, but one thing he decided to do eventually was to more or less retire and get a coadjutor with right of succession.'

Tom Garvin, *Preventing the Future: Why was Ireland so Poor for so Long?* (Dublin, 2004); McQuaid to McCourt, 12 February 1966, *John Charles McQuaid: What the Papers Say*, Esras Films for RTÉ; RTÉ Authority, minutes, 16 February 1966; Joseph Dunn, *No Lions in the Hierarchy* (Dublin, 1994), p.39.

playwright and member of the Radharc documentary team, reckoned that *The Late Late Show* had 'probably done more than any other single factor to form the national consciousness on a hundred different topics' during its first ten years.[57] As successive taboos were broken, the 'danger line' shifted: but it always remained in the eye of the beholder. Not everyone drew it in the same place. As Gageby emphasised when crediting the programme with 'a crucial social role', what at first had seemed blasphemous or obscene 'very soon was taken to the heart of the viewing public as ordinary tea-time chat.'[58]

The novelist Colm Tóibín grew up in a house where the children were banned from watching the programme, which made them all the more curious. 'The door was closed and the children were sent to

57 Desmond Forristal, 'The Late Late Show', *Furrow*, 23/10, October 1970, p.655.
58 Douglas Gageby, 'The Media, 1945-70', in Joe Lee, *Ireland: 1945-1970*, p.133

WINDOW AND MIRROR

Gay Byrne with the Harley Davidson motorbike which was presented to him as a surprise thank you gift by Bono and Larry Mullen of Irish rock group U2, on his last edition of *The Late Late Show*, 21 May 1999.

bed and as you got to a certain age you'd say: "When I'm what age will I be able to watch *The Late Late Show*?" which was a sort of rite of passage'. It was especially exciting because Byrne never announced in advance who was coming on next 'and it could be a nun who didn't believe in being a nun or it could be someone talking about sex and there had never been talk about sex in our house.' It could not be easily turned off – no one had a zapper – and to 'run over to turn it off ... would have been considered square.' So for Tóibín, it began by being forbidden, 'and then became immensely interesting with great moments of pure embarrassment', all mixed in with show business 'and whatever things that were unsayable in Irish life'.

There were many opinions considered 'unsayable'. The notably conservative politician Oliver J. Flanagan opened up one debate with his claim that there had been no sex in Ireland before television. While this occasioned much humorous comment, Ferriter explores the point that Flanagan was attempting to make. He concludes that such could be the silence on the subject in many family settings that there was a whole generation of people who would have lived and died in twentieth-century Ireland without having heard any discussion of sex were it not for *The Late Late Show*. To that extent, at least, 'perhaps Oliver J. Flanagan was accurate'.[59]

John Naughton, long-time television critic of *The Observer*, was among many international admirers of how RTÉ had developed this programme: he reckoned it the 'only example in history of an intelligent chat-show with a large audience'. He gave the main credit to Byrne, who, if asked, 'would probably still describe himself as an entertainer. Someone once said that reading a great newspaper was like listening to a nation talking to itself. Viewers of Mr Byrne's programme over the years have had much the same experience.'[60]

59 Ferriter, *Occasions of Sin*, 374-76.
60 *The Observer*, 19 June 1988.

This was Byrne's own perspective on the programme from the beginning, facilitating the nation to talk to itself and to listen to opinions whether or not they agreed with them. The present author can still recall a debate he chaired on *Right of Reply* in 1968 when Byrne defended the programme along these lines after he had been accused by the historian and archaeologist Liam de Paor of 'treating serious issues trivially and trivial issues seriously'. Nor was de Paor alone in this assessment of Byrne at that juncture. At a meeting of the RTÉ Authority in 1968, T.W.Moody, the Trinity historian and long-serving member of the Authority, referring to a recent *Late Late Show* on racism, said 'that this was a good example of Gay Byrne taking on something he was just not intellectually fit to cope with'.[61] But a decade later, following a debate on nuclear energy, Moody had manifestly come to a wider appreciation of Byrne. He congratulated him on the nuclear debate which had proved 'unforgettable' on many levels, 'intellectual, moral, spiritual and artistic'. This was due to 'the high quality, informativeness and fluency' of the panels on both sides of the debate and to 'the deadly earnestness' of the audience but also to Byrne's exceptional combination of professional skill 'with perceptiveness, sincerity, sense of responsibility, and fair-mindedness'.[62] Many commentators have attempted to explain Byrne's gifts as a broadcaster, among the most perceptive being Anthony Clare. He believed that Byrne's 'inimitable, astonishing, unique televisual skill' might well rest on the fact that he was 'a confessor who needs neither to forgive nor punish, a psychiatrist who does not need to diagnose nor to prescribe, a facilitator whose only task is to ensure that the client talks, reveals, spills the beans, performs.'[63]

---

61 RTÉ Authority minutes, 19 April 1968.
62 T.W.Moody to Gay Byrne, 13 January 1979, RTÉWA.
63 Anthony Clare, 'The man who nobody knows', *Sunday Tribune*, 1 October 1989.

the citizen with a television 'will have more to come home to'
– Maurice Gorham, 1949

IN CONCLUDING THIS BOOK how does one measure the impact of television on Irish society over the past half-century? The first change was behavioural. It was only when Telefís Éireann had commenced broadcasting in 1962 that set ownership became widespread and that the habit of watching television began to be part of Irish daily life. This was the most profound change of all. And it was especially so for those living in the huge swathes of rural Ireland which had been without electricity until the mid-1950s. To now have access to their own television service was modernisation at a pace equal to anything in the developing world. For many in Ireland from the 1960s onwards, television became a pastime – literally: a significant fraction of each day was given over to it. Television brought information, education and entertainment; it brought solace, humour, escapism and fantasy; it revealed how other people – especially suburban Americans – lived. Refrigerators, telephones, modern kitchens – and motor cars – did not seem to be luxuries to the families portrayed. Television also introduced new radical ideas, although these were more likely to find expression in indigenous Irish programmes than in the imported series which were anodyne since they could not afford to offend any Americans. Television provided all this and envy too – or begrudgery, as some insisted on defining its Irish variant. Moreover, RTÉ provided another service – becoming, for many, the nation's Aunt Sally, available as a favourite cock-shy. It was rather akin to a parent: a taken-for-granted essential resource, but available to be railed against when the mood suited.

Television introduced skills to farmers and housewives; and it raised the expectations of children and probably encouraged them to speak their minds more than their parents ever had at their age. It introduced viewers to opinions contrary to their own. Even those who took the trouble to exercise their personal in-house censorship – avoiding debates on subjects which they did not care to contemplate

Justin Keating presenting *Telefís Feirme* in 1965. This was an educational programme with many farmers viewing in groups and discussing its lessons at the end of transmission. It attracted attention as an innovative use of television from as far away as Japan.

– could find themselves obliged to confront such topics if they emerged as dilemmas in a programme such as *The Riordans*, which they did not care to switch off.

Older viewers who knew a world before television, might recall Gorham's optimism after the war about the new medium. When so many others were decrying it, he showed prescience in suggesting that the citizen with a television 'will have more to come home to'.[1] He believed that its net effect would be to bring a wider appreciation of the arts, music, science, sport and so much else. Leif Jerram reminds us that for thousands of years 'most people's homes were so unpleasant, that the desire to leave them meant that they had to invent something to do, and somewhere to do it, when they were "out".' Television had transformed the European home. The expectation that the living room would be 'a warm, safe place', entrance to which was controlled by those living in the house, 'and which was quiet, well-lit, and packed with things to do, gave to the working and lower-middle classes a domestic world which the rich had been enjoying for two hundred years'. This amounted to 'a democratisation of space as well as a democratisation of taste'.[2]

Ireland was not alone in finding that poorer families were more likely to own a television set, even if it was bought on hire purchase: did it not provide an extraordinary range of entertainment for a modest investment? Did it not bring the family together to share a common experience? A further change has occurred in more recent years. Set ownership and technology have reached a stage where communal TV viewing – one of the profound changes in family life in the latter half of the twentieth century – is now giving way to a new pattern where the individual can identify his or her preferred programmes and choose to watch them privately when and where they like.

Television could not be other than subversive of the establishment. And especially of that strand of the establishment – epitomised by de Valera – which sought to maintain Ireland as a sheltered arcadian utopia whose people were content to live 'the life that God desired that men should live'. Whatever chance there was of de Valera's ideal of 'frugal comfort' being realised was scuttled by the arrival of television. The cameras were indeed interested in chronicling any pockets of this old way of life, but in the spirit of an anthropologist, capturing for posterity what once had been: not as a blueprint for what ought to be or ever could be. Whatever viewers aspired to in the consumerist culture embraced by television, it was not frugality.

Tom Inglis wrote of the impact of television that, instead of the family 'kneeling down around the fire to say the rosary, they now sat around the television'. Leif Jerram wrote that television throughout Europe had brought culture indoors and had 'reconfigured the micro-geography of family life, so that relatives no longer sat facing each other, and no longer talked to each other for large chunks of their time at home. Instead, they faced in one direction – the layout of the cinema was brought into the living room. It was a revolution in family life.'

Inglis, *Moral Monopoly* (first edition, 1987), p.90; Leif Jerram, *Streetlife: the Untold History of Europe's Twentieth Century* (Oxford, 2011) p.229.

---

1   Maurice Gorham, *Television: Medium of the future* (London, 1949), p.140.
2   Leif Jerram, *Streetlife: : the Untold History of Europe's Twentieth Century* (Oxford, 2011), p.228.

well-intentioned, do-gooders; or self-appointed busy-bodies?

IN 1962 IRELAND WAS a sheltered society. And there were many forces at work to attempt to keep it that way. The establishment seemed to fear the outside world: Cardinal D'Alton and Eamon de Valera had said as much at the opening of the television station. Both enjoyed their status in what was a society rooted in hierarchical power. De Valera was by intuition an isolationist. To his party he was headmaster and guru: many of his followers thought him infallible – an accusation he did not deny. Had he not famously said that to know what the Irish people wanted, he had only to look into his own heart? This was a society that was smug enough to believe it was holier than pagan Britain. Yet we now know – thanks partly to RTÉ television – that it had its own shameful secrets of child sexual abuse, sometimes by clergy and, worse, a preference to protect the perpetrators and the church as an institution rather than the victims.

Ireland by 1960 was a nation with its fair share of censors, prudes, snoops and vigilantes. Some were officially appointed by the state: others worked in a voluntary capacity for sporting organisations or for the church. Murphy believed that the official censorship created 'layers of unofficial, self-righteous, busybody censorship in many a local community'.[3] There was indeed no shortage of do-gooders who were willing to act as gate-keepers for their fellow citizens: an organisation with the GAA's extraordinary achievements could still recruit vigilantes to spy on fellow members who might be watching the forbidden 'foreign games'; there were bishops forbidding catholics from attending Trinity College; the censor's writ ran in bookshops, libraries and in the cinema; the official film censors snipped even a few phrases from John Ford's *The Quiet Man*. Ireland was a society where many seemed intent on keeping the twentieth century at bay: there were campaigns against the circulation of British newspapers; serious books on sexuality were considered worthy of the censor's attention; novels on the reading lists of third-level English literature courses could also be banned by the Censorship Board. There were busy-bodies everywhere protecting their fellow-citizens from jazz on the radio, from all dances during Lent, from sharing the beach at Salthill in Galway with members of the opposite sex – even if married to them. Men and women in rural Ireland sat in separate aisles at Catholic churches on Sunday; and in the town of Clones the parish priest even insisted – successfully – in imposing the same rule in the local cinema! And

Historian John A. Murphy believed that the official literary censorship had the effect of 'provoking evasion, and thus contributed further to the superficially conforming, furtive, under-the-counter mentality which is one of the more unlovely facets of the Irish heritage.'

The Irish film censor even found it necessary to make two cuts in John Ford's classic *The Quiet Man*.

---

3   John A. Murphy, 'Censorship and the Moral Community' in Brian Farrell (ed.), *Communications and Community in Ireland* (Cork, 1984), p.62.

state funerals of former presidents could be divisive. In 1949 the Taoiseach of the day, John A. Costello and the Fianna Fáil leader, Eamon de Valera, had both stayed outside the Church of Ireland cathedral during the State funeral of Ireland's first president, Douglas Hyde, because the service was in a protestant church. As the poet, Austin Clarke observed, worried lest listening to the Lord's Prayer in English they 'hear that *which* for *who* and risk eternal doom.'[4]

There were much bigger issues too: why should women by law resign civil service jobs on marriage? Or from RTÉ for that matter? Why should the sale of contraceptives be a criminal offence? Women's lib as an agenda had not yet been formulated but it would provide even bigger challenges than those represented by some of the petty regulations just cited. And what sort of society was it that tolerated such rulings?

Ireland was in transition from de Valera's Ireland to that of Lemass. And the latter's government, in introducing the new television service, rather inattentively entrusted to the broadcasters more independence than Lemass himself may have suspected was wise. He often stated that he might revisit this legislation were he dissatisfied with how the broadcasters exercised their responsibilities. What Lemass failed to appreciate was that the public approved of a television service with this degree of independence. Once the genii was out of the bottle, there was no going back. The *status quo ante* was not an option. Lemass remained grumpy about what he saw as a television station that did not know its place: what he failed to appreciate was what an ally it would prove in accelerating his own modernising agenda.

---

4 Austin Clarke, 'Burial of an Irish President'.

As Telefís Éireann opened on New Year's Eve 1961, Irish society was already in transition from the Ireland of Eamon de Valera to that of Seán Lemass. The emphasis in de Valera's politics had tended towards isolationism, idealism and a preoccupation with the past; Lemass, in contrast, was a pragmatist who wanted to end protectionism and was impatient to embrace a future within the European Community. Both men had been colleagues since 1916, had founded Fianna Fáil in 1926 and had served together in government for all but six years since they had first won power in the 1932 election. They are photographed at the Benediction ceremony as the station was inaugurated.

GIVEN ITS CENTRAL IMPORTANCE in Irish life in the past half-century there have been relatively few specialist studies of Irish television. But many of those writing more general surveys – historians and others – have commented on its role. The popular notion that the modernisation of Ireland flowed from the Lemass-Whitaker policy seemed to Naughton 'unduly deterministic'. After all, many societies had engineered economic prosperity 'without any liberalisation in social or intellectual life.' Naughton believed that in the Irish case other factors had been in play. 'One was undoubtedly the advent of Radio Telefís Éireann in 1962, and in particular the evolution of Gay Byrne's *Late Late Show* as the first truly national forum for the discussion of social, sexual and intellectual issues.'[5] Historians of twentieth-century Ireland expressed broad agreement in assessing television's impact. Lyons's verdict was that the new television service 'matured remarkably quickly, breaking through taboos of all kinds to discuss before a startled public such issues as birth control, drugs, premarital relations, pornography, and the place of the Church in the modern world.' Lyons believed that television was but one factor in the early 1960s which rendered Ireland into a 'pushing and restless society', the mood possessing the country being 'one of impatience, and of criticism, but also one of hope and excitement'.[6] Cathcart emphasised that society was on the cusp of change when television arrived and mentioned especially that 'the place of urban life in the national psyche could not continue to remain at a discount'.[7] Kennedy made a similar observation, television entering Irish life 'at a time when Ireland was crossing the Rubicon between a rural and urban society'.[8]

Brown saw television as 'a major instrument in Ireland's conversion to consumerism'.[9] Garvin recalled how 'quite revolutionary' it had been in the early decades of television, 'to see bishops, priests and politicians trying, often ineptly, to defend their opinions and policies in front of increasingly emboldened lay audiences'.[10] Fennell recalled programmes in which the young – talking of Irish Catholicism – brought 'shocks, amazement, gratification and displeasure into many homes'. But he believed that an 'intensity of feeling' on their part had been 'mistaken for knowledge and thought' and he found that a great

---

5   John Naughton, 'A Breath of Fresh Eire', *The Observer*, 12 November 1995.
6   F.S.L.Lyons, *Ireland Since the Famine* (London, 1971), pp.679-80.
7   Cathcart, 'Mass Media', 693-94.
8   Finola Kennedy, *Cottage to Crèche: Family Change in Ireland* (Dublin, 2002), p.250.
9   Terence Brown, *Ireland: A Social and Cultural History: 1922-2002* (London, 2004), p.249.
10 Tom Garvin, *Preventing the Future: Why was Ireland so Poor for so Long?* (Dublin, 2004), p.274; hereafter, Garvin, *Preventing the Future*.

deal of this debate had been 'bedevilled by ignorance and provincial-mindedness'.[11]

Fanning, in his history of *Independent Ireland*, noted that the station's political broadcasting – indebted to British and American models – 'was more confrontational and inquisitorial than deferential'; leaders of church and state 'were soon asked to submit to interrogation on television'.[12] Most proved shy. In fact the discussion programmes in the early years had been largely neglected by the establishment – or, in the case of McQuaid, never even visited by them – and this left the airwaves open to less orthodox, or even, some considered, heretical opinions. McQuaid's hope that he could somehow win control over Catholic programmes – on the grounds that the studios were located in his diocese – persisted into the late 1960s, despite the fact that he was constantly disabused of this notion by RTÉ executives.[13] Besides, the only programmes which could be thought of as strictly denominational were the brief bedtime homilies by individual speakers which were allocated between the different churches: doubtless McQuaid exerted as much influence as possible in selecting those Catholic priests who contributed. For the rest, religious programming reflected the democratic culture of television.

Whyte, in his *Church and State in Modern Ireland*, commented on the call for freer discussion which had been encouraged by the Vatican Council in the 1960s and suggested that the response of the Irish bishops had been, 'on the whole, not to denounce it but to participate in it'. But Whyte's criteria for participation may appear paltry to modern readers as he then listed out the eight bishops who between 1962 and 1970 had 'allowed themselves to be interviewed on television'. That he had compiled this list with the help of two friends in RTÉ and hoped that no bishop had been 'inadvertently omitted' provided its own insight into the period. Whyte also noted that television as a medium required controversy. A discussion programme would prove 'intolerably dull' unless the participants were in disagreement.[14] Foyle reckoned that RTÉ included in such programmes 'a disproportionate number of non-Catholics' whose religion made them 'more argumentative and confused' than would be the case 'with mature Catholics'. He believed that the 'scope for propagating error' had 'greatly increased' with the coming of television: and he feared that 'respect for the mental acumen of the commentators' could grow at the expense of respect for the

In the papers of John Charles McQuaid, there is a letter from some priests of his diocese, who advise that they are his 'own diocesan priests' who 'as a result of a discussion' had decided to write to him. Writing on 22 January 1970, they warned of 'a sinister campaign against celibacy' which had been abetted by a recent 'scandalous' *Late Late Show* which had featured 'Religious Order Priests making fools of themselves. One was an English Jesuit and the other was an Oblate on holiday from Australia.' They reassured McQuaid that they did not want to add to his work burden but suggested that 'the Faithful could do with some reassurance and the ordinary honest-to-God priests would value a word of authoritative praise.'

The letter is simply signed 'Group of Priests'.

---

11 Desmond Fennell, *The Changing Face of Catholic Ireland* (Washington, 1968), p.32.
12 Ronan Fanning, *Independent Ireland* (Dublin, 1983), p.200.
13 Esras Films, *John Charles McQuaid: What the Papers Say*, interview Todd Andrews RTÉ film archives.
14 J.H.Whyte, *Church and State in Modern Ireland: 1923-1970* (Dublin, 1971), pp. 355, 358.

judgement of clerics, 'traditionally thought to be well-nigh infallible in all matters'.[15] The truth was that television reserved for infallibility a producer's code, WBD: worthy but dull.

What the medium desired most was two rival exponents of diametrically opposed positions: and if each reckoned him or herself infallible, so much the better! Controversial debates concerning hitherto taboo subjects proved especially popular, Chubb noting the emphasis in the 1960s on topics all of which were 'unthinkable' as subjects for broadcasting a mere ten years before. But Chubb also found a 'marked sensitivity of unacclimatised politicians to political broadcasting, and especially to even the mildest criticism in this medium'.[16] Keogh surmised that the strikes and industrial unrest which marred the years between 1961 and 1966 might have accounted for 'the barbed statement' in Lemass's 'instrument of public policy' speech.[17] Ferriter reckoned this speech important and concluded that RTÉ had not been 'allowed the autonomy it hoped for'. Citing the inability to send reporting crews to Vietnam and Biafra 'and a sometimes censorious approach to current affairs', he concluded that it had been 'perhaps unsurprising that there was an undue emphasis on less serious television'.[18] Cathcart disagreed, arguing that RTÉ had not been intimidated: 'The broadcasters quickly acquired the confidence to mount programmes critical of government performance and policy.' He also believed that there was no doubt that television 'stimulated the whole process of change by promoting the free movement of ideas'. And although the national newspapers – presuming 'on the unchanging allegiance of their respective political constituencies' – were at first slow to respond, Cathcart considered that that they had been forced to follow television's path.[19] Sheehan argued that television had proved influential on another level, 'a sort of subliminal seduction into the whole pace and texture of its dense and discontinuous flood of stimuli'; she believed it 'most likely' that this had even more far-reaching consequences, 'though much more difficult to assess or even express'.[20]

The archbishop of Dublin Dr John Charles McQuaid had never made any secret of his dislike of anything approaching what would now be called ecumenism. He had cajoled, rebuked, stymied and generally obstructed those catholic intellectuals who had opened up dialogue with like-minded Jews and separately with protestants in the early 1940s. He had observers report regularly to him about their meetings. Jews and Protestants would be tolerated at such meetings provided they were there as listeners, open to conversion to the Roman Catholic position. When Catholics such as Frank Duff did not respond to such discouragement, McQuaid invoked Canon 1325, paragraph 3, of the church's code of canon law: 'Catholics should avoid having any debates or encounters (*disputationes vel colationes*), especially in public, with non-Catholics without the permission of the Holy See or, if the situation be urgent, of the local Ordinary.' That error had no rights would fairly summarise the McQuaid line. With such a cast of mind he was not well placed to appreciate the robust discussion of religious topics which appealed to television producers.

Finola Kennedy, *Frank Duff, a life story* (London, 2011), pp.158-70; Esras Films, *John Charles McQuaid: What the Papers Say*, RTÉ television.

15 Joseph Foyle, 'The Mass Media Apostolate', *The Capuchin Annual*, 1965, 356-64.
16 Basil Chubb, *The Government and Politics of Ireland* (London, 1970), pp.135-37.
17 Dermot Keogh, *Twentieth-Century Ireland* (Dublin, 2005), p.261.
18 Diarmaid Ferriter, *The Transformation of Ireland: 1900-2000* (London, 2004), p.602.
19 Cathcart, 'Mass Media', 693-94, 702-03.
20 Helena Sheehan (2004a).

Hello Divorce ...Good-bye de Valera

Desmond Fennell complained in 1986 that RTÉ had 'a parochial, blinkered and unconsciously arrogant mentality in relation to Ireland as a whole'. It was 'largely negative, rather than largely affirmative, in relation to the values and beliefs of the national community' which it purported to serve. This was a reversal of the proper function of a national broadcasting service. It was, he argued, 'a disservice, an offence, and a highly undemocratic state of affairs'. RTÉ took the licence fees of Irish Catholics 'as the established Church of Ireland used take their tithes', and repaid them, as that Church did, 'with hostility to their religion and clergy'.

Desmond Fennell, 'What I really think of RTÉ', *Nice People and Rednecks: Ireland in the 1980s* (Dublin, 1986), pp.51-55.

THE INITIAL ESTABLISHMENT of an Irish television service was, as Patterson has noted, the consequence of 'a traditionally nationalist and Catholic' impulse: this was to match what Northern Ireland already enjoyed, two stations both with signals which could be received through much of the Republic. Some politicians who would have preferred if the medium had never been invented took the view that if you had to tolerate this nuisance, better that it be an Irish nuisance. But Patterson reckoned that Lemass's attempts to 'curb unruly broadcasters', whether made in private or in public, had had little effect. Increasingly it was becoming clear 'to all but the most obdurately reactionary politicians and clergy that the rules by which they exercised power and authority were being remade and that the mere invocation of the value of traditional forms of life and thought would be insufficient to defend them.' Patterson suggested that television as a medium had concentrated on 'the defects and shortcomings of the Republic' and thus proved a 'potent threat to traditional values'.[21] That such values had been denigrated by most RTÉ producers, presenters and interviewers was Desmond Fennell's persistent complaint in the 1980s: he suggested that by and large they adhered 'to the ideology which is predominant both in the American media and throughout the capitalist world'. This was 'consumerist liberalism' which did not reflect the community's religious values and traditions, nor 'to any significant degree', its standards of taste, decency and justice. Implicit in his argument is that RTÉ liberals foisted an agenda on viewers who would have preferred to take their opinions as their parents largely had from the Irish establishment and especially from the Catholic church.

But this argument failed to recognise that, irrespective of RTÉ programming, Irish Catholicism was undergoing profound change. Although this was a church which seemed as late as the 1980s to have a 'cultural and political grip' on Irish society which seemed 'quite intact, pervasive and impervious to change', there was a seismic shift underway which some sensed earlier than others. One indicator for Garvin was the second revised edition of Inglis's book on the church in Ireland, *Moral Monopoly*, published in 1998 and which read 'almost like a different book about a different country' to its first edition a mere decade before.[22] If in the 1980s the more effective preachers were to be found in television studios rather than pulpits, this was not because

---

21 Henry Patterson, *Ireland since 1939* (Dublin, 2006), p.165-66.
22 Garvin, *Preventing the Future*, 273. Tom Inglis first published *Moral Monopoly: The Catholic Church in Modern Irish Society* (Dublin, 1987); his revised second edition was entitled *Moral Monopoly: The Rise and Fall of the Catholic Church in Modern Ireland* (Dublin, 1998).

of any RTÉ conspiracy. Rather, it was owing to the interests – in both senses of the term – of the audience. Younger Irish Catholics were no longer prepared to defer on sexuality and other issues to celibate males quoting an infallible source in Rome. Bagehot had warned in the nineteenth century – he was referring to the British monarchy – not to let daylight in on magic. Television represented daylight: this could be of no comfort to the traditional church.

Irish attitudes to divorce was another indicator of the speed of the change: in 1980 there was no *politician in the Dáil* who openly advocated divorce; yet by 1995 there was no *political party in the Dáil* which opposed its introduction.[23] That the pace of that shift in opinion had been quickened by television could be argued. But that it would not have taken place were it not for RTÉ is scarcely tenable. Garvin suggests that, as far as the church was concerned, it was a case of 'educate them and lose your control'. It was manifestly the case that 'a huge divide existed between the increasingly educated young and the still devout and unquestioning culture of the older people of the de Valera era'.[24] This change, although incremental, was also rapid. Was there a tipping point? It would not be an exaggeration to argue that one of the most profound changes in all human history was the development of the oral contraceptive: enabling women to control their own fertility had the most profound consequences. For the church to expect Irish Catholic women to ignore this revolution was naive: yet this was the Pope's response for the entire church with the publication of *Humanae Vitae*. In terms of church influence, this was historically catastrophic. And there were more priests willing to uphold the encyclical's teaching and advise sexual abstinence to a woman in the confessional than were ever willing to debate the same issue with women in a television studio. Likewise, procedures such as *in vitro* fertilisation and sterilisation have long since become matters between Catholics and their medical advisers, whereas their mothers might have sought – and would certainly have been expected to seek – the guidance of their religious advisers.

The church had been losing ground ever since its 'victory' in the Mother and Child church-state clash of 1951. The state had taken over social welfare and health and was in the process of taking over education. These major changes were probably accelerated by television – and even more by radio since the phone-in programmes offered so much more airtime to testimony, advocacy and debate. Was Fennell shooting the messenger? Was the director-general, Oliver Maloney,

The employment of the above poster by the No Divorce Campaign proved controversial in the 1995 campaign. In the event – as was said on the RTÉ results programme as it became clear that the Yes side would win by less than 1 per cent – it was a case of 'Hello Divorce … Good-bye de Valera'.

Television, radio and the media in general, according to Tom Inglis, had encouraged 'self-realisation and self-expression' while the message of the Church had essentially been one of 'self-abnegation or denial'. Interpretation and debate in the public sphere about social life had shifted 'from bishops, priests and theologians to journalists, commentators, producers and spin-doctors'. Prestige followed: it was now associated with media gurus who tended to be 'more self-confident and extrovert and skilled in speaking in the media's preferred format – keeping their sound-bites simple, short and sexy.'

Inglis, *Moral Monopoly* (second edition, 1998), p.232-33.

23 RTÉ Referendum results on Divorce 1995.
24 Garvin, *Preventing the Future*, 272.

Some found it 'quite revolutionary' to find the clergy obliged to defend their opinions 'in front of increasingly emboldened lay audiences'. In this edition of *The Late Late Show*, on 13 May 1967, the audience was comprised of priests and laity. Fr Michael Cleary is in the second row, second from the right and below the woman who is speaking.

shooting the messenger when in 1975 he expressed his concern that the station 'appeared to have slipped into a pro-contraception stance'.[25] This was asserted at an interesting moment in the history of this issue in the Republic. The previous year the Dáil had failed to legalise contraception when Taoiseach Liam Cosgrave voted against his own government's bill. And soon Fianna Fáil would bring in their 'Irish solution to an Irish problem' that would make contraception legal for 'bona fide' family planning purposes. However, it was clear to most informed social commentators at the time that the politicians, the bishops – and much of the medical profession – were all straggling behind a major shift in public opinion and in sexual behaviour on this question. For those to whom it was of most practical concern, women of child-bearing years, it had rapidly become an issue of private morality and civil rights. This would inevitably be reflected in how the question was dealt with on RTÉ programmes. In making his complaint, Maloney demonstrated that he was a straggler in the company of the politicians and the bishops rather than with the younger women on this issue.

Fennell himself from the start of the station had called on it to prove itself as more than a 'wonder-box or a time-killer for the very young and the old'.[26] By debating these issues and being awake to the historic shift in Irish Catholicism, was RTÉ not doing what any broadcaster would do in such a setting? What has been witnessed is the empowerment of the individual, the strengthening of rights based on individual choice rather than the old hierarchical society with answers handed down from those already characterised as 'well-nigh infallible in all matters'.[27] Some were insightful enough to see that the Church's influence was rapidly fading. When the first referendum offering provision for divorce was rejected by a two to one majority, Cardinal Ó Fiaich suggested that this was no victory for the conservatives: he believed that the reversal of that constitutional decision was only a matter of time. He based this on an examination of the evidence of opinion polls and attitude surveys on the topic. The crucial figures for Ó Fiaich were those of the younger, educated, urban females. How they thought about such an issue would, he believed, eventually determine the question.[28] And so it proved – and within a decade.

25 Horgan, *Broadcasting and Public Life*, 145.
26 *Hibernia*, December 1962.
27 Foyle, *The Capuchin Annual*, 1965, 356-64.
28 RTÉ Referendum results on Divorce 1995.

The first referendum on divorce was held on 26 June 1986. After early opinion polls had shown a majority in favour of divorce, the referendum was eventually lost after a hard-fought campaign by gaining the support of only 538,279 votes in favour to 935,843 against. Within a decade a second referendum was held on 24 November 1995. This was carried by 818,842 votes in favour to 809,728 against. In percentages this showed 50.28 per cent in favour. Although this was narrowly carried, the detail of exit polls and the constituency results show how much the opposition to divorce came from older rural voters. The highest 'No' vote was in Cork North-West at 66.06 per cent; the highest 'Yes' vote was in Dun Laoghaire at 68.21 per cent. Other constituency results show a predominant urban-rural divide and exit polls confirm that support for divorce came from younger, urban voters. Cardinal Ó Fiaich, noting this trend in 1986, had then predicted that some provision for divorce was inevitable.

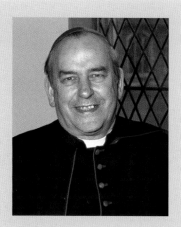

'till the eyes tire, millions of us watch the shadow of shadows and find them substance'

THAT RTÉ TELEVISION has come through its first half-century relatively intact does not mean that such an outcome was guaranteed; nor is it any indication that the station's future is assured. Television and how it is watched and on what platforms has been revolutionised during the past half century. Competition has intensified and Irish viewers have enjoyed an ever-widening choice, all on a scale unimaginable in 1962: there are three further Irish terrestrial channels, RTÉ 2, TG4 and TV3; an additional two British channels, BBC 2 and Channel 4; and, with the digital revolution, a proliferation of further options through cable, satellite and subscription. Nor, any longer, are there issues concerning ares of marginal reception areas – the world has shrunk and geography is no longer a barrier in accessing coveted channels. During that half-century there had been many strategic choices to be made by RTÉ management to ensure that the RTÉ channels remained relevant and economically viable. For this they needed to retain sufficient loyalty from Irish viewers, despite their being wooed by so many rival television providers.

Although much of the credit for holding their audience must belong to the station's strategists and broadcasters, a considerable accolade is also due to the viewers for their serious engagement with their own society and their sustained interest in how its challenges were debated on home-produced programmes. There may be very few, if any, western democracies where public service programming was so focused on such an agenda. RTÉ has managed to attract audiences for such programmes on a scale per head of population

In the early months of 2011, RTÉ was obliged to quickly cover an Irish general election, and shortly thereafter, within the space of a week, the visits of Queen Elizabeth II and of President Barack Obama. And there was a state funeral of Garret FitzGerald to be televised on the Sunday between the two state visits. The recently appointed director-general, Noel Curran (right), drew attention to the fact that it was RTÉ's Outside Broadcast pictures which had been 'made available to all broadcasters worldwide and to TV3 in Ireland 'to maximise access'. They were seen 'on countless channels and sites worldwide'. Curran observed that while this service was 'tightly budgeted' it was not a commercial undertaking for RTÉ. Rather was it, 'in the plainest terms' an example of public service broadcasting: delivering access to the audience 'and serving a shared public purpose'.

Irish Times, 10 June 2011.

far in excess of any similar programmes in Britain, for example.

Of course not all the programmes broadcast by RTÉ were popular. Some were found offensive, dull, corrupting, irrelevant or simply badly made. As the station opened, Eamonn Andrews declared:

'Show me a library in which you will like to read all the books, and then I will show you a television service in which you will like all the programmes.'[29] RTÉ television failed to please all of the people all of the time: but over its first half-century it has pleased more of them more of the time than might have been envisaged on New Year's Eve 1961. Whatever would the owner of that carping

29 Eamonn Andrews, 'What a tremendous achievement it is!' *RTV Guide*, 29 December 1961.

Queen Elizabeth II at the Garden of Remembrance, Parnell Square, Dublin in May 2011 at the start of her state visit. Her first public engagement was highly symbolic: to lay a wreath to those who had died in the cause of Irish nationalism.

voice overheard by Gabriel Fallon on the opening night have made of it? That voice which proclaimed that the new station was 'a far too ambitious project'.[30]

RTÉ television has managed over its first half-century to maintain a central position in Irish life, its share of viewers the envy of many other national public service broadcasters. But being a national brand and enjoying a large following is no guarantee of survival in the modern world. When Telefís Éireann was launched, the *Irish Press* circulation was a multiple of that of the *Irish Times*. The challenge for RTÉ's management for the next half-century will be to ensure that the ethos of public service broadcasting survives. It was born out of necessity, the then scarcity of available wavelengths. That scarcity no longer applies. Multinational media empires – and based not alone on television but also including film, audio, newspapers, magazines, books and internet – are becoming so powerful that such concentration of ownership is being seriously considered as a threat to democracy.

Whatever happens the television industry, it seems inevitable that as a medium it has captured a significant fraction of the daily attention, span of mankind throughout the developed world. Television has

College Green in Dublin had once been the traditional venue for monster rallies by Irish political parties. Had it ever seen a crowd so large as that which greeted U.S. President Barack Obama in May 2011? And they were joined by a further 1.1 million viewers watching live on Six-One News on RTÉ. Drawing attention to the millions more watching throughout the world via RTÉ's pictures, director-general Noel Curran argued that a tipping point was approaching. The prize was 'simply that of sustaining public broadcasting. If, in three years time, the Irish public once again wished to share in a sequence of major public events such as the royal and presidential visits, RTÉ must be there to provide that.'

Irish Times, 10 June 2011.

30 *RTV Guide*, 5 January 1962.

Barack Obama paid the shortest visit ever to Ireland by a serving United States President on 23 May 2011. He is photographed here with Taoiseach Enda Kenny at the major public meeting in College Green, Dublin which concluded his visit and was broadcast live on RTE *Six-One News*. Because an encroaching ash cloud threatened the possibility of air travel, Obama's security advisers insisted that he leave directly after this speech and fly to London that evening. His visit – despite its brevity – made an enormous impact with day-long coverage on television. The late George Hodnett's song 'Monto' written in 1958 had marked an earlier state visit by Queen Victoria. It included the lines:

'Now the Queen she came to call on us,
She wanted to see all of us
I'm glad she didn't fall on us,
She's eighteen stone.'

Obama's visit prompted this parody:
'At nine Obama called on us,
Then left for Moneygall on us,
But managed to see all of us,
By six-fifteen.'

George Hodnett was, incidentally, the first ever guest on *The Late Late Show*.

become a habit, part of the daily routine of most people's lives. As Raymond Williams put it:

> Till the eyes tire, millions of us watch the shadow of shadows and find them substance; watch scenes, situations, actions, exchanges, crises. The slice of life, once a project of naturalist drama, is now a voluntary, habitual, internal rhythm; the flow of action and acting, of representation and performance, raised to a new convention, that of a basic need.[31]

What those with the custodianship of RTÉ television must ask, as it contemplates the future, is how much of that basic need will they fulfil in the next fifty years? And with what programme content? And through what means of communication? Will the medium which we now call television be recognisable when the centenary is celebrated in 2061?

These are questions for the future. This book has been concerned with the first fifty years. It seems to the author probable that Irish television – no matter what the future brings – has been fortunate that its beginnings owed so much to the tradition and ethos of public service broadcasting. Initially, the custodianship of this new medium had been tardily granted to the station, by the government of the day. It is for readers and viewers to decide how that challenge and responsibility was discharged. Was there not in the 1960s and '70s an historic conjunction of a repressed, sheltered society willing to embrace change and to participate with its national broadcaster in creating the forum for that agenda to be debated? Too much of RTÉ's history (this book itself could be culpable) has been about programmes that were vetoed – foreign reporting of Vietnam and Biafra; or censored – through Section 31; or not broadcast – the end of *The Spike* series. These dimensions are instructive and important. But they are not the whole story. There was also the assiduous use of the Broadcasting Act by successive directors-general who called the bluff of would-be political influencers by inviting them to exercise their influence through the Act. And might not T. P. Hardiman's insistence that he would work the Act in his initial altercation with Charles Haughey have provided the political establishment with its clearest message that the new television station had a mind of its own?[32] Might this not have been a tipping point in the relationship between the young station and the government? It seems to this author that whatever the next fifty years brings, RTÉ television's best years may yet prove to have been its earliest faltering steps when it established that broadcast journalism would be its purpose, rather than being merely 'an instrument of public policy'.

---

31 Alan O'Connor, *Raymond Williams* (London, 2006), p.44.
32 See pp. 111-12 above.

A CONSIDERABLE variety of sources has been used in researching and writing this book: interviews, private papers, public archives, newspapers, periodicals, memoirs, biographies and specialist books. Because of the thirty year rule many papers covering the last three decades remain closed for research. It may also be noted that the arrival of the photocopier in the 1970s has had a considerable influence on research in contemporary history: on the one hand it facilitated the multiple copying of some documents which might otherwise have been lost; but it also encouraged profligate copying of routine material with the result that the management of archival material has proved daunting to an organization such as RTÉ whose primary duty must be the production of tonight's broadcast programme rather than the station's history. So often when papers were being considered for the Written Archive – in the first instance by the possible donor – it must have seemed as if they were of little value: filing cabinets crammed with photocopies and old scripts. To dump them must have seemed the appropriate response for many: but how many clues to aspects of the station's history might be hidden among the chaff? And, if sent to the archives, such voluminous material is costly to store and process. In consequence – or so it seems to this researcher and through no fault of its own – the RTÉ Written Archive must have material of considerable quality but, as yet, it is obscured by the sheer quantity of routine duplicated papers which have been generated by the original donors. And this probably applies whether the donor be departments, programmes or individuals. The photocopier has proved to be both friend and foe to the historian.

The following list of secondary sources makes no claim to be a comprehensive bibliography and should be considered in conjunction with the references cited throughout the book. For instance, the one quotation from Galbraith's *The New Industrial State* is fully referenced on page 44. Only his very interesting verdict on television commercials is quoted in this book and there seemed little virtue in citing this again in a bibliography. Quoted from the original 1967 Penguin edition, Galbraith's classic remains in print from Princeton University Press.

Andrews, C.S. Todd, *Man of No Property*, Dublin (2001);

Erik Barnouw, *Tube of Plenty: the Evolution of American Television* (Oxford, 1990);

Asa Briggs, *The History of Broadcasting in the United Kingdom: Sound and Vision: iv, 1945-55* (Oxford, 1995);

——, *The History of Broadcasting in the United Kingdom: Competition: v, 1955-1974* (Oxford, 1995);

Barry, Michael, *From the Palace to the Grove* (London, 1992) Royal Television Society;

Battersby, Eileen, 'Last of the soap: Thursday interview: Wesley Burrowes', *Irish Times*, 8 January 1998;

Byrne, Gay, *To whom it concerns* (Dublin, 1972);

Cathcart, Rex, *The most contrary Region: The BBC in Northern Ireland: 1924-1984* (Belfast, 1984);

Comiskey, Rev. Brendan, 'Should the Christians always lose?', *Irish Broadcasting Review* (12) (Autumn/Winter 1981). pp.7-11;

Cooney, John, *John Charles McQuaid: ruler of Catholic Ireland* (Dublin, 1999);

Day, Robin, 'Troubled reflections of a TV journalist', *Encounter*, May 1970, pp.78-88;

Doolan, Lelia, Dowling, Jack, and Quinn, Bob, *Sit down and be counted: the cultural evolution of a television station* (Dublin, 1969);

Dowling, Jack, 'Broadcasting: An Exercise in Deception', *Aquarius*, 3 (1973);

Duignan, Seán, *One Spin on the Merry-go-round* (Dublin, 1998);

Dunn, Joseph, *TV and Politics* (Dublin, 1971);

Edwards, Hilton (1973), 'RTÉ: Drama on Television' [interview by Cyril Farrell], *Aquarius*, 1973, pp.104-109;

Feeney, Peter (1984), 'Censorship and RTÉ', *The Crane Bag*, 8:2 (1984);

Fisher, Desmond, *Broadcasting in Ireland* (London, 1978);

Harris, Eoghan, *Television and terrorism, 1987*, mimeo. RTÉ reference library;

Hickey, Tom 'A farm drama that gripped the nation', *Irish Times*, 7 February 2009;

Horgan, John, *Lemass: The Enigmatic Patriot* (Dublin, 1997);

——, *Irish Media: A Critical History Since 1922* (London, 2001);

——, 'Journalists and Censorship: A Case History of the NUJ in Ireland and the Broadcasting ban 1971-94', *Journalism studies*, 3:3. (2002);

Inglis, K.S., *This is the ABC: The Australian Broadcasting Commission: 1932-1983* (Melbourne, 1983);

Irvine, John, 'Broadcasting and the Public Trust' (Thomas Davis Lecture, 1976), mimeo;

Kelly, Mary, 'Twenty years of current affairs on RTÉ' in Martin McLoone and John McMahon [eds.], *Television and Irish society: 21 years of Irish television* (Dublin, 1984), pp.89-106;

Kelly, Mary J., and O'Connor, B., *Media audiences in Ireland: power and cultural identity* (Dublin, 1997);

McCague, Eugene, *My Dear Mr McCourt* (Dublin, 2009);

Manning, Maurice, 'Brian Farrell: political scientist, teacher, broadcaster and colleague' in Tom Garvin, Maurice Manning and Richard Sinnott, [eds.] *Dissecting Irish politics: Essays in honour of Brian Farrell* (Dublin, 2004), pp.1-5;

Morash, Christopher, *A history of the media in Ireland* (Cambridge, 2010);

O Broin, Leon, *Just Like Yesterday* (Dublin, 1982);

O Morain, Donal, 'The Irish Experience', *Irish broadcasting review*, 10 (Spring 1981);

O Tuathaigh, Gearoid, 'Language, literature and culture in Ireland since the war', in Joe Lee, [ed.] *Ireland: 1945-70* Dublin (1979) pp.111-23;

Purcell, Patrick, 'TV or not TV', *Irish Monthly*, December 1950, pp.573-79;

Rugheimer, Gunnar, 'Irish television in trouble', *The Irish Times*, 20 October 1969;

Savage, Robert J., *Irish Television: The Political and Social Origins* (Cork, 1996);

——, *A Loss of Innocence? Television and Irish Society: 1960-1972* (Manchester, 2010);

Sheehan, Helena, *Irish Television Drama* (Dublin, 1987, first edition); revised edition is included as CD in Sheehan's later book, *The continuing story of Irish television drama: tracking the tiger*, (Dublin, 2004);

Thornley, David, 'Television and politics', *Administration*, XV Autumn 1967, pp.217-25;

Wyndham Goldie, Grace, *Facing the nation: television and politics: 1936-76* (London, 1977);

Smith, Anthony, [ed.] *Television and political life: studies in six European countries*, (London, 1979).

WITHIN A VERY SHORT TIME of the public announcement that I was writing this book I received a surprise gift: the research notes and many other important materials from John Horgan, historian of RTÉ news and current affairs. My indebtedness to him is not only based on this generosity but also on the encouragement which it gave me to plunge in immediately at the deep end in my own research. I am also immensely indebted to RTÉ's former chief archivist, Brian Lynch, for drawing my attention to some important files, for providing copies of others and for his continued interest and support, not least in locating some relevant files in the National Archives of the United Kingdom at Kew in London. Historian Ciara Meehan has been supportive in a number of ways, by drawing my attention to some important material in the National Archives of Ireland and in contributing to other aspects of the book

The library staff in RTÉ have been exceptionally supportive: Pearl Quinn in RTÉ Stills has provided support well beyond the call of duty as has Michael Talty in the main library and Eibhlín Ní Oisín: also to be thanked are Lara Harte, Natalie Milne, Jimmy Galvin and Liam Wylie. Tina Byrne and Claire McLoughlin in Written Archives were also supportive as was Brid Dooley in numerous ways.

I have always believed that there are some truths which can best – only? – be captured by the cartoonist: and I am especially pleased at the number of outstanding Irish cartoonists whose work is included in this book: Ian Knox, Martyn Turner, Nick Robinson, James O'Donovan, Tom Mathews and Tom Halliday, along with a variety of *Dublin Opinion* cartoons from the 1960s.

I am indebted to Ronnie Tallon for providing the outstanding drawing by Patrick Collins of Michael Scott's original idea of how the first Television building might look. And I am indebted to architect Cathal O'Neill for permission to reproduce his watercolour of Ronnie Tallon's Administration Building. I must thank Declan McCourt and Seán Ó Mórdha for the loan of some very valuable private papers; and I wish to thank Paul Durcan for permission to reproduce his poem for Liam Hourican and for some minor amendments to the original *Irish Press* version.

Also to be thanked are the following: at Fáilte Ireland, Mary Cosgrave and Derek Cullen; at the National Library of Ireland: Mary Broderick, Keith Murphy and Berni Metcalfe; at Trinity Library Manuscripts Department, Bernard Meehan and Aisling Lockhart; at UCD Archives Department, Seamus Helferty for his kind permission to reproduce some documents and also to Orna Somerville for her advice and courtesy; at TG4, Pádhraic Ó Ciardha; at An Post, Anne O'Neill; at the Irish Film Institute, Rebecca Grant; at Esras Films, Peter Kelly; at Scott Tallon Walker Architects, Sue Watters; also photographer Peter Barrow; at the Ordnance Survey of Ireland, Seán Tobin and Nancy Costello; at *The Kerryman*, Declan Malone; at the *Irish Times*, Mary Sheridan, Niall O'Connor and Peter Murtagh; at the *Irish Examiner*, Anne Kearney; at Gill & Macmillan, Teresa Daly; at the Irish Traditional Music Archive, Nicholas Carolan; at the GAA Archives, Mark Reynolds; at the Dublin Diocesan Archive, David Sheehy and Noelle Dowling; at the National Archives of Ireland, Aideen Ireland.

The project has also been aided in many diverse ways by Ruth Baker, Bob Baker, Karina

Buckley, Bob Collins, Maura Connolly, John Cooney, Colm Crowley, Pat Deane, Ted Dolan, Mark Duncan; Clare Duignan, Madelyn Erskine, Katell Guillamot, Gabrielle Gilmartin, Godfrey Graham, Jim Jennings, Michael Johnston, Joe Kavanagh, Mary Keane, Louise Kearns, Avril Lynch, Grainne McAleer, Vicky Moran, Joe Mulholland, Mairead ni Nuadhán, John O'Regan, Seán O'Rourke and Robert Savage.

Beverly Hanly and Adrian Moynes were exceptionally helpful with access to the RTÉ Authority papers; Betty Purcell has been a colleague for very many years and also a member of the Authority and shared many insights with me. I must also thank Diarmuid Breathnach for exceptional support. And I would like to thank the late Kevin McCourt, T.W. Moody, Jim McGuinness, David Thornley and Leon O Broin for interviews in the past which have proved invaluable to me in this task.

My broadcasting colleagues with whom I was working in radio and television while this book was being researched and written were also very supportive and I wish to thank Deirdre Younge, David Nally, Shay Howell and Stephen Wallace; also Loreli Harris, Dave McHugh, Robert Canning and Brian Rice. Also supportive were Cathal Goan and Noel Curran as directors-general. I must also thank Glen Killane, Kevin Dawson and Peter Feeney. And I compliment Cliff Murphy for compiling an exceptional index; and the staff of The Collins Press for their courtesy, professionalism and support.

My indebtedness to Ciara Baker who shared the research with me is difficult to express. Not only was she indefatigable in pursuit of many of the needles – which I had long abandoned as lost causes – but she tended to find others in the same haystack. And her enthusiasm and 'can-do' approach to all research challenges reminded me only of the pioneering spirit of that first generation of television learners who launched the station in 1962 and who quickly became expert professionals. I know no higher compliment. Susan Waine undertook much of the picture research and designed the book by integrating the graphics and photographs into the storyline. Her commitment, enthusiasm and willingness to discuss challenges at any time of the day or night was hugely supportive. And her judgement on all matters concerning book production is impeccable. I would also wish to record my warm appreciation to my literary agent, Jonathan Williams – a walking Fowler – who saves his authors from any number of errors and who himself is close to infallible. I should add that any remaining errors in the text are the sole responsibility of myself. To Shelley McNamara of Grafton Architects and her colleagues Philippe O'Sullivan and Matt McCullagh I am indebted for the exceptional work-space which they have designed for me. I would also like to record my appreciation of the support of Fintan Drury.

My indebtedness to my family should also be recorded: to my late son Jonathan for sharing many memorable conversations on the subject of this book and to his son Saul for keeping me in touch with all aspects of popular culture; and to Emma, Abie and Daniel whom I have always encouraged to be forthrightly critical in judging my work and who embraced that advice with enthusiasm when considering early drafts of the present work. They proved more influential than may have appeared likely when we were first discussing their detailed criticisms. My wife Eimer also read the text and made very many invaluable suggestions, many of which I acted on. She must also be thanked for enduring what she assured me was my 'absence' – even when present – during the final writing period. I do not plead guilty but I have no doubt that she is being fair. She also contributed tellingly to one of the captions.

Finally, I feel that I have been working on this book ever since I was a viewer myself on the opening night of what was then Telefís Eireann. I have always had an interest in the history of the media in Ireland and have been fortunate to have had the opportunity to present a range of specialist media programmes on both radio and television since *Right of Reply* in 1968. During the course of such programmes, I have had occasion to interview virtually all the key players in the history of RTÉ television and I have also shared more informal conversations with many of them about all aspects of the subject. I feel I have drawn on this experience here and feel an obligation especially to those colleagues whose insights I may have appropriated to a point where I even believe them to be my own.

The Spike controversy, 147
Lynch, Joe, 160c
Lynch, John, 162b
Lynch, Mairin, 121
Lyons, F.S.L., 227
Lyons, Tommy, 208c
Lyster, Michael, 208c

M

McAleese, Mary, 127, 127c, 199, 199c
MacAnally, Ray, 84
MacAonghusa, Prioinsias, 57–58
MacAongusa, Brian, 175c
McCabe, Eugene, 47, 156c
McCafferty, Nell, 127
McCann, Hugh, 100, 100c
McCann, John, 31
McCarthy, Canon Cathal, 7c
McCarthy, Kathleen, 218b
McCauley, Leo, 18b
Mac Coille, Cathal, 140b
McColgan, John, 153c, 166, 185
Mac Conghail, Muiris, 74, 90, 191b, 192c
    7 Days Biafra proposed coverage, 100, 101
    7 Days programming boundaries, 102, 126
    current affairs broadcasting, 187
    The Spike controversy, 146, 147c
McCourt, Kevin, 58c, 65c, 69c2, 76c, 77, 88c, 220b
    7 Days Biafra proposed coverage, 99, 100–1
    7 Days move to newsroom, 102
    Eamonn Andrews and business, 87b
    Blythe, Ernest, Irish Language instruction lobbying, 109
    Catholic religious programming appointment, 66, 67, 67c, 68, 68c, 69, 69c1
    director-general, appointment as, 65–66, 73–74
    Fianna Fáil government, conflicts with, 70b, 95
    Government broadcasting policy, 90, 94c
    Insurrection series, 83
    Irish language policy, 78, 78c, 79–80, 92, 93
    J.F. Kennedy visit, 71, 71c
    Tibor Paul, 105
    resignation, 111
    RTÉ, ministers views on, 95b
    Rugheimer as controller, retention of, 85–86, 88
    Rugheimer's replacement, search for, 87b, 88
McDarby, John, 161c
MacDonagh, Donagh, 32
MacDubhghaill, Uinsionn, 185n12
MacEntee, Seán, 5c, 18
McEvoy, Mary, 160c
McEvoy, Peter, 150
McGetigan, Charlie, 211c
McGilligan, Patrick, 13–14, 13c

McGrath, Pat, 219c
McGrath, Tom, 46, 46c, 219c
McGuinness, Jim, 97, 119, 119c, 202
    7 Days, management of, 102
    Broadcasting Review Committee criticisms, 125
McHugh, Kevin, 50c, 162b
McHugh, Roger, 30
McInerney, Kathleen, 152c
McKiernan, Eoin, 11, 78
McLendon Investment Corporation, 15
McLendon, Gordon, 15, 15c
MacMahon, Bryan, 4
MacMahon, Tony, 108c, 109
MacManus, Ed B., 86c
MacManus, Francis, 78c, 79b
MacMathuna, Ciaran, ix, 107c, 109c
Macmillan, Harold, 23–24
McQuaid, Archbishop John Charles, 15, 15c
    Dublin theatrical community, 67
    ecumenism, opposition to, 229b
    Joe Foyle, funding request from, 122
    T.P. Hardiman interview approach, 112b, 112c
    industrial schools, documentary, 212–13
    Late Late Show, The, 'Bishop and the Nightie affair' 220b
    religious programmes, control of, 66–67, 68, 68c, 69, 69c
    RTÉ concentration on religion, 193
    Telefís Éireann opening night, 6c, 7, 8, 8c
    Telefís Éireann, dissatisfaction with, 57
    and television, 8–9, 228
McRedmond, Louis, 135, 136c
McRory, Avril, 219c
Mac Stiofián, Seán, 123, 123c, 124c, 127
McStay, Kevin, 208c
Mack Kyle, C., 49b
Madigan, Siobhán, 208c
Magee, Jimmy, 219c
Magill, 164, 170b
Maguire, Aidan, 203c
Maguire, Conor A., 5c
Maloney, Oliver, 117, 138c, 231–32
    as director-general, 138c, 141–44
    newsroom problems, 144–45
    press treatment of, 141–42
    The Spike controversy, 146–47
    RTÉ Authority, 141
    RTÉ reform agenda, 141–45
    second television channel, 148
Manchester, 177
Manchester Guardian, 21
Manning, Maurice, 194b
Mant, Pamela, 161c
Marcus, David, 128
Marian College, Dublin, 8b
Martin, Gus, 76b
Martin, Linda, 210
Masterson, Bat, 75
Masterson, John, 219c

Mathews, Brendan, 161c
Mathews, Niall, 108c, 162b
Mathews, Tom, 178
Maynooth College, 7c
Mayo, County, 135
Media coverage of the Irish elections of 1981–82, 197n
Melly, George, colour television, 139b
Men for the Harvest, 7c
Menzies, Robert, 23
Mercier, Vivian, 8, 11c
    drama in Irish society, 155
Meredith, Fionola, 205b
Mexico, 64
MGM, 59b
Michelson, Charles, 15, 15c, 16c, 18b, 18c
Miles na gCopaleen, see O'Nolan, Brian
Miller, Liam, 167c, 181
Minority Report: the Anatomy of the Southern Irish Protestant, 57c
Mitchel, Charles, 39c, 55c
Mitchell, Jim, 169, 199
    Ray Burke and RTÉ, 167
Molloy, M.J., 47–48
Moloney, Paddy, 152c
Monaghan, County, 156c
money-lending and *7 Days,* government tribunal, 116, 116c
Monica Sheridan's Kitchen, 203c
Monkees, The, 77
Montrose gremlins, interrupting broadcasts, 64b
Moody, Janet, 53c, 54
Moody, T.W., 27, 60, 82, 86c, 89b, 124
    Gay Byrne and Late Late Show, 222
Moon Shines on Kylenamoe, The, 50–51
Mooney, Ria, 2c
Moore, Butch, 107b
Moore, Fr Henry, 212
Moral Monopoly: The Catholic Church in Modern Irish Society, 143b
Morash, Christopher, 75–76
Morgan, Dermot, 166b
Morning Ireland, 179b
Morris, Archbishop Thomas,
    Catholic religious programming appointment, 67, 68–69
    Telefís Éireann, dissatisfaction with, 57
Morrissey, Eamon, 150c
Morrissey, Marty, 208c
Morton, Peggie, 161c
Moynihan, Maurice, 17
Muggeridge, Malcolm, 31c
Mulally, Phil, 206c
Mulcahy, Noel, 112
Mulcahy, Richard, 5c
Mulcahy, Tomás, 208c
Mulhall, Ed, 202, 202c
Mulholland, Annie, 219c
Mulholland, Joe, 140b, 170b, 202, 219c
Mullen, Larry, 221c

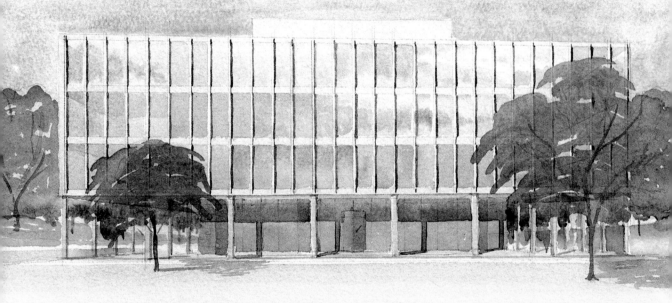

In Cathal O'Neill's estimation the RTÉ Administration Building – painted here by O'Neill – is 'perhaps the finest office building in Dublin'. Yet although thousands of commuters pass it by on the Stillorgan dual carriageway each day it remains 'almost unknown to the general public'. Designed by Ronnie Tallon in the late 1960s, O'Neill describes it as 'a sympathetic and skilful interpretation of the ideas of Mies van der Rohe'. This four-storey building represents 'the vertical element in an otherwise horizontal group of outstanding buildings', on the RTÉ campus all of which were designed by the firm of Scott Tallon Walker. O'Neill studied under Mies van der Rohe and worked in Mies's private office before returning to Dublin to become Professor of Architecture at UCD. He believes the Miesian genre of architecture to have been 'widely copied but seldom understood'. With Tallon's Administration Building, O'Neill suggests that 'the beauty of the structure depends on the refinement of the composition as the proportion of each part unerringly relates to the whole.' He finds the building 'exudes a calm presence and is equally pleasing from all sides, like a Palladian villa. The glass box floats above the ground as if not wishing to obstruct the views of the landscaped gardens.' O'Neill believes that it should serve 'as a reminder to us all of the importance of restraint in architecture'.

Cathal O'Neill, *Cathal O'Neill's Dublin* (Dublin, 1998), pp.102-03.